Indigenous Identities

Indigenous Identities

Edited by Jaune Quick-to-See Smith

Jane Voorhees Zimmerli Art Museum
Rutgers, The State University of New Jersey

Hirmer Publishers

HERE

NOW

& ALWAYS

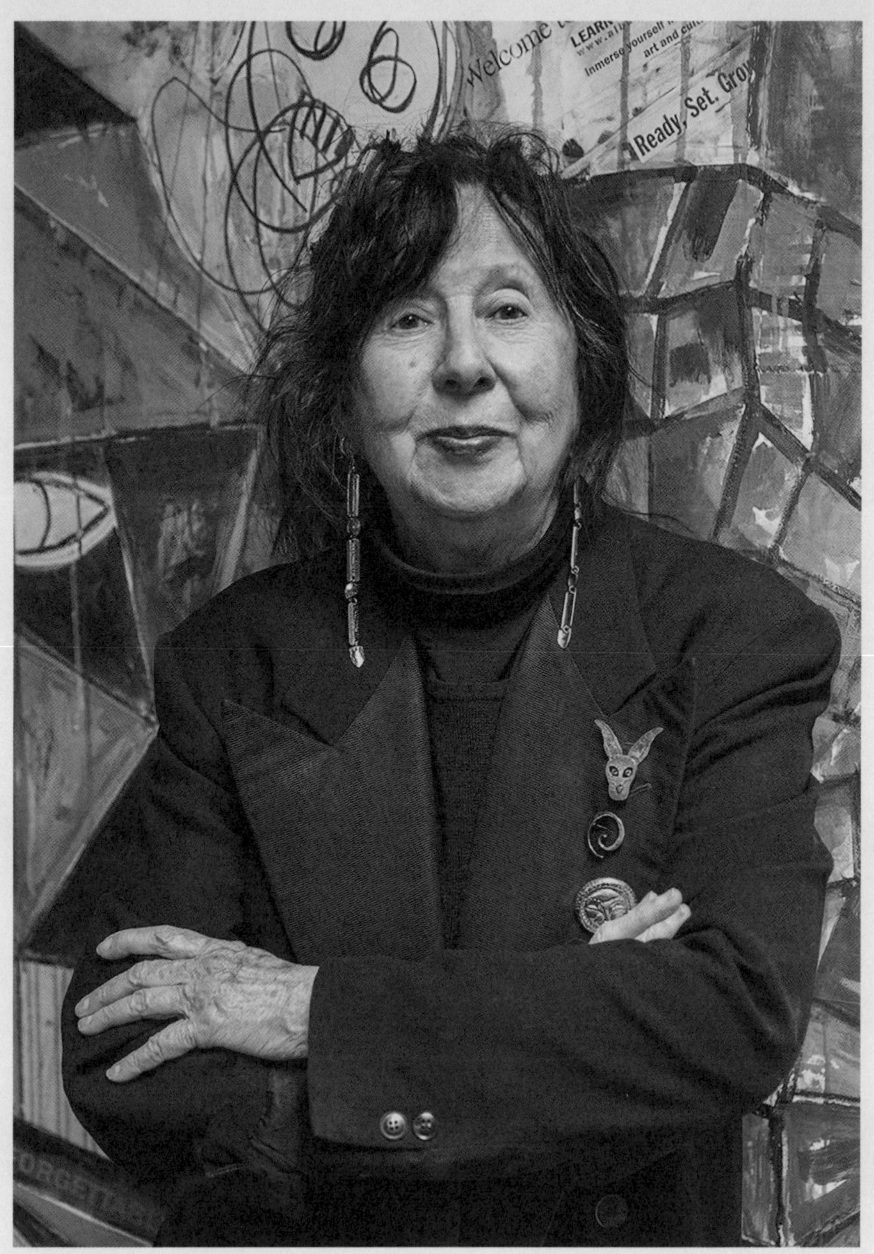

Jaune Quick-to-See Smith
1940–2025

Contents

Foreword

JAUNE QUICK-TO-SEE SMITH and I first met in New York City in 2015. As part of that year's *Performa* biennial, I was asked to participate in a panel discussion with Emory Douglas and Vernon Ah Kee, convened at Richard Bell's *Aboriginal Tent Embassy*, the artist's multipurpose space for activism and dialogue supporting Indigenous rights globally. After the talk, Jaune approached me regarding Bell's first museum retrospective, which I organized in 2010 and which traveled nationally. Our conversation naturally turned to contemporary Native American art—its brilliance, its neglect, and, ultimately, the dearth of large-scale exhibitions. Together that day, we vowed to organize an exhibition to showcase the diverse and exceptional art of the nation's many Native communities. *Indigenous Identities: Here, Now & Always* began with that first conversation, and now, over a decade later, I am so pleased to see it realized at the Zimmerli Art Museum.

The exhibition's opening on February 1, 2025, was a bittersweet moment; just one week earlier, Jaune passed away, at the age of eighty-five. While this exhibition is testament to three years of her work, it is also, in a larger sense, a symbol of her immense contribution to our shared American histories.

Jaune's legacy is immeasurable. An artist, activist, pedagogue, mentor, curator, and citizen of the Confederated Salish and Kootenai Nation, Jaune catalyzed a living Native art history, not only through her own artistic contributions to the field but also through the thirty-plus exhibitions she curated over the course of her career. She ceaselessly endeavored to challenge assumptions around Indigenous identity and contemporary Native American art. She championed justice, amplified Indigenous narratives, and inspired countless individuals to use their voices and creativity to enact change. Many of those voices are on display in *Indigenous Identities*.

This exhibition marks Jaune's largest curatorial endeavor. It is also one of the largest museum exhibitions of contemporary Native American art in the United States to date. According to Jaune, it is also the very first exhibition of Native American art focused exclusively on identity versus craft: weaving, glass, photography, and other artistic categories. The exhibition is, in her words, "a celebration of life." Comprising over one hundred works across a wide range of media, from beadwork, basketry, and jewelry to video, sculpture, and painting, *Indigenous Identities* foregrounds the significance of identity in art making through the diverse practices of ninety-seven artists collectively representing more than seventy-four Native American nations and communities across the continental United States. Featuring works made within the last fifty years by both well-established and emerging artists, the exhibition crosses several generations and examines subjects with historic and continuing relevance to Indigenous communities in North America, including stolen lands, genocide, lost languages and cultures, survivance and invisibility. Celebrating the breadth of groundbreaking contemporary art made by Native artists, *Indigenous Identities* brings to light a series of guiding concepts—land, social, tribal, and political—that unify the works on view and speak to the permeability of art in Native American life. The exhibition also confronts the idea that traditional forms of making are artifacts of a past time and acknowledges these practices and their contemporary resonance.

On view concurrently with *Indigenous Identities* and organized in conjunction with the survey is a focused exhibition of artwork by Smith from the Zimmerli's own collection, curated by Raven Manygoats (Diné), the museum's curatorial assistant in the department of the Art of the Americas, who also aided Jaune in the monumental task of organizing *Indigenous Identities*. Featuring nine works created between 1986 and 2001, *Hope with Humor: Works by Jaune Quick-to-See Smith from the Collection* explores how Smith honors Indigenous survival and resilience in her own artistic practice and reflects her approach to preserving Native cultures, ceremonies, and traditions through both wit and optimism. Also on view is an exhibition of illustrations by Steph Littlebird (registered member of Oregon's Grand Ronde Confederated Tribes) from the children's book *My Powerful Hair* by the best-selling author Carole Lindstrom (enrolled member of the Turtle Mountain Band of Ojibwe). That exhibition is organized by Nicole Simpson, curator of prints and drawings.

As a director deeply committed to decolonizing museums, it was imperative to me that each of these projects embodied key principles integral to that process. Thus, our goal was to ensure that each endeavor was principally Indigenous-led, from curation and didactics to book and exhibition design. The remarkable *Indigenous Identities* publication was led by a team of Native American collaborators: RoseMary Diaz (Santa Clara Pueblo) managed its astute editing; Kathleen Sleboda (Celetkwmx / Nlaka'pamux) provided its inspired design, within which she utilized a typeface by Typotheque, a firm that works directly with Indigenous communities to develop fonts that support Native American language revitalization and preservation efforts. In addition to an interview with the guest curator and her son, Neal Ambrose-Smith, the publication includes essays by seven Native American scholars and artists and one by an expert in Native American jewelry and fashion. The art historian Chelsea M. Herr (Choctaw Nation of Oklahoma) provides an overview of Native American art history; the artist Mario Caro (Colombian Mestizo) contributes an essay on Native American photography; the scholar Lou Cornum (Diné) writes about Indigenous Futurism and artist collectives; the poet Heid E. Erdrich (Turtle Mountain Ojibwe) offers an overview of Native American poetry; the art historian Lara M. Evans (Cherokee Nation) authors an essay on Native American sculpture; the curator Anya Montiel (Tohono O'odham) discusses Native American ceramics and basketry; the scholar Stacy Pratt (Mvskoke) writes about Native American painting; and the scholar Jennifer Woodcock-Medicine Horse contributes an essay on Native American jewelry and fashion. The publication was project managed by Stacy Smith, publications specialist; Kiki Michael, associate registrar, oversaw the many rights and reproductions. The book has been meticulously copyedited by editor Carolyn Vaughan and proofreader Carrie Wicks and thoughtfully indexed by Emily Bowles. We also thank our publisher Hirmer and, in particular, Elisabeth Rochau-Shalem for supporting this project from the outset.

Many other hands and minds helped realize this exhibition within the Zimmerli's galleries. Erin Bradford, registrar, attended to every loan detail, shipment, contract, and internal coordination. The stellar exhibition design and presentation owes much to the skill of Mark Steigelman and Cara Giddens, as well as to framing specialist Alex Cuschieri. Brandon Truett, head of learning and community engagement, and his team, Claire D'Amato, associate curator, and Barbara Cepeda, assistant curator, organized a robust program of public and educational programs that foregrounded the voices of the artists and that benefited our broad audiences. All these individuals worked diligently over the past three years to move this project forward, and their efforts have my deepest appreciation.

On behalf of the Zimmerli Art Museum, I extend my thanks to the many lenders who graciously agreed to part with works in their care so that additional audiences might enjoy them. Many of the artists in *Indigenous Identities* made their works available, as did public collections, including the Ganondagan Seneca Art and Culture Center, C.N. Gorman Museum, and Montclair Art Museum. Private foundations and collectors generously enabled us to borrow works, including the Forge Project, Gochman Family Collection, JoAnn Gonzales Hickey Collection, and, especially, the Tia Collection. We thank also Nanobah Becker as well as the many anonymous donors. For assistance with other loans, we thank Garth Greenan Gallery and Bockley Gallery.

An exhibition as ambitious as *Indigenous Identities* requires multiple committed funders. The exhibition and its accompanying publication and public programs are supported by the National Endowment for the Arts, the Nissan Foundation, the Middlesex County Board of County Commissioners through a grant award from the Middlesex County Cultural and Arts Trust Fund, and Rutgers University. Additional support was provided by donors to Zimmerli's Major Exhibitions Fund: Kathrin and James Bergin, Sundaa and Randy Jones, and Heena and Hamanshu Pandya. Generous support for the bilingual text was provided by Art Bridges Foundation's Access for All program. The Zimmerli's operations, exhibitions, and programs are funded in part by Rutgers, The State University of New Jersey, and income from the Avenir Endowment Fund and the Andrew W. Mellon Endowment Fund, among others. Additional support comes from the New Jersey State Council on the Arts, Bloomberg Philanthropies, and the donors, members, and friends of the museum.

Above all, we thank Jaune for her brilliance, kindness, warmth, and generosity. It has been the honor of a lifetime to have worked so closely with her on realizing this historic exhibition. Enormous thanks are also due to her son and collaborator, Neal Ambrose-Smith, without whose assistance this exhibition would not have been possible.

The Zimmerli's core mission is to offer a platform for under-represented artists. By addressing historical gaps in representation and incorporating more works by BIPOC, LGBTQIA2S+, and women artists into permanent gallery and exhibition rotations, the Zimmerli represents its diverse audiences. *Indigenous Identities* reflects this expansive vision. My hope is that this presentation will set the stage for the Zimmerli to continue its decolonization efforts and that it encourages other institutions to support Native artists through visibility, funding, and advocacy. *Indigenous Identities* gestures to many possible futures.

Maura Reilly, PhD
Director, Zimmerli Art Museum

Identity Is a Living Thing: Reframing Stereotypes

Conversation with Jaune Quick-to-See Smith (Confederated Salish and Kootenai Nation) and Neal Ambrose-Smith (Descendant of the Confederated Salish and Kootenai Nation)

We thank the ancestors, for without them, we would not be here.

JAUNE QUICK-TO-SEE SMITH

Although this discussion is not meant to be a "complete urban Indian compendium," it will serve as a glimpse from and into our perspective.

You and I used to go every summer to the Medicine Lodge ceremonies at Badger Creek with our cousin Gerald "Jerry" Slater (Confederated Salish and Kootenai Nation), an educator and the founder of Salish Kootenai College. Jerry was married to a Blackfeet woman, Lois LaFrombois McClure. Darrell Robes Kipp (Blackfeet Nation) was always in attendance for he was our Camp Crier and teacher throughout the ceremonies. He was a scholar through and through and would talk to everyone who would listen about what he had read lately. When we asked what led him to found the Piegan Institute when he wasn't a speaker, he told us it had to get done. He said, "Don't ask permission, just do it." He challenged all of us to contribute to our communities. I think we tried with this exhibition.

I'll start with a phrase we've heard many times: "We are still here." We hear it at conferences, meetings, gatherings, and powwows. An MC will call it out at the grand entry just to remind people how miraculous it is that through genocide, boarding schools, disease, hunger, rape, and abuse we are still here. I remember when President Jimmy Carter signed the American Indian Religious Freedom Act (AIRFA) into law in 1978 that said it was finally legal for us to use eagle feathers and practice our own religions.[1] Of course, the Code of Indian Offenses, enacted in 1883, didn't stop us from dancing, singing, and practicing our faith for the past ninety-five years, but that the law existed is paramount.[2] No other ethnic group in this land of religious freedom was forbidden, by law, to practice their faith. Only we Native Americans were forbidden to do so. This created a bond among us from tribe to tribe, with the sharing of jingle dances, grass dances, chicken dances, fancy dances, and much more. At one time these dances were regional or even tribal but now are spread across the nation.

NEAL AMBROSE-SMITH

The concept of full-blood Native or some percentage of Native has plagued our identity since the beginning of the nineteenth century. All humans are of mixed ancestry, especially today. It's quite inconceivable that people haven't mixed or aren't mixing, even when it's frowned upon by the culture. Look at war, invasions, and even ordinary travels, that's where people mix. It's going to happen. So even the idea of full-blood is a colonial construct, designed to eliminate reservations and, ultimately, the Native people. It is really the end of us as Native peoples. It's a genocidal tool. Measuring one's blood quantum is not a measure of one's identity. Blood quantum is not culture, but that's our current metric to determine who is Native American.

JQTSS

Another phrase that comes at us from the mainstream is "But you don't look Indian." This happens on a regular basis, no matter whether we are light, dark, or in between—it's the same old same old because, as many Americans say, they've never met a real American Indian except on TV or in the movies. Of course, as we all know, Hollywood has consistently hired Greek, Italian, or Chinese actors to represent Natives. We can respond that they wouldn't know one if they saw one. So we're supposed to match those stereotypes, but we don't because we embody multiple body types, hair color, and skin color. Some of this is due to the initial rape and pillage that came with the Great Invasion. We sometimes think we should respond to these comments by saying, "Well, you don't look English," or "You don't look Spanish."

NAS

Our identity is our culture, not our hair, skin, or eye color. It's how we're raised and it's how we identify ourselves. Sometimes an individual's identity may even change as they grow and move through life. So how do we recognize a Native person? Sometimes, as Native people, we wear our culture. Dentalium shell earrings worn with a heavy silver bracelet could reflect different tribes and trades. Sometimes our culture is present in conversation.

Trade is definitely part of our identity, and the giveaway, the Potlatch, for sure. [Potlatch was against the law in Canada from 1885 until 1951 and was also forbidden in the United States from 1883 to 1978 as part of the Code of Indian Offenses.][3] Gifts are a little reminder to ourselves of how we honor each other. It's about honoring something else, somebody else. We love to wear things that somebody else created, and we love to give gifts to each other for that same reason. We carry each other around. There is always a story, and who doesn't love stories? We're covered with stories. We are what we wear. That's identity. That's my identity. It's an affirmation of my identity when I meet another Indigenous person from the Americas. We "powwow" every time.

JQTSS

Well, I can repeat that by saying that blood quantum has nothing to do with culture. We do not all have the same creation stories or the same ceremonial clothing. We do not all have the same designs in our beadwork; in fact, many of our tribes do not bead. We do not all have casinos. Many of our tribes have some land and some land bases are called reservations, but not all tribes have land and are seeking land. Some land bases are as small as one acre. The US Congress [generally composed of elderly White men who know nothing about Native Americans] has to give us approval to identify as Native Americans. No other ethnic group needs government approval to identify their ethnicity. So far, the government has approved

574 federally recognized tribes with hundreds still awaiting recognition.[4]

Many of our reservations have blond, blue-eyed people who were raised in the culture and who know the stories, the dances, the drumming, the songs, and the ceremonies. They have grown up on the reservation or in our Native communities. Seventy percent of Native people now live in urban centers.[5] That makes for a lot of different kinds of identity through foods and dress for ceremonies and dances, such as a stomp dance, a fancy dance, or a chicken dance or grass dance. There are Southern dances and Northern dances. There are dances from the East Coast and the West Coast, all with different styles of dancing and regalia.

Another tip-off would be to ask someone where they are from. If they are Native, they will not tell you where they live currently, they will tell you their tribe, even though they might have never lived there. It is their identity. All the genocidal plans that mainstream government has sand-trapped us with by attempting to integrate us into the main society have failed. Boarding schools, Relocation, forcing their form of government on our reservations, giving us new Anglo names, and on and on.[6] None of this has worked, nor has taking away our languages.[7]

Some reservations are now going back to their old languages and their old form of government. They're returning to their original names that they used to call themselves, which generally translate to "We the people," "We the human beings," or "We are the first peoples" in their own language. Names that trappers, traders, and White people laid on them were Blackfeet, Flathead, Big Earrings, and so on. It is part of the genocide, to take away names, languages, form of dress, manners, and, of course, stealing the land so we couldn't eat our traditional foods. First, they gave us moldy flour and wormy beef, and later canned surplus foods laden with salt and sugar, which caused a multitude of physical ailments. And so, in today's world, with better food, better health care, and more agency, Indian people are going back and retrieving their original tribal names and trying to revive many parts of their culture, their ceremonies, the places they used to go to worship, old dances, and gambling games that they used to play, like the feather game. We're bringing our languages back.

Culture and identity are very complex and complicated issues. One example might be how the jingle dance has caught on like wildfire across Indian Country. [Indian Country is our name for the whole United States.] Now there are Navajo jingle dancers and Pueblo jingle dancers, even though this dance originated in the Great Lakes region and can represent women's strength.[8] Though the dance and the decorative design elements of its regalia, with the rolled snuff-can lids, started as a healing dance, it sometimes flows out into other tribal communities and is now a remembrance of a new time and new events.

Our cultural philosophies are being shared, like when we say we look seven generations into the future when making our decisions. And though nearly all tribes are using this concept now, it was originally a Haudenosaunee traditional way of making a decision and considering the future of our great-grandchildren.[9] Another Native expression that has spread is the reference to the United States as Turtle Island, meaning the turtle holds the world on its back. This, too, is part of the Haudenosaunee origin story and many are using it now. When we're in a group of people, if somebody speaks up and uses an expression like that, bam! we know that person is Native.

Some people say we're becoming pan-Indian. You could make the case that because of our vast trade routes we shared our cultures going way back in time. Today's highways in America, including passes in the mountains, are laid down on our old trade routes.[10] What we used to call "the Indian Grapevine," which referred to the many ways of communicating we had long before modern media, we now call social media, which has sped up the process of sharing cultural information. We have jumped into new media with Tim Giago's [Oglala Lakota Nation] *Indian Country Today* and Frank Blythe's [Eastern Band of Cherokee Indians/Sisseton-Wahpeton Dakota Nation] Vision Maker Media film institute because they changed with the advent of new technology.

Other cultural signifiers are hand gestures, phrases, humor, or terms that make us know the person we are conversing with is Native. Like when we shake hands, there's the soft slide or the pump, which come from Washington, DC. If they've been in a government job, they might have trained with Dale Carnegie Training, so we know where that Indian person has been or what their job has been in the past—it marks their identity. Another thing is eye motion or eye movement. When Indian people are gathered together, they don't always stare at each other but look down or look aside because eye contact is so intimate, and we learn early that it's not particularly polite to stare into another Native person's eyes. Those things are changing now with the urban Indians because they've picked up more and more of mainstream society's ways, but we still retain those old ways on a reservation or in a Native community.

Our foods are another thing that connects us: corn, beans, squash, and chile are the main dishes of the day whether you're up in Haudenosaunee Country or in the Southwest, as well as most other parts of Indian Country. Buffalo meat and salmon are considered to be Indian foods, along with shellfish and other wild foods like nuts and berries. Wild rice is another Native food that moves around the country, given as gifts when visiting friends or relatives and used in feasts throughout Indian Country. It grows around the Great Lakes and is under threat right now due to pollution and climate change. There are many more wild foods that are traditional to the Native diet and coming back to the dinner table and feast days.

I've watched these transitions happen slowly, and more connections in Native America have emerged, especially with social media. Indian people, especially Indian artists, keep in touch with each other, and the fact that we continue to do that, the fact that we love to come together to eat and spend time together, means there is much laughter and storytelling. We share what's going on in our communities. We talk about what the government is doing. Our tribal colleges also connect us, and we have many other ways that we connect with each other that show our identity, that show our colors. We don't need a headdress or traditional regalia; we show our colors in other ways. It might be with a hatband, a watchband, or a shell necklace. In our colonization, we didn't always wear beadwork or anything that identified who we were. Many Natives tried to pass, and many married out. The racism was so debilitating, we had to hide our identity.

I think the advent of Bacone College, the Haskell Institute, and the Institute of American Indian Arts gave students permission to show their street, to show their colors. The early 1970s was also the beginning of transnationalism because many Natives had gone to colleges and universities all over the country, or maybe in Europe and other countries, as did Nicholas Galanin (Tlingit/Unangax̂), Jeffrey Gibson (member of the Mississippi Band of Choctaw Indians and of Cherokee descent), Jolene Rickard (Tuscarora Nation, Turtle Clan), and others. So their work is showing not only their identity, but also their exposure to world art as well as reflecting their life experiences.

When I was a kid, Indian people had no money for plane fare. And there weren't even jets flying at that time, that I know of, so we couldn't have traveled far. You know, my family was one of three families living in a one-room cabin, and we were next to starvation, living on dried salmon jerky. We had no running water in the house and only an outhouse. A lot of Indian people my age grew up in circumstances like these. Today, those things have gotten better and most of us are not using outhouses anymore and our life experience is different. But this is not true for everyone; we can still go home to our communities or reservations and find no running water and outhouses in daily use.

Native people constitute the poorest populations in this country and that is very little known. Those of us who have gone to college often have parents who were illiterate. My father didn't read or write. I mean, that's pretty common in Indian families, especially with someone my age. Nobody in our family went to college. And forget about getting a high school degree, maybe sometimes a GED. And that makes a difference in how we view our world, our life experiences, and how we make art. Now, because we're exposed to all kinds of European and world art, we're not just learning at the kitchen table on the reservation—we're exposed to everything, including the media. And many of us have been to Europe and other countries, to the museums, and have seen worldwide art. And it doesn't mean that we don't value our traditional arts, because what I see right now is a kind of turning back, referencing tradition and regalia and inventing new ways of using it.

When I was growing up, Baptist ministers and priests were putting beadwork into bonfires, burning it up because it was evil stuff. And now people are trying to retrieve those old designs and use them in paintings and beadwork. But many other things are happening too. Our Salish weavings were destroyed by the Christian churches 150 years ago, though Salish weavers would say instead that the weavings were sleeping. Recently, some contemporary Salish weavers have been studying mountain goat and woolly dog hair weaving at the Peabody Essex Museum to learn the knots and techniques, and they are now teaching numerous new Salish weavers. The weaving is now being awakened. Salish weaving is similar to Plateau basket designs.

Well, they taught other weavers, and they also have continued teaching and now we have forty-four Salish weavers. They just had a conference where nearly every speaker cried onstage about how thrilled they are with this revival. One speaker said, "Please, let's not say this art form was destroyed, let's say it was sleeping," and that brought tears to my eyes. We are in recovery.

The diversity in this exhibition reinforces the fact that there is no one single definition to describe Native art. But through the artwork, each artist describes how they feel about their identity. We Natives can walk through the exhibition and see each artist's identity in the work. Some viewers may not be able to see it, being unfamiliar with Native cultures, but each piece contains a story.

You see, everything we create, harvest, or perform is connected to a religious aspect of our lives, our spiritual world, and our metaphysical world. Two other aspects of Native culture are that storytelling is always a part of it, and the creative process itself is considered the most important part of any creative act. And there is often a certain prayerful overview that goes with it that might be called meditative. A lot of our old traditional ways, whether it's forging silver or doing beadwork as one of our premier beadworkers, Marcus Amerman (Choctaw Nation), does, that too is a meditative process. Many Indian people are doing these kinds of things because they tie us to our traditions, to our ancestors. These enterprises make us feel good and they are healing to us. I can say that about a lot of the things we make, such as ribbon shirts and the new ribbon skirts. And we've been putting ribbons as well as beadwork on suit jackets, shirts, skirts, trousers, everything. We've moved to a place where we can show our street. We can show our colors now, legally and publicly.

NAS

It's not about posterity, exhibiting, presenting, or sharing our cultures and our identity and traditions. It's about going back and learning what we've lost in order to move forward. We're talking about the seven generations and the importance of observing the Seventh Generation Principle to get to the eighth generation. You must know from where you've come to move forward. So much information about the history of the earth is in our stories and in our languages and our cultures. These stories are vital today for the survival of Native peoples and our relatives, the animals, the trees, and all of nature. Now is a very important time to bring that information and those stories forward.

Everything we do is art in some form; it is all tied together. Europe has one word for art that generalizes and blankets everything and puts it into boxes or categories. I don't think there's a Native language in the Americas that has a separate word for art because everything is holistic. Everything is connected. All things are part of our world. We are all artists in many ways and with many facets. There aren't many other cultures today that can say that. I think many cultures had that way back in time, but it's been colonized out of them. It's been eradicated, removed, and lost. I think, as human beings, as a species, one of the things that connected us to everything, holistically, was that everybody was some type of artist at some level, because art was connected to a functional place in our lives.

Fortunately, identity is a living thing. Culture is a living thing. Traditions are a living thing. This exhibition can reintroduce the world to Native America and our unique and beautiful identities. It can exhibit traditions and cultures that are connected and not in stasis. It can reframe stereotypes about Native America. Americans need to recognize the fact that Native peoples of the Americas are multifaceted, multilingual, and have many different stories, identities, cultures, and traditions.

This exhibition contains the work of ninety-seven Indigenous artists with over seventy-four nations and communities represented, which can be translated into ninety-seven different identities and stories. We have multiple generations of living artists in this exhibition, ranging in age from their twenties to their eighties.

It is also a great honor to have many elder mentors represented, such as Peter Jemison (Seneca Nation of Indians) and Hulleah Tsinhnahjinnie (Navajo Nation), among many other very important influential artists, who have given back for decades. Viewers will have an immediate picture in their minds when reading about the show and may have expectations. Once it's witnessed, however, their ideas and expectations may change.

JQTSS

Well, you know, we're speaking out and telling people that we believe we are the true scientists of the Americas because in our languages we convey thousands of years of science about the plants, the animals, the water, and the environment. The White people don't realize that when they forced us to learn the Christian Bible, everything in that book was from the other side of the earth, the biblical plants and animals were alien to us. We have no connection to them or to the cultures in the Bible. People say we are closer to the Shinto religion, which is about animism. Everything is in constant motion. Leroy Little Bear (Blackfoot Nation), Vine Deloria (Oglala Lakota Nation), Greg Cajete (Santa Clara Pueblo), Joy Harjo (Mvskoke Nation), and Dan Wildcat (Yuchi Tribe/Mvskoke Nation) are scholars who have lectured and written about this. Of course, there are many other Native scholars who address this as well. Animism is such an important facet of our science and our epistemology, as well as our metaphysics.

This is just the tip of the iceberg, learning that Indian peoples, as fractured as we've been from the genocide, as difficult as our struggles have been, still retain a lot of that knowledge. And that, too, is part of our culture because it's so embedded and so ingrained in our study of our languages, our food, our housing, and our clothing, everything that comes out of our original environments. And you can see the tracks and the traces of it, including when the traders came in and swapped moose hair embroidery or quillwork for glass beads or trade cloth for hides, and we still track that knowledge in understanding about that history. And even though the art historians have not paid much attention to this, mainly because they're busy studying in Egypt and Italy or somewhere in Europe and are not paying attention to what is here in the Americas. They are the aliens here; they have no attachment to our natural world. This is not their history. Their ancestors don't reside here. And when they talk about the Mexican people being aliens, that's just a crock because the Mexican people are related to everybody here. They are Indigenous peoples of the Americas—that border is a political border; it split families and tribes. We had trade routes here for thousands of years that went from the Atlantic to the Pacific and from Point Barrow to Patagonia.[11]

I think this is the first time we've had an exhibition that is just purely about identity. There are exhibitions about glass, weaving, painting, crafts, and so on. There are exhibitions about Native women, dance regalia, photography, and clothing but no exhibitions purely about identity, and there is so much to say. Writers who record cultural changes are not keeping up with the changes in Native identities. There are extreme changes from eighty years ago or even fifty years ago. Twenty years ago would also be a benchmark because of social media. This exhibition demonstrates these changes in various ways, some personal and some tribal, and all are meaningful and revelatory for any viewer. This exhibition is a celebration of life.

NAS

It's good medicine for us all.

1. "American Indian Religious Freedom Act Summary," NOAA Office for Coastal Management, accessed on September 25, 2024, https://coast.noaa.gov/data/Documents/OceanLawSearch/Summary%20of%20Law%20-%20American%20Indian%20Religious%20Freedom%20Act.pdf.

2. Hiram Price, "Rules Governing the Court of Indian Offenses," US Government Documents Related to Indigenous Nations, Department of the Interior and Office of Indian Affairs (47th Congress, 2d Session, Washington, DC, 1883), https://commons.und.edu/indigenous-gov-docs/131/.

3. Taylor C. Noakes, "Potlatch Ban," *The Canadian Encyclopedia*, June 14, 2023, https://www.thecanadianencyclopedia.ca/en/article/potlatch-ban.

4. "Tribal Nations & the United States: An Introduction," National Congress of American Indians, Washington 2020, https://archive.ncai.org/about-tribes

5. "Learn More about Urban Indian Health Care and Urban Indian Organizations," National Council of Urban Indian Health, 2021, https://ncuih.org/about/urban-indian-health-facts/.

6. 84th Congress, "Relative to Employment for Certain Adult Indians on or Near Indian Reservations," S.3416, Public Law 959, August 3, 1956, https://www.congress.gov/bill/84th-congress/senate-bill/3416/text.

7. "1887: Indian Affairs Bans Native Languages in Schools," *Native Voices*, National Library of Medicine (Bethesda, MD), https://www.nlm.nih.gov/nativevoices/timeline/369.html

8. Catherine Tynjala, "The Jingle Dress," American Indian Studies, College of Liberal Arts, University of Minnesota, January 17, 2019, https://cla.umn.edu/ais/story/jingle-dress

9. "Who We Are," Haudenosaunee Confederacy, https://www.haudenosauneeconfederacy.com/who-we-are/.

10. Gary Hoover, "Persistence of our Paths: From Native American Trails to Hyperloops," Business History, American Business History Center, December 12, 2019, https://americanbusinesshistory.org/the-persistence-of-our-paths-from-native-american-trails-to-hyperloops/.

11. Bob Joseph, "Indigenous Trade Networks Thrived Long Before the Arrival of Europeans," *Indigenous Corporate Training Inc.* (blog), July 5, 2017, https://www.ictinc.ca/blog/indigenous-trade-networks-thrived-long-before-the-arrival-of-europeans.

Native Art Overview: How Do We Consider the "Contemporary" in Indigenous Arts?

Chelsea M. Herr, PhD (Choctaw Nation of Oklahoma)

TO CONSIDER CONTEMPORARY NATIVE ART simply as that which has been created in the last fifty years would not only be disingenuous, but it would also be reductive of the complexity and diversity of Indigenous ontologies. Often, conversations and scholarship that address the characterization of "contemporary" (or any circumscribed era, for that matter) Indigenous art interrogate Euro-Western art historical notions of chronology, medium, and identity, and social, cultural, and political critique. While even within larger art historical discourse the notion of the "contemporary" is ambiguous, nebulous, and often arbitrary, the term is further complicated when considering the artistic production of Indigenous peoples. The problem with temporality as a marker of contemporaneity is that it insists upon the linear chronology that is the foundation of post-Enlightenment Euro-Western thought. It assumes that there is a shared beginning, middle, and eventual end of time that originates in Judeo-Christian philosophy, which only reinforces the colonial project of subsuming non-Euro-Western peoples—or eliminating them entirely.

As such, this text does not aim to provide a definition of what is or is not contemporary Indigenous art. Rather, I reflect on how contemporaneity is inextricably tied to our own histories and intergenerational knowledge systems. To provide a basic framework while discussing such a complex topic as contemporaneity, I address what I perceive as two shared aspects of recent Native art (although there are many that could be considered): an advocacy for the perspectives and agency of Indigenous peoples in an extant settler-colonial state and an embodiment of many Native communities' long-held traditions of both verbal and visual storytelling. These aspects are not necessarily discrete; rather, they are interdependent and buttress one another.

Recent Indigenous art grows out of generations of survival and advocacy—in particular, a sociopolitical legacy of Red Power and the growing activism of Native thinkers like Vine Deloria Jr. (Standing Rock Sioux), who championed tribal self-determination and sovereignty in the wake of the federal Termination Era. One of the earliest works featured in *Indigenous Identities*, G. Peter Jemison's (Seneca Nation [Heron Clan]) *Red Power* (1973; pp. 190–91), speaks to what I view as a foundational aspect of contemporary Indigenous art: advocacy and agency. *Red Power* textually and visually invokes the energy with which Native activists demanded recognition for the rights of sovereign Native nations. Sharp, angular fields of red and orange burst forth from the surface of the canvas, creating an abstracted representation of a barbed plant. At the left of the picture's plane, one of the plant's offshoots seems to wither, yet the remainder of its thorny protuberances erupt with dynamism and vitality, as if challenging the viewer to invade its space.

There were two pivotal moments in Jemison's life that he attributes to his work during this time period. The first was his "increased contact with Seneca . . . singers, dancers, [and] fluent Seneca language speakers."[1] The second poignant influence on Jemison's artwork in the early 1970s was his interaction with other artists and activists who grew up during the Red Power movement. He describes this period as: "The time when Indian activists began to say that it was time for us to stand up for who we are. It was time for us to acknowledge that we have a proud tradition. The Indian activists were young people, guided by elders, who stood up to speak of some of the injustices that were happening in this country—injustices to our own people that had to stop."[2] Jemison's invocation of Indigenous activism in the arts is certainly not unique. Artists such as Oscar Howe (Yanktonai Dakota), who wrote a protest letter to the Philbrook Art Center in 1958, and Jaune Quick-to-See Smith (Salish and Kootenai Confederated Tribes), who curated the exhibition *Submuloc Show/Columbus Wohs* in 1992 in response to the Columbus Quincentenary, have demonstrated how effective Native artists and their work can be in both representing and advocating for Indigenous peoples.

Artists working today have inherited this legacy of advocacy, and the approaches to this inheritance are myriad. Self-determination and sovereignty encompass *all* aspects of life for Native people, as individuals and as members of a Native community. This includes our cultural lives, which are built upon intergenerational traditions, such as storytelling. In addition to advocacy, I view storytelling as one of the foundational aspects of contemporary Native art. Regardless of time period, medium, or style, Indigenous art is fundamentally a form of storytelling. It is dialogic and instructive, and it often takes the form of a call-and-response, inviting the viewer to contribute as a participant in the life of the artwork. In telling stories, whether visual or verbal, we not only perpetuate our worlds, but we create, deconstruct, and reimagine them.

Many of the works in *Indigenous Identities* explicitly invoke narratives that reference Indigenous ontologies, such as Jason Clark's (non-enrolled Algonquin/Creek; Swiss/Scottish) *Winona and the Big Oil "Windigo"* (2014; pp. 114–15). In this print, Clark depicts Anishinaabe environmental activist Winona LaDuke as a bear, battling the fossil fuel industry, which is represented as a Windigo, a spiritual being often understood as vicious and malevolent who embodies "excess, and by extrapolation . . . encourages moderation."[3] With his use of an Ojibwe or Woodlands-style aesthetic, Clark embeds a present-day scene in the long history of the Anishinaabe peoples. The artist creates a reciprocal dialogue between his artwork, his community, and the viewer, demonstrating what the Indigenous Australian artist Fiona Foley describes as a crucial facet of contemporary Indigenous art—that it is "no longer just about ideas, but about actual encounters: the direct confrontations of the everyday, which demand mutual involvement, commitment and responsibility."[4] Contemporary Native artists also engage in dialogue with one another in works such as Cara Romero's (Chemehuevi) *Arla Lucia* (2019; pp. 208–9), in which the model, Arla Marquez (Seneca-Cayuga/ Shoshone-Bannock/Blackfoot), dons a Wonder Woman outfit accompanied by beadwork by Jamie Okuma (La Jolla Band of Luiseño Indians/ Shoshone-Bannock/Wailaki Tribe/Okinawan) and jewelry by Keri Ataumbi (Kiowa). Romero's photograph is more than a collaboration among artists. It exemplifies the ways in which Indigenous peoples have always been in contact, conversation, and exchange with one another.

Storytelling in Native art is also evidenced in the materiality and phenomenology of the artworks themselves. In other words, the physical existence of the artwork as object tells a story in and of itself. The artist and scholar Sherry Farrell Racette (Métis/ Timiskaming Algonquin/Irish) eloquently describes the potential for contemporary Indigenous art to offer "an alternative mode of translation and expression" that can avoid "the flattening effect of the printed word."[5] She argues that we honor an artwork when we understand it as an autonomous object, with a life, a history, and a purpose that are indelibly linked to its creator, its materials, and everyone who encounters it. In this sense, "the meaning of objects is under continuous construction, altered and fluctuating by the knowledge and memories projected onto it."[6] This can be seen in Gail Tremblay's woven-film baskets and Marie Watt's (Seneca Nation) reclaimed wool blanket structures (see pp. 96–97), as both artists bring the object, its materials, and its viewer into a dialogic interaction that is constantly in flux.

In maintaining the examination of storytelling and advocacy as key components of contemporary Native art, where does our field go from here? Current Native American art historical scholarship contends with an array of methodological approaches, many of which seem to contradict or discount one another. The polyvocal nature of the field is arguably unprecedented, and its contemporary history can be traced to the 1980s, when Indigenous peoples' voices became part of the curatorial and academic spheres of Native artistic production. That decade marked the emergence of diverse objectives and approaches to Native art, when the perspectives of Native peoples were no longer seen exclusively through artworks themselves but also through the inclusion of Native voices in dialogues that continue to narrate, situate, and prioritize Native ways of knowing and being. What I argue in the confluence of advocacy and storytelling in contemporary Indigenous art is that Indigenous artists, scholars, curators, and community members are the ones both telling and responding to our own stories. For decades now, we have demanded not just a voice in arts institutions and publications but a permanent and meaningful space that is long overdue.

This determination to advocate and speak for ourselves is embedded in both our diverse traditions of storytelling and our understanding that our continued existence is an act of resistance. Returning briefly to Jaune Quick-to-See Smith's 1992 exhibition, we see the effect of Native participation in our own storytelling. Carla Roberts (Delaware Nation), one of the organizers of the *Submuloc* exhibition, traces how cultural institutions regarded Native peoples during the twentieth century. She argues that we "have evolved from object, to subject, to practitioner" in museum displays, and that the "*Submuloc Show*, in conjunction with other Native-led projects in 1992, marked the turning point from Indigenous cultures' participation in institutions as 'subject' to 'practitioner.'[7] This turning point could be considered a further qualification for what we consider "contemporary" Native art: that being contemporary for Indigenous peoples is simply existing in spaces that were never intended for us—the settler-colonial state and its institutions.

To conclude, I offer a possibility of what contemporary Native art *might* be, with the understanding that it will never have only one definition. The Australian art historian Terry Smith illustrates how elusive the definition of the "contemporary" is, describing it as: "That which emerges from within the conditions of contemporaneity . . . as an art of that which actually is in the world, of what it is to be in the world, and of that which is to come. Its impulses are specific yet worldly, even multitudinous, inclusive yet oppositional and anti-institutional, concrete but also various, mobile, and open-ended."[8]

Building upon Smith's observation that contemporary art is that which is of the world and what is to come, I contend that contemporary Indigenous art recognizes that "the world" is not the singular, universal, colonial construct that has been a constant presence in our lives for over five centuries now. Our cultural production has always been an expression of what it means to be in the world—and, arguably, in multiple worlds—and it has always considered what is to come. Thus, Native art is, has always been, and will always be contemporary.

1. G. Peter Jemison, quoted in "Q&A: Native Artist G. Peter Jemison Stretches the Canvas," *Native News Online*, June 18, 2020, https://nativenewsonline.net/currents/q-a-native-artist-g-peter-jemison-stretches-the-canvas.

2. Jemison, "The Journey," *St. Thomas Law Review* 7, no. 3 (Summer 1995), 435.

3. Grace Dillon, foreword to *Dangerous Spirits: The Windigo in Myth and History* by Shawn Smallman (Victoria, British Columbia: Heritage House Publishing, 2014), 18.

4. Fiona Foley, *The Art of Politics/The Politics of Art: The Place of Contemporary Indigenous Art* (Queensland: Keeira Press, 2006), 70.

5. Sherry Farrell Racette, "Encoded Knowledge: Memory and Objects in Contemporary Native Art," in *Manifestations: New Native Art Criticism*, ed. Nancy Marie Mithlo (Santa Fe, NM: Museum of Contemporary Native Arts, 2011), 42.

6. Ibid., 40.

7. Carla Roberts, "Object, Subject, Practitioner: Native Americans and Cultural Institutions," *Native Americas: Akwe:kon's Journal of Indigenous Issues* 11, no. 4 (Fall–Winter 1994): 4.

8. Terry Smith, "Contemporary Art and Contemporaneity," *Critical Inquiry* 32, no. 4 (Summer 2006): 692.

Indexicality as Kinship: The Relationality of Native Photography

Mario A. Caro, PhD (Colombian Mestizo)

PHOTOGRAPHY, AS A MEDIUM AND PRACTICE, has always occupied a unique place within the arts. Since its inception, the practice has required that the photographer establish and be cognizant of their relationship with or to the subject. Whether considering the intimacy required in developing a portrait, the engagement with the environment in composing a landscape, or the care needed to document an event, the photographer is always, in some way, already part of the picture.

In the West, the indexical quality of the photograph—the direct contiguity between the subject and the resulting image—has always made photography a special category of image making. If we consider photography as medium—the physics involved in controlling and capturing fleeting light—the immediacy captured between the subject and the apparatus has led to the resulting image being coded as truth. The mechanical way in which light from a subject is captured as an image—an immediacy perceived as unmediated—offers the photographic image as the result of objective witnessing.

Within the broad range of functions performed by photographs, from artistic subjectivity to scientific objectivity, the imagery produced by Native photographers, I will argue, conveys an approach to relationality that is specifically Indigenous. This is not an essentialist claim. It is, instead, an approach to reading Native photographs within an Indigenous framework that considers relations as the result of kinship. And the onus is not just on the reader to consider this relationality framework as a way to read the photograph; here also needs to be a consideration of the agency of the photograph itself. In the dialectical exchange of meaning between subject and viewer, there should also be a consideration of the photograph as an actor in the process of meaning making.

Whether a memorial of a distant relative, a formal military portrait, a faded color photograph from one's youth, a graduation picture, or an image of a special place we've visited, photographs act on us. Photographers initiate this phenomenon, but the intentionality of the artist, informed by their worldview, influences the way in which photographs behave in the world. And this is what makes Native photographs act differently.

The following are quick observations on a selection of photographs that I hope will help to illustrate this point.

Traditional Design as Community Bond

Tom Jones
(Ho-Chunk Nation of Wisconsin)
Forster Nash from the *Strong Unrelenting Spirits* series, 2015, digital photograph with beadwork
(pp. 136–37)

An excellent example of Indigenous photography that displays and enacts familial ties is the vibrant *Forster Nash* by Tom Jones (Ho-Chunk). The image is a colorful portrait that features a happy infant smiling delightfully, comfortably swaddled in his cradle board. He occupies the center of the image, which is set against a dark background within a delicately beaded traditional Ho-Chunk design. The image is from a series of large-scale portraits titled *Strong Unrelenting Spirits*, which follow this same composition. They all feature members of the Ho-Chunk community against backdrops of beaded traditional floral designs. As an ensemble, the group of portraits conveys a sense of community; the sitters are all enveloped and united by cultural iconography. The designs are beaded directly onto the photographs, breaking that direct indexical relationship between the present of the photo and the past of the image captured. The vibrant presence of the beadwork points to the continuous transfer of knowledge that makes the enhancement possible—an imaging of tradition that promises its futurity.

Colonization and Climate Change

Larry McNeil
(Tlingit Nation/Nisga'a Nation)
Tonto's Earthen House from the *Tonto & Lone Ranger* series, 2013, platinum print

The figures of Tonto and the Lone Ranger have appeared in many of McNeil's compositions. These complex images reconfigure the Western stereotype of the colonizer savior and his oftentimes not-so-faithful sidekick. In this instance, Tonto stands next to a brightly colored car—a Tlingit-blue Cadillac to be precise—looking as though he has just put the Lone Ranger in jail. McNeil has developed a narrative that makes the image a metaphor about the present ecological crisis: Tonto attempts to reverse the detrimental effects of fossil fuel pollution. (McNeil's own commuter bicycle is seen at the right as an obvious alternative.) The relationship between the two protagonists has been reversed: the colonized has taken control and is enacting a strategy of reversal, reversing power relationships as well as the causality between car culture and climate change. McNeil has suggested that Tonto's immediate pursuit is the conversion of the gas-guzzling classic to an electronic vehicle, a stylish alternative.[1]

The Spectacle of Indigenous Feminisms

Cara Romero
(Chemehuevi)
Arla Lucia, 2019, photograph (pp. 208–9)

Women are the main protagonists in Cara Romero's oeuvre. Their forceful agency is made highly visible through the ways in which Romero portrays their engagement with their surroundings. In *Arla Lucia*, we encounter a Native superhero—an Indigenous Wonder Woman. The colorfully clad figure is set against a dark background, suggesting a timeless space and highlighting an eternal hero. Her outfit, though highly Indigenized, references the classic costume of comic books and movies. She wears beaded earrings and a large medallion; in her headband stands an eagle feather. The powerful figure confronts the viewer head-on, forcing them to consider how differently justice would be meted out if it were done by a Native woman. Her Lasso of Truth would extract a very different truth. This is an Indigenous feminist approach that aims at rematriating the relationship between Native women and the photographic apparatus.

Mastering Medium

Will Wilson
(Diné)
Self-Portrait—DAM, 2013, tintype (pp. 224–25)

Will Wilson is one of the most technically mindful photographers working today. His practice employs a range of radical techniques, from early analog processes using large-format cameras, plates, and handmade lenses to the latest image-recognition technology that bring his imagery to life. However, it is his Critical Indigenous Photographic Exchange (CIPX) project, a monumental ten-year project, that has taken most of his efforts. His practice has rewritten the history of photography as it pertains to Native American subjects—both in terms of technology and as the relationship between photographer and subject. The project has been in development for more than a decade and uses the wet-plate collodion photographic process, a laborious and unforgiving approach to making photographs. It requires time and focused engagement. The project has resulted in thousands of powerful images over the years, each representing an ever-expanding web of relationships he has nurtured through the project. Ultimately, his effort with the project—and with his practice overall—is to produce images that "return agency and subjectivity to the Indigenous people they represent."[2]

The CIPX has been discussed as social engagement art. The aim of the project is to produce portraits in collaboration with the sitter. This contrasts with non-Native photographers at the turn of the twentieth century who would simply, and at times forcibly, "take" their image. Instead, Wilson engages in a friendly and respectful exchange, a mutual giving and taking, with the sitter. This intimate relationship leads to a moment in which the sitter gives their image, along with a verbal relaying of who they are, in exchange for a copy of the photograph produced. Through this project, Wilson aims to "Indigenize the photographic exchange."[3]

This very brief selection of photographers is meant to illustrate my claim that Native photographers are employing the medium of photography and its many processes—studio photography, street photography, portraiture, landscape, documentary, and so on—in ways that are attentive to the relationships that constitute Indigenous communities. And their photographs play a role in producing, conveying, and maintaining these relationships. The Western notion of indexicality, which considers the photograph as capturing the trace of photons bouncing off a subject, is supplanted by a consideration of our relatedness, of our kinship. Native photographers know that we are all related, and the photograph helps to maintain those relations.

1. Larry McNeil, "Indelible," National Museum of the American Indian, accessed August 2, 2024, https://americanindian.si.edu/indelible/tontos-earthen-house.html.

2. Will Wilson, "On Ten Years of the Critical Indigenous Photographic Exchange," in *In Our Hands: Native Photography, 1890 to Now* (New Haven, Connecticut: Yale University Press, 2023), 198–203.

3. Ibid., 201.

Indigenous Futurism, Collaboration, and Spatial Intervention

Lou Cornum, PhD (Diné)

INDIGENOUS ARTISTS WORKING in the twenty-first century are creating within the churning changes of innovative technologies. These technologies have had profound effects on formations of Indigenous consciousness, whether cultural or political, and aesthetics, influencing not only how art is made but how it circulates. The ubiquity of online media and information economies that are heavily reliant on the image has meant a much wider reach for Indigenous art generally, and particularly for Native art that does not fit neat definitions or institutional parameters for inclusion. This is also the age of decolonization, if not as political reality, then certainly as a mobilizing idea. The desire to decolonize relations, epistemologies, and systems of governance often animates artistic production, not only in its capacity for critical intervention but also in the imagining of alternatives. The transformational aspect of recent Indigenous-made work then is located in experiments with forms both visual and social, and otherwise. I refer here to artist collectives and public-facing artists emerging in the past decade who have faced the pressures of outside recognition and the rubrics of authenticity in irreverent, critical, and imaginative ways.

This manifests most explicitly in the movement and discourse described as Indigenous Futurism. Indigenous Futurism spans a range of media and in its artistic manifestations takes up visual vocabularies from pop culture, outer space, and digital infrastructures. Native American artists defy their imposed or perceived isolation from the (post-)modern world and internet age by directly engaging its images and materials and extending them within the context of Indigenous cosmologies and traditions. This can result in work that truly takes us to the outer limits of scientific possibility. For instance, the Oglála Lakȟóta artist and performer Suzanne Kite, part of the COUSIN Collective, works with machine learning programs, making kin with the rare earth minerals that power our digital devices. The work of the Cochiti Pueblo artist Virgil Ortiz adapts alien and cyborg forms that bear striking resemblance to sci-fi bounty hunters in the *Star Wars* movies, cast in the materials and color schemes of traditional Pueblo pottery. His figural sculpture *Tracker* (2012), a ceramic work built from and slipped with black clay, presents a time-traveling vision of Indigenous creation and land defense. *Last Son* (2019; pp. 218–19), a digital print by Jeffrey Veregge (Port Gamble Band of S'Klallam), with its spray-paint stencil aesthetic, holds even more direct pop-cultural reference: Superman, recast in Salish visual style. Artists like Veregge and Ortiz perform a reappropriation of science fiction's reliance on colonial tropes of the alien and the "new world" to make culturally specific references to modern mythologies.

Indigenous Futurism plays on genres of mass appeal and also engages the world-building aspect of science fiction imaginaries. This constructive practice is shared by the large-scale installation works of groups like Postcommodity and New Red Order (see pp. 84–85). The fact that these installations—often involving elements of performance, sculpture, and video all at once—come into being through the work of collectives is also telling: the more people involved, the more ambitious in scope and scale these socially engaged art practices can become. Collaboration as a method disrupts the Western ideal of singular genius and also makes possible more material disruptions. The 2015 installation *Repellant Fence*, a two-mile-long installation of balloons tethered to the ground and extending one hundred feet into the sky while cutting north–south across the US-Mexico border, was envisioned by Postcommodity and brought into existence by several different groups based on either side of the divided nations. Both Postcommodity and New Red Order have flexible notions of membership, with the groups expanding and contracting over time and depending on the project at hand. The work forges an artistic relationship to the sorts of organization that occur in contemporary leaderless social and political movements. In *Repellant Fence*, Postcommodity's work with a cross-border contingent coalition made possible a physical and symbolic reinscription of a scarred geography. One of the collective's former members, Raven Chacon (Diné/Chicano), has carried through this engagement with on-the-ground struggle in his own sound-based and installation works. Political protest is not confined to metropolitan streets; it also exists in the reservation border towns and rural lands to which many Native artists have connections. That is to say, what constitutes "street art" in the worlds of Indigenous visual cultures has to be slightly stretched. Sometimes the street is a dirt road or a highway through the plains. Chacon's recent work at the Whitney Biennial 2022 highlighted the quiet spaces between the flare-ups of confrontation between land protectors and law enforcement in a sound piece titled *Silent Choir (Standing Rock)* (2017). Also included in the Biennial were the lithograph scores from the *For Zitkála-Šá* series (2019; see pp. 58–61), all made for specific Indigenous women (Suzanne Kite again appears as a performer for one score), which highlight in another medium Chacon's insistence on working with others and in honor of figures of Native struggle over the generations.

Since its inception, the New Red Order collective has played with the language of being a "public secret society," both a nod to the Improved Order of Red Men, a nineteenth-century fraternal organization wherein White American men played Indian, and an invocation of the group's interest in bringing people into temporary coconspiracy across lines of difference. New Red Order casts this kind of collaboration in terms of gathering "informants" and accomplices, as in their 2019 exhibition at Artist's Space in New York, *Informants Get Paid!*, which transformed the downtown gallery space into a combination art show, recruitment center, lecture series, and punk rock music venue. (Full disclosure: I was a participant in this programming.) These projects bring together local and transnational communities, both Indigenous and non-Indigenous, into all-night symposia, remixing academic lectures, participant rituals, video screenings, and musical performances that play with the notions of "Indian play" and the desires that animate them. The group seeks to reroute those who want to momentarily embody the exotic commodified sense of the symbolic into actual material forms of solidarity, whether that be the repatriation of museum items or of land itself.

Like the social movements these particular collectives are in conversation with, Postcommodity and New Red Order amplify and assert Indigenous claims to land and public space. This speaks to circuits of artists who travel between the rural and urban nodes of Indian Country. To follow the cutting edge of Indigenous art is to pay as much attention to what's happening in Gallup, New Mexico, and Tulsa, Oklahoma, as in downtown New York City. Street art is another method of spatial intervention that also speaks to larger communities, particularly through engagements with public space and everyday experience. It can also be a way of bringing aesthetics associated with urban life into the reservation and bringing reservation concerns to the city, as in the work of Tomahawk GreyEyes, who is Navajo and grew up all around Arizona (see pp. 122–23). His work demonstrates the innovations within street art found across Indian Country. GreyEyes's outdoor works include mixed-media collage-like statements against mining in Oak Flats, plastered on the side of a water drum near Snowflake, Arizona, and screen-printed posters hung across Albuquerque walls to put in front of passersby the history of the Indian Child Welfare Act (ICWA) of

1978. These very site-specific interventions highlight the immediacy of producing visual culture in contexts of continuing colonialism.

The styles of Indigenous street art are increasingly appreciated by larger public institutions, especially as forms of community-engaged historical knowledge sharing. Cameron Decker, who is a member of the Navajo Nation and a Salish descendant, was commissioned by the Ronan School District, in Ronan, Montana, to complete several large murals for their high school's hallways. One of these, titled *Sophie Moiese* (2022), depicts the eponymous, knowledgeable ceremony keeper in a spray-painted stencil style. The figure, rendered in black and white and outlined with a deep orange halo of paint, radiates from the plywood surface. There is a kinetic energy to this representation of an elderly Salish matriarch that demonstrates the power of illustrating collective memories through the meaning-making techniques of the twenty-first century. Moiese was a leader of the Bitterroot ceremony, which marked the reemergence of fresh life from the cold, hard ground of winter. When she was twenty-seven, the Salish were forcibly removed by the United States government from the Bitterroot Valley. That was in 1891, and she lived to tell that story until her passing in 1960, at the age of ninety-six. Decker's work makes Moiese and other key figures of Salish history, whom he also painted for the school, into icons.

Much of the recent work produced by Native artists in the vernacular associated with graffiti and street murals also seems descendant, even if indirectly, from the wide-ranging creations of Edgar Heap of Birds, or Hock E Aye Vi, who is Cheyenne and Arapaho and based in Oklahoma but has shown work all over the world. *Indian Never Safe* (2006–12; pp. 76–77), a series of prints made over six years, from 2006 to 2012, is paradigmatic of the text-based explorations Heap of Birds has undertaken over multiple series that merge poetics and paint. As in the viscosity print series *Columbus Day* and *Our Red Nations Were Always Green*, *Indian Never Safe* consists of evocative messages written in bold, informal print, like tags on the walls of the world. Some in this set read, "Indian Still Target Obama Bin Laden Geronimo," and "Plains to Beach Capture and Collect." Over the decades, Heap of Birds has also participated in several large-scale public works, many of which use the street sign as a template to remind viewers not of speed limits and turnoffs but instead of the claims of local Native nations. The *Today Your Host Is* series takes the same outline and on simple, two-post signs addresses the place of its location, written backward as if seen in a rear-view mirror. Alaska, for instance, is told, "Today Your Host Is Haida." Throughout British Columbia, some on the grounds of the University of British Columbia, there are many signs: "Today Your Host Is Musqueam," "Today Your Host Is Wet'suwet'en." Throughout his career and into the current day, Heap of Birds has always pushed the bounds of artistic practices, challenging himself and the viewer to imagine new connections across time and place. This evinces the long-standing tradition of political aesthetics and messaging that has emerged again in works from recent years.

There is—even in the most futuristic or strikingly novel art being made by Indigenous peoples today—an abiding commitment to cultivating intergenerational transmission. Eric-Paul Riege's (Diné) work encompasses weaving, costuming, performance, and sculpture across media that incorporate the materials of Navajo aesthetic forms and recasts them in uncanny scales and durational embodied movement. In certain moments, such as with the work titled *Hólǫ́—it xistz* (2020), Riege wears his art to make himself into an Earthen Cyborg, arms striped with ash and face covered with a spiny shield. Born in 1994, Riege has exhibited his work in cities across the Americas, bringing an esoteric Southwestern index of narrative symbols to various locations and activating across boundaries of human and other than human, subject, and landscape. Riege is part of a network of collaborators and peers creating in New Mexico that also includes Grace Rosario Perkins (Diné/Akimel O'odham), a self-taught painter who has lived across New Mexico and, more recently, in the Bay Area (see pp. 206–7). From April to October 2022, the Museum of Contemporary Art (MOCA) in Tucson was host to Perkins's *The Relevance of Your Data*, a paradoxically termed first "solo" exhibition, given that the artist immediately made space for several other artists to show work and bring programming into the space. These are just a couple of the people to watch as the emerging generation of Indigenous artists increasingly widens the scope of what it means to create work for each other and for their people, not just for a hungry market driven by momentary trends.

We come full circle to the ethos of collaboration, a commitment to working in groups to transform spaces as well as the practice of art making itself. The future of Native American and Indigenous art is one of breaking boundaries and moving beyond outmoded conventions of cultural institutions. Indigenous artist collectives and individual artists working in tandem with community and political causes insist—even from within the gallery spaces they fill—on upholding the responsibility to respond to ongoing struggles for land and life. Like the visuals of the Indigenous Futurists, the tendencies toward street art, public space installations, and reciprocal exchange highlighted in these pages represent images of what can be drawn from the long memories of what has been.

Always Quakes: Native American Poetry as Tectonic

Heid E. Erdrich, PhD (Turtle Mountain Ojibwe)

WHO IS TO SAY WHEN POETRY BEGAN in these lands where our Indigenous nations formed?

There's no doubt that something like what Europeans called poetry arrived when we did—whether in canoes or walking on ice or crawling out of a passage from another world or fallen from the stars, poems were probably in our pockets when we skidded along on the fault lines of geography. These first poems might not have been written in words or even memetic images or any systems of symbology, but I know from a life of being a poet that a rock or shell can tell a poem, a bit of bark can keep dream words, a pattern woven into a basket can save a song poem. I once kept a pecan cookie on my desk for a year because it held a poem.

Imagine the poem on its own—
the act of the poem—the catch.
The poem first set foot on this land
in times untold. Except, sometimes
as metaphor. The tale of the younger sibling.
The one afflicted in speech and motion,
the one who wouldn't attempt
the usual acts of war. Who loved
butterflies and birds. Who made some
shapes in the sand. Then spoke those shapes.
Then POEM in our homelands.

When we started using English and the written versions of our Indigenous languages, we started making poems that the rest of the world would recognize and that we can now claim. In fact, our poems were in some of the first books made in what would become the United States. The first Bible published here was translated into the Natick dialect and printed by Indigenous people, including James Printer, or Wowaus, a printer whose many times great-grandchildren are today known as Nipmuc people. Often called *The Eliot Bible*, in reference to the missionary who engaged Indigenous interpreters and printers in the project, the book's formal title is *Mamusse Wunneetupanatamwe Up-Biblum God*. We know the Christian Bible contains poetry, and translation of poetry is a form of poetic production. In the Nipmuc- and Natick-centered production of what many now refer to as *The Algonquin Bible*, I'd say we produced what is considered poetics by European terms. We did so as soon as we were asked to translate from English into our Native tongues.

Let's resist defining Native American poetry by European terms alone. Perhaps theory says more about them than it does about us. Let's use the great abstractor and innovator: Indigenous imagination. Imagine us bringing poems here to these continents—North, Center, and South. Maybe we took them everywhere we went. Some say we went to Europe and back, some say we traveled to the Pacific Islands, China, and even Turkey, where some of our relatives started out, and where some of us have returned, perhaps to visit. It's certain that many Indigenous people of the Americas traveled to Siberia and back, as they have in my lifetime, and as they have recently to escape Russian conscription. The poet Joy Harjo (Mvskoke/Creek) suggests that no human route is a vacuum.

Carrying our poems, we shifted with the cracks in the globe, perhaps not knowing if we would ever go back across a rift but keeping track of where we had been: The art we make consists of maps of human comings and goings. When I look at Aboriginal Australian art, as I have had the good fortune to do recently at Dartmouth College's Hood Museum, the poetry of Indigenous life comes clear. The ways in which poems relate to our songs, our dances, our maps, our ways of marking kinship and making art—these all come clear to me as Indigenous ways that are intrinsic to our being. We have always made poetry. We are made of poetry.

Everywhere became poem. All at once,
like a good idea. The sibling,
The Poet Misfit, celebrated, made
ribald jokes and danced. Badly.
On purpose. The Poet Misfit
might have named the flowers,
and sang for esoteric ceremony.
The Poet Misfit might have amused
and inspired—but I never heard if
The Poet Misfit found love or glory.
Except in the love and glory of words.

Alongside any inherent Indigenous poetics, we had a long and important tradition of conventional publishing that is all but unknown. We can follow a two-hundred-year timeline of authors starting with William Walker (Wyandot, born 1800) and Bamewawagezhikaquay/Jane Johnston Schoolcraft—whose bilingual Anishinaabe and English poems written in the 1820s are likely the oldest Native poems. We can mark that timeline with the poems of Alexander Posey (Mvskoke/Creek, b. 1873) and Louis Little Coon Oliver (Mvskoke/Creek, b. 1904) to Joy Harjo (Mvskoke/Creek b. 1951), the longest-serving poet laureate of the United States, whose first book was published in 1975. These poets, and many between them, illustrate how we have always adapted English poetics to Indigenous worldview. And vice versa.

However, in the first half of the twentieth century, if our poetry made it into the literary canon at all, most often it was through anthropology and the transliteration of songs collected in sometimes dubious circumstances. Sometimes an anthology included a "chant" in English often unattributed to an individual but rather to the entire tribe, or lines presented as an excerpt from a speech attributed to a "chief." One such collection of Native American poems was gathered under the title *American Indian Poetry* edited by George William Cronyn in 1918. It was still a bestseller in 2018.

Many new voices of Native poets lacked representation in the late twentieth century, but at the same time, we began to see important regional or tribally specific anthologies such as *Traces in Blood, Bone, and Stone* edited by Anishinaabe poet Kimberly Blaeser. The trend continued to *Dawnland Voices* edited by Siobahn Seiner in 2014, an extensive book of collected writings and poetry from "colonial" times to the present by Indigenous people of the Northeast United States. And there were many other anthologies in the past fifty years that gathered Native poets in mostly stereotypically themed collections.

There was also a huge gap in publications of anthologies between the late 1970s (Duane Niatum's excellent *Carriers of the Dream Wheel*) and 2018, when Graywolf Press published the anthology I edited, *New Poets of Native Nations*.

I find it remarkable that it was not until 2020 that the first *Norton Anthology of Native Nations Poetry*, edited by Joy Harjo, was published. In the Norton, beginning with an elegy by "an Indian student" from 1678 and to the present, Native American poets represent five broad regions of the country in more than four hundred pages. I can tell you those pages were not nearly enough to hold everything editors wanted.

Our representation of our own poetry was a long time coming. Perhaps because so few of us were PhD literary critics until the 1990s. In the late twentieth century—not because Native poets weren't writing all along, but because a White literary critic had an idea—the literary world discovered Native American poetry. I find it odd that the term "Native American Renaissance" given by Kenneth Lincoln in 1985 holds as the name of an era in Indigenous intellectual production today. I understand the term as meaning a flourishing, but there's that other connotation and our Indigenous poetics never died, so why would being published in English bring them back to life? The writers of this "renaissance" era include N. Scott Momaday (Kiowa), James Welch (Blackfeet and A'aninin), Duane Niatum (Jamestown S'Klallam Tribe), nila northSun (Shoshone/Chippewa), Gerald Vizenor (enrolled member of the Minnesota Chippewa Tribe, White Earth Reservation), Joy Harjo, and others. There are poets who bridge this period, such as Roberta Hill Whiteman (Oneida Nation), Luci Tapahonso (Navajo), and Louise Erdrich (enrolled citizen of the Turtle Mountain Band of Chippewa Indians of North Dakota), but the poets who first published collections in the 1960s and 1970s held sway as the recognized Native writers for decades.

What came after that period came like the patience of tectonic movements. An event key to the development of Native American poetry was the 1992 Returning the Gift gathering in Oklahoma, supported by poets considered part of the "renaissance." In the years after the gathering in Oklahoma, in a slow shifting of the poetic plates, the poets I consider my generation—Eric Gansworth (enrolled member of the Onondaga Nation), Gordon Henry (enrolled member of the White Earth Chippewa Tribe of Minnesota), Elise Paschen (member of the Osage Nation), Tiffany Midge (Hunkpapa Lakota enrolled member of the Standing Rock Sioux), Deborah Miranda (enrolled member of the Ohlone-Costanoan Esselen Nation of California), Laura Tohe (Diné), and others—began the push toward publishing first books in the 1990s to early 2000s. There were not a lot of us, and few of us gained the immediate recognition of the previous generation or the one that followed. Perhaps we were that quiet sound of a few rocks giving way before a landslide. Perhaps we were the force of the magma itself.

Since 2000, dozens and dozens of poets have published books and chapbooks. Growing national recognition of Native poets such as Natalie Diaz (Mojave and an enrolled member of the Gila River Indian Tribe) and Layli Long Soldier (Oglala Lakota) made it a good time for Joy Harjo and her editorial team of Native poets to launch the Norton. But part of the reason we can open the canon now is because many of us have literary training and because a Native poetry community of support began in 1992 at Returning the Gift. Now there is a mountain of Native poetry rising up, sometimes through the editorial efforts of established Native poets, sometimes in their noticing the surge. In gathering the poets for *New Poets of Native Nations*, I determined to select from the work of poets whose first books were published from 2000 to 2018. I looked at the work of seventy-two Native poets. I chose twenty-one poets for the twenty-first century. I'll never feel it was a perfect process, but seeing the diversity of voices, the anthology led me to claim *There is no such thing as Native American poetry* in an essay I wrote for *Poetry* magazine in 2018. There are poets of Native Nations and Indigenous poets. There are poetries of Native and Indigenous groups. There's a plurality of schools that might not yet be recognized or name themselves—the Diné writers, the Anishinaabe authors, the poets of the Institute of American Indian Arts—these might one day be discussed as collective. But there is no one literature we can call Native American poetry. There's just so much and more and more after that. Our poetries are the tectonic linguistics bonding Indigenous languages to English, the shifting sound of the world remade.

The Poet Misfit liked the taste
of words in the mouth, yes—
but in the eyes as well. The face
of a letter, the shape of type,
the movement on the page,
the white against dark,
the cypher, punctuation marks
all brought back the magic. The Poet Misfit
began to paint again, collage images,
make them move, and construct
concrete rooms of poems.
This work made The Poet Misfit hungry.
But most poets are good cooks.
Can you smell that poem?
All the ingredients are Indigenous.
In fact, it's a recipe. Poetry tastes so damn good.
The Poet Misfit wanted more and more.
Impatient. One foot stomp
and another stomp and the world broke.
Halves and quarters and quakes—new places.
New poets tremble up from the earth
where it cracks. The Poet Misfit says
. . . hmmm you little ones sure shake.
Welcome to a noisy world. Welcome back.
Sing when you can. Dance. Make it quake.

Native Sculpture: More than Object

Lara M. Evans, PhD (Cherokee Nation)

IN ART HISTORICAL TRADITION, sculpture is defined as three-dimensional, that is, having height, width, and depth. Euro-American art preferences generally consider large-scale sculptural works made of durable materials, metal and stone particularly, as the most desirable. Conceptual categories of sculpture expanded dramatically in the twentieth century with the addition of assemblage, installation, environmental art, land art, and site-specific sculpture as viable categories. Positioning Native artists' work in relationship to these art historical definitions can be a simple task, and many artists included in this exhibition deliberately engage with these movements. However, many are also simultaneously engaging with practices that are deeply rooted in Native cultural practices and theoretical underpinnings that predate these art historical definitions.

Native cultures, historically and in the present moment, are wonderfully diverse, but we all have been affected by the same governmental oversight as well as the imposition of Euro-American intellectual, religious, and political frameworks. But regardless of how varied our cultural practices are, they are repeatedly bifurcated into either the anthropological or the artistic. The anthropological view prioritizes generalized cultural norms, sometimes frozen in an imagined moment of cultural authenticity from early encounters between European interlopers and Indigenous peoples. The "art" lens prioritizes individual creativity and innovation; it is the search for newness, which, also in response to the world wars of the twentieth century, sometimes expresses a desire to jettison outdated traditions. This dichotomy is manufactured and closely related to the false dichotomy Stacy Pratt (Mvskoke) writes about in her essay *A Condensed History of Native American Painting* in this volume: traditional and contemporary are not oppositional. One hundred years ago, Native sculpture as a category included Northwest Coast carved masks and what are now called crest poles, and katsinas (kachinas) from the Southwest. Yet the continuance of these sculptural practices embodied cultural traditions that the colonial imposition of Christianity and wage labor economics could not tolerate. Museum collections are full of plundered objects being stored and exhibited under circumstances never intended by their makers; Native artisans might instead be commissioned to create replicas for museums or tourist venues. The ability to depart from a narrow range of styles, materials, and forms was very limited until Allan Houser (Chiricahua Apache) began creating modernist abstract figurative sculpture in the late 1940s and into the 1950s, part of a movement of Native modernism across multiple artforms that helped establish Native artists as contemporary and innovative. The success of Houser's sculptural practice marked a clear departure from an art economy that aimed to remove sacred objects from Native communities and replaced it with one that began to accept the agency and intent of Native artists to create works that deliberately engage with Euro-American art as an equal in dialogue.

Many items that fit the criteria for sculpture, that is, three-dimensional objects made by humans, do not end up being categorized as sculpture but may instead be classified as furniture, jewelry, or fashion. Container forms, like baskets and clay vessels, are associated with craft and decorative arts but—literally—carry other purposes and meanings for Native cultures, historically. Many "containers" are included in this exhibition. Douglas Miles's (White Mountain Apache-San Carlos Apache-Akimel O'odham) *Forced Removal Series: Victoria in Blue and Gold* (2023; pp. 82–83) is a suitcase, but it is also a container for historical narratives of colonial governance, forced removal, and assimilation. Mikayla Patton (enrolled member of the Oglala Lakota Nation) creates handmade paper "boxes" based on the sturdy, lightweight rawhide parfleche containers used throughout the Plains. Parfleche exterior surfaces are customarily painted in geometric patterns that are abstract representations of terrain, plants, animals, and relational concepts. Containers, in Euro-American aesthetics, are often considered to be craft objects rather than fine art. By altering the materials and color palette and suspending the forms in the air, Patton helps viewers separate from this cultural blind spot and see parfleche as sculpture.

Once we can think of Patton's *Enduring* (2023; pp. 86–87) as sculpture, we may also ask ourselves to consider Jackie Bread's (Amsakapi Pikunni/ Blackfeet) *Triangular Beaded Trinket Box, Chief Joseph* (2007; pp. 112–13) as sculpture. And why stop there? Consider Joe Feddersen's (Okanagan and Arrow Lakes) *Country Road* (2024; pp. 120–21), a Plateau-style twined sally bag as sculpture too. Excluding tools and objects created for practical uses from being considered as "art" is inconsistent with Indigenous aesthetic values and knowledge systems. This is one of the significant artistic philosophical chasms between Native and settler cultures. Practical tools are often created in ways that simultaneously function as art and as objects of use, such as Linda King's (enrolled member of the Confederated Salish and Kootenai Nation) peyote-stitched beaded makeup brushes in *Beauty Set* (2020; pp. 142–43).

Native artists working in sculptural modes engage with the conventions of Western art practices but also engage additional sets of practices, meanings, and traditions. It's not that non-Native artists do not also break those disciplinary boundaries, but Native artists often choose to break them in culturally specific ways. For example, Bently Spang's (enrolled member of the Tsitsistas/Suhtai Nation) *Modern Warrior Series: War Shirt #3—The Great Divide* (2006; pp. 92–93) is a sculptural object composed of photographs. It also references a culturally significant article of clothing: a war shirt. It is not just sculpture—it is a performative garment. The landscape photos that compose the shirt also connect the (unwearable) garment to a specific place and even times of day. Native Art Department International's *Double Shift* (2018; pp. 204–5) is simultaneously garment and object to be used in performance. Sculptor Eric-Paul Riege (Diné) also creates large-scale sculptures that are used in performances, and his soft sculptures are based on historical jewelry forms executed in monumental scale. Spang and Patton are working with non-sculptural foundations—photography, fashion, accessories, parfleche containers—to present their work in ways that clearly allow it to become categorized as sculpture. In this context, might we also consider Keri Ataumbi's (Kiowa) *Antler Earrings* (2022; pp. 102–3) and Carly Feddersen's (enrolled member of the Confederated Tribes of the Colville Reservation and of mixed European heritage) *(Dis) Embodied: Fingers Necklace II* (2023; pp. 118–19) as sculpture too? Deer antlers are worn by ceremonial dancers in multiple Native cultural traditions. Ataumbi transforms the scale dramatically by miniaturizing the antlers and presenting them to be worn as earrings. Feddersen presents beautifully macabre metalwork and stonework in necklace form, with embellished nails on the dangling fingers. Attaching sculpture to the body makes it shareable and portable, and, historically, the portability of sculptural objects has been highly significant for Indigenous peoples. Seasonal movements and extensive trade routes across long distances make portability a highly valued feature. In Indigenous aesthetics, changing the scale of an item calls attention to scale as relational, rather than invoking Euro-American art's penchant for scale as hierarchical.

Site-specific and environmental sculpture, assemblage, and installation are all categories of sculpture that were formed in the twentieth century; Native American artists, however, have been creating works that fit under these descriptors for thousands of years. The problem is that the Western art category of "sculpture" was too narrow and works by Native artists were considered primitive or ethnographic, with limited opportunities to be considered as art. The scale and site-specificity of these types of works make it difficult to include them in museum exhibition spaces. Some artists, such as Alan Michelson (Mohawk member of the Six Nations of the Grand River) and Sky Hopinka (Ho-Chunk Nation/Pechanga Band of Luiseño Indians), sometimes use video installations to adapt place-based works for gallery settings (see pp. 202–3; 128–29).

The sculptures in this exhibition have been created with many complicated intents. They were made to be shared, to move about the world, to be ambassadors and educators, to tell stories, to inspire, to observe, to criticize, to destabilize, to act upon, to restore—to satisfy expectations as well as defy them.

A Community of Knowledge:
The Ceramic Art of Roxanne Swentzell, Rose Bean Simpson, and Raven Halfmoon

Anya Montiel, PhD (Tohono O'odom)

If one wishes to make a bean pot, they should also know the appropriate cultural steps that represent a specific cosmovision. What prayers should one make while collecting and preparing clay? How should a potter center their thoughts and feelings while working? In addition, the skill possessed by an individual is not unique to the particular person but is the accumulated skill of countless generations of knowledge-bearers who passed these gifts on to their descendants. One should never forget that their creations are part of a community of knowledge in which they are privileged to share.

—Porter Swentzell

PORTER SWENTZELL, THE SON and brother of the Kha'po Owingeh (Santa Clara Pueblo) ceramicists Roxanne Swentzell and Rose Bean Simpson, respectively, provided insight into the ancestral teachings, cultural protocols, and mindfulness rooted in creating a ceramic vessel like a bean pot. For the Tewa people, the knowledge and skills required to make such a work of pottery, a vessel that provides nourishment to others, are viewed as a gift and a privilege. The clay artist Raven Halfmoon (Caddo Nation), along with Swentzell and Simpson, is also rooted in that "community of knowledge," whereby the teachings and epistemologies of ancestors and elders provide a foundation for the art they make. From that foundation, these artists create large figurative artworks that speak uniquely to their worldview as Native women.

The art form of ceramics has been practiced and fostered by Indigenous cultures of North, Central, and South America for many millennia. In the process, Native people have developed ceramic traditions and shared materials, designs, and technologies across their many expansive trade networks. For example, while the Caddo Nation is based in Oklahoma, their ancestral homelands also include parts of Texas, Louisiana, and Arkansas. Three thousand years ago, Caddo ancestors were part of the Mississippian trade complex and built massive earth mounds. They also used local clay and shell and clay tempers to build pots and jars with intricate rectilinear and curvilinear designs and effigy jars portraying humans and animals like alligator gars. The local Red, White, and Washita Rivers contain rich red, buff, and dark clay.

A citizen of the Caddo Nation and of Choctaw, Delaware, and Otoe-Missouria descent, Halfmoon learned to make pottery from Caddo elders such as Jereldine "Jeri" Redcorn, who is credited with reviving Caddo pottery in the 1990s. While at university, Halfmoon studied ancient Indigenous pottery, the rock sculptures of the Olmecs and Easter Island, and earthworks in the Mississippian region. "A lot of those earthworks my ancestors made," explains Halfmoon. "Caddo ancestors, especially in the Mississippi region, so I was always interested in large scale works and being a part of that, the idea of community being in those works."[1] Representing the community of knowledge spanning from thousands of years ago to now, it is no wonder that Halfmoon works with clay on such a monumental scale: Last year, she sculpted a figure of a woman rising twelve feet and weighing more than eight hundred pounds.

Another important work by Halfmoon, which reaches more than five feet in height, is *E-a'-ti-ti* (2021, pp. 186–87), a double figure depicting two women positioned side by side. Both figures have multiple faces stacked above their heads, referring to matrilineal ancestry. The stoneware sculpture is covered in red, black, and cream glazes, representing the colors of local natural clay. Halfmoon's works are very textural, and, as the artist explains: "I have always been drawn to clay because it is a direct reflection of land, placement, time. You can see my exact fingerprints in the way I use clay: you can see who made those pieces, and I leave it. I leave every single human touch visible on the surface because I want it to be recorded. You pull clay from the earth and it's definitely a powerful tie to where we are, what age we're in."[2] Halfmoon is both a storyteller and a historian.

In the American Southwest, ceramics are practiced among many Native communities, and most artists, including Swentzell and Simpson, come from multiple generations of ceramicists who are part of an unbroken line of clay artists whose knowledge has been passed down from generation to generation. In *X-Ray* (2021; pp. 164–65), Simpson created a ceramic figure encased in metal. The head, which sits atop an elongated neck, has tattoo-like markings reaching from the top of the head down to four horizontal lines along the front of the neck. The vertical box in which the figure resides includes a cutout that reveals black-and-white geometric designs. As in an X-ray, the figure's internal skeletal framework is visible, in this case composed of ancestral Pueblo pottery designs. No matter what the exterior might be, the figure is unequivocally Pueblo, even down to its bones.

Swentzell also creates clay figures that reveal her worldview as a Pueblo woman from Kha'po Owingeh. Her art often draws from personal experiences that connect to universal emotions and lessons. She has expressed the importance of "seeing the connectedness we have with everything around us and being in touch with ourselves on both the spiritual level and in the physical sense."[3] Swentzell understands the interconnectedness and importance of balance. She established the Flowering Tree Permaculture Institute, a nonprofit organization that draws from Indigenous knowledge systems of the local ecosystem to offer teachings in sustainable home building, high-desert farming and irrigation, solar energy, seed saving, beekeeping, and animal husbandry.

In Swentzell's clay figure *Touched* (2011; pp. 168–69), the woman is seated and looks upward. Her body, including the side of her face, is covered in handprints of different colors. Swentzell commented that when creating the sculpture: "I was thinking about all the people in my life who have affected me in one way or another. This piece is about how our touch does leave a sort of fingerprint on whatever it is we come in contact with. So my question is . . . What kind of touch do I wish to leave in the world?"[4] Through such a deeply emotive work, Swentzell communicates a personal experience that speaks to all people and brings attention to the impact of others' actions and the toll it leaves on the body.

As Porter Swentzell explained through the example of the bean pot, creating in clay represents knowledge and responsibilities for many Native artists. Along with being shaped from the earth itself, the artworks by Swentzell, Simpson, and Halfmoon exist on a continuum that connects them to their histories. For some Native nations, cosmologies link clay to their ancestors, including the creation of the first humans from clay. And as Simpson so beautifully expressed to the *New York Times*: "Clay was the earth that grew our food, was the house we lived in, was the pottery we ate out of and prayed with. So my relationship to clay is ancestral and I think it has a deep genetic memory. It's like a family member for us."[5] Clay is more than an artistic medium: it is an ancestor and a relative.

The epigraph is from "Museums and Beans: A Transformative Stew," in *Lit: The Work of Rose B. Simpson* (Santa Fe, NM: Wheelwright Museum of the American Indian, 2019), 15–16.

1. Chadd Scott, "Raven Halfmoon's Monumental Homage to Indigenous Women," *Forbes* (July 6, 2023), https://www.forbes.com/sites/chaddscott/2023/07/06/raven-halfmoons-monumental-homage-to-indigenous-women/.

2. Tara Escolin, "Past, Present, Future, Always: A Conversation with Artist Raven Halfmoon," *Arkansas Times* (November 10, 2023), https://arktimes.com/rock-candy/2023/11/10/past-present-future-always-a-conversation-with-artist -raven-halfmoon.

3. Lawrence Abbott, "Roxanne Swentzell," *Indian Artist* (Fall 1997): 23–24.

4. Roxanne Swentzell, "Touched," artist's website, https://www.roxanneswentzell.net/Pieces/roxo_Wlottery_Touched_f.htm.

5. Jori Finkel, "Rose B. Simpson Thinks in Clay," *New York Times* (June 16, 2022), https://www.nytimes.com/2022/06/16/arts/design/rose-b-simpson-clay-sculpture.html.

A Condensed History of Native American Painting

Stacy Pratt, PhD (Mvskoke)

EUROPEANS GENERALLY characterize painting as the practice of applying paint or other medium to a solid, usually two-dimensional, surface. Painting in the Americas, both in ancestral times and today, is conceptually more comprehensive in terms of materials and surfaces. Cave and rock painting, like that of the Chumash at the Cooper's Ferry site in what is now Idaho, have been carbon-dated to 13,000 BCE. Long before colonization, Indigenous people painted on hides and pottery, tipis and totem poles, among other ceremonial and mundane "canvases"—a practice that continues today. Native painters have retained cultural identity through eras of tenacious survival to now, when Jeffrey Gibson (member of the Mississippi Band of Choctaw Indians and of Cherokee descent) is the first Native American artist to have a solo exhibition in the US Pavilion at the Venice Biennale (see pp. 72–73).[1] This very condensed history of Native painting provides a starting point for considering the ongoing impact and influence of Native painters.

Like all Native American art, painting has suffered for decades under critical reception that assumes the false dichotomy of "traditional versus contemporary." In 2013, the Cherokee painter America Meredith founded *First American Art Magazine (FAAM)* in part to combat this dichotomy by presenting critical writing, primarily by Native scholars and critics, on "Ancestral, historical & living arts by Indigenous peoples of the Americas."[2] In her powerful essay, "Why Categorizing Native Art as 'Traditional' and 'Contemporary' Is Toxic," Meredith examines the myriad reasons why this polarity is not only incorrect but harmful: "[T]hese words don't advance thoughtful discourse about Indigenous art. Rather, they cripple it. Separately, they can be misused, vague, or trite, but when paired together in a false dichotomy, they are insidious." She asks: "How can there be a traditional style or a contemporary style? Several Native art markets and shows cleave artwork in categories called contemporary and traditional. This implies some underlying timeframe divides these concepts: Indigenous peoples made certain arts prior to European contact and other arts post-contact; however, upon closer examination, this assumption falls apart."[3] Understanding the history of Native painting requires keeping Meredith's warning in mind.

In ancient times, our ancestors painted on cave and rock walls; today, Native graffiti artists and muralists paint on buildings and other structures. Jaune Quick-to-See Smith (Confederated Salish and Kootenai Tribes) explains that ancestral artists using dyed porcupine quills woven into birchbark or hide could be considered painters in relation with today's artists who incorporate collage, beading, or weaving onto their canvases.[4] For ages, moose hair, yucca, grass, willow, bark, and other plants have been bitten, marked, and dyed before being woven into functional and decorative items. Today's quillworkers, birchbark biters, and beadworkers are clearly as "contemporary" as painters working in acrylics or digital art—and painters working with the latest technology and mediums are part of an ancient tradition of expression through painting.

Throughout the nineteenth century (and beyond), the US government continued its attempts at exterminating Indigenous people through forced relocations and war. Ledger drawing developed during this time. These drawings, made with fountain pens, pencils, crayons, and watercolor in ledger books, bore stylistic resemblance to those traditionally drawn on animal hides. They recorded feats of war and memories of tribal life as well as the artists' experiences as prisoners of war. Ledger books were used to keep track of land sales, among other tools of colonization, so their use in Native art is an act of defiance as well as one of historical witness. Current artists such as Bobby C. Martin [Mvskoke Nation] recall that reclamation in their work, utilizing printmaking to superimpose images over historical documents or photographs.

Federal boarding schools attempted with devastating effect cultural assimilation throughout the twentieth century. The schools exposed students to Western European art history, methods, and materials, and forbade them from speaking their Native languages or creating any form of Native art. In the 1930s, the ban on teaching Native arts at boarding schools was lifted. Mable Morrow began an Indian arts and crafts program at Santa Fe Indian School, intending to teach women to become professional artists. In 1932, Dorothy Dunn opened the Studio, also at the Santa Fe Indian School. She emphasized historical, tribe-specific "authenticity" and encouraged the linear style of painting [influenced by San Ildefonso Pueblo pottery painting] that came to be known as Flatstyle.

Artists influenced by this style—and the market for it—developed the various Flatstyle schools: Studio [Dunn's], San Ildefonso [in New Mexico], Bacone, and Southern Plains. Along with an emphasis on draftsmanship and precision, Flatstyle painting is characterized by light backgrounds and solid colors, most often painted in opaque watercolor. Bacone College in Muskogee, Oklahoma, opened Ataloa Art Lodge to expose students to Indian art traditions. The most prominent Flatstyle painters were the Kiowa Six: Spencer Asah, James Auchiah, Jack Hokeah, Stephen Mopope, Lois Smoky, and Monroe Tsatoke, who were part of the University of Oklahoma's art program under the direction of Oscar Brousse Jacobson. During the Great Depression, several Works Progress Administration murals by Flatstyle artists, including the Kiowa Six, were painted and can still be seen today. The work of the Kiowa Six was exhibited around the world, including at the 1932 Venice Biennale.

In 1946, the Philbrook Museum of Art in Tulsa began its annual juried exhibition of Indian painting, affecting the careers of several painters in that generation, including Oscar Howe [Yanktonai Dakota Nation], who famously wrote a letter to the museum when his experimental work was rejected for not being "traditional Indian." Howe wrote: "Whoever said that my paintings are not in the traditional Indian style has poor knowledge of Indian art indeed. There is much more to Indian Art than pretty, stylized pictures. We are to be herded like a bunch of sheep, with no right for individualism, dictated as the Indian has always been, put on reservations and treated like a child, and only the White Man knows what is best for him."[5]

By the 1950s, Native painters such as George Morrison [Ojibwe] and Leon Polk Smith [Cherokee Nation] were contributing to the abstract expressionism movement based in New York. Their paintings were part of the 1952 Annual Exhibition of Contemporary Painting at the Whitney Museum of American Art, exhibited alongside the work of non-Native artists like Willem de Kooning and Jackson Pollock. An essay accompanying a current traveling exhibition of Native abstract paintings and prints explains: "For Native Abstract Expressionists, the Modernist period did not invent abstract imagery. However, the movement's experiments with abstraction did provide inspiration: Native artists explored intuitive expressions from their own art traditions, which manifested in geometric, expressionistic, and symbolic representations of shapes, forms, and colors."[6] In later generations, painters like Jaune Quick-to-See Smith, G. Peter Jemison [Seneca Nation [Heron Clan]] [see pp. 190–91], and Lloyd R. Oxendine [Lumbee Nation] continued to exhibit, curate, and write in New York, further establishing the Indigenous art presence in that important art center.

In 1962, the Institute of American Indian Arts [IAIA] opened on the campus of Santa Fe Indian School. A high school within the federal boarding school system, its focus was on freeing Native art from previous constraints. The founders Lloyd Kiva New [Cherokee Nation] and George Boyce encouraged students to experiment, and all students were required to try working in a variety of mediums, from writing to sculpting to painting. The painter Fritz Scholder [La Jolla Band of Luiseño Indians] was among the influential instructors at the school, which later became a college. The work of revolutionary IAIA painters like Linda Lomahaftewa (Hopi/Choctaw) (pp. 148–49), Kevin Red Star (Crow Tribe of Montana), and T. C. Cannon (Kiowa Indian Tribe of Oklahoma/Caddo Nation) continues to influence later generations of Native painters.[7]

The 1980s and 1990s saw young painters of the 1960s move into their professional careers and the next generation work with fewer, or at least different, constraints than previous ones. In 1990, the Indian Arts & Crafts Act (IACA) and the Native American Graves Protection and Repatriation Act (NAGPRA) passed. While the IACA defines who can market work as "Indian art," NAGPRA seeks to return ancestral art and other objects, including human remains, to their descendants. Both acts affected Native painters in practical and artistic ways, as several began to incorporate newly accessible ancestral imagery into their work.

IAIA remains an important center for Native artists and arts workers. Student painters like Avis Charley (Spirit Lake Tribe of North Dakota/Navajo Nation), George Alexander (Muscogee [Creek]) (see pp. 230–31), Chaz John (Winnebago Tribe of Nebraska/Mississippi Band Choctaw/European) (pp. 240–41), and Dyani White Hawk (Sicangu Lakota Nation) continue the school's tradition of innovation. Other painters make their mark on mainstream art programs, such as the prominent landscape painter Kay WalkingStick (member of the Cherokee Nation of Oklahoma and Anglo) (see pp. 252–53), who received her education at Pratt Institute in Brooklyn. The painter and muralist Yatika Starr Fields (Osage Nation/Mvskoke Nation) attended the Art Institute of Boston. (His mother, multimedia artist Anita Fields (Osage Nation), is an IAIA alumna.)

From ancestral works waiting to be reclaimed from museum cases to paint drying on canvases in studios to digital works held together by pixels in a new kind of cloud, Native painting continues to bear witness to the traumas and triumphs of history. Exhibitions like this one place Native American paintings in conversation across time—with each other and with all who experience them, here, now.

1. The Kiowa Six participated in the US Pavilion of the Venice Biennale in 1932.

2. *First American Art Magazine* tagline.

3. America Meredith, "Why Categorizing Native Art as 'Traditional' and 'Contemporary Is Toxic," *First American Art Magazine* 8 (Fall 2015), 12; revised February 6, 2020, https://firstamericanartmagazine.com/traditional_contemporary/.

4. Jaune Quick-to-See Smith, email to author, 2024.

5. Susannah Gardiner, "Who Gets to Define Native American Art?," *Smithsonian*, April 5, 2022, https://www.smithsonianmag.com/smithsonian-institution/who-gets-to-define-native-american-art-180979968/. Howe went on to exhibit and judge future Philbrook Indian Annuals.

6. "Native American Art & Abstract Expressionism," *Action/Abstraction Redefined*. IAIA, https://abstraction.iaia.edu/assets/pdfs/Native-American-Art-and-Abstract-Expressionism.pdf.

7. *Action/Abstraction Redefined* is an exhibition of early student art from the IAIA Museum of Contemporary Native Arts.

A Condensed History of Native American Jewelry and Fashion

Jennifer Woodcock-Medicine Horse, PhD

NATURE AND NOVELTY, constraint and creativity, stitched together with exacting attention to detail, have defined the exuberant field of Indigenous clothing and personal adornment on Turtle Island for tens of thousands of years. In ancient times, people followed game migrations and tended plant harvests in their traditional territories, becoming eminently knowledgeable about the resources available to them locally and how to most skillfully and artfully create clothing to accommodate the conditions of their environments.

For the past several hundred years, both scientists and the popular press have plied the public with singularly inaccurate visions of and ideas about Native people, the nature of their daily lives, and their clothing. This fictive misinformation became institutionalized in the 1800s, when anthropologists promoted the ludicrous theory that the evolution of all human cultures was divisible into three categories or basic stages of development: savagery, through barbarism, to civilization. Not surprisingly, this concept coincided with the widespread acceptance among Europeans and European immigrants that settler colonialism was a legitimate way to establish a presence in the Indigenously occupied lands of our globe. Needless to say, many European traders, politicos, and entrepreneurs were quite happy to colonize any lands that held trafficable resources—human, animal, plant, or mineral. However, for those with questions regarding the morality of displacing human populations, doubts were assuaged by the scientific community's assertion that these populations were savages, possibly the Missing Link, and even, shockingly, cannibals.

These scientific tracts, as well as newspaper cartoons, visually conveyed the horrific aspects of these cannibals and their savage kin—the denizens of Africa, Australia, and the Americas—dressed in tattered scraps of animal skins, scruffy bones pushed through their noses, and who clearly never bathed. In some cases (not cannibals), artists presented an opposite but equal reaction—the romanticized savage, or the lovely, sexualized siren of Polynesia, a favorite of Gauguin, for example. Equally skimpily attired but bathed and alluring to the Western Gaze. But not someone you would sit down with to knock out a trade agreement or discuss the fine points of existentialism.

These dismissive depictions of Indigenous peoples, whether lustful or sneering in tone, codified them in the public mind as savage—simplistic, unsophisticated peoples of no intellectual or cultural weight. This was catastrophically off the mark, and to the present day it has underlain the popular portrayal of Indigenous peoples and their clothing, often in great contrast to their actual attire. Often this has meant sexualizing Indigenous women, and in some cases men, in ways that would be appalling to them if they could hop in a time machine and take a look. One of the prime examples of this is the historic poster child for Murdered and Missing Indigenous People—Pocahontas. The portrayal of Pocahontas is almost always as a happy-go-lucky young woman in her twenties, wearing a fringed buckskin minidress suitable for a 1970s hippie and enraptured by the English settler colonists. But there are a couple of problems with this narrative. First, Pocahontas (born c. 1596) was in her early teens when she was taken captive by the English at Jamestown and coerced into marrying John Rolfe, who took her away from her family to England, where she died of an unidentified illness, possibly tuberculosis, at the age of twenty-one. It is a story of the trafficking of a child, not of romance. The other problem is that portrayals of Pocahontas's attire are wildly inaccurate when compared to the modest clothing worn by Powhatan women of the time: she would never have been dressed so immodestly, and, as a chief's daughter, she would have been dressed in the finest of clothes and jewelry, denoting her social rank. Major Pocahontas films in 1995, 2005, and 2022 reiterate the same misrepresentations of this beleaguered woman.

What this kind of pervasive misrepresentation and oversimplification engenders is a lack of curiosity about what life was actually like for Indigenous people of the Americas and, specifically, how people were dressing and adorning themselves for the tens of thousands of years before Europeans pulled up on the beach. And that is a travesty, because precontact clothing in the Americas, Turtle Island, is a riveting topic. For example, the residents of the Aleutian Islands, between what are now Russia and Alaska, primarily made their living for millennia by fishing and hunting marine mammals from kayaks, designed to be the perfect, maneuverable boat for the rough seas of the North Pacific Ocean. There was no neoprene in the millennia of old, and the North Pacific is very cold and wet with bracing winds and drenching ocean spray, so the ancient Aleut people used the resources at hand—in this case, marine mammal intestines—and perfected featherweight, waterproof parkas with drawstring wrists and hoods and connections at the waist to secure waterproof kayak covers to keep the interior of the vessel dry despite rough water. These parkas were sewn with a waterproof stitch, most commonly from strips of seal intestine. The seams were often embellished with bird feathers, which added color and served as a beautiful design element, but also, functionally, wicked water away from the seams.

Every unique environment on Turtle Island has its own materials and conditions to accommodate. In radical contrast to the frigid arctic, the center of Turtle Island was home to vast agricultural empires. A persisting myth is that Europeans did Native people a giant favor by bringing glass beads and industrially woven cloth as trade goods. But the reality is that there were ancient trade networks crisscrossing and linking North and South America. There was a lively flow of people, ideas, foods such as cacao and maize, ceramics, portable art, knappable stone like obsidian and cherts for making tools, fine gemstones including turquoise and jade, all manner of shells, metals such as copper, and finely woven cotton cloth, among many other attractive items.

Mesoamericans and ancestral Puebloans were manufacturing and dying fine cloth for millennia before the arrival of European fabrics and weaving technology. Indigenous people adorned their cloth or leather clothing with a wide array of decorative elements, such as ceramic, shell, bone, and stone beads;

porcupine and bird feather quillwork; bird feather plumage; dentalium shell; and painting with natural pigments, to name but a few. If these options were not locally available, they could be obtained through the trade networks, as could fully constructed clothing like moccasins. Jewelry was ubiquitous in the form of earrings, necklaces, rings, bracelets, and cuffs created from tanned hide—painted, quilled, or beaded—metals, shell, stone, and ceramic, and sometimes crafted using materials and techniques traded from other Indigenous communities. Pueblo artisans in the Southwest specialized in the manufacture of incredibly fine shell or stone beads called heishi, miraculous in a time prior to modern electric tools.

What was notable about European trade goods like beads and cloth is that they were both novel and time-saving compared to hand drilling stone or shell beads or weaving cloth from scratch. The introduction of mass-produced glass beads permitted a degree of artistry previously challenging for women of the Northern Plains; the work involved in preparing and sewing designs with porcupine quills is extremely labor intensive. The introduction of glass beads, uniform in size and color, meant that these women could bead the entire upper half of their dresses—and matching horse regalia in some cases!—with complicated designs. This kind of dense beading persists to the modern day. But this was a devil's bargain because, with the introduction of European trade goods in exchange for furs, women's work in preparing furs for trade skyrocketed without compensation. Because of the dismissive attitudes toward Indigenous people at the time, the individual artists remain anonymous for the most part—their names were rarely noted when items were collected.

While the nineteenth century as a whole was a time of denigration at best and genocide at worst, early to mid-twentieth-century tourism and affluent collectors brought a fresh perspective regarding Native people, at least in the Southwest. Instead of being burned in boarding school bonfires, traditional Native clothing was being purchased by museums. Pueblo pottery, Zuni jewelry, and Diné (Navajo) weavings were purchased in large quantities by tourists, creating significant profits for the trading posts that brokered the art. Again, this was also a devil's bargain: although there were ready markets for their work, these artists were expected to produce what was deemed "Indian looking" and sellable to tourists at a cheap or moderate price, so creativity was hampered and artists frequently worked beneath their artistic capability. However, this was not solely an extractive bargain. Much of what is now considered traditional Southwest art—wool weavings, silver jewelry—includes key components that Native artists adopted from the Spanish and made their own. Native artists all over the country sought novel materials and incorporated them into new designs. For example, during the 1918 influenza pandemic, Ojibwe women cut tobacco can lids and formed them into tinkly jingles for their new cultural expression, the jingle dress, with each jingle's bell tone carrying prayers for the sick to the Creator. By the mid-twentieth century, these adaptations were perceived as traditional.

Mid-century manufacturing brought a plethora of new synthetic materials with which Native artists began to experiment and later incorporated into their work. Santo Domingo Pueblo artists used vinyl records to make heishi beads; Aleutian seamstresses use modern waterproof materials to make parkas; powwow regalia incorporates mirrors, hearkening back to nineteenth-century trade goods, and eye-catching neon fabrics. In 1962, the textile artist and designer Lloyd Kiva New (Cherokee Nation) and Dr. George Boyce cofounded the Institute of American Indian Arts (IAIA), in Santa Fe, which was supported by Bureau of Indian Affairs (BIA) funding. New was already a well-established fashion designer and artist, which lent credibility to the institution in its formative days, and, from the very beginning, he brought in phenomenally talented artists as faculty. From its first cohort, IAIA has graduated brilliant artists in each of its offered fields, but the importance of New as a cofounder cannot be overestimated in the validation of Native fashion design and jewelry as important arts in the latter twentieth century.

Native artists creating jewelry and clothing are breaking down cultural barriers more rapidly than academia, museums, or the popular media can keep up with. The 2015 Peabody Essex Museum's exhibition *Native Fashion Now* was a tipping point, showcasing the jewelry and clothing of dozens of exceptional Native artists. Art and cultural museums are finally commissioning and exhibiting wildly popular contemporary work, such as Jamie Okuma's (Luiseño/Shoshone-Bannock Tribes/Wailaki Tribe) spectacular Indigenized Louboutin knee-high boots, fully beaded with bird and floral designs. Charles Loloma

(Hopi) incorporated all manner of interesting stones and woods into his jewelry designs, rather than using just the simple palette of turquoise and coral, and experimented with new inlay techniques; Diné (Navajo) weavers such as Melissa Cody explode "traditional" weaving styles into brilliant Escheresque patterns; Wendy Ponca (Osage Nation) uses materials such as Mylar to evoke traditional cosmological cultural references in her clothing; Jackie Larson Bread (Amsakapi Pikunni/Blackfeet; see pp. 112–13) and Marcus Amerman (Choctaw Nation) use very fine glass beads to create historical and contemporary photorealistic portraits and scenes beaded onto leather bags and bracelets. Federal legal protections have created opportunities for Native artists to fight and discourage cultural appropriation in the fashion industry, namely, on the runways of New York, Paris, and Milan, but also in the ready-to-wear market. Ready-to-wear, until recently, was the sole domain of appropriative imagery for companies such as Pendleton and American Apparel, but, more recently, many Native designers, including Bethany Yellowtail (Northern Cheyenne/Apsáalooke), have successfully launched their own lines of culturally specific clothing that is free of any designs that should not be replicated for the public.

For modern Native designers and jewelers, nature and novelty and constraint and creativity are still expressed in their work. Sho Sho Esquiro (Kaska Dena/Cree Nation) incorporates animal skulls, tanned fish skin, and seal fur into her runway designs, integrating nature and novelty into her work. Designers in rural Montana are constrained by their location but availing themselves of the creative freedom offered through custom fabric printing and social media–based sales. It is a bright day when Native art and clothing are found in art museum exhibitions and gift shops and being worn on the street, rather than relegated to dusty, natural history museum collections.

PLATES

Through genocide, boarding schools, disease, hunger, rape, and abuse, we are still here.
—Jaune Quick-to-See Smith

Native American artists have often used their work to confront both contemporary and past violences of settler colonialism in the United States. For a few generations, many Native Americans have walked between two worlds—reservation life and off-reservation life. Moving off reservations generally offers a better quality of life with more educational and economic possibilities. Recently, with growing economic stability and the rise of social media, Native Americans have fostered intertribal connections and revitalized political action. The mobilization of water protectors at the #NoDAPL protests in 2016–17, for instance, was the direct result of such changes.

POLITICAL

Norman Akers

Citizen of the Osage Nation (b. 1958)

Drowning Elk, 2020
Oil on canvas

Floating in a blue aquatic scape surrounded by plastic water bottles, the Great Elk calls out. In a desperate plea, he acknowledges a world in crisis: one where water, essential to life, is bottled and sold. This commodification of water, a vital life-giving element, is now complicit in adding to the human-made waste that suffocates our world, which should concern us all. —N.A.

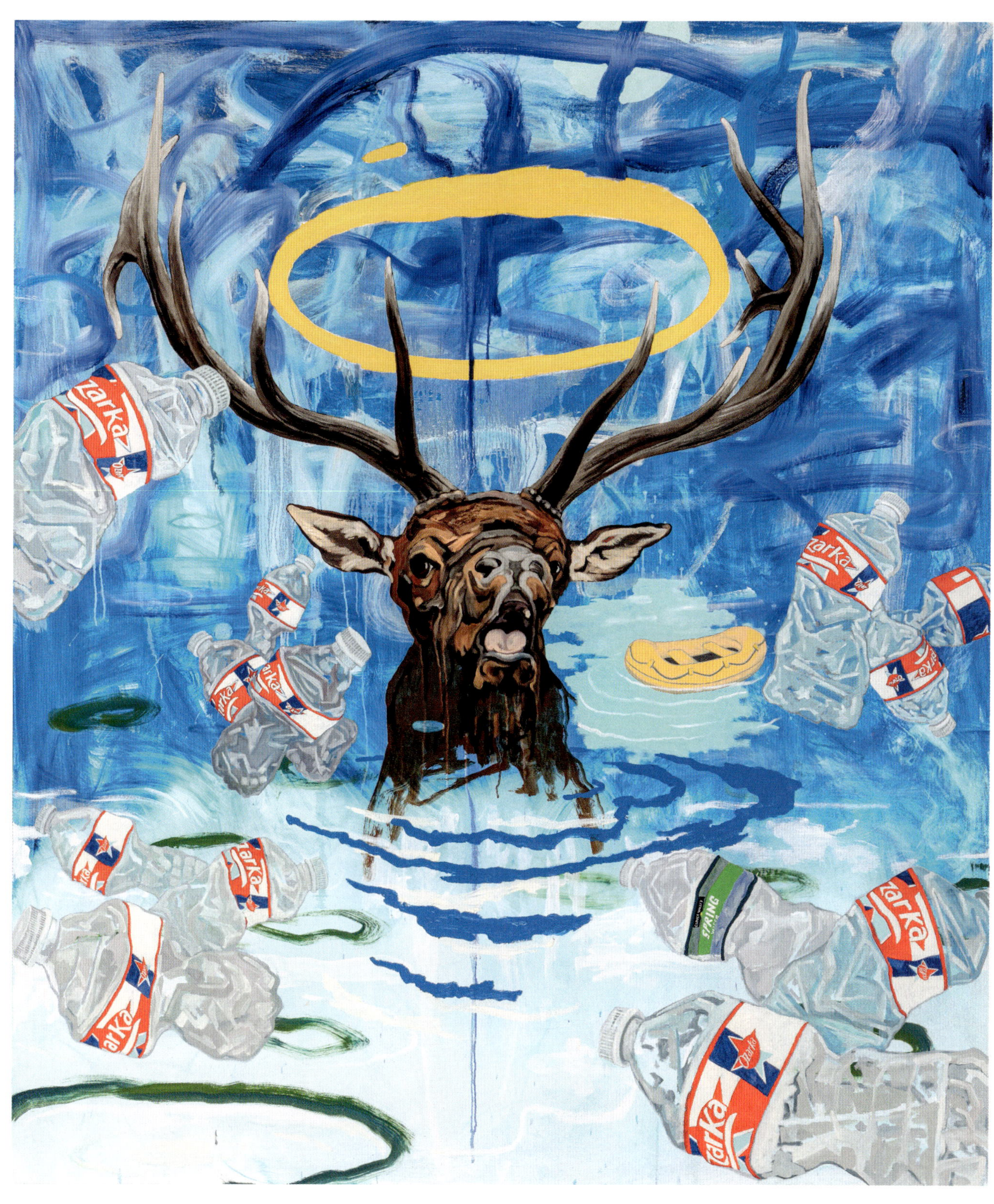
Zarka
SPRING

Neal Ambrose-Smith

Descendant of the Confederated Salish and Kootenai Nation of Montana (b. 1966)

Abstract in Your Home, 2009
Neon, mixed media

It was no surprise to me upon first seeing Pier Paolo Calzolari's piece *Abstract in Your Home* (1970) that I saw a tipi. I thought the statement inside the tipi was pretty cheeky, but the triangle wasn't meant to be read as a tipi. It may be abstract to have a tipi inside a building or dwelling, which is like a home within a home. We often dwell in our kitchens with family, for instance. We dwell within our bodies, and home is where the heart is. Our cousin married into the Blackfeet, and so for several summers my mom and I traveled up to Blackfeet in Montana for the Okán (Sundance). Each summer we put up lodges and lived in them during the ceremonies. The tipi or triangle will always take me home. —N.A-S.

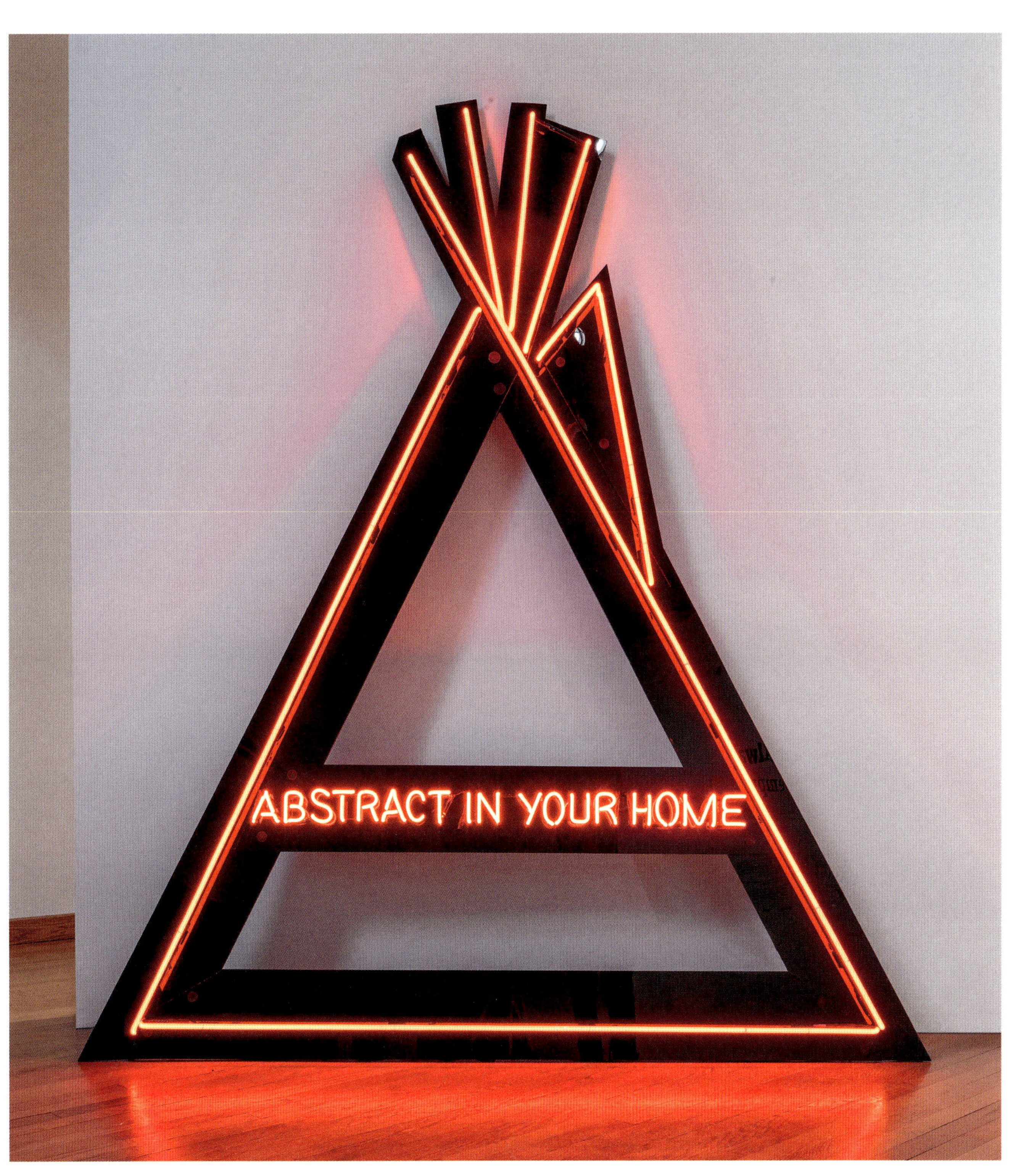
ABSTRACT IN YOUR HOME

Natalie Ball

Klamath/Modoc (b. 1980)

Sheriff's Star, 2022
Neon glass, textiles, Billy Jack hats, ribbon, paint, deer hide

Sheriff's Star was born from my lithography print series during my artist-in-residence at Crow's Shadow Institute of the Arts in March of 2022. I started the Crow's Shadow residency the same week that I was sworn into the Klamath Tribal Council and took my seat as an elected official of the Klamath Tribes. My first Tribal Council meeting was after the official swear-in, and I was given the opportunity in my new role to vote "e" (yes) for a large Land Back acquisition. I learned that much of my Tribal Council work is done through emails. —N.B.

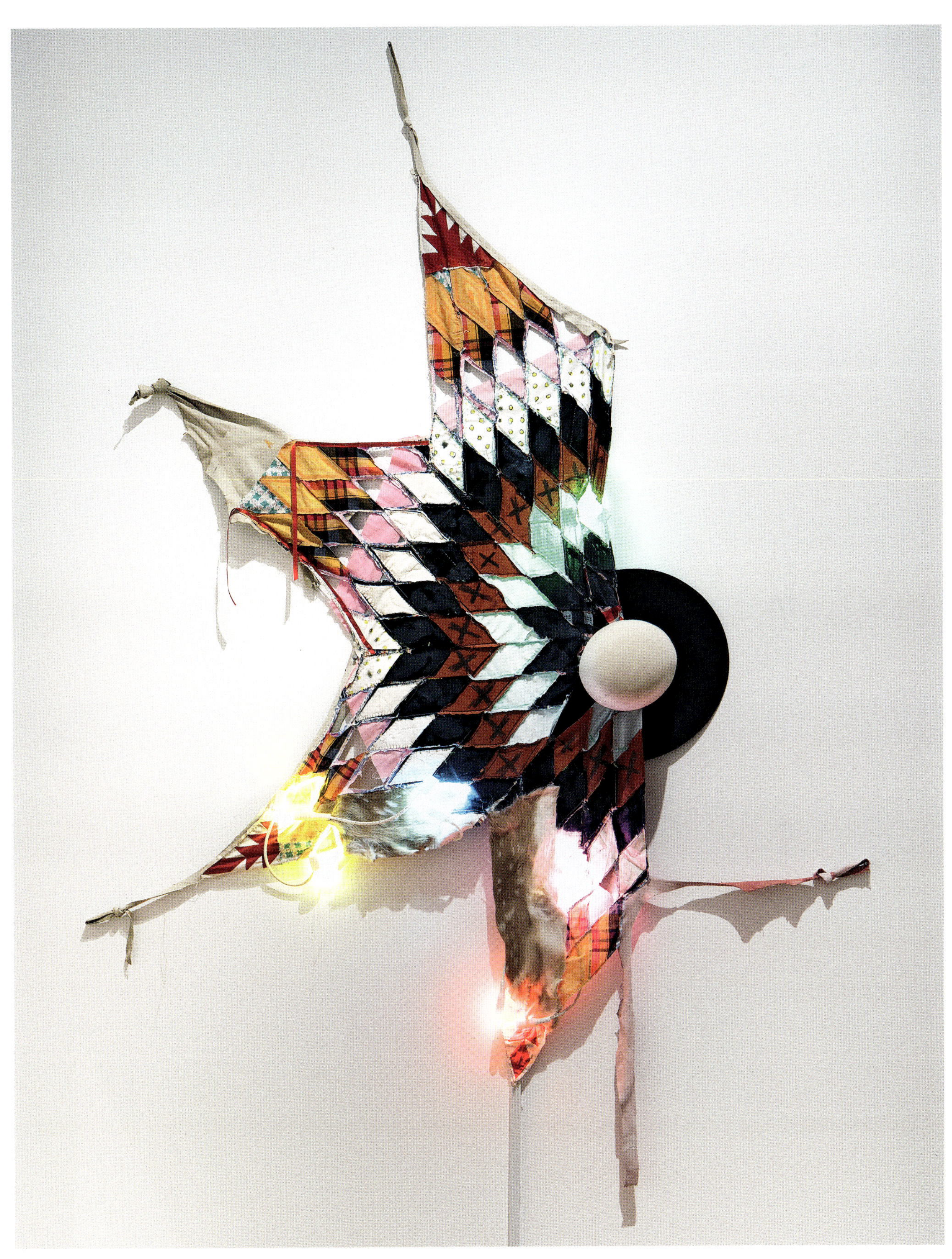

Raven Chacon

Diné/Chicano (b. 1977)

For Zitkála-Šá (For Carmina Escobar), 2019
Lithograph

From Chacon's *For Zitkála-Šá* series, named after the Yankton Dakota composer and musician (1876–1938), the artist crafted scores and lithographs dedicated to contemporary Indigenous and mestiza women musicians. In *For Carmina Escobar*, inspired by the Mexican sound and intermedia artist of the same name, Chacon grapples with the erasure of Indigenous peoples, languages, and traditions in Latin America.

When you have no tongue to speak your original language, what is the sound of that scream? What is the sound of the horror of not having the words of your true name because that name in your language no longer exists? Is this the stifled scream hidden behind a mask?
—from *For Zitkála-Šá* by Raven Chacon

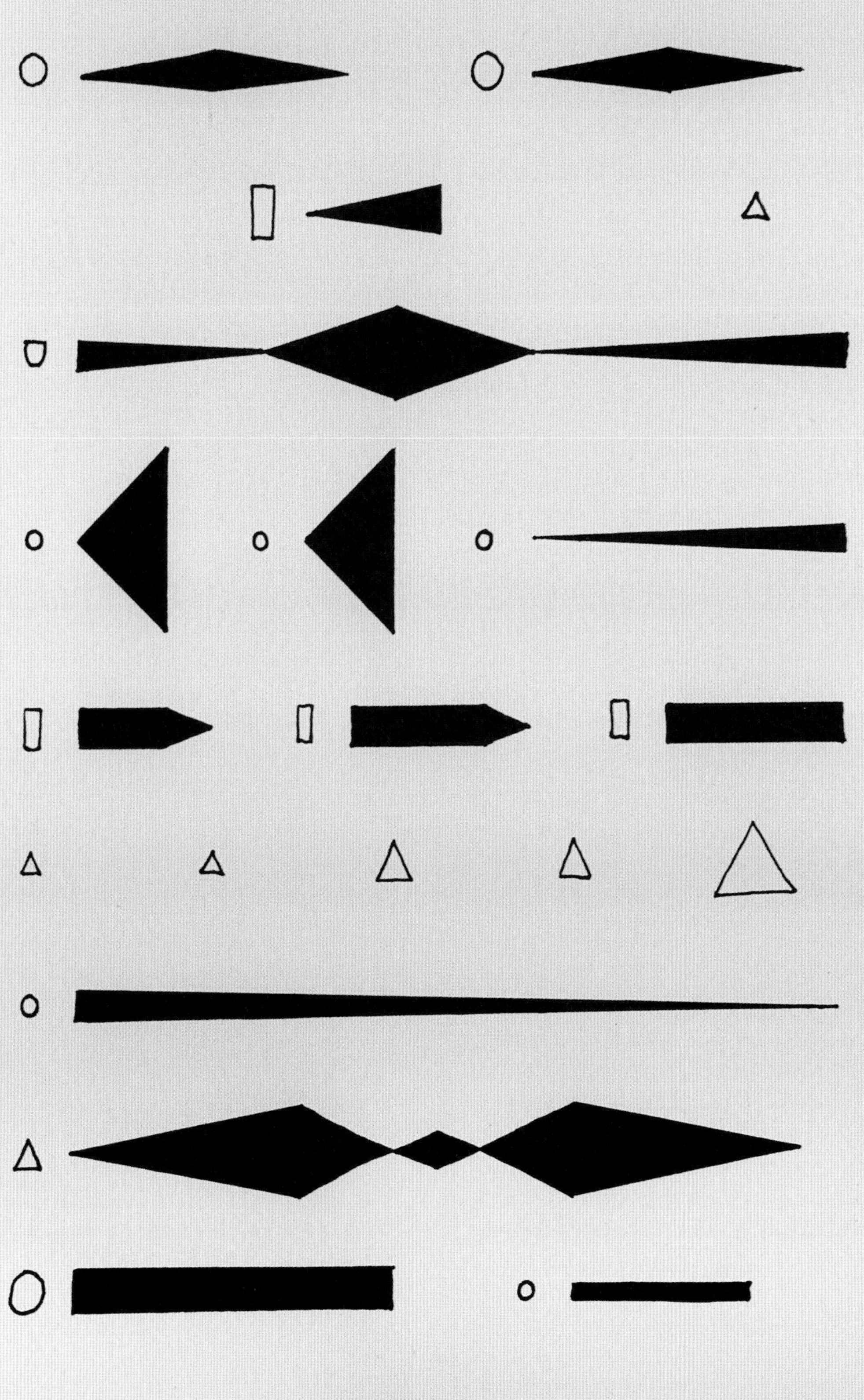
FOR CARMINA ESCOBAR

Raven Chacon

Diné/Chicano (b. 1977)

For Zitkála-Šá (For Suzanne Kite), 2019
Lithograph

For Suzanne Kite is inspired by the award-winning Oglála Lakȟóta artist, composer, and academic. The artwork represents instructions for a performance from Raven Chacon. "For any electronic or non-electronic instrument. Starting at the top, perform the given value, interpreted as a changeable parameter of music (pitch, tempo, volume, etc.), or as rhythms, preset buttons, code, etc. As you proceed to other values, you may be confronted with a new path, which may also climb back up the page. When you arrive at the end of a path, you may turn around, unless that path is at the bottom of the page. The Xs are any value you desire."—from *For Zitkála-Šá* by Raven Chacon

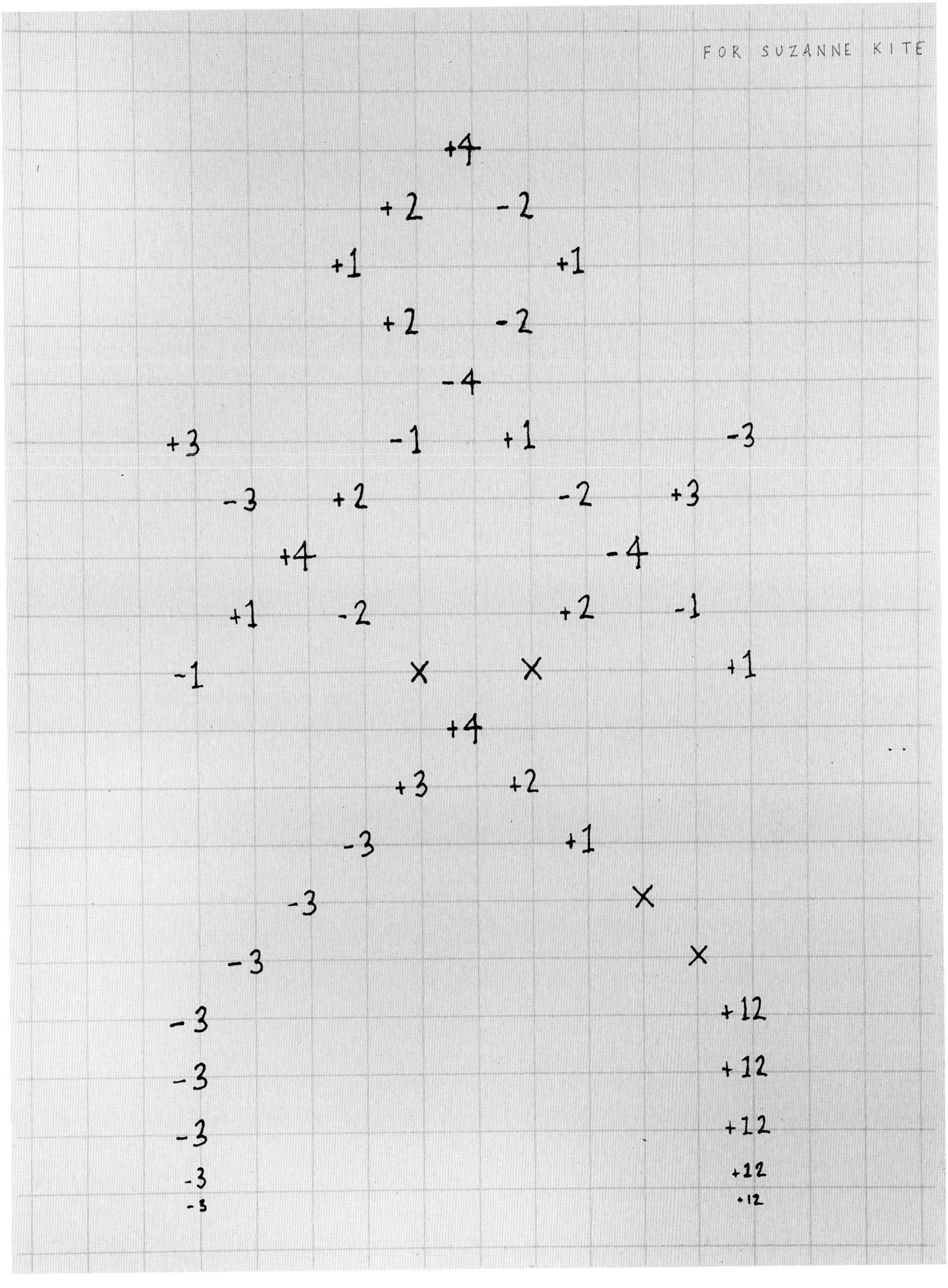

FOR SUZANNE KITE

+4

+2 -2

+1 +1

+2 -2

-4

+3 -1 +1 -3

-3 +2 -2 +3

+4 -4

+1 -2 +2 -1

-1 X X +1

+4

+3 +2

-3 +1

-3 X

-3 X

-3 +12

-3 +12

-3 +12

-3 +12

-3 +12

Corwin Clairmont

Member of the Confederated Salish and Kootenai Tribes of the Flathead Nation (b. 1946)

Raven Speaks to His Friends, 2020
Serigraph

Raven Speaks to His Friends was created in response to the COVID-19 virus and President Donald J. Trump's handling of the pandemic and his seeking of another term in office in 2020. Raven represents a significant wise Grandfather and cultural leader; the animals, birds, fish, and insects are his friends. Raven and his friends are our relatives and are often referred to as nonhuman beings of the natural world who came before we humans to prepare the way for us. They are our teachers on how to survive. Their many lessons are found in our traditional coyote stories and legends that have been passed down to us for thousands of years. Speaking to his friends, Raven is warning everyone that the Trump Virus is deadlier than the Hudson Bay smallpox blankets and that the only cure is to mask up and vote. —C.C.

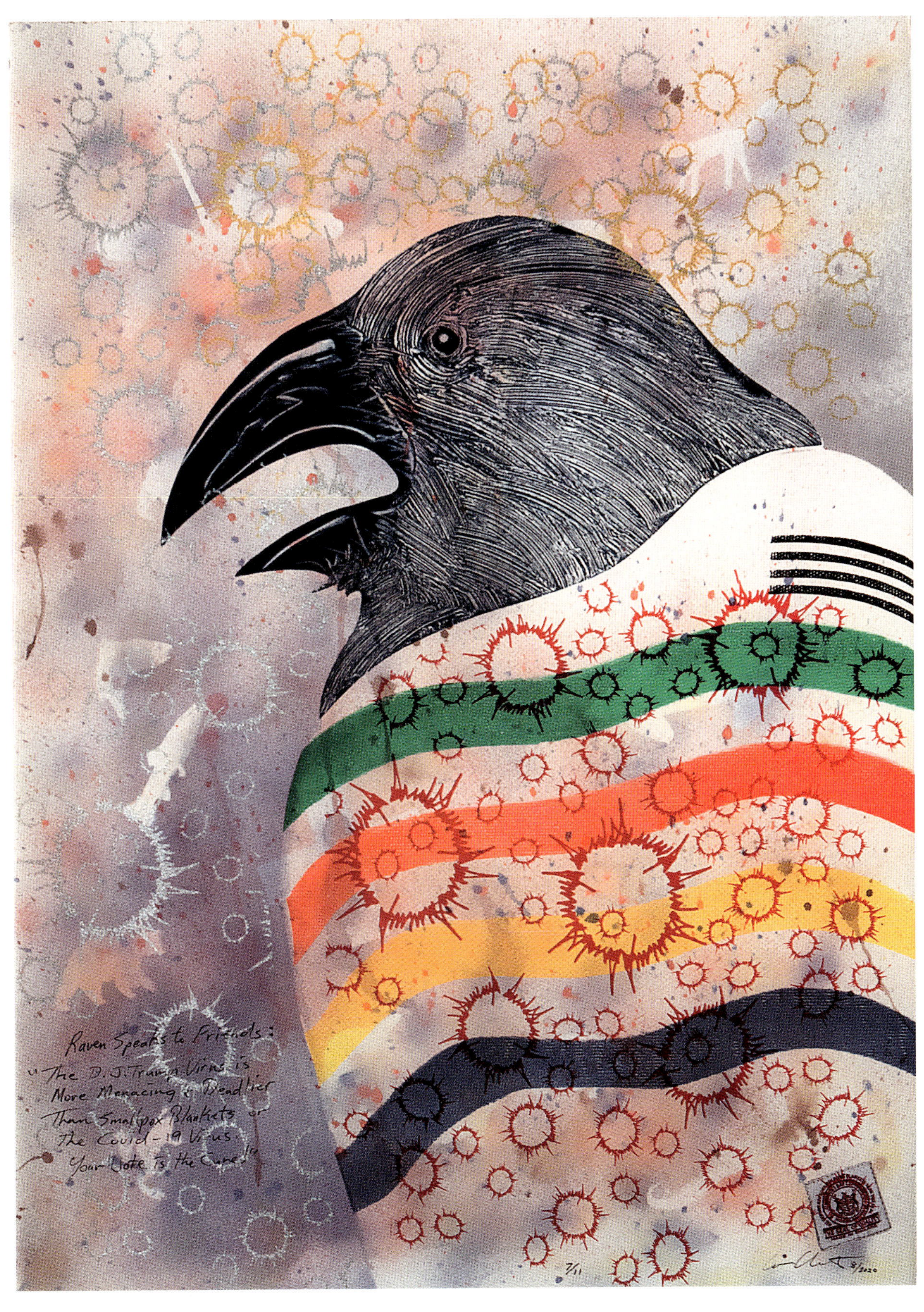
Raven Speaks to Friends:
"The D.J. Trump Virus is
More Menacing & Deadlier
Than Smallpox Blankets or
The Covid-19 Virus.
Your Vote is the Cure!"
7/11

Gerald Clarke Jr.

Cahuilla (b. 1967)

Native Land, 2019
Burnt paper

I aspire not to romanticize the subjects or content of my work. I strive to "keep it real" and have found that my best works are inspired by my personal experiences. Beer cans, branding irons, and gourd rattles represent aspects of my reality. These materials reflect who I am and not how the mainstream might understand the contemporary Native American experience. They represent my community as well: a community that struggles with various issues but that also laughs, loves, and continues to evolve. As you view my work, I ask that you do not simply compare or contrast it to "traditional Native American art," but that you understand that it exists within a spectrum of Indigenous expression that is simultaneously ancient and contemporary. I'm proud and humbled to contribute to the Indigenous intellectual tradition. I am not simply a contemporary artist who happens to be Indian. I am a Native American artist. I am a Cahuilla artist. —G.C. Jr.

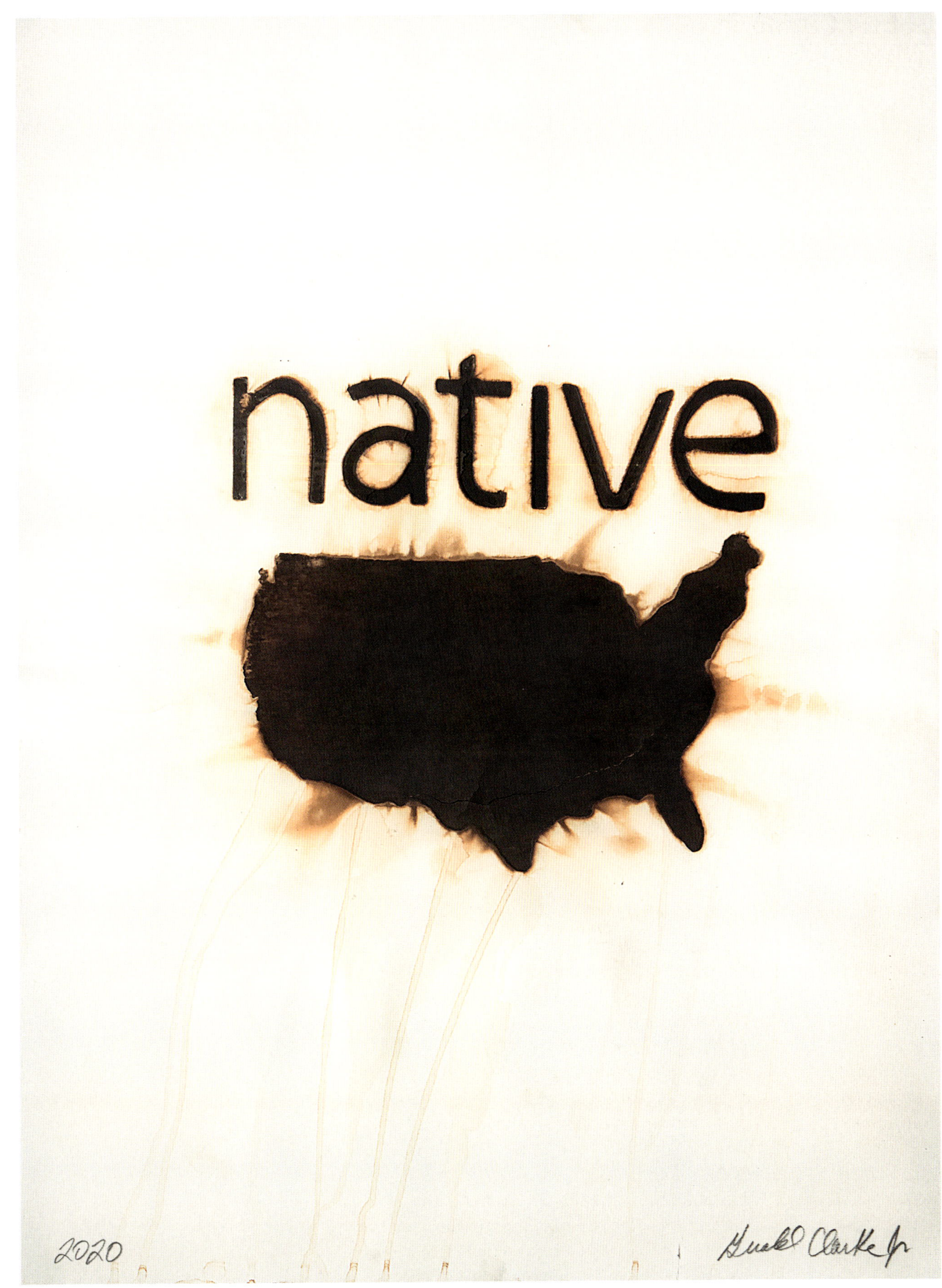
native
2020
Gerald Clarke Jr

Demian DinéYazhi'

Diné (b. 1983)

my ancestors will not let me forget this, 2020
Letterpress print

Inspired by DinéYazhi''s large neon work of the same title, this piece addresses the entangled relationship between the land, Indigenous peoples, and the United States.

"The work suggests the American flag isn't an innocent emblem of patriotism, rather a signal of devastation to be read as a warning from those who may be waving or wearing it." —D.D.

EVERY american flag is a WARNING SIGN
EVERY american flag is a WARNING SIGN
EVERY american flag is a WARNING SIGN
EVERY american flag is a WARNING SIGN
EVERY american flag is a WARNING SIGN
EVERY american flag is a WARNING SIGN
EVERY american flag is a WARNING SIGN
EVERY american flag is a WARNING SIGN
EVERY american flag is a WARNING SIGN
EVERY american flag is a WARNING SIGN
EVERY american flag is a WARNING SIGN
EVERY american flag is a WARNING SIGN
EVERY american flag is a WARNING SIGN

RYAN! Feddersen

Confederated Tribes of the Colville Reservation and of Mixed European Descent (b. 1984)

Bison Stack Crane, 2018
Archival pigment print

Bison Stack Crane ties the mass slaughter of the bison and systematic removal of Native peoples from their lands to current continuing trends of rapid redevelopment and displacement of people and animals in many of America's major urban centers. The imagery adds layers of meaning to an unattributed photograph from the mid-1870s, where two settlers are shown atop and before a mountain of bison skulls. In *Bison Stack Crane*, the men are removed and replaced by a more contemporary symbol of irresponsible development and displacement: the tower crane. —R.F.

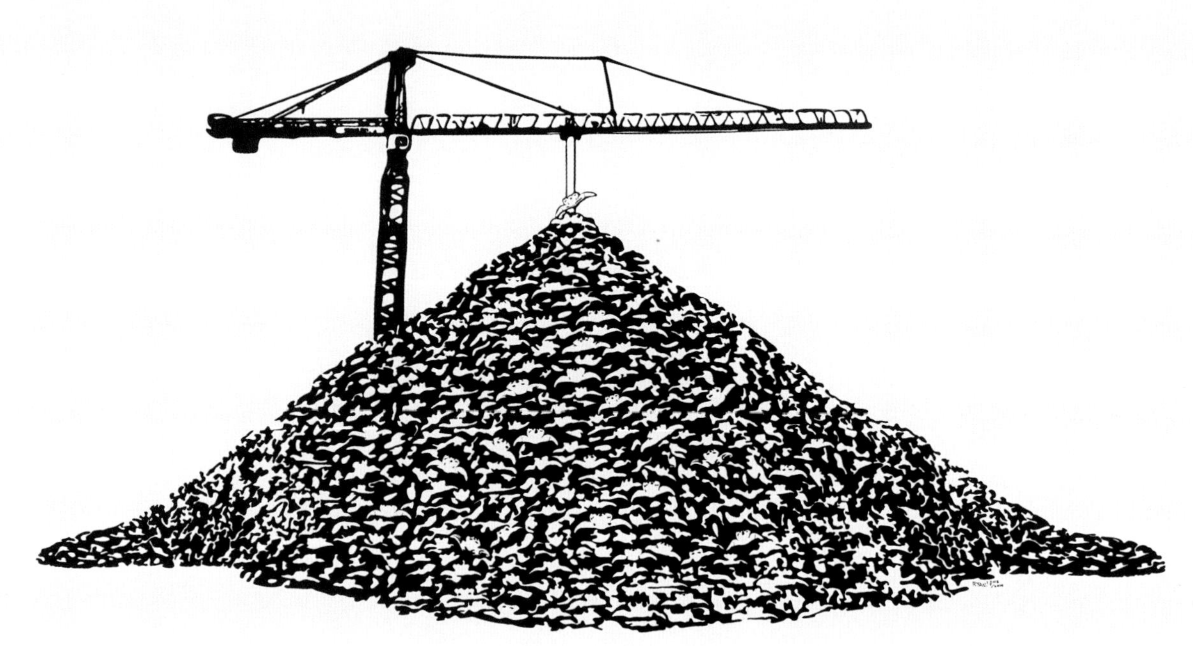

Nicholas Galanin

Tlingit/Unangax̂ (b. 1979)

Never Forget, 2021
C-print

Colonial entities, the United States Constitution, and the current United States government refer to people Indigenous of the continental United States collectively as "Indian." Hollywood's misrepresentations of Indigenous people reflect and attempt to justify United States policy. The term "Indian" is a refusal to acknowledge tribal sovereignty and attempts to erase the diversity of over five hundred distinct nations. Indigenous land and Indigenous communities remain unique, resilient, complex, and beautiful despite over five hundred years of occupation by violent settler states. *Never Forget* refuses to legitimize settler occupation and reframes a word of generic reduction to call for collective action. It is a monumental invitation to landowners to seek out Indigenous leadership for land relationships, to center Indigenous knowledge in creating sustainable practices, to contribute to real rent initiatives, and to transfer land titles and rights to Indigenous nations and communities. —N.G.

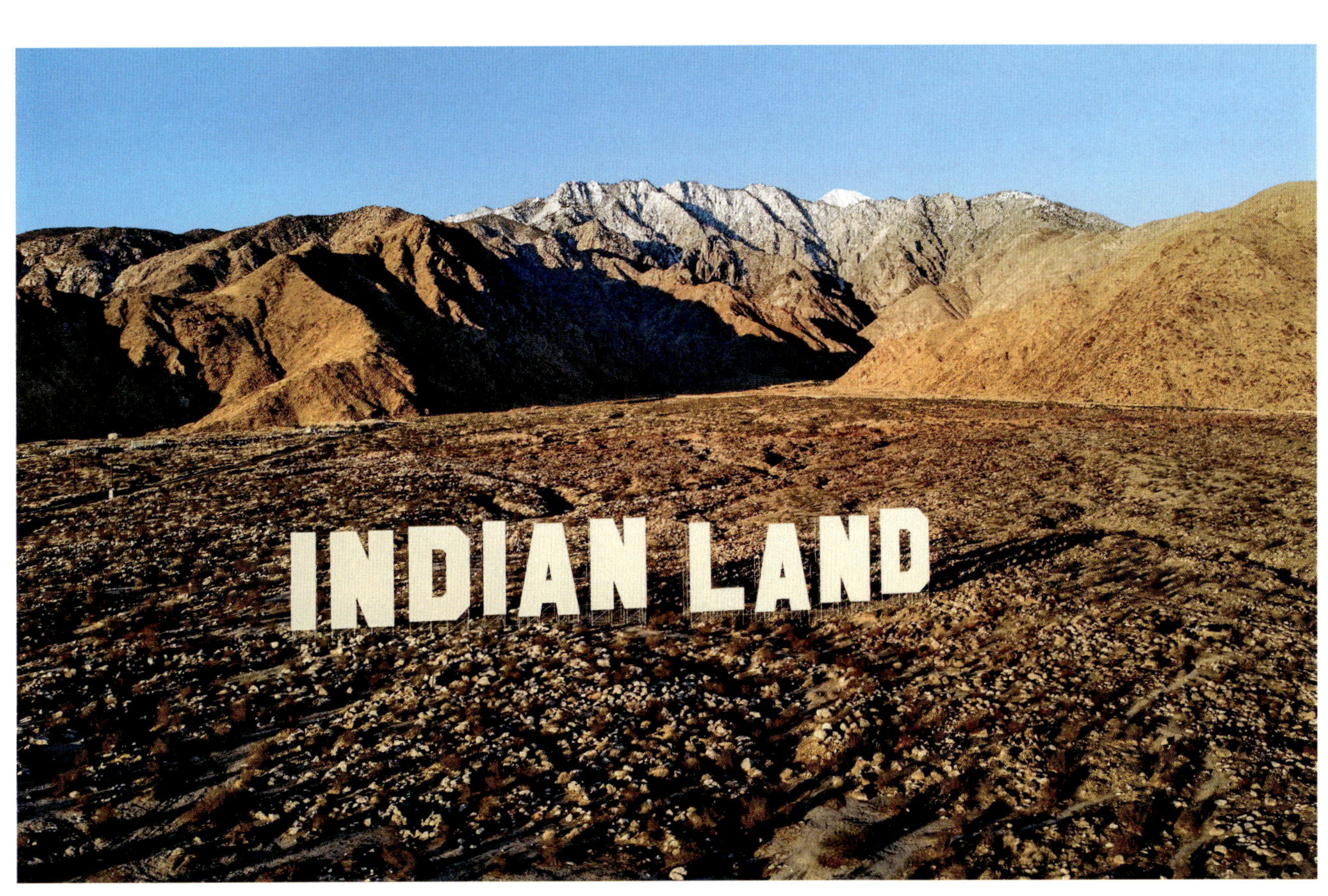
INDIAN LAND

Jeffrey Gibson

Member of the Mississippi Band of Choctaw Indians and of Cherokee Descent (b. 1972)

SHE NEVER DANCES ALONE, 2021
Acrylic on canvas, archival pigment on cotton, archival pigment on rice paper, inset in custom wood frame, glass beads, artificial sinew

Made in conjunction with a video piece of the same title, which was broadcast in Times Square in 2020, Gibson's work both celebrates Indigenous matriarchy and raises awareness of the ongoing crisis of Murdered and Missing Indigenous Women (MMIW). Both the painting and the video center on the jingle dress dance, a powwow dance that originated with the Ojibwe tribe and is traditionally performed by women to call upon ancestors for strength, healing, and protection.

Of the piece, Gibson has said that it "is an ancestral call for strength and healing for all Indigenous people, and a recognition of the power of Indigenous women."

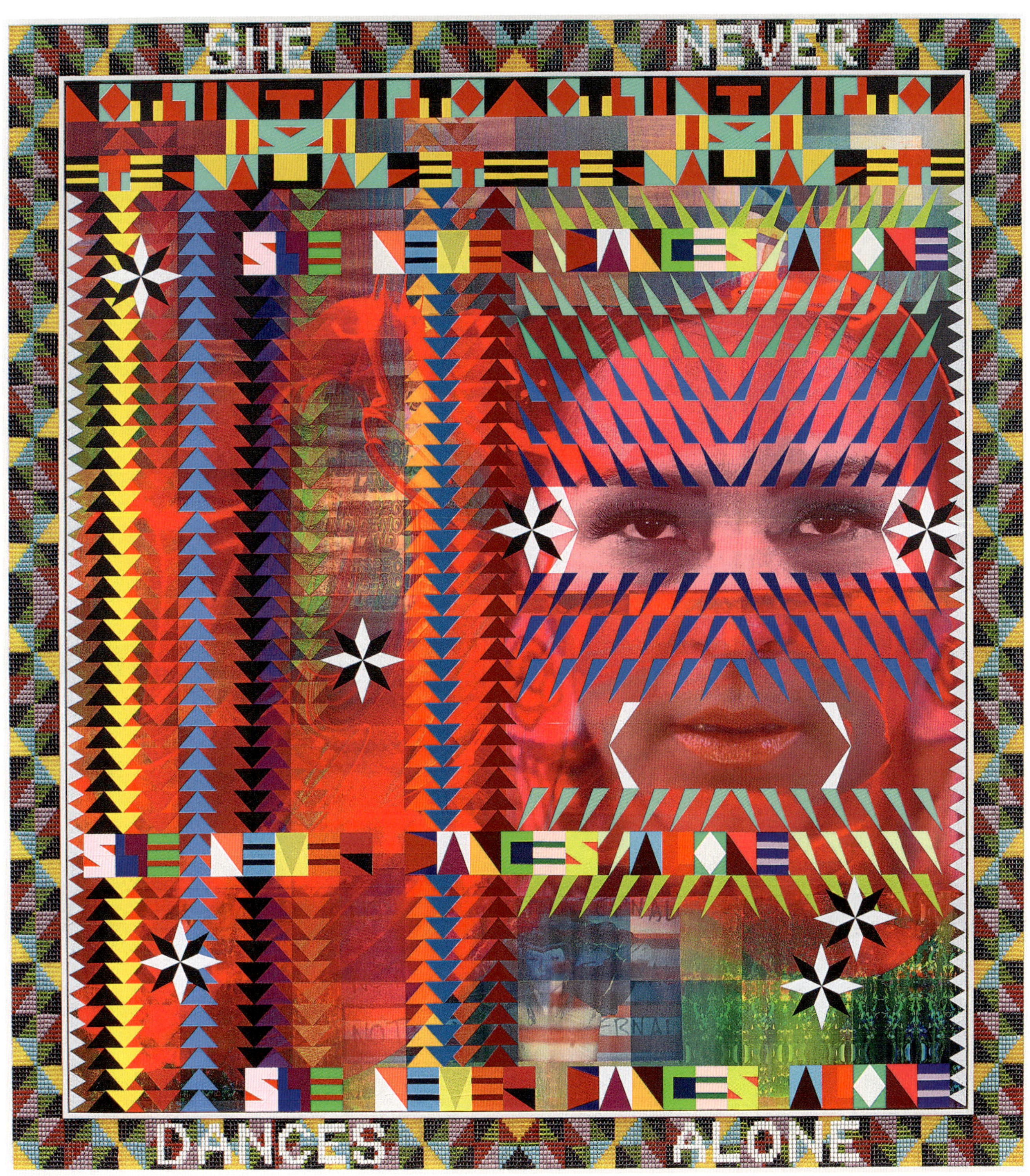
SHE NEVER
DANCES ALONE

Richard Glazer-Danay

Caughnawaga Mohawk and Jewish Descent (b. 1942)

Divided We Stand, 2020
Ink on paper

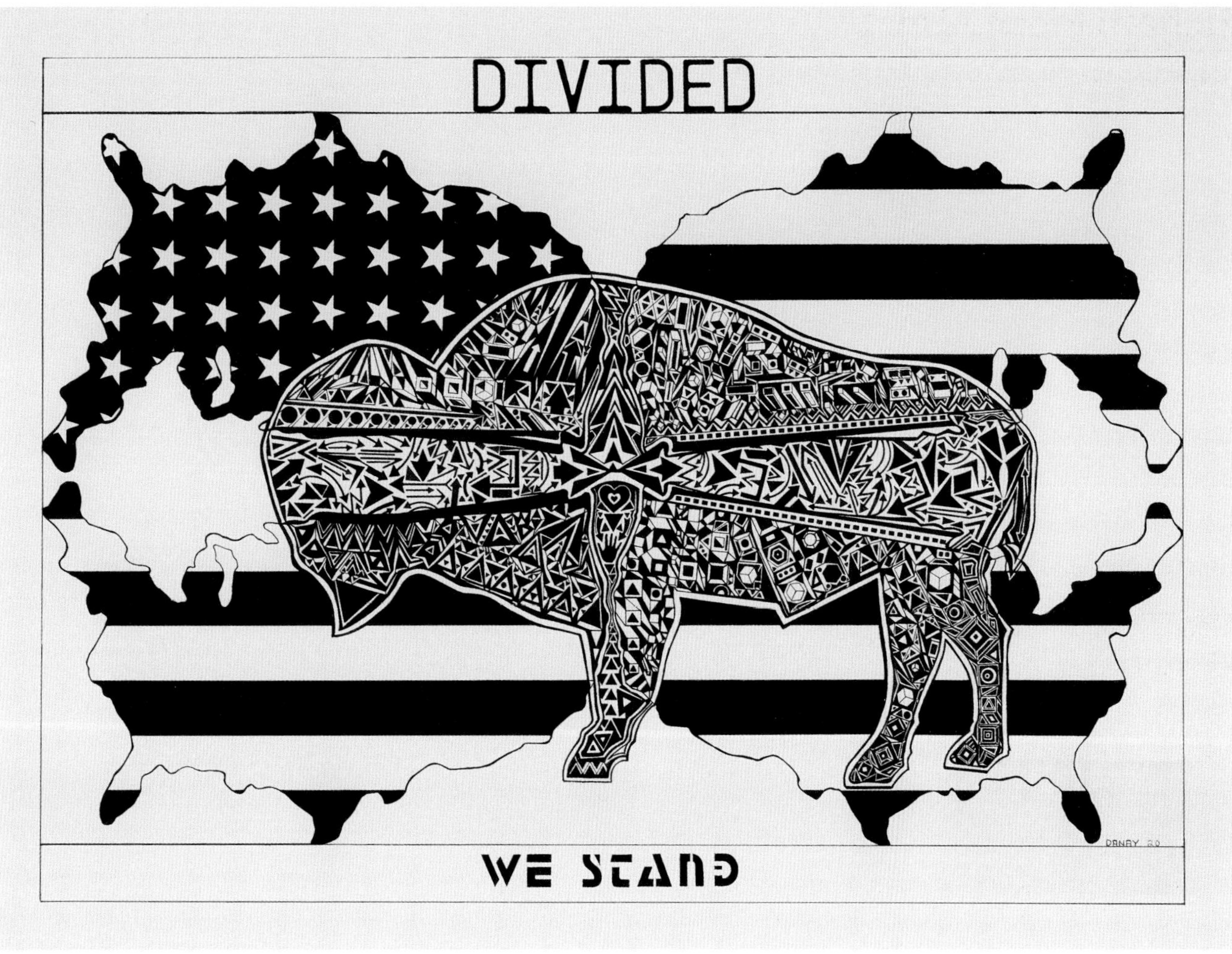
DIVIDED
WE STAND

Edgar Heap of Birds

Cheyenne and Arapaho Nations (b. 1954)

Indian Never Safe, 2006–12
Monotype

Three forts were built to attack and attempt to control the Cheyenne and Arapaho Tribes in Oklahoma Indian Territory.

Fort Supply was constructed to resupply Custer and his army, which enabled the Washita Massacre. Cantonnment Reno and Fort Reno were later formed to serve as enforcers over the tribes. Fort Reno is still an active institution, and the tribes continue to seek reclamation of the land. Part of Fort Reno was retooled to be used as a federal penitentiary, where Oklahoma City bomber Timothy McVeigh was detained.

Throughout history, United States forts have never brought peace to Native peoples, only the front line of violence.
—E.HoB.

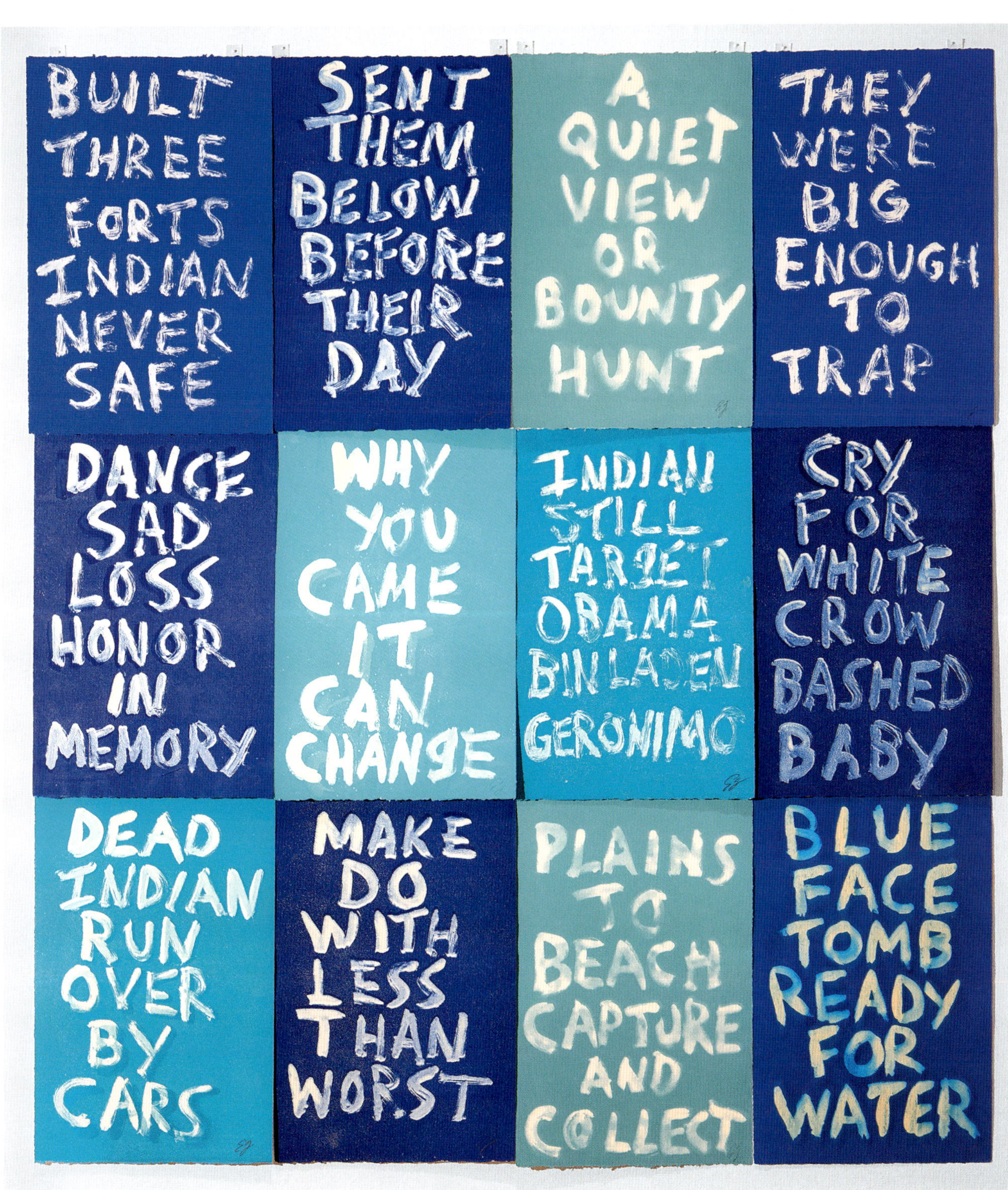
BUILT THREE FORTS INDIAN NEVER SAFE
SENT THEM BELOW BEFORE THEIR DAY
A QUIET VIEW OR BOUNTY HUNT
THEY WERE BIG ENOUGH TO TRAP
DANCE SAD LOSS HONOR IN MEMORY
WHY YOU CAME IT CAN CHANGE
INDIAN STILL TARGET OBAMA BIN LADEN GERONIMO
CRY FOR WHITE CROW BASHED BABY
DEAD INDIAN RUN OVER BY CARS
MAKE DO WITH LESS THAN WORST
PLAINS TO BEACH CAPTURE AND COLLECT
BLUE FACE TOMB READY FOR WATER

Luzene Hill

Enrolled Member of the Eastern Band of Cherokee Indians (b. 1946)

Enate, 2017
Video

Enate is an exposition of the numbers of Native American women who are sexually assaulted each year, presented as material volume in 6,956 silk taffeta female figures. The silhouettes, dyed with cochineal, are motifs from the earliest images of females in the Americas (4000–3500 BCE); 6,956 is the average reported number of Native American women who are sexually assaulted each year. The silhouettes are layered in threes in reference to the fact that Native women are three times more likely to be assaulted than other women in the United States and 90 percent of the assaults are by non-Native men. Each trio forms a cluster, resembling feathers, and is attached to the cloak, metaphorically unifying the women into a solid mantle of protection and empowerment. —L.H.

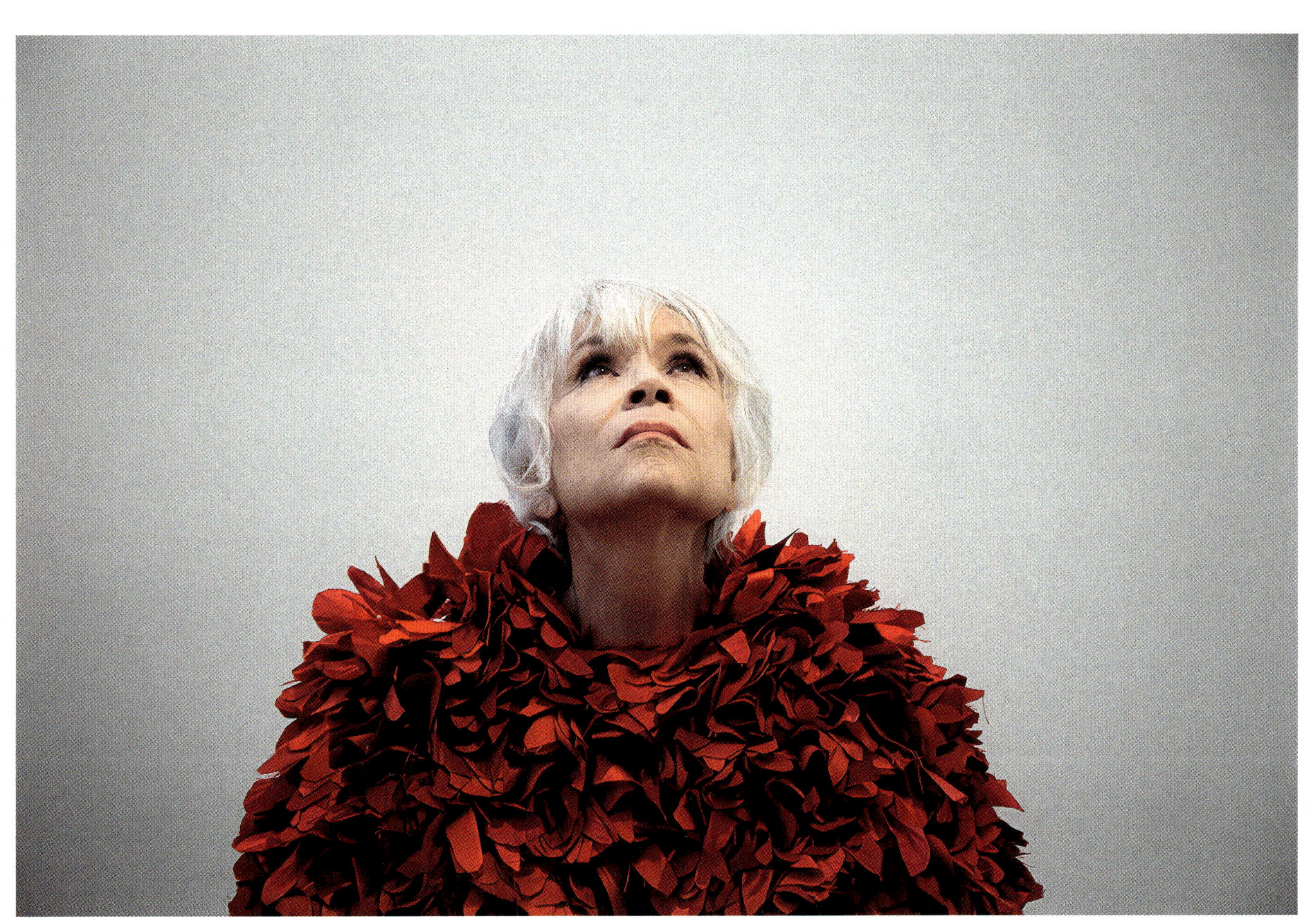

Cannupa Hanska Luger

Enrolled Member of the Three Affiliated Tribes of Fort Berthold and is Mandan, Hidatsa, Arikara and Lakota (b. 1979)

Mirror Shield Project, 2016–ongoing
Social collaboration, video, sculpture, land art performance

Art can be an incredible tool when you're fighting aggression—it's a language that transcends hostility. The *Mirror Shield Project* was initiated in 2016 in support of the water protectors standing up against the Dakota Access Pipeline on my ancestral homelands. Through a tutorial video shared on social media, I invited people to create durable mirrored shields that would be used in on-site frontline actions. The *Mirror Shield Project* continues to be an open-source artwork and has been utilized in various resistance movements across the world. This project allows for those not able to be on the front line to contribute to those who are. As artists, we live on the periphery—but we are the mirrors. We are the reflective points that break through a barrier. —C.H.L.

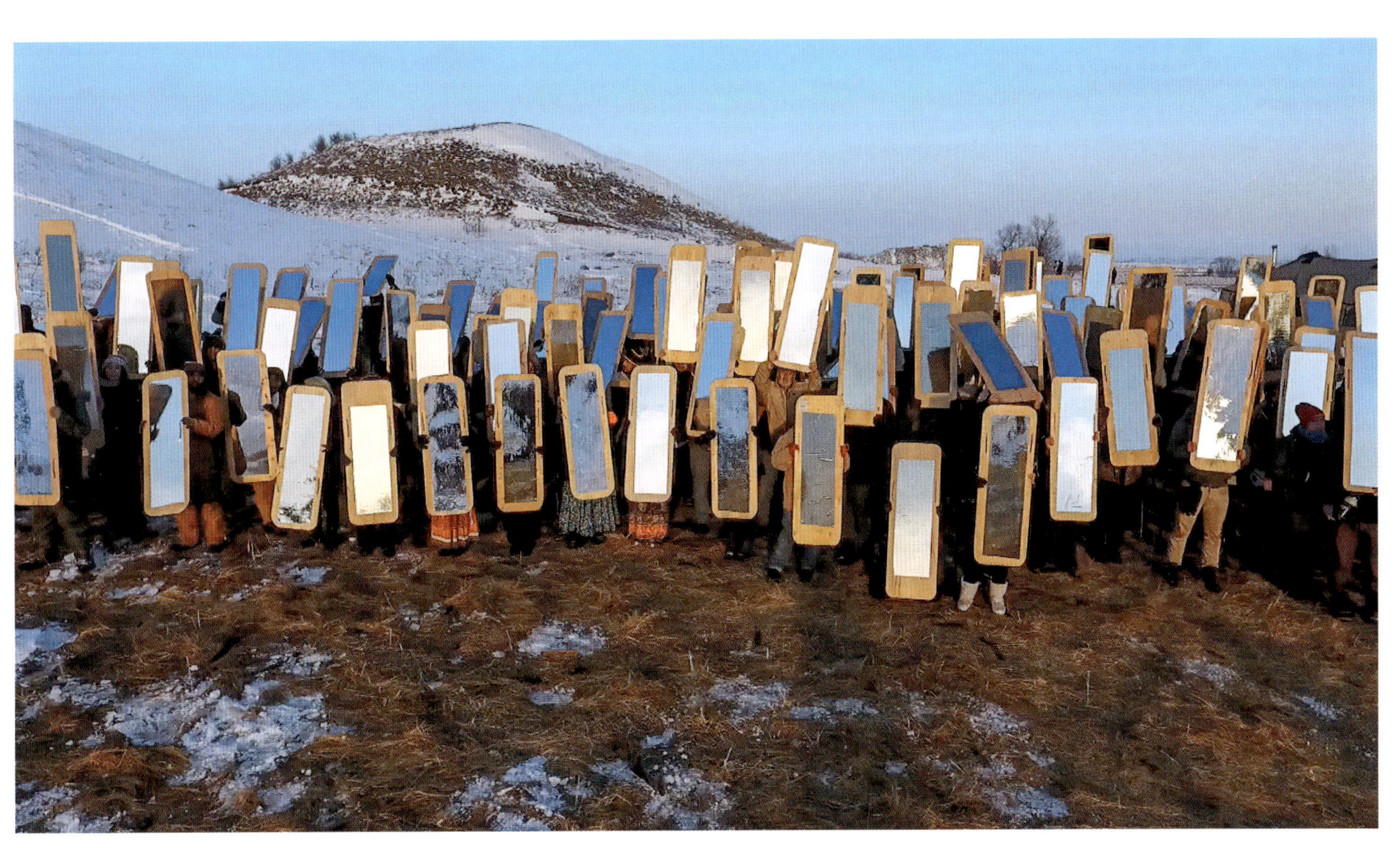

Douglas Miles

White Mountain Apache-San Carlos
Apache-Akimel O'odham (b. 1963)

Forced Removal Series: Victoria in Blue and Gold, 2023
Vintage suitcase, spray paint, and appliqué

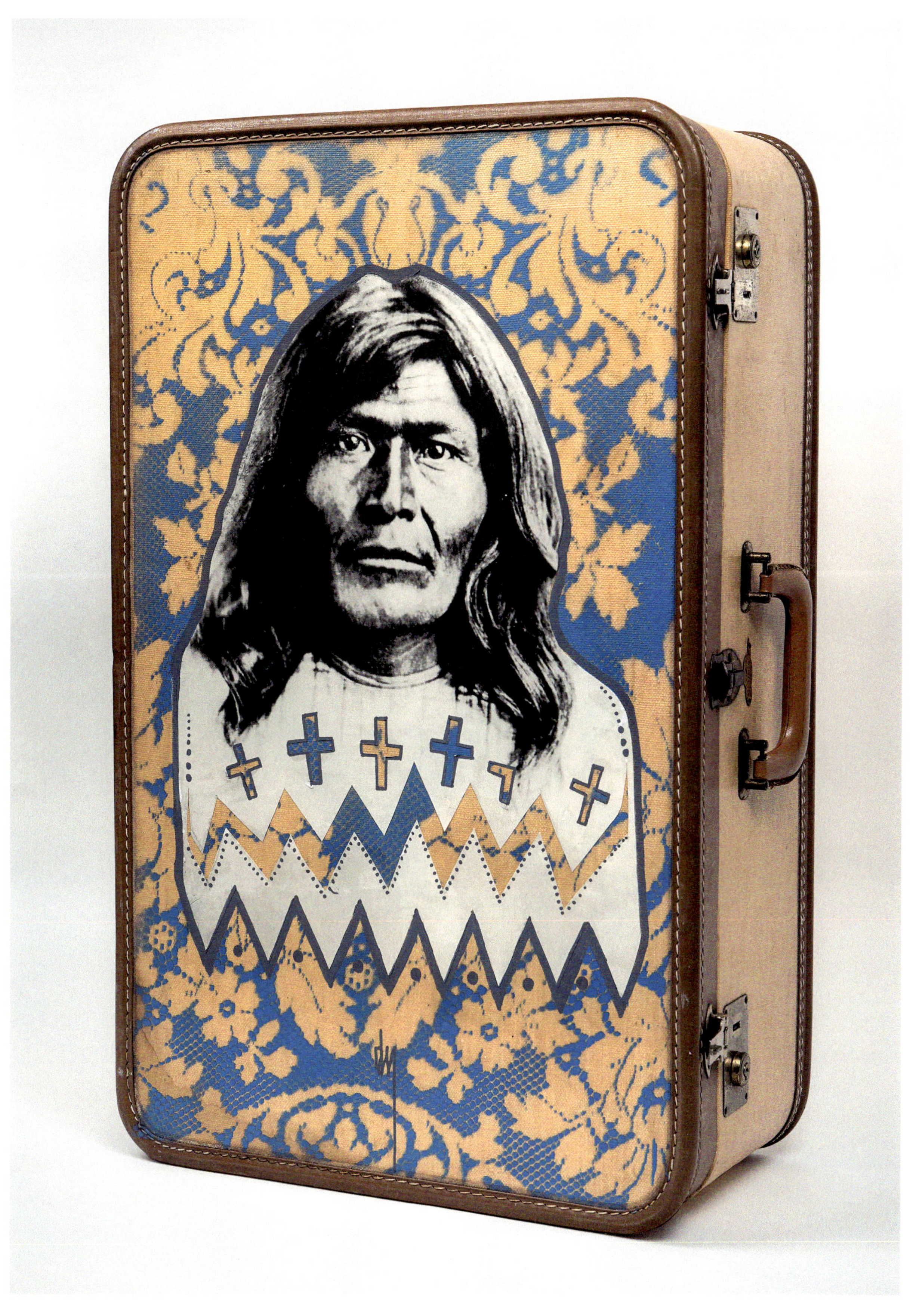

New Red Order (NRO)

Ojibway, Tlingit

Culture Capture: Crimes Against Reality, 2020
Video

Culture Capture: Crimes Against Reality examines desires for monumentality and its dissolution, pursuing fantasies of removal by morphing monuments into metastasizing flesh via ritualized photogrammetric capture and virtual manipulation to perform a sort of sympathetic magic. The piece literalizes the violence of settler-colonial propaganda and features high-profile monuments such as the equestrian statue of Theodore Roosevelt, which stood in front of the American Museum of Natural History (AMNH) in New York City from 1940 until its removal in 2022, and sculptures by American sculptor James Earle Fraser. The video mines the archives of Fraser, moving beyond simple iconoclasm to probe deeper, investigating desires for capturing the Indigeneity that motivated the artist—desires that continue to pervade myths, dreams, and political foundations of the so-called Americas. —NRO

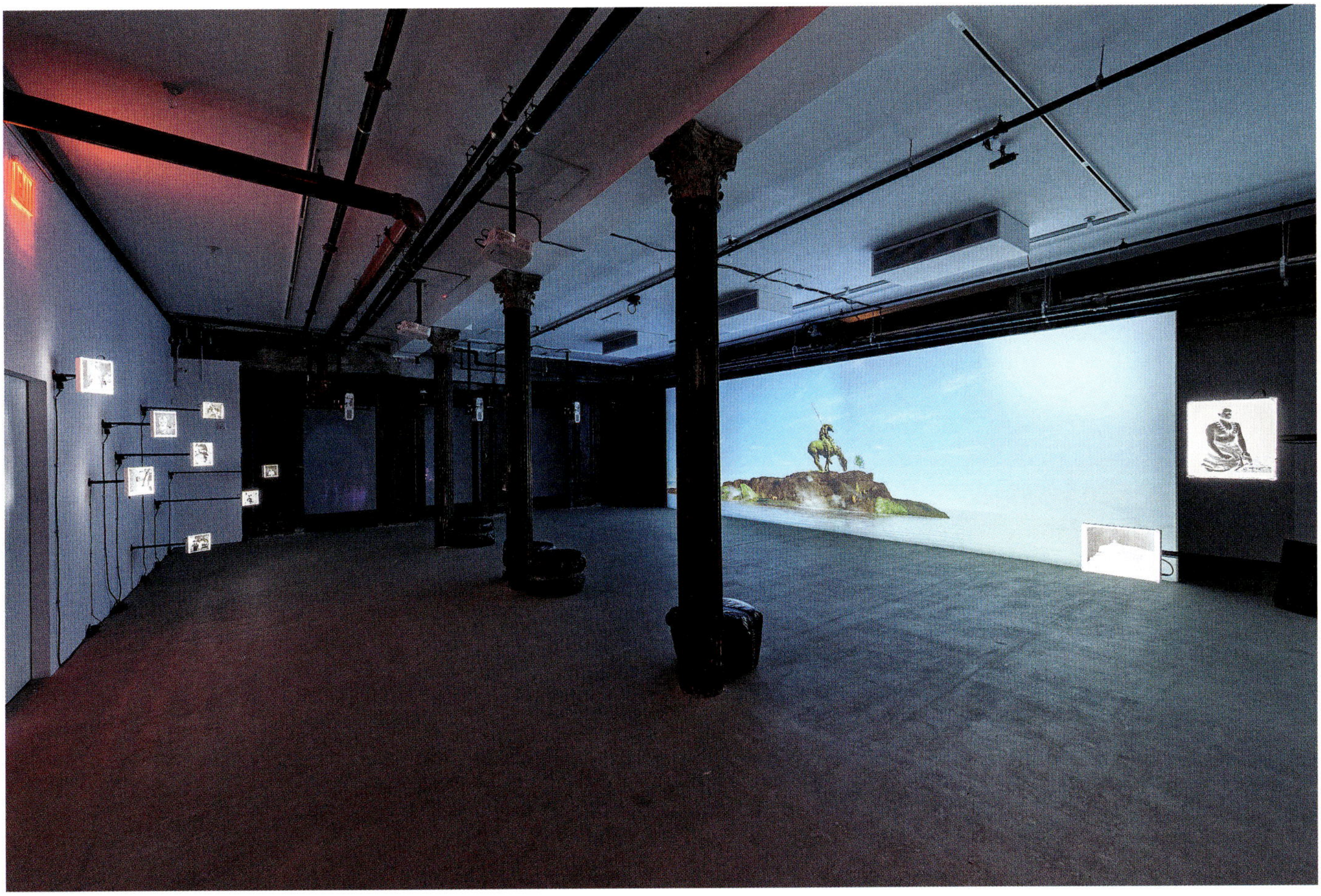

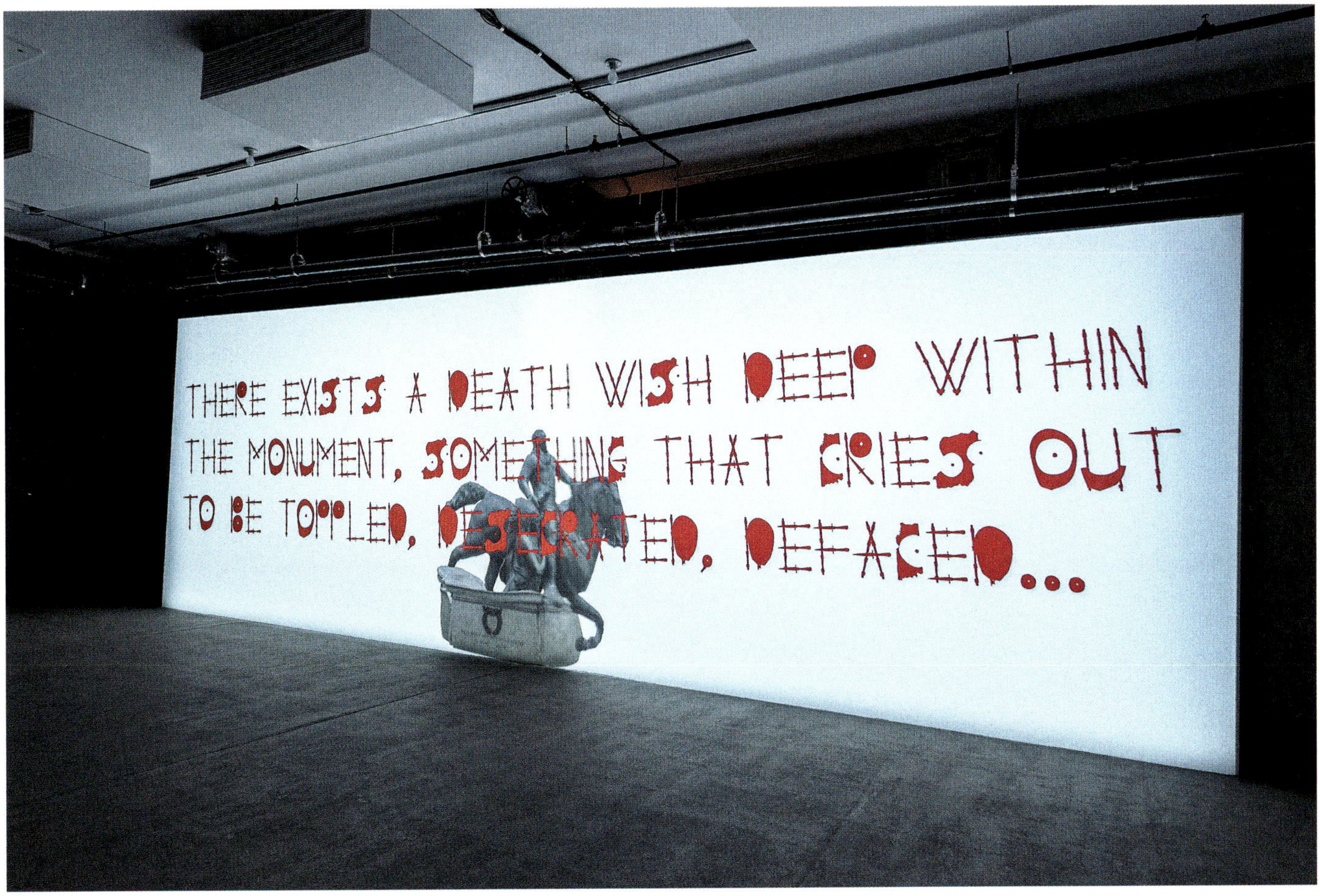
THERE EXISTS A DEATH WISH DEEP WITHIN
THE MONUMENT, SOMETHING THAT CRIES OUT
TO BE TOPPLED, DESECRATED, DEFACED...

Mikayla Patton

Enrolled Member of the Oglala Lakota Nation (b. 1991)

Enduring, 2023
Paper, deer lace, porcupine quills, medicine ash

Enduring reflects the delicate balance between vulnerability and protection through the interplay of recycled handmade paper and found porcupine quills. The floating sculpture comprises two traveling-trunks bound together with leather that fringes to the ground and spills out, evoking a sense of journey and movement. The smaller ends of the boxes, dressed in porcupine quills, are intricately stitched into checkered and linear patterns, like quillwork used for generations by my people. Porcupine quills, a symbol of strength and self-preservation in many Indigenous cultures, embody protection while paper is often viewed as fragile and delicate. When layered and manipulated, paper reveals an innate strength and resilience, much like the spirit. —M.P.

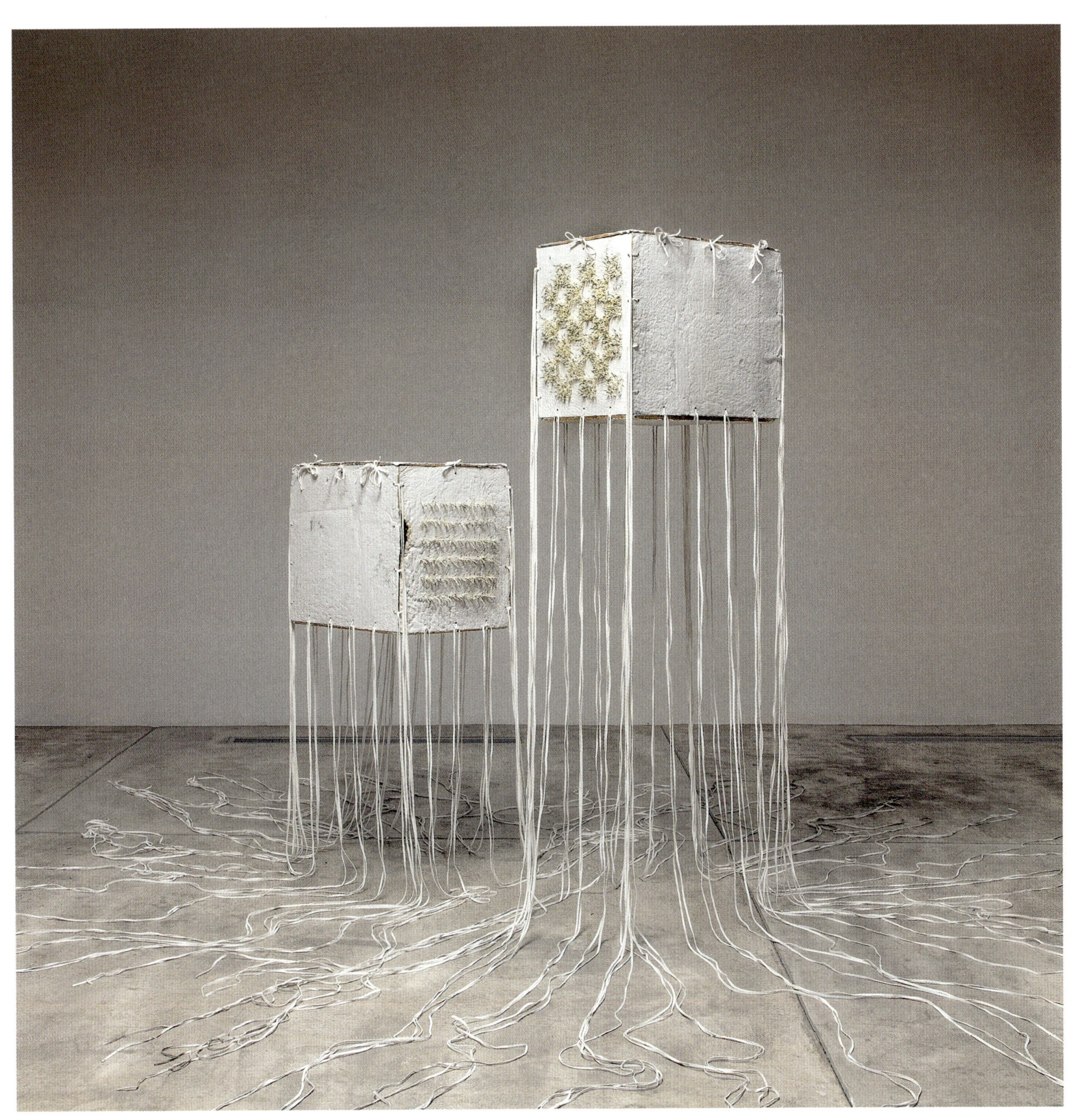

Diego Romero

Cochiti Pueblo (b. 1964)

Girl in the Anthropocene, 2017
Lithograph

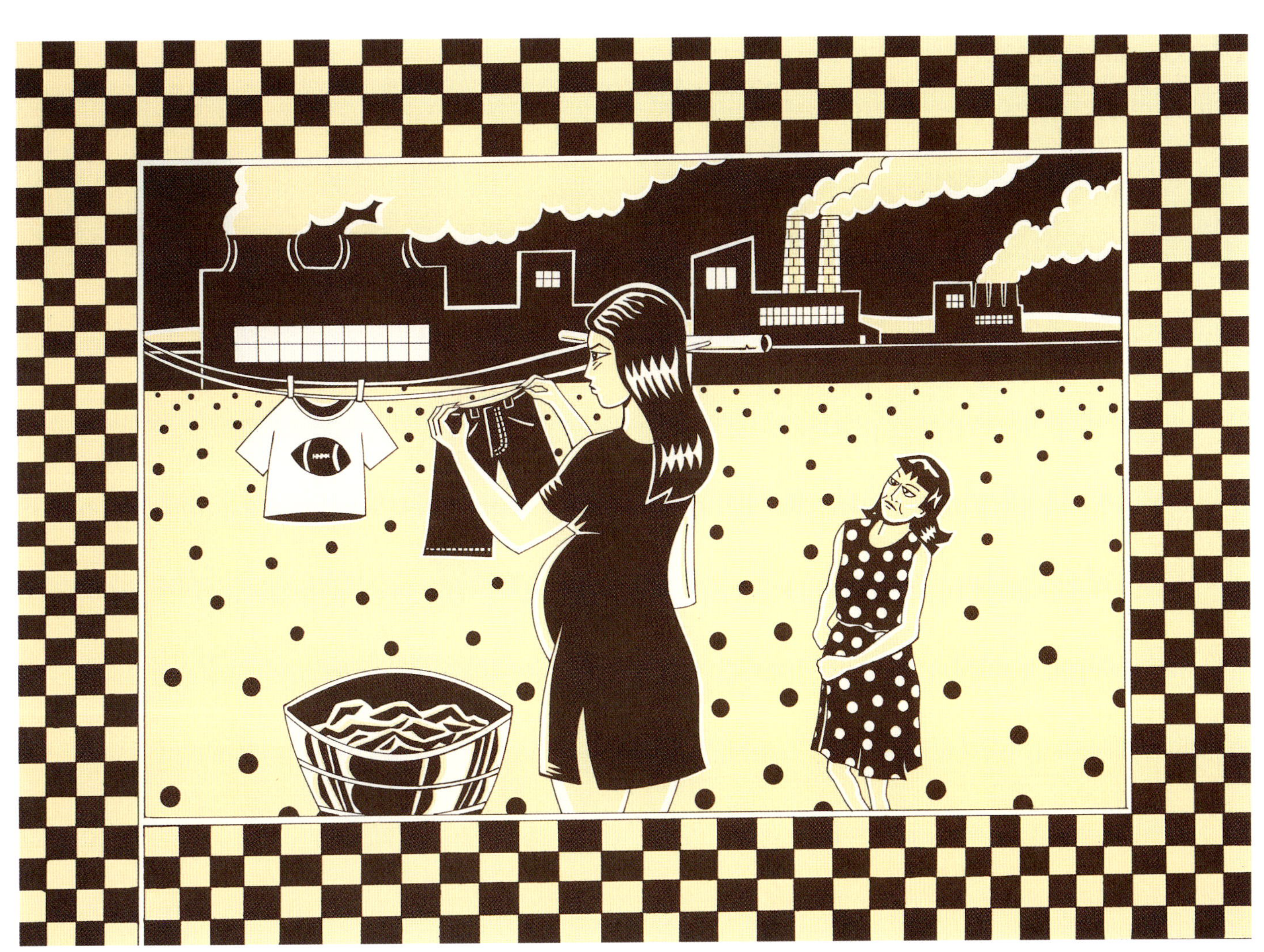

Philip Singer

Diné (Navajo) (b. 1963)

Pink Triangle, 2019
Wool

This two-color design consists of bands and a spiral triangle. It was woven during the month of June, which is also Pride Month in the LGBTQ+ community. The idea of a round spiral was borrowed from Anasazi rock art. But rather than round, why not a triangle and the symbol of identity? The spiral denotes a maze, a path, and a never-ending cycle of growth and change. Struggles with identity are hard for many as one maneuvers within the maze. The exit within the spiral is there when one has found contentment and acceptance. This tapestry consists of hand-processed, natural white wool and cochineal-dyed yarn. It is constructed in the Navajo closed-loom technique. —P.S.

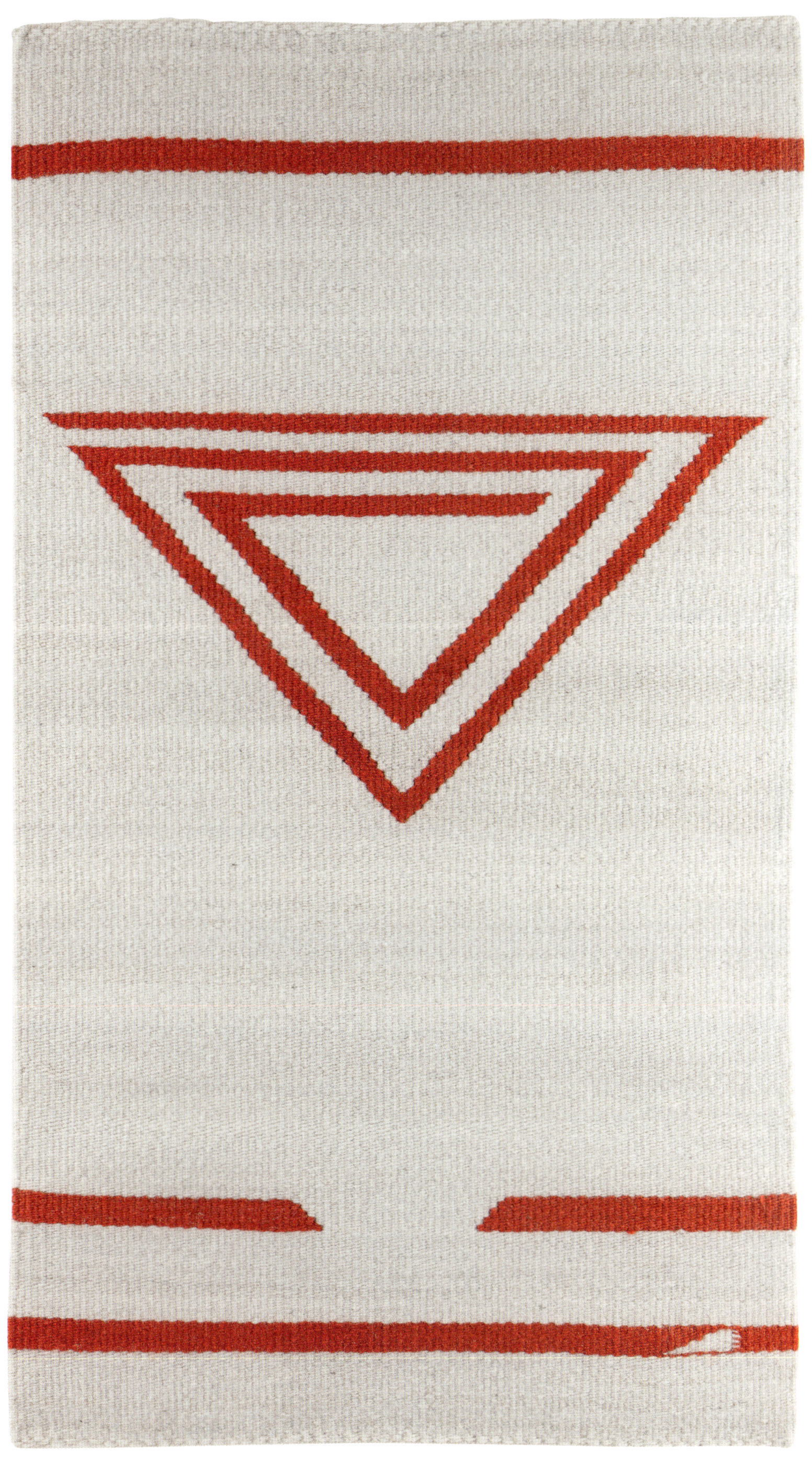

Bently Spang

Enrolled Member of the Tsitsistas/
Suhtai Nation (b. 1960)

Modern Warrior Series: War Shirt #3—The Great Divide, 2006
Mixed media

I use photography in my work to counter misconceptions about Native culture and history. We are still here because our relatives built strong, sophisticated cultures with objects like the war shirt as central elements of protection. My photo war shirts, though not meant to be actual war shirts, draw from the reciprocity built into the shirts of the past. Those shirts were made by relatives of the wearer and were adorned with hair from those same relatives and other symbols and objects of power to protect the wearer. The photos and objects in my shirts are conceptual representations of the power we draw from today as modern warriors in continuity with our past. This piece celebrates a place we call "The Divide," an immense mountain ridge on my homelands. —B.S.

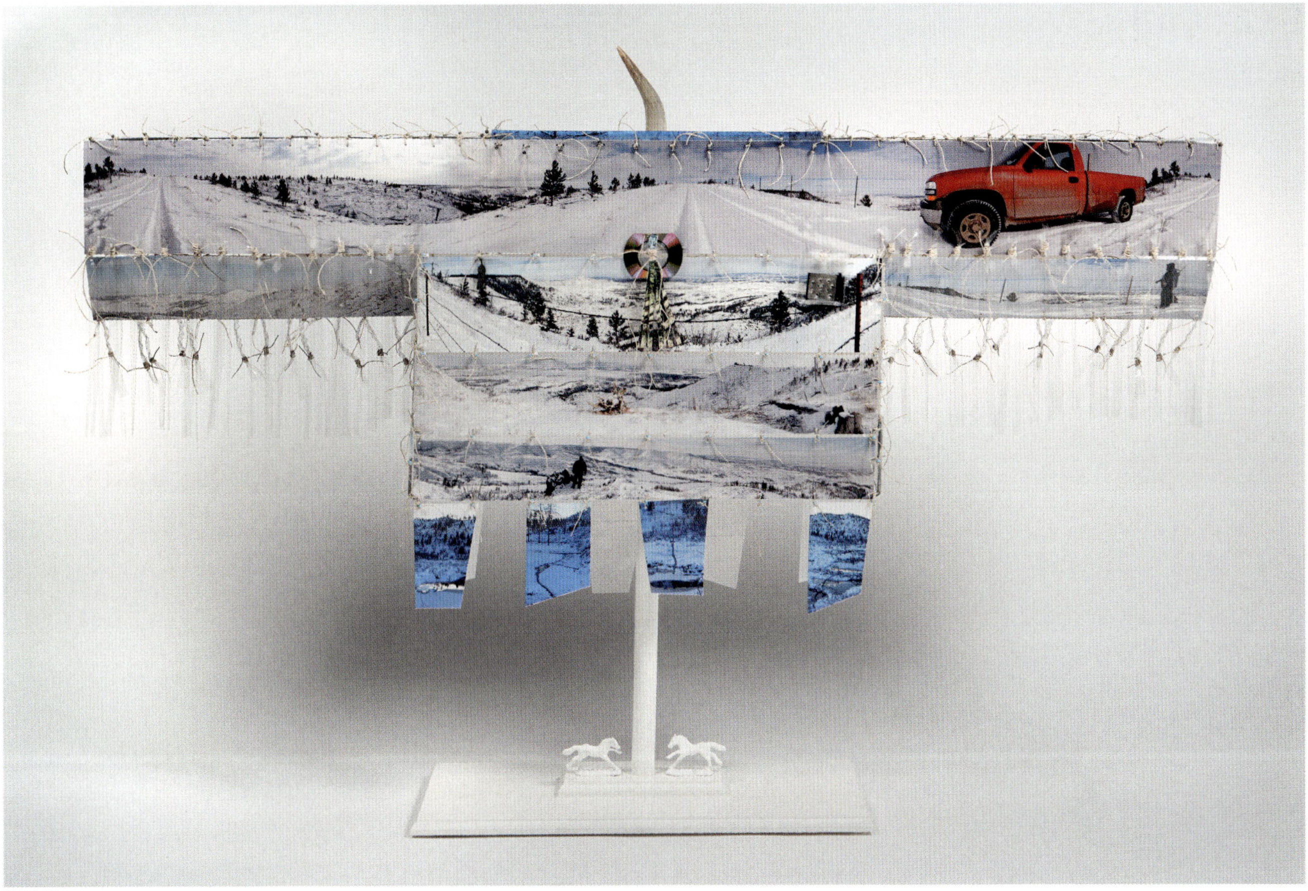

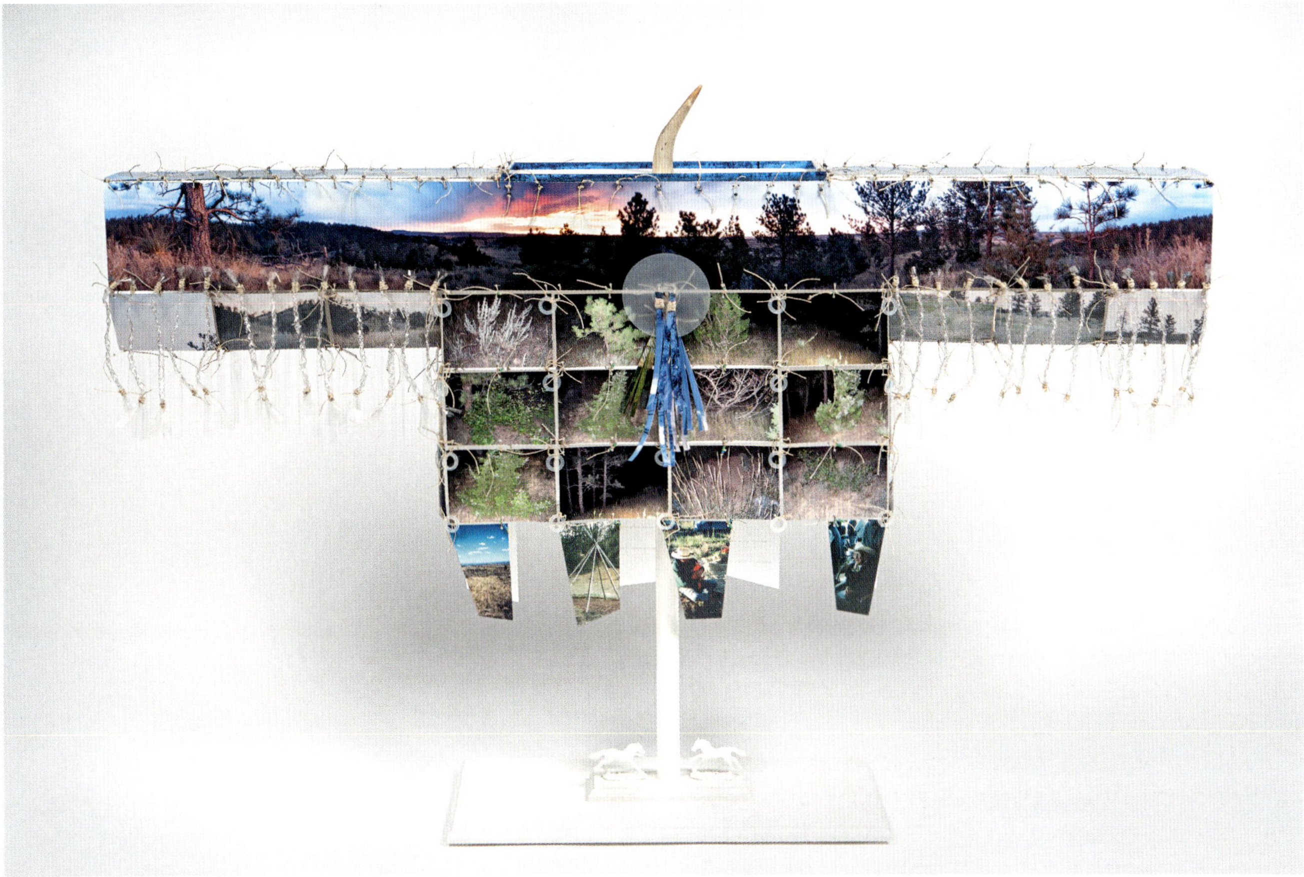

Charlene Teters

Spokane (b. 1952)

Way of Sorrows, 2020
Video

The caravans of refugees coming to the United States' Southern border are part of an uninterrupted history of forced migrations and trails of tears. The installation *Way of Sorrows* looks starkly at the birth of savior mythologies, asking, "On whose shoulders does responsibility reside?" Are we truly at a point of some fearing having a little less in order to welcome the stranger who has nothing: no earthly possessions, no place to call home, no place of safety or ceremony?

The installation seeks a spirit of hope represented through photo murals of the artist robed in silver and gold emergency blankets. She represents the mother-savior—Our Lady of Survival—and hopes that we can finally be seen as human. —C.T.

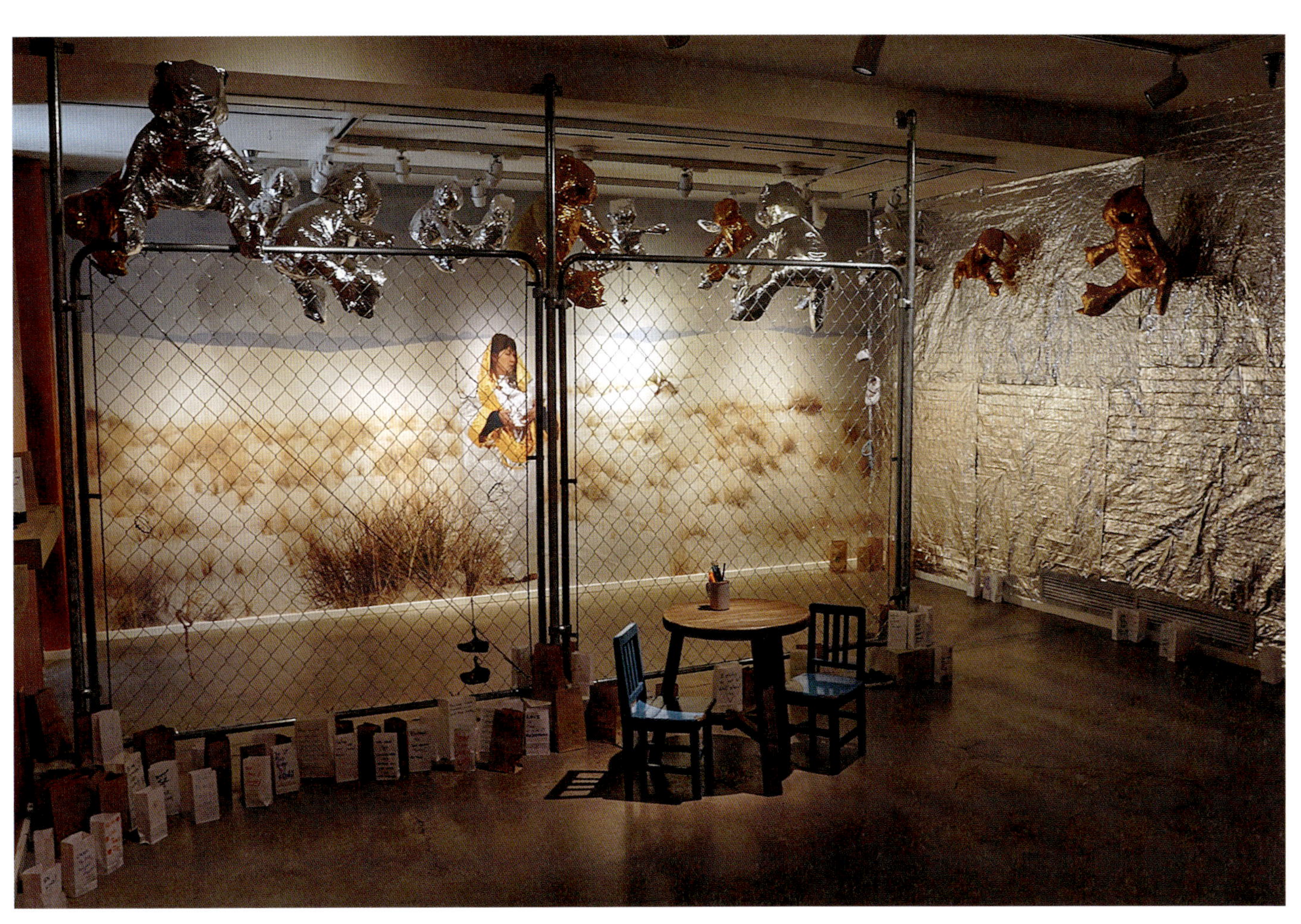

Marie Watt

Enrolled Member of the Seneca Nation of Indians/European Descent (b. 1967)

Skywalker/Skyscraper (Twins), 2020
Reclaimed wool blankets, steel I-beams, two textile towers

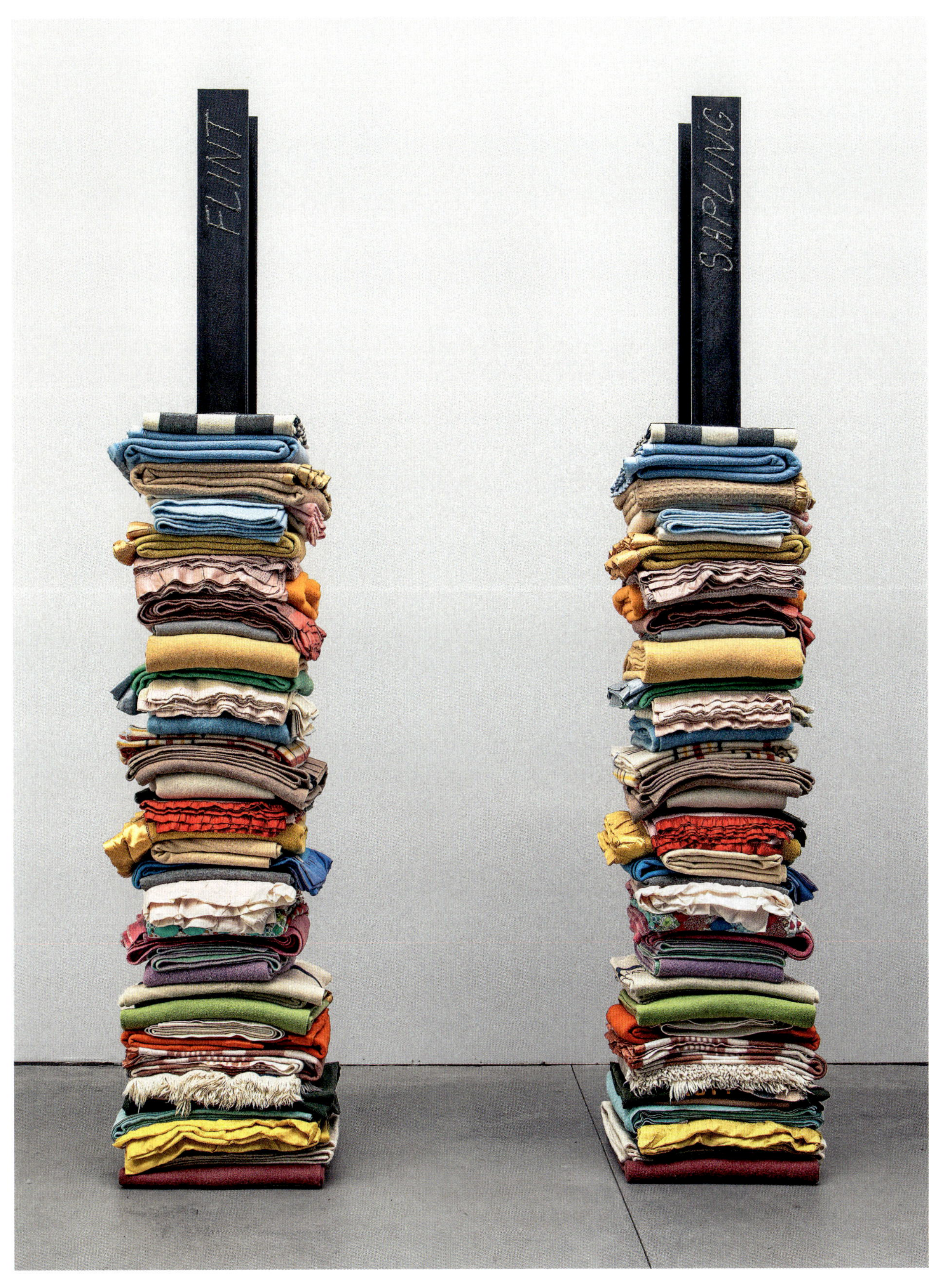
FLINT
SAPLING

Everything we create, harvest, or perform is connected to a religious aspect of our lives, our spiritual world and our metaphysical world.
—Jaune Quick-to-See Smith

Artworks centered around tribal identity have a distinct cultural component that illuminates, honors, and describes traditions and practices from daily life. These include songs, origin stories, oral histories, plants, terrain, climate, and food sources relevant to specific tribal nations. From beadwork to the honoring of the animal spirit world as well as adaptations of traditional craft, each artist reflects their tribal nation's unique beliefs and art practices.

TRIBAL

Tony Abeyta

Diné (Navajo) (born 1965)

Dispersion, 2018
Micaceous clay and acrylic medium, historical Native beads, encaustic wax on archival wood panels

This painting represents seeds that lay dormant in winter, then, as the wind might disperse them about the dry desert, their awaiting of rain and the possibility of sprouting upon the next spring monsoons. The central panel depicts seeds and spores, vegetal shapes, and medicinal plants, and these forms create an abstracted deity that represents germination. The adjacent side panels also echo fields that might be planted for a later fall harvest. Overall, the tonality of soft-spoken colors is calm, meditative, and patient, aspiring to illustrate the seasons. —T.A.

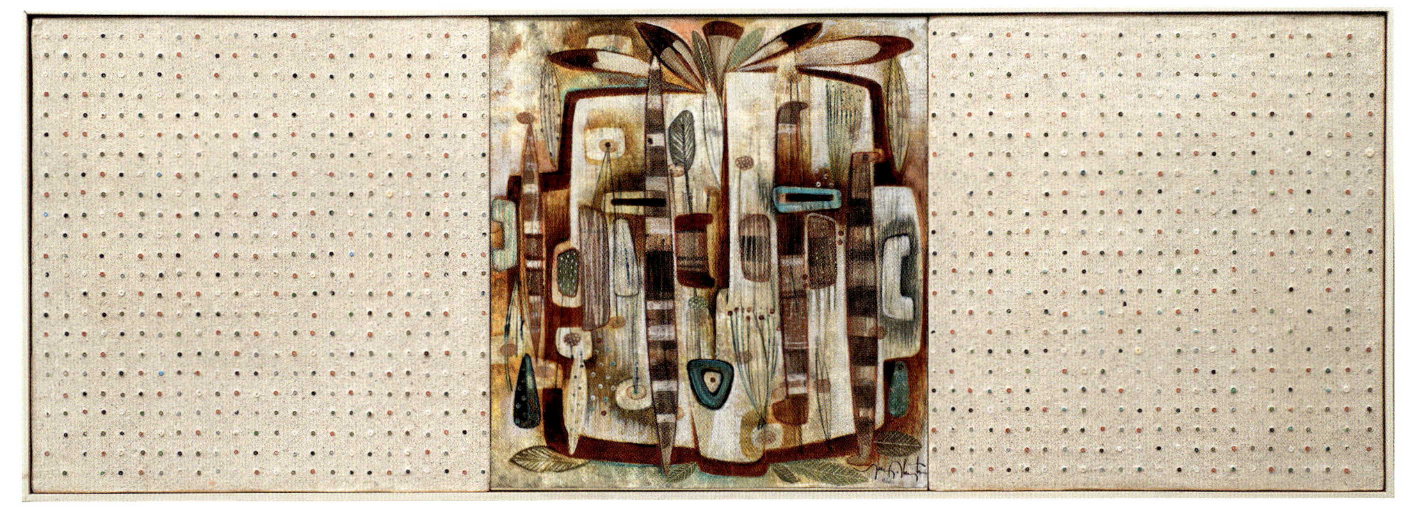

Keri Ataumbi

Kiowa (b. 1971)

Antler Earrings, 2022
Silver, gold, and diamonds

I am a member of the Kiowa Tribe of Oklahoma. Our name for ourselves is Cáuigú and my family comes from the Kogui/Elk band. I grew up in Wyoming, which is historically Cáuigú northern territory where my family would hunt and harvest elk. All parts of the elk are used, from the meat to the teeth. My family is Ownday and my mother raised my sister and me to understand the refinement and extraordinary knowledge that is inherent in our traditional clothing and adornment. These earrings are a contemporary reflection of my connection to who and where I come from. The combination of elk imagery and diamonds set in gold reflects the refinement and ancestral allegiance of being Ownday, Kogui, and Cáuigú. —K.A.

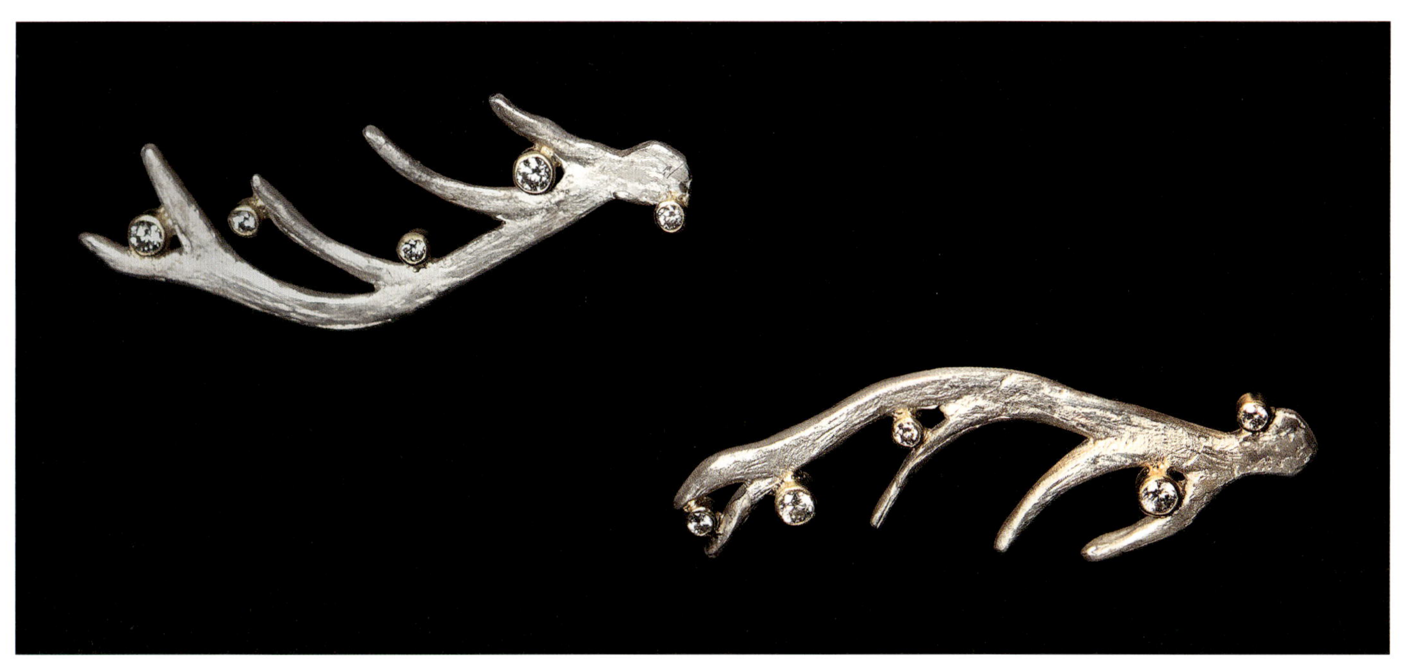

Joe Baker

Enrolled Member of Delaware Tribe of Indians of Oklahoma (b. 1946)

Bandolier Bag, 2014
Fabric, wool, and glass beads

The same practices that began in 1609 with the arrival of the Dutch West India Company, that unraveled life for my ancestors and saw our forced removal from our lands here in the Northeast, followed us through the generations to Oklahoma. These practices continue to erase Indigenous histories, cultures, and experiences—a genocide that haunts American identity to this very day. The bandolier bags that I make are part of a restorative arts practice determined to return the beauty and dignity of our Indigenous aesthetics to our community. These belongings were taken from us for the benefit of private collectors. The first Lenape (Delaware) bandolier bag that I saw in person was in the collection of the National Museum of the American Indian (NMAI) in the early 1990s. I was in the presence of a great teacher and was determined to honor that experience by making a contemporary bandolier bag. Five have been made since that beginning. —J.B.

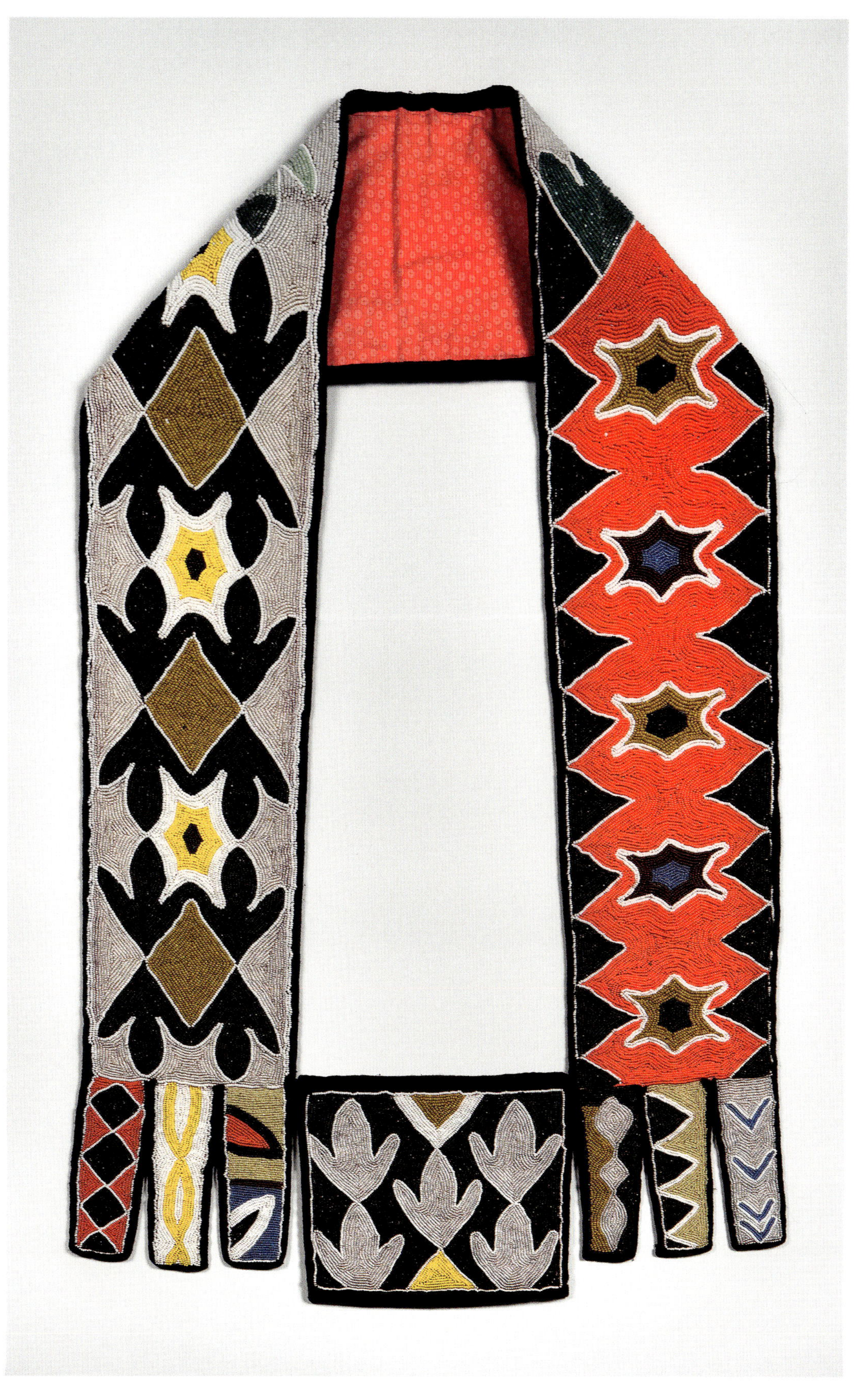

Jamison Chās Banks

Enrolled Member of the Seneca-Cayuga Nation of Oklahoma (b. 1978)

Untitled, 2015
23-layer serigraph on cedar

Untitled was the beginning of a series of works that sought to analyze seemingly mundane objects from my past. With this particular work, I wanted to challenge my printing skills by laying down twenty-three layers of ink for each individual VHS box. Technically, this was one of the more challenging designs that I have attempted to re-create. Conceptually, it speaks about the nature of wood as a recordkeeping device. It also speaks to the ephemerality of memory.

Personally, when these items are laid out or stacked upon the floor together, they begin to symbolize nostalgic notions of teenage freedom and escape. —J.C.B.

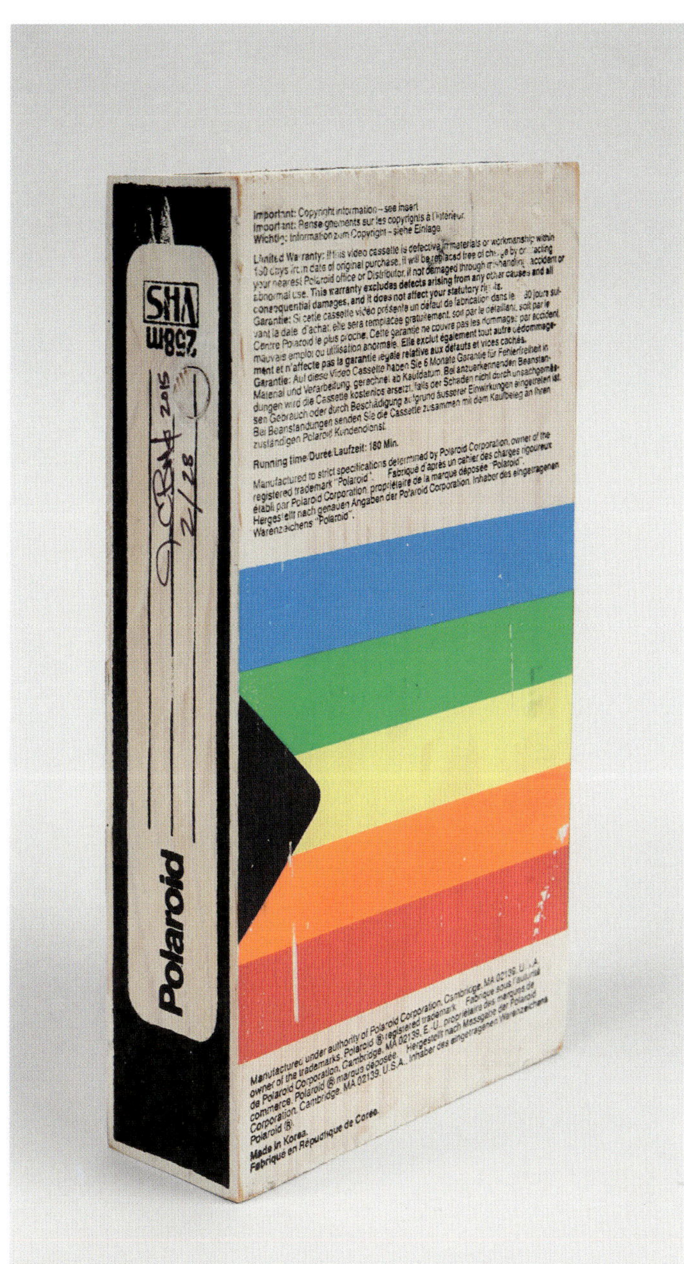
Polaroid

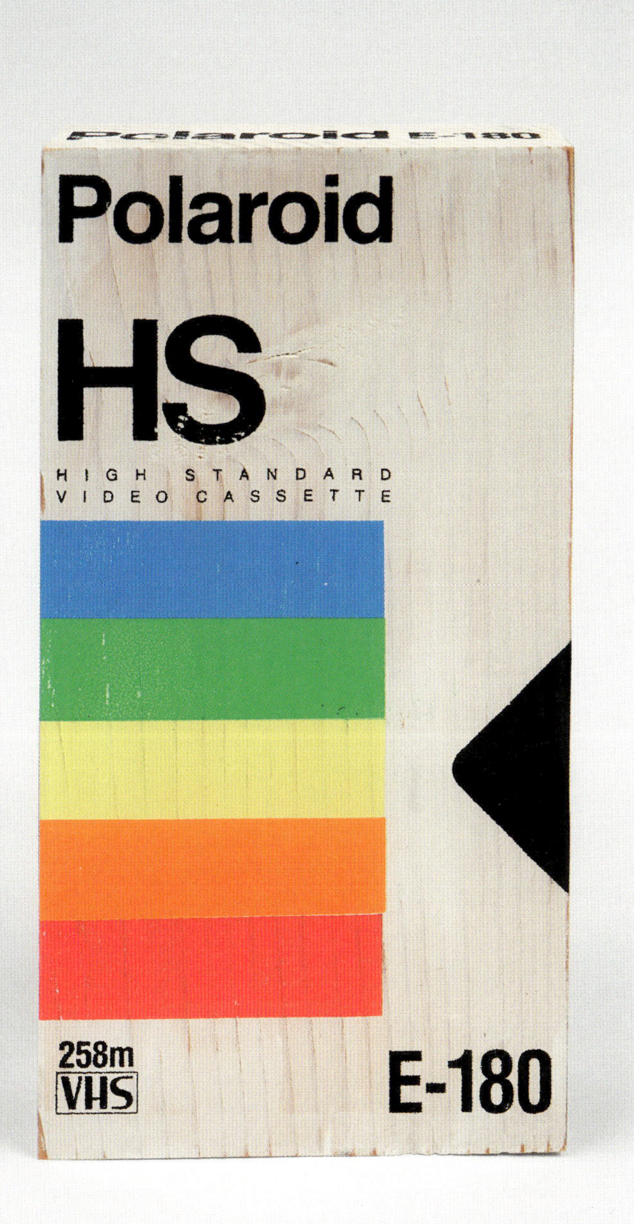
Polaroid E-180
Polaroid
HS
HIGH STANDARD
VIDEO CASSETTE
258m
VHS
E-180

Marwin Begaye

Navajo (b. 1970)

Columbia River Custodian, 2018
Lithograph

When I was invited to Crow's Shadow Institute of the Arts for their artist's residency, I wanted to know about the Columbia River Gorge and the Indigenous people and their histories in relationship to their location. As I continue making work about birds and the important roles they have within Indigenous cultures, I wanted to honor the condor. This bird of prey has been a part of the Columbia River landscape for centuries and is now endangered. One oral story told to me about the condor described how he showed the eagle where the salmon people lived so the people could survive. My local research also included visiting with tribal cultural materials from the region. While on the Confederated Tribes of the Umatilla Indian Reservation, I visited and researched the collections of the Tamastslikt Cultural Institute. I was looking for locally significant design elements that I could make into a pattern that would fit with the concept of the condor. —M.B.

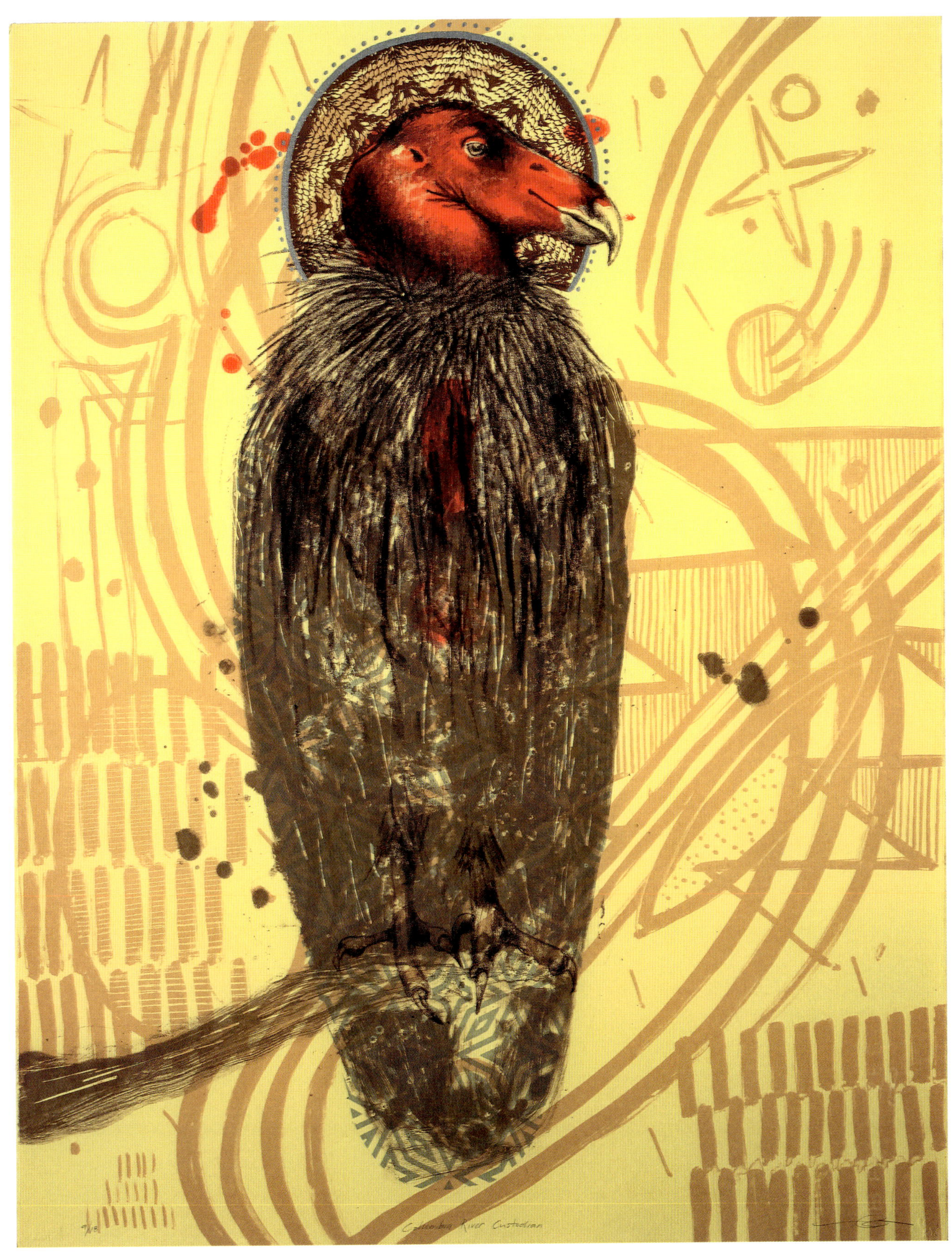
9/18
Columbia River Custodian

Roy Bigcrane (and Thompson Smith)

Séliš, member of the Confederated Salish & Kootenai Tribes (b. 1968)

The Place of the Falling Waters, 1990
Video

The Place of the Falling Waters is a documentary told by the Indigenous people who live here: the Séliš, Qlispé, and Ksanka (Salish, Pend d'Oreille, and Kootenai). They tell the history of how the people lived before reservation life, how the Séliš Ksanka Qlispé Dam (formerly Kerr Dam) came to be built, and the possible things that can be done once we take over the dam. This is the story from our people, telling our viewpoint of history. —R.B

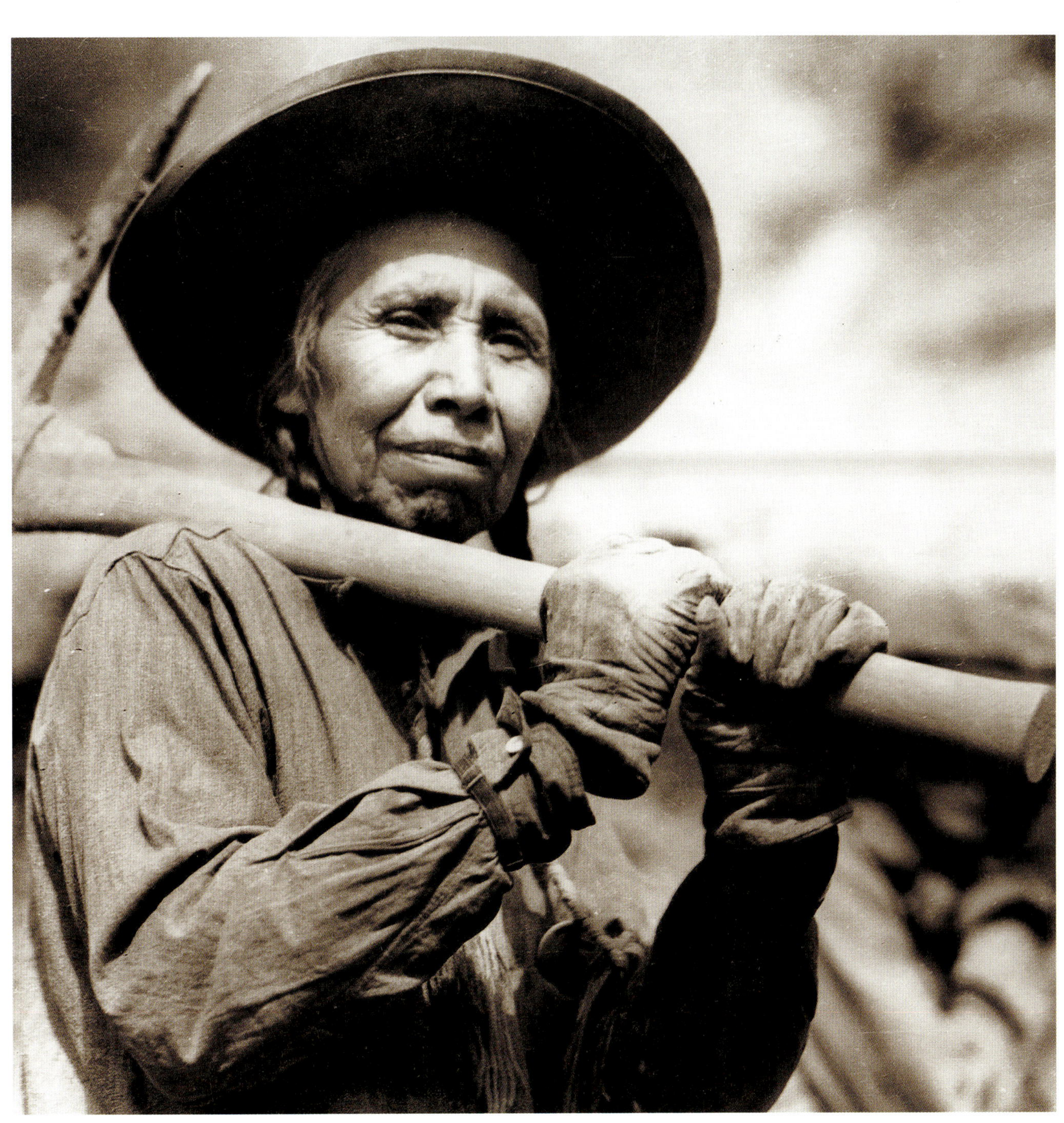

Jackie Larson Bread

Amsakapi Pikunni/Blackfeet (b. 1960)

Triangular Beaded Trinket Box, Chief Joseph, 2007
Beaded satin-lined box

The images of the beautiful people are all Blackfeet—Fish Wolf Robe, Yellow Kidney, and Heavy Breast. The designs are a collection of Blackfeet parfleche and lodge designs that speak of the importance of how we as a nation designed and did things. —J.L.B.

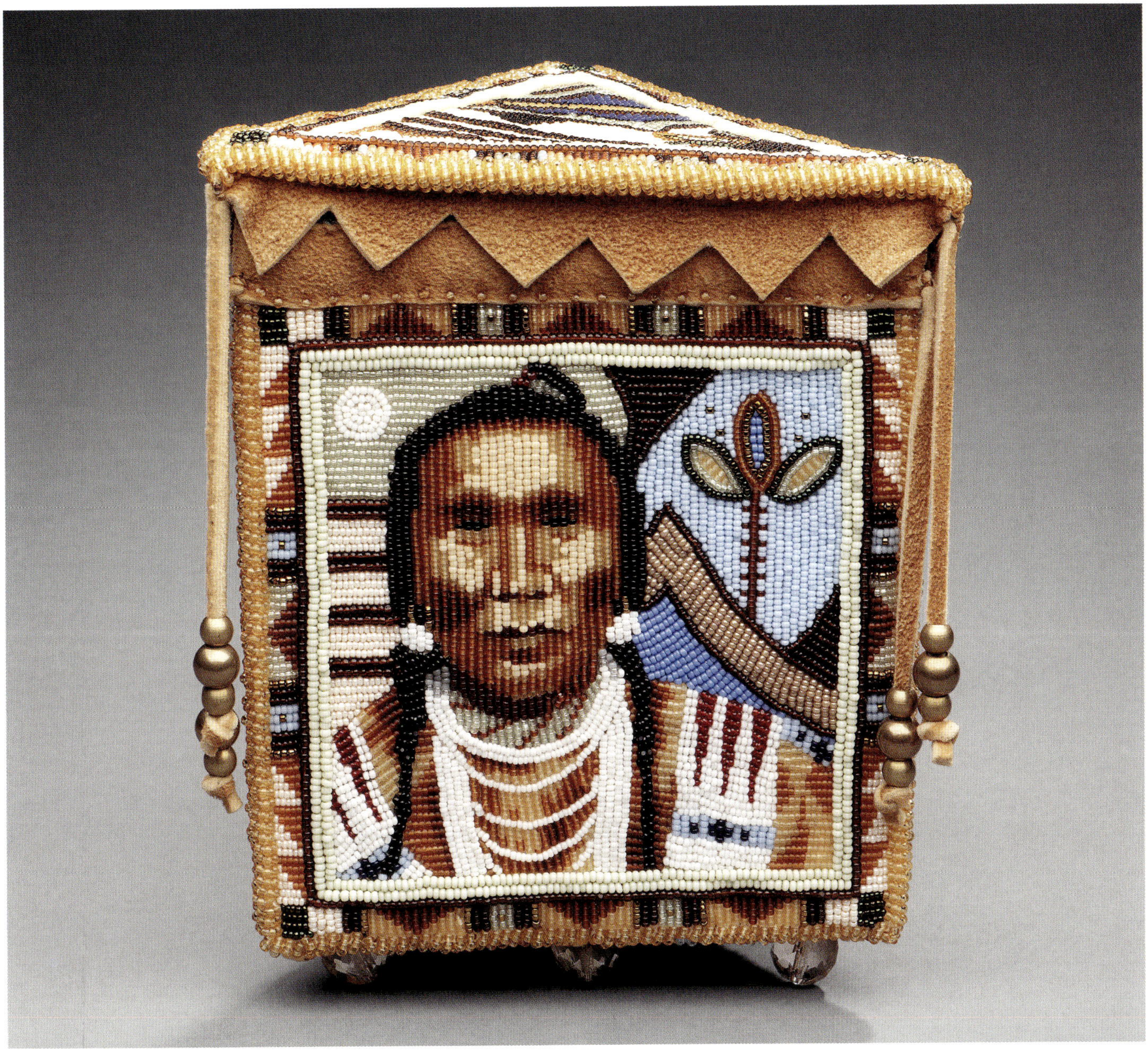

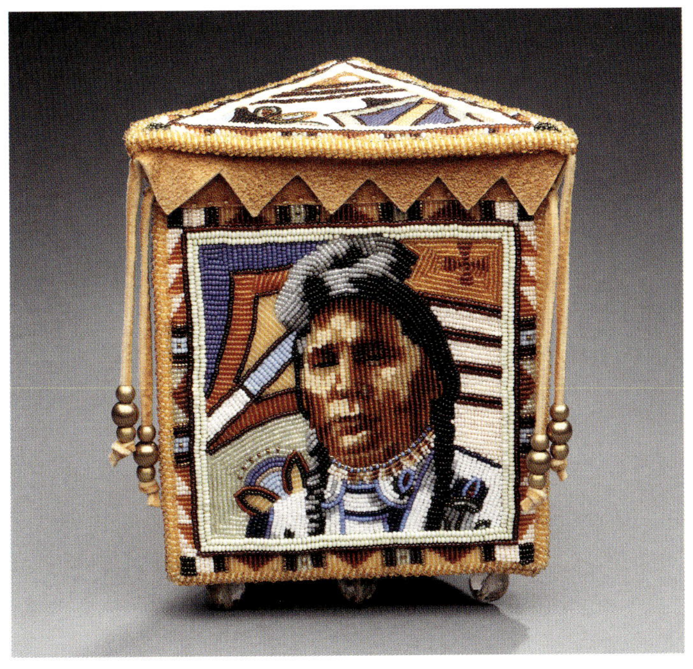

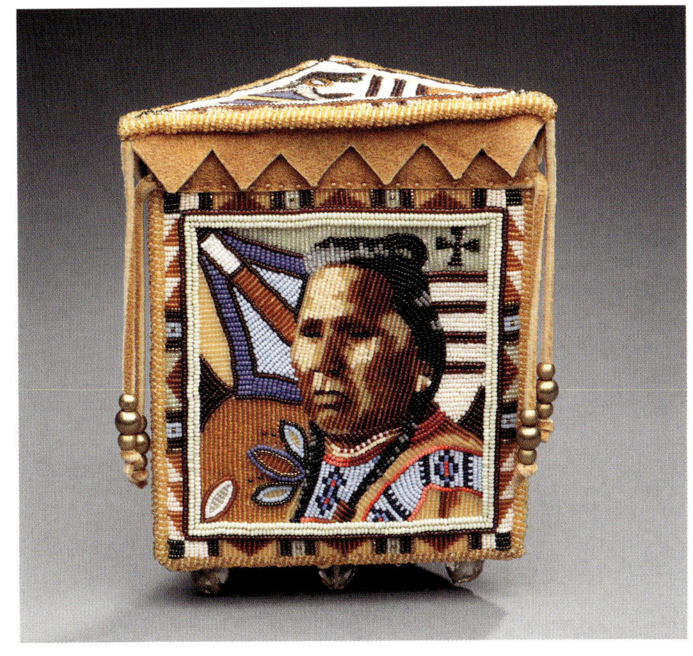

Jason Clark

Non-enrolled Algonquin, Creek, Swiss, and Scottish (b. 1967)

Winona and the Big Oil "Windigo," 2014
Woodcut

This piece was inspired by a quote from Winona LaDuke, an Anishinaabe activist, who said, "Someone needs to explain to me why wanting clean drinking water makes you an activist, and why proposing to destroy water with chemical warfare doesn't make a corporation a terrorist." I used the image and idea of a protective mother bear to represent Winona in this print because the belief system of my forefathers considers the bear to be the guardian of nature and the giver of knowledge. In contrast to the protective mother bear figure, I used the image and concept of the Windigo and attributed it to the big oil corporations. —J.C.

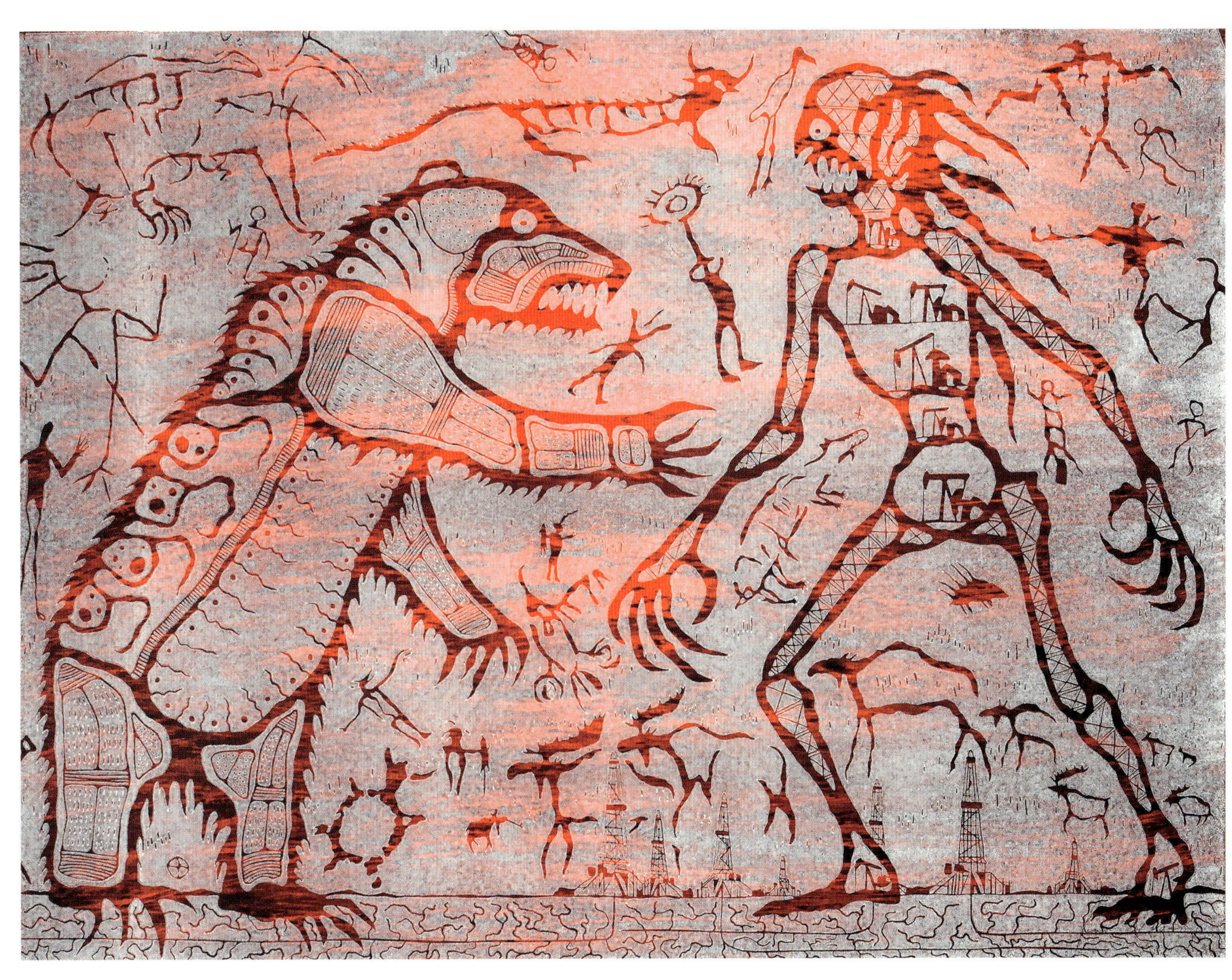

Jordan Anne Craig

Northern Cheyenne (b. 1992)

Colliding Clouds, 2020
Acrylic on canvas

In Roswell, New Mexico, the vast skies light up with lightning storms during the warm summer nights. My sister and I would sit on the back porch and watch the lively storms, often too far away for us to feel rain or hear thunder. It was like watching a massive argument in the sky play out. I made this painting in reaction to these intense evening shows. Like a silent film, *Colliding Clouds* is black-white and relies on symbols, shapes, and lines to tell the story. —J.A.C.

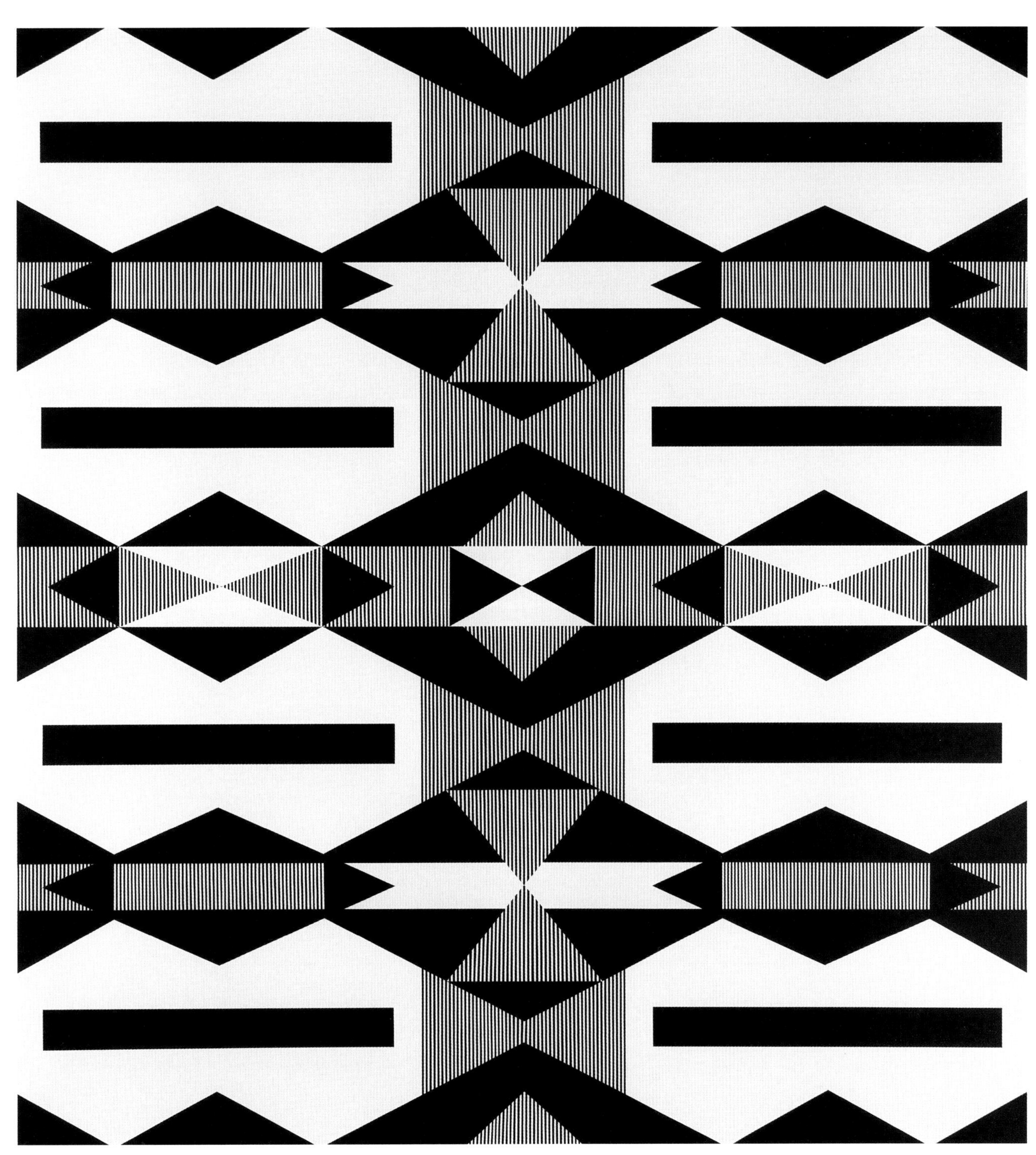

Carly Feddersen

Enrolled Member of the Confederated Tribes of the Colville Reservation and of mixed European Heritage (b. 1982)

[Dis] Embodied: Fingers Necklace II, 2023
Mixed media

Following a long tradition of stone carving in the Columbia Plateau, *[Dis] Embodied: Fingers Necklace II* is carved from river stones collected on the traditional land of the Wenatchi and Yakama Tribes in Wenatchee, Washington. The fingers personify the land from which they are created and illustrate its capacity to sense and touch us. Giving the stones a human form enhances our ability to imagine this. Hanging from hand-formed beads, the severed fingers move eerily with the wearer while the fine finish of sterling silver obscures palpable references to violence, colonization, and trophy-taking in warfare. —C.F.

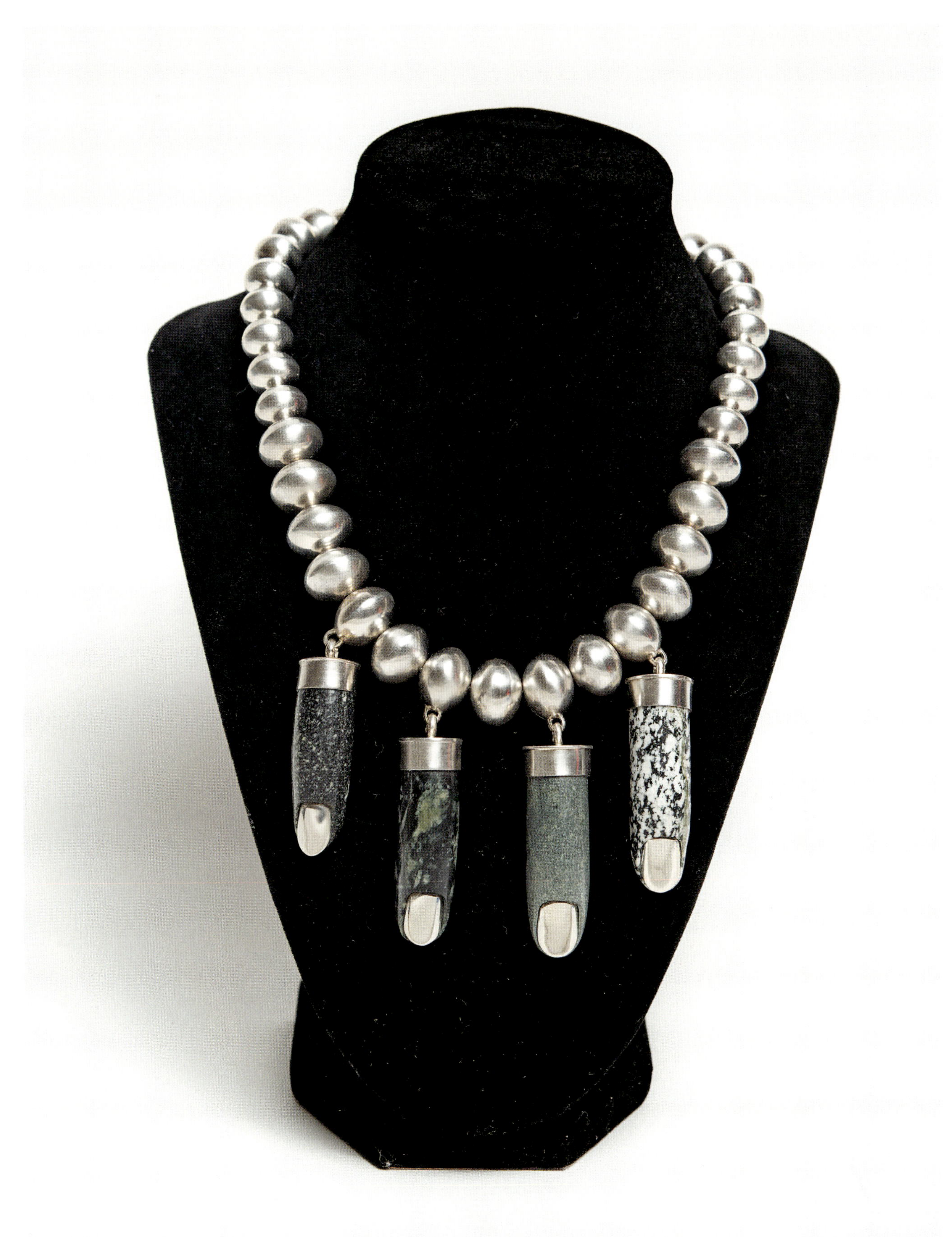

Joe Feddersen

Okanagan and Arrow Lakes (b. 1953)

Country Road, 2024
Sally bag

My work is grounded in the landscape and in my cultural heritage. The land in all its forms has fueled my curiosity for over twenty years. In this particular piece, and others like it, I study representations of the land through Native basket and blanket designs. I use the root baskets of home as a source of inspiration in my work. I learned to twine them. I twine in the traditional form but embellish them with contemporary designs, in this case high voltage towers and a highway pattern. These showcase my interest, which lies in the zone where the signs tenuously dissolve into a modernist aesthetic while still maintaining direct ties to the Plateau designs of my Native American ancestors. —J.F.

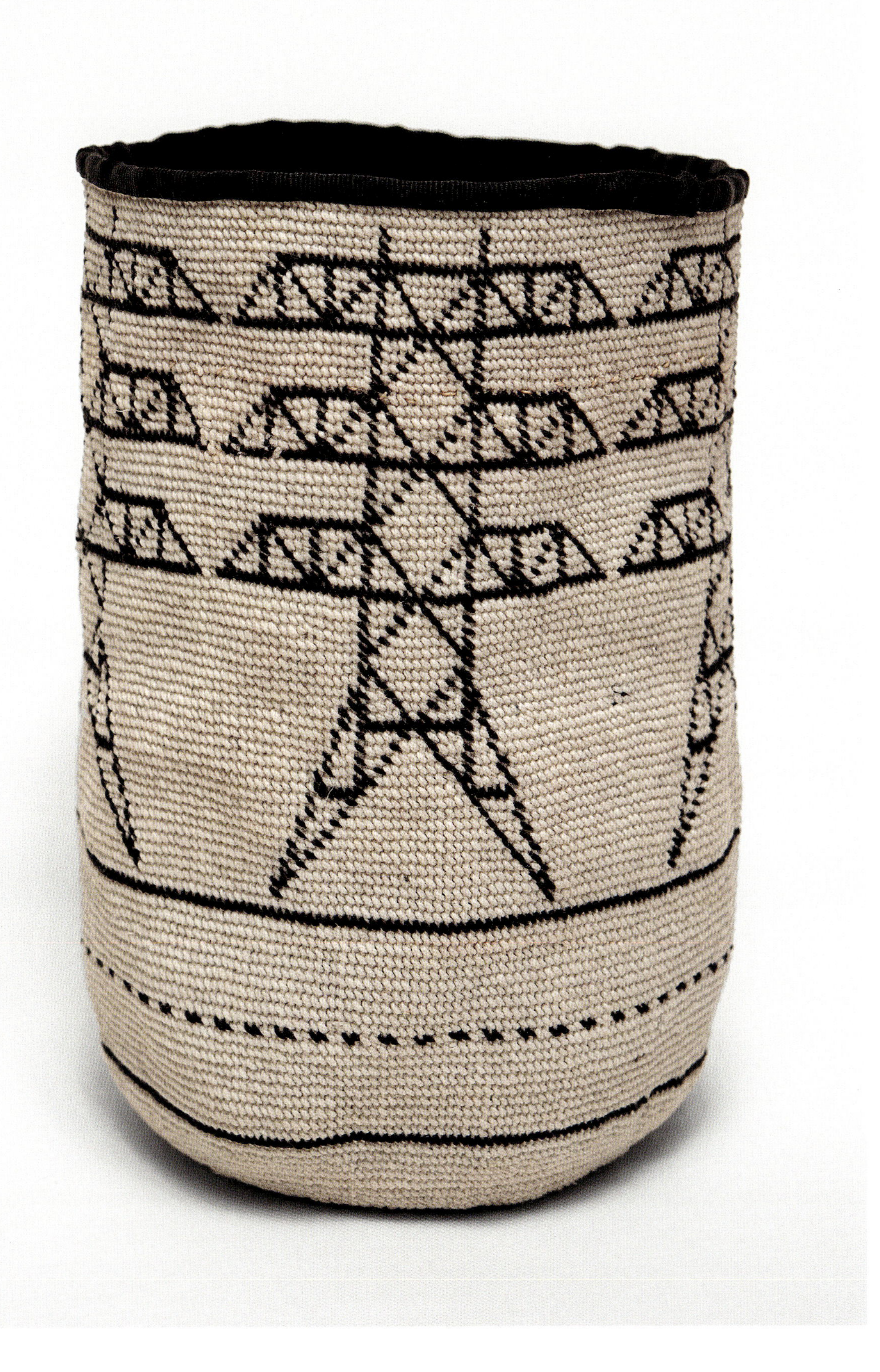

Tomahawk GreyEyes

Navajo [b. 1989]

Eyes Like Arrows, 2013
Digital media

Eyes Like Arrows is part of a larger series from early in my career as an artist. In the series, I utilize vintage portraiture of Navajo people and rework them by adding in Navajo geometric patterns and landscapes found on the Navajo Nation. This particular artwork showcases an image of an anonymous Navajo man taken by an unknown photographer. The image comes from the public domain, which is how I sourced all of the images in this series. The landscape featured in *Eyes Like Arrows* is of a portion of Black Mesa, near a community called Chilchinbito, on the Navajo Nation reservation. The series has no political agenda but tries to add energy to old and forgotten photographs. It is meant to highlight the beauty of our traditional styles and the land we come from. —T.G.

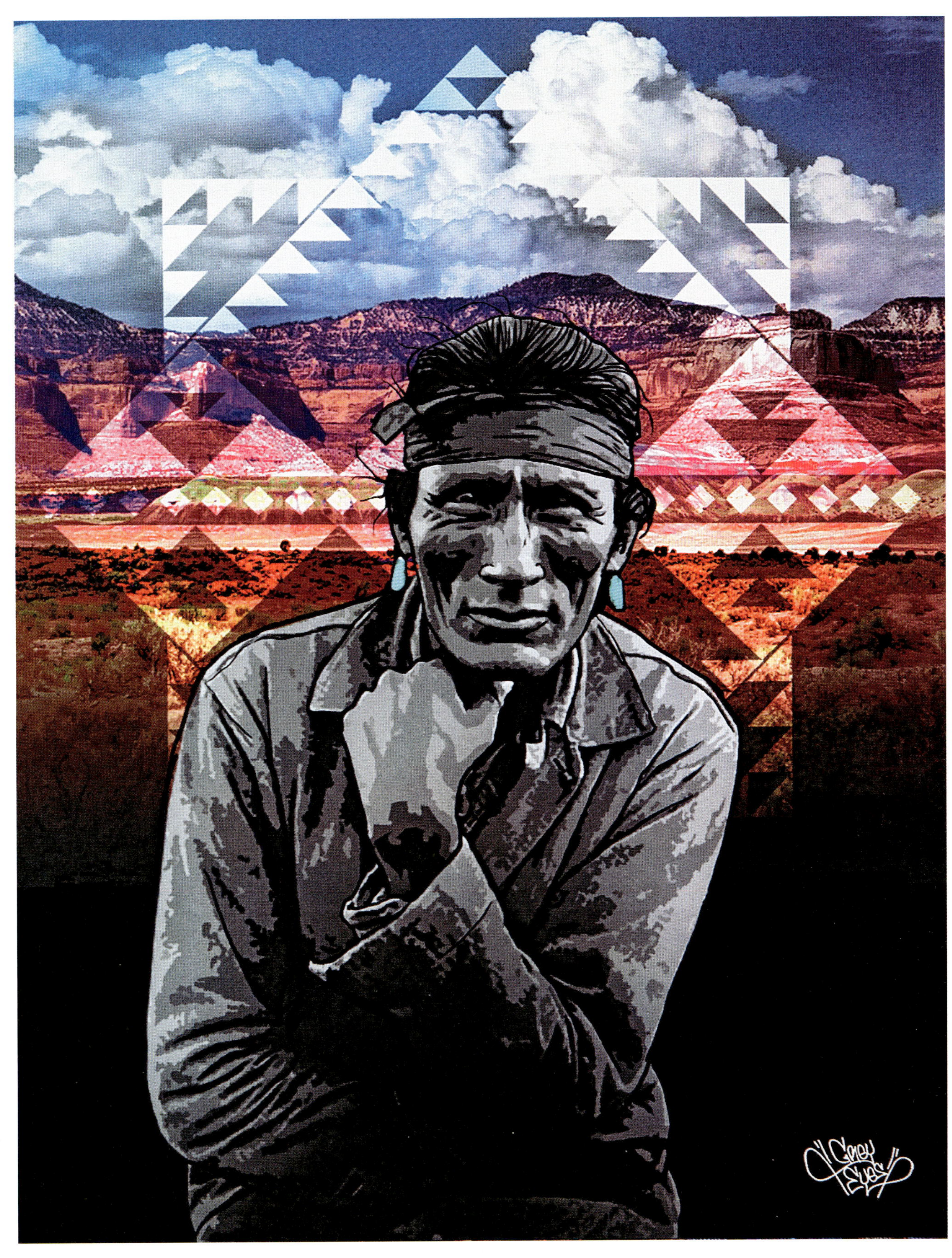

John Hitchcock

Comanche, Kiowa, and Northern European Ancestry (b. 1967)

Shouting Lightning from Their Eyes (Winter Birds), 2021
Lithograph

Shouting Lightning from Their Eyes is a series of drawings and prints based on horse masks made by Plains tribes, created to honor, remember, and respect the Kiowa, Comanche, and Cheyenne people and their horses. In 1874, the United States military leader Ranald S. Mackenzie ordered the 4th United States Cavalry troops to slaughter an estimated two thousand horses and mules in Tule Canyon, which belonged to the Comanche, Kiowa, and Cheyenne people who had set up camp in Palo Duro Canyon, Texas. The Battle of Palo Duro Canyon was a military act of genocide that contributed to the forced removal and relocation of the Kiowa and Comanche people to the present-day Wichita Mountain area of Lawton, Oklahoma, which is my tribal homeland. My artworks are based on my memories and stories of growing up in the Wichita Mountains of Oklahoma, on Comanche tribal lands next to the United States field artillery military base, Fort Sill. —J.H.

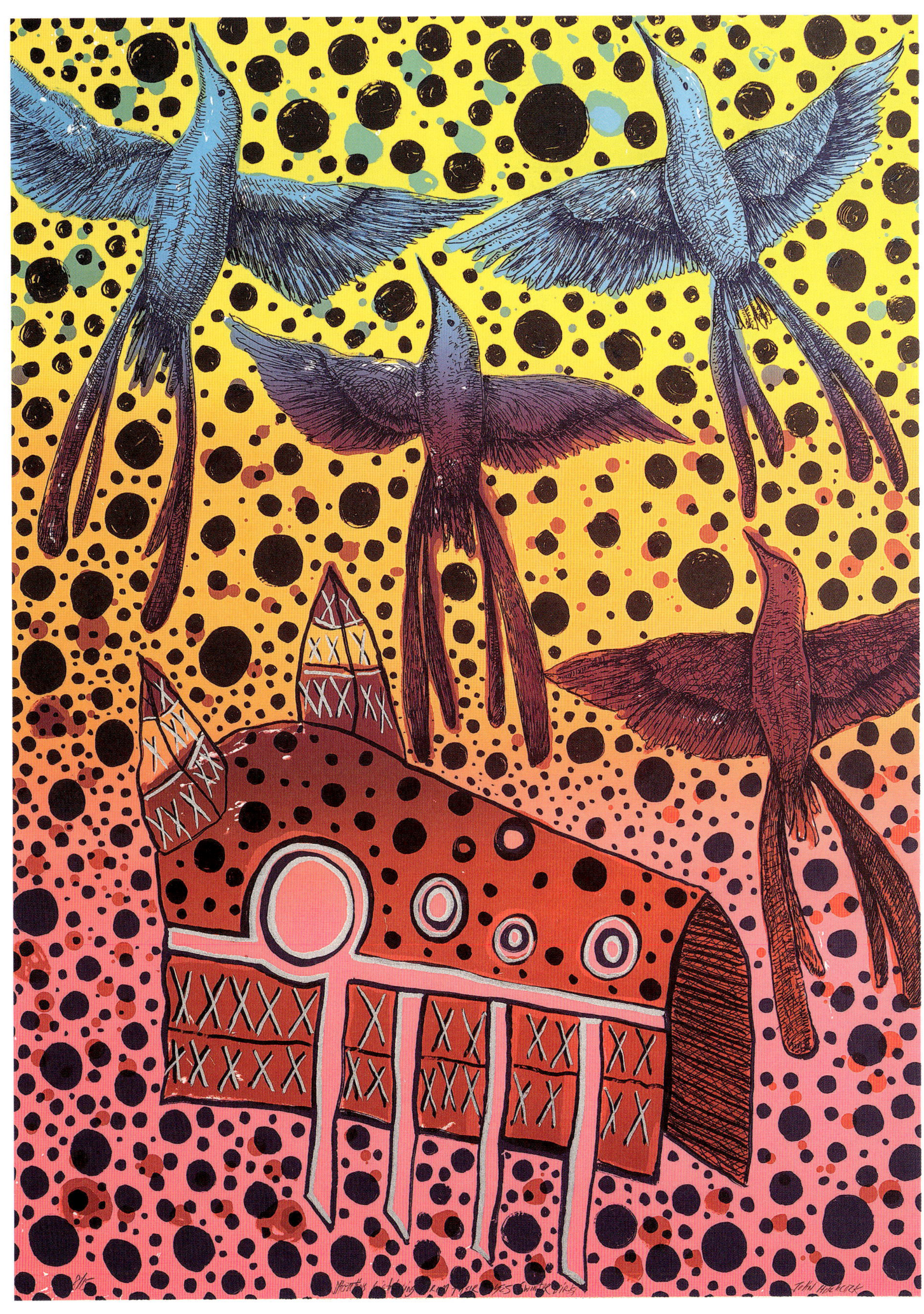

Anna Hoover

Norwegian/Unangax̂ (b. 1985)

Salmon Reflection, 2021
Video

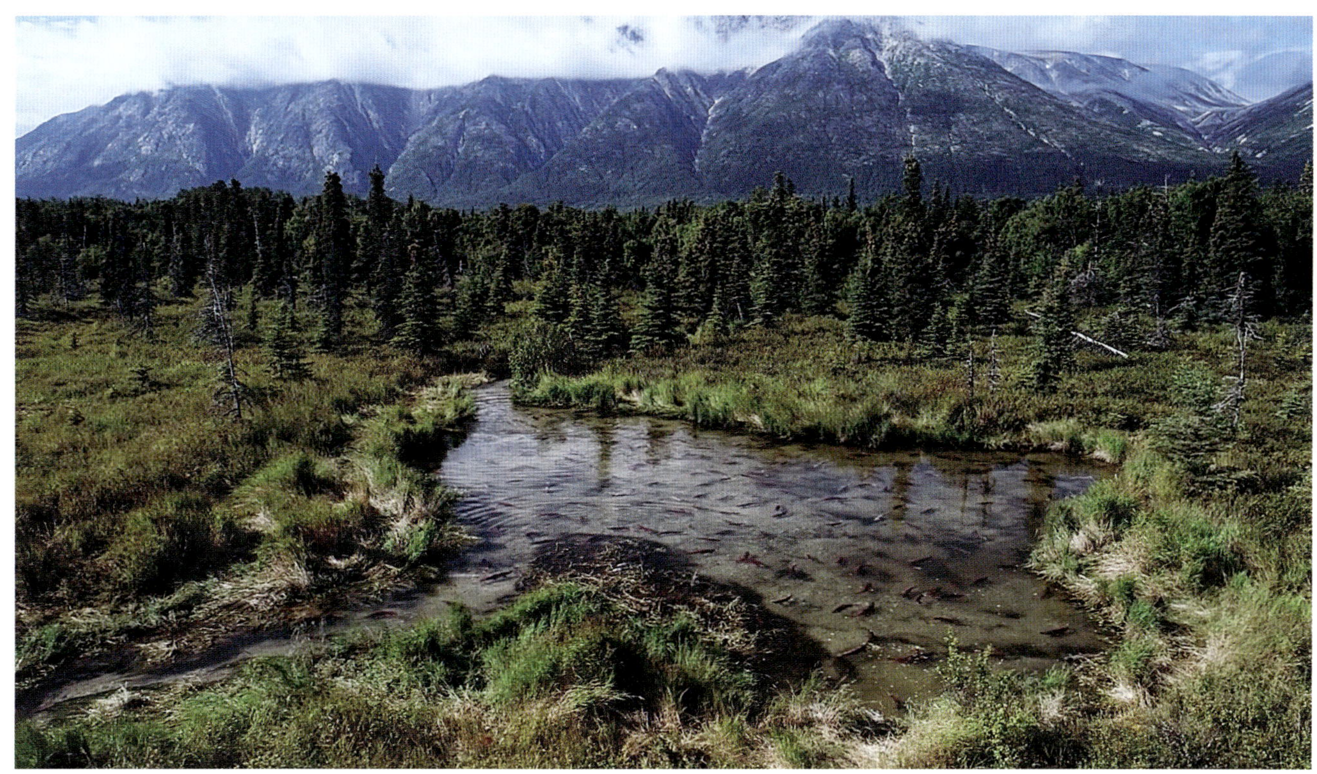

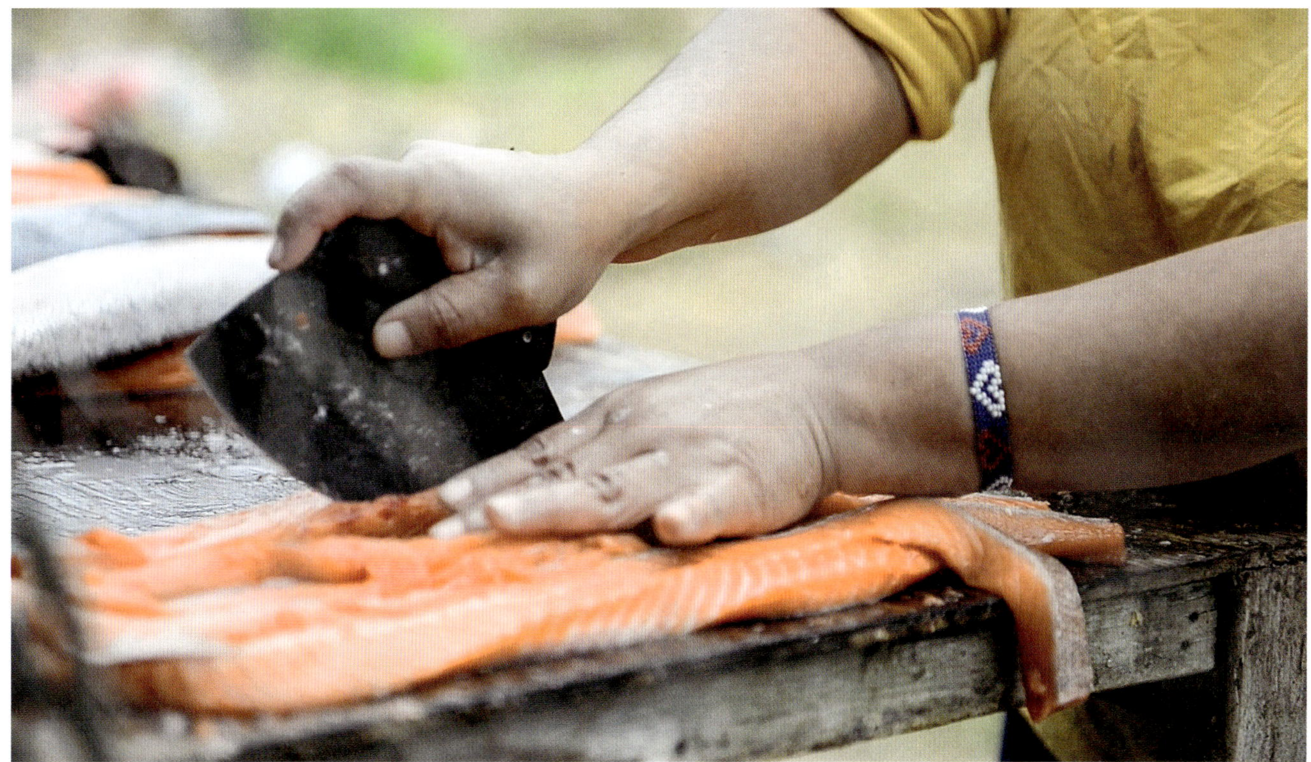

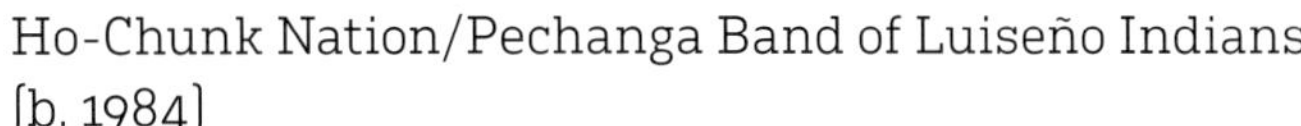

Sky Hopinka

Ho-Chunk Nation/Pechanga Band of Luiseño Indians
(b. 1984)

Here You Are Before the Trees, 2020
HD video, stereo, color, 3-channel synchronous loop

Here You Are Before the Trees traverses Indigenous presence in the Hudson River Valley, Wisconsin, and the areas in between. Presented in three channels, each screen focuses on different homelands and their complex relationships with history, landscape, power, and institutional means of oppression. One channel is set in and around the Mahicannituck (also known as the Hudson River, in upstate New York), the homelands of the Stockbridge-Munsee Band of Mohican Indians, and another is set in the Waazija, the homelands of the Ho-Chunk Nation of Wisconsin. The third channel is situated between the two and is a single take—a glimpse of the road and the static yet transient stretches spent traveling. —S.H.

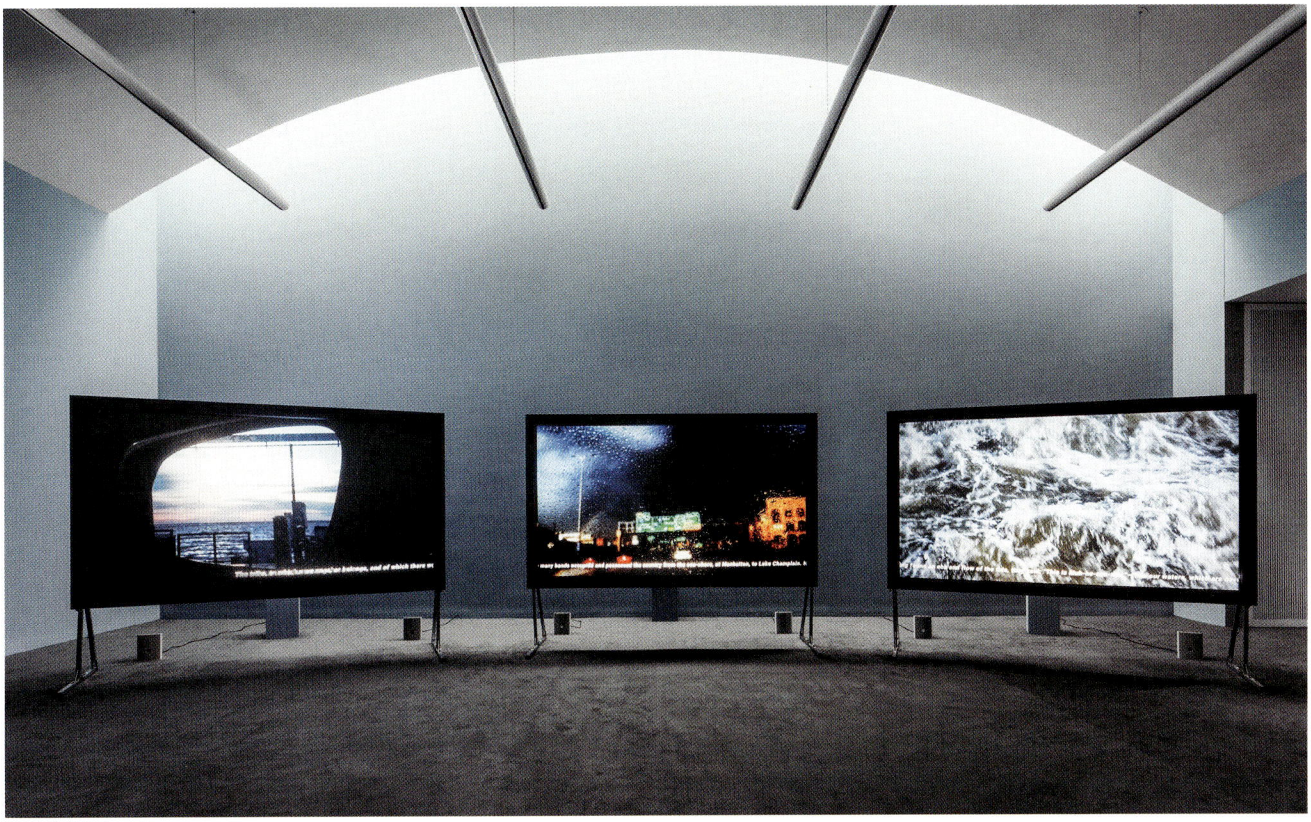

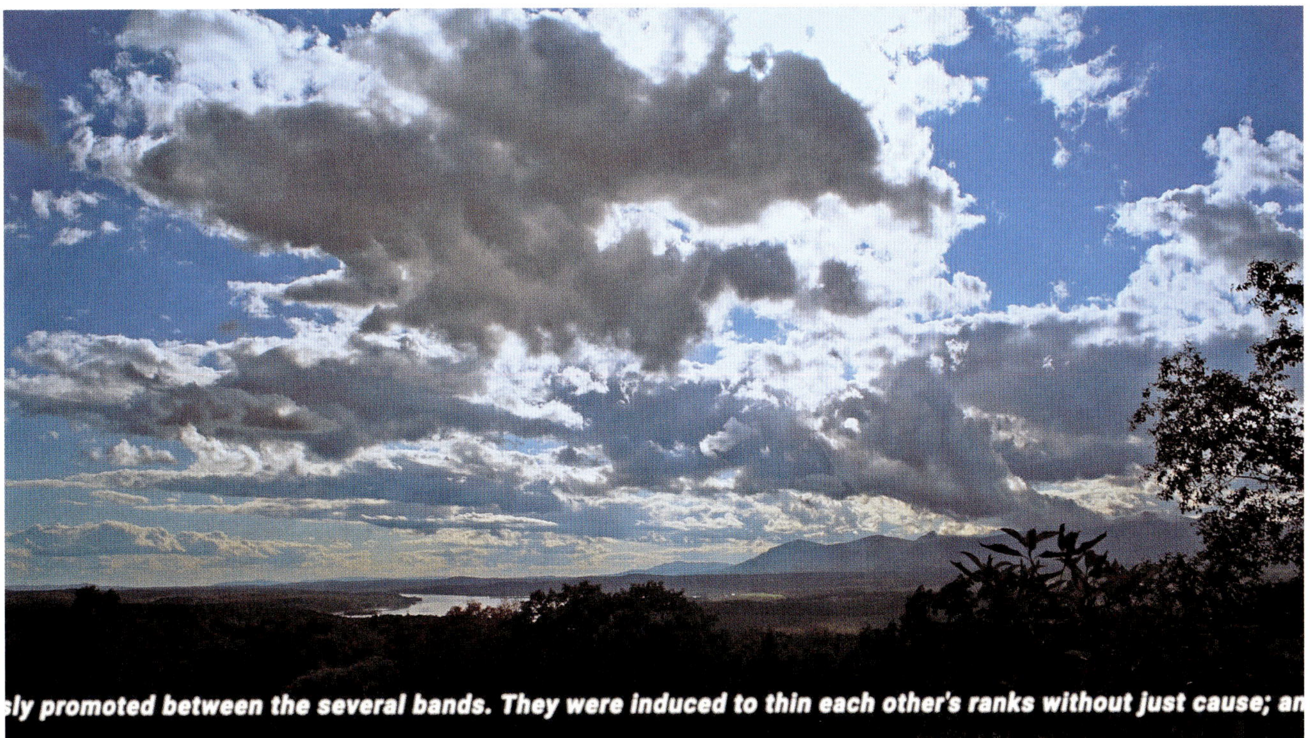
sly promoted between the several bands. They were induced to thin each other's ranks without just cause;

Norma Howard

Choctaw and Chickasaw (1958–2024)

Miniature Storefront, 2019
Watercolor on paper

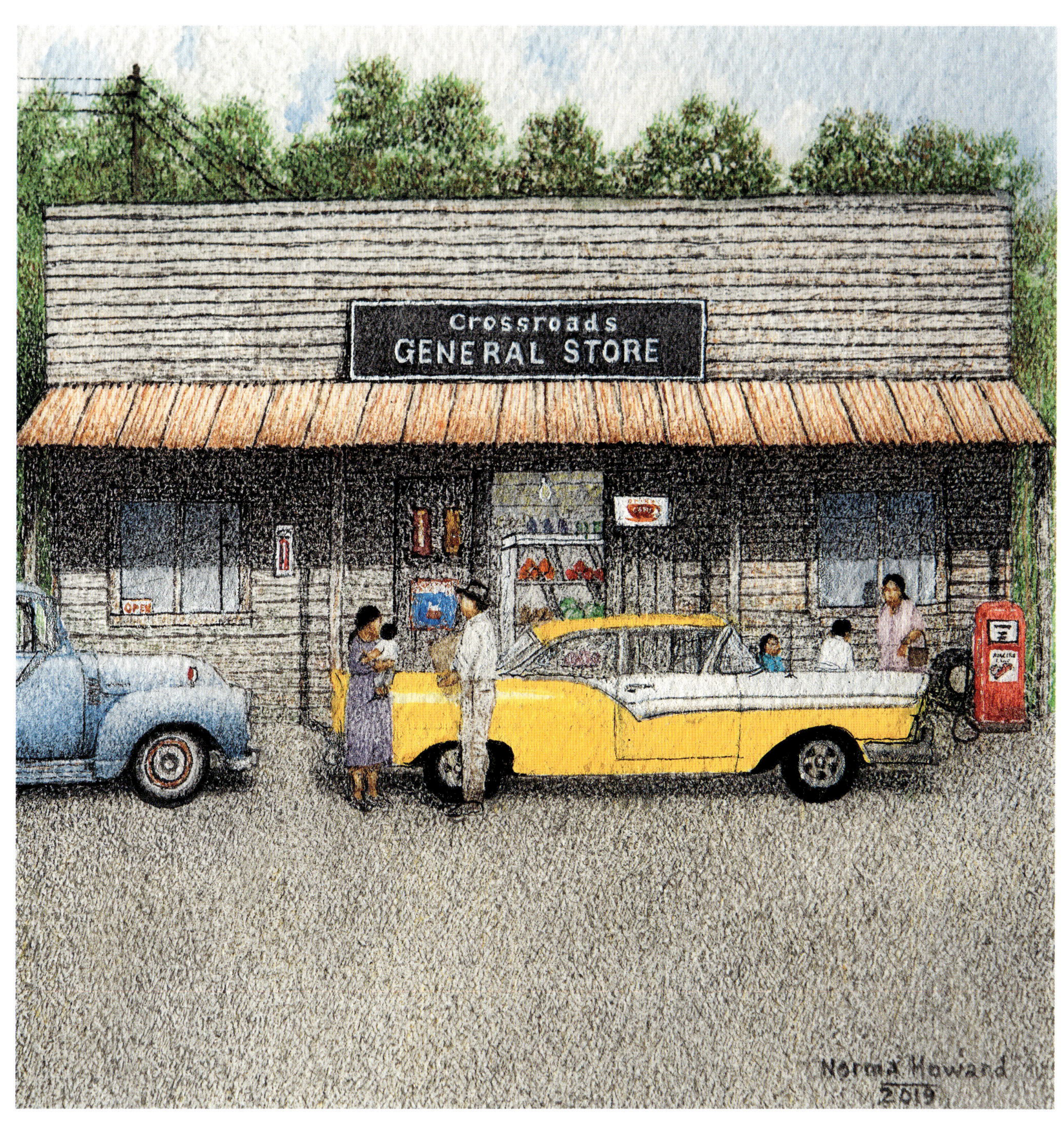
Crossroads
GENERAL STORE
OPEN
Norma Howard
2019

Patrick Dean Hubbell

Diné (b. 1986)

You Protect Us Day and Night, 2020
Oil, acrylic, spray, and natural earth pigment on canvas

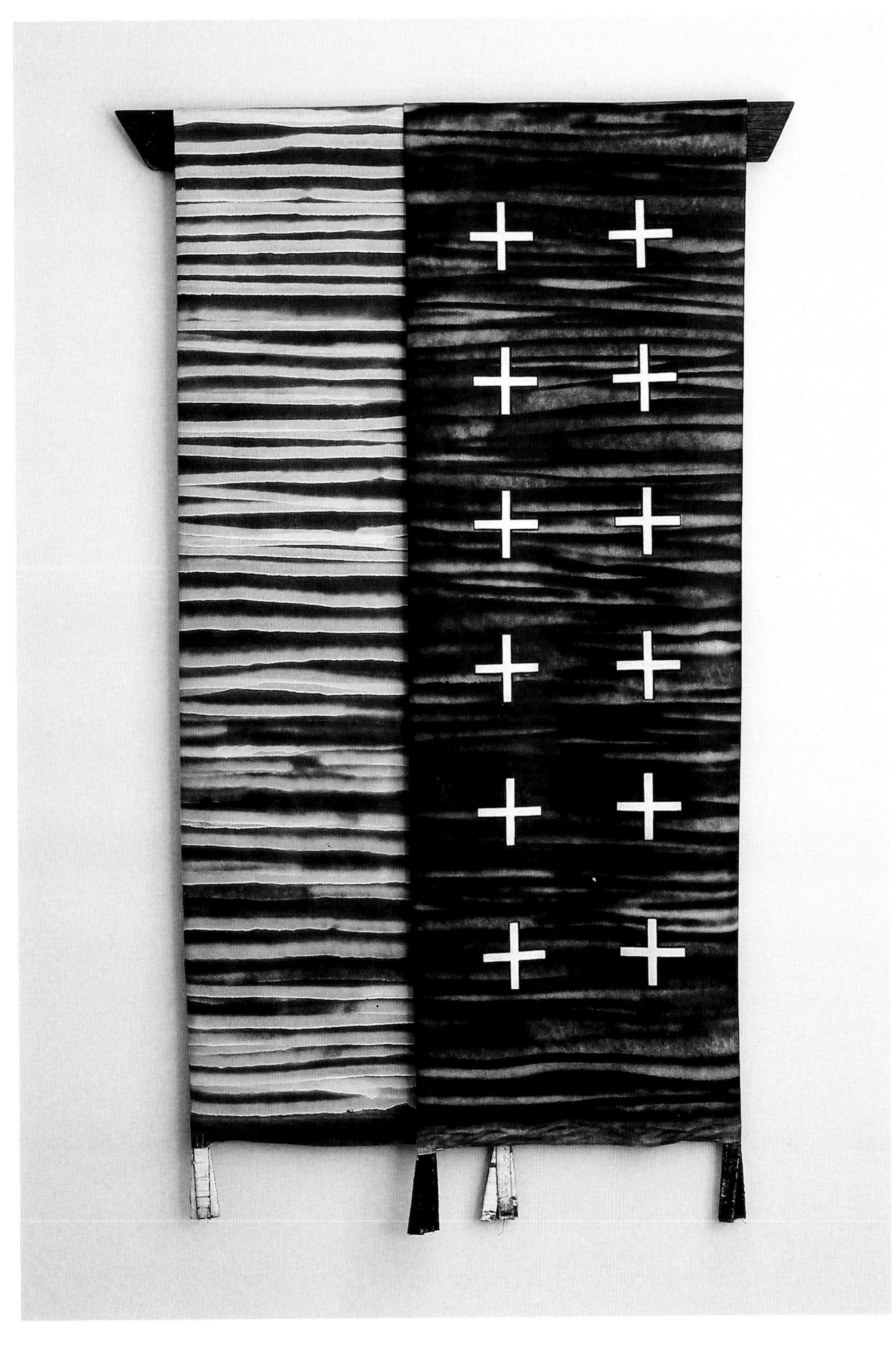

Erin Ggaadimits Ivalu Gingrich

Nome Eskimo Community, culturally affiliated
Koyuokon Denaa & Iñupiaq (b. 1990)

Spawning Iqalukpik Double from Tustumena Lake, 2022
Basswood, acrylic, glass beads, and salmon vertebrae

The iqalukpik (salmon) my family and I harvest from the Kenai Peninsula fill my freezer and my dreams. Feeding both me and my work, these carved representations depict the reality of subsistence harvesting and taking care of the gift of salmon. Adorned with beaded blood strands and connected, these salmon live and die together as a gift to those who care for and steward the waters that they call home. The depiction of them as a pair represents the abundance of the gift of salmon, which are hopefully never caught alone. These carved bodies stand as a count or tally of the gifts we are given. —E.G.I.G.

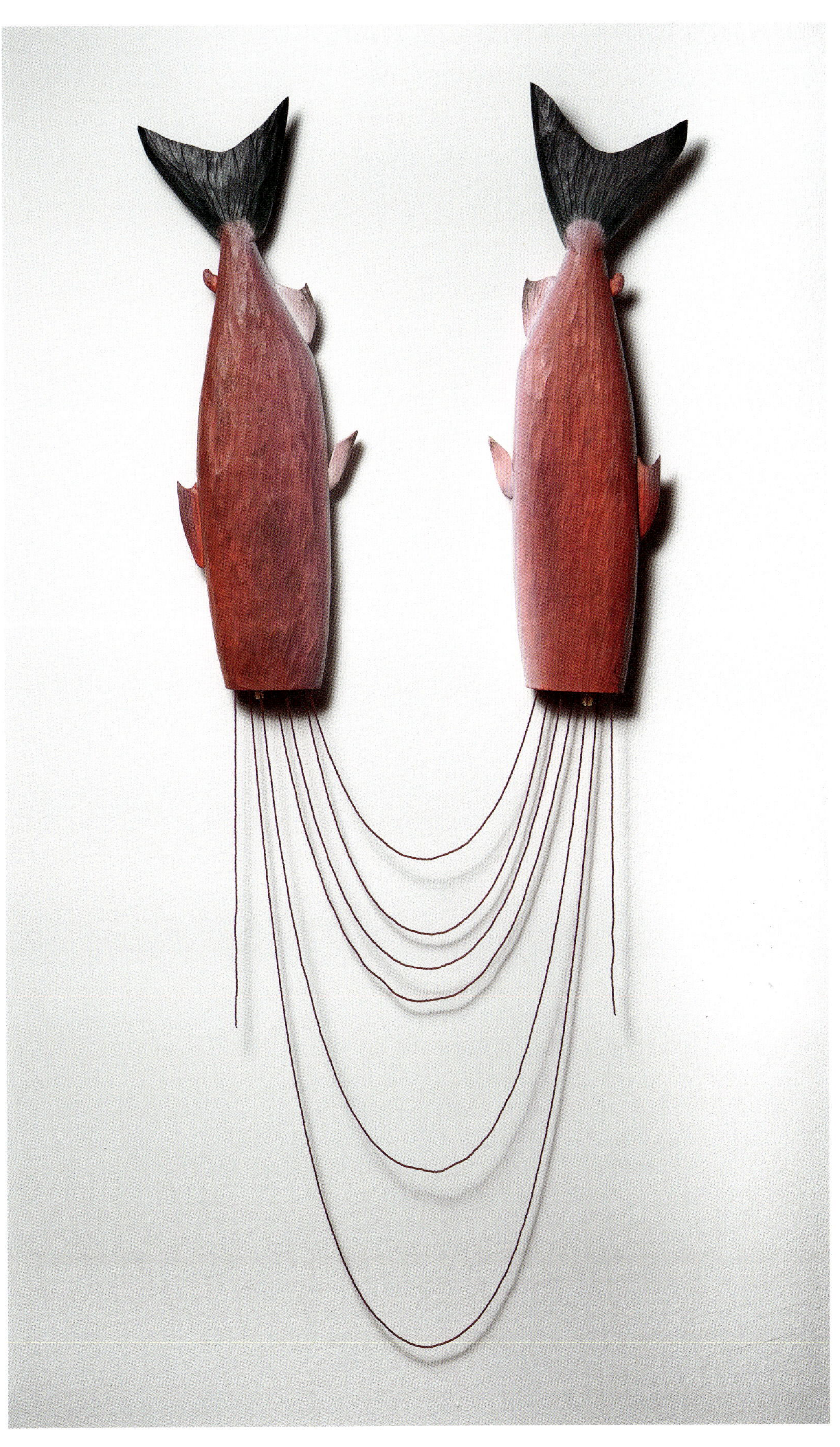

Tom Jones

Ho-Chunk Nation of Wisconsin [b. 1964]

Forster Nash from the *Strong Unrelenting Spirits* series, 2015
Digital photograph with beadwork

Strong Unrelenting Spirits is a body of work rooted in Ho-Chunk identity. A pivotal childhood memory informs this work. I went with my mother to see the Sioux medicine man Robert Stead, on the Rosebud Indian Reservation, for a healing ceremony. We sat on the floor along the walls with many other people. When the lights were turned off, the women started to sing. They were asking for the spirits to come in, and it was at this time that small orbs of light began to float around the room. I am visually representing this experience through beading Ho-Chunk floral designs directly onto the photograph, symbolizing our ancestors who are constantly watching over us. Celebrating the pride, strength, and beauty of my people, I am expanding the conversation of portraiture in mainstream art. —T.J.

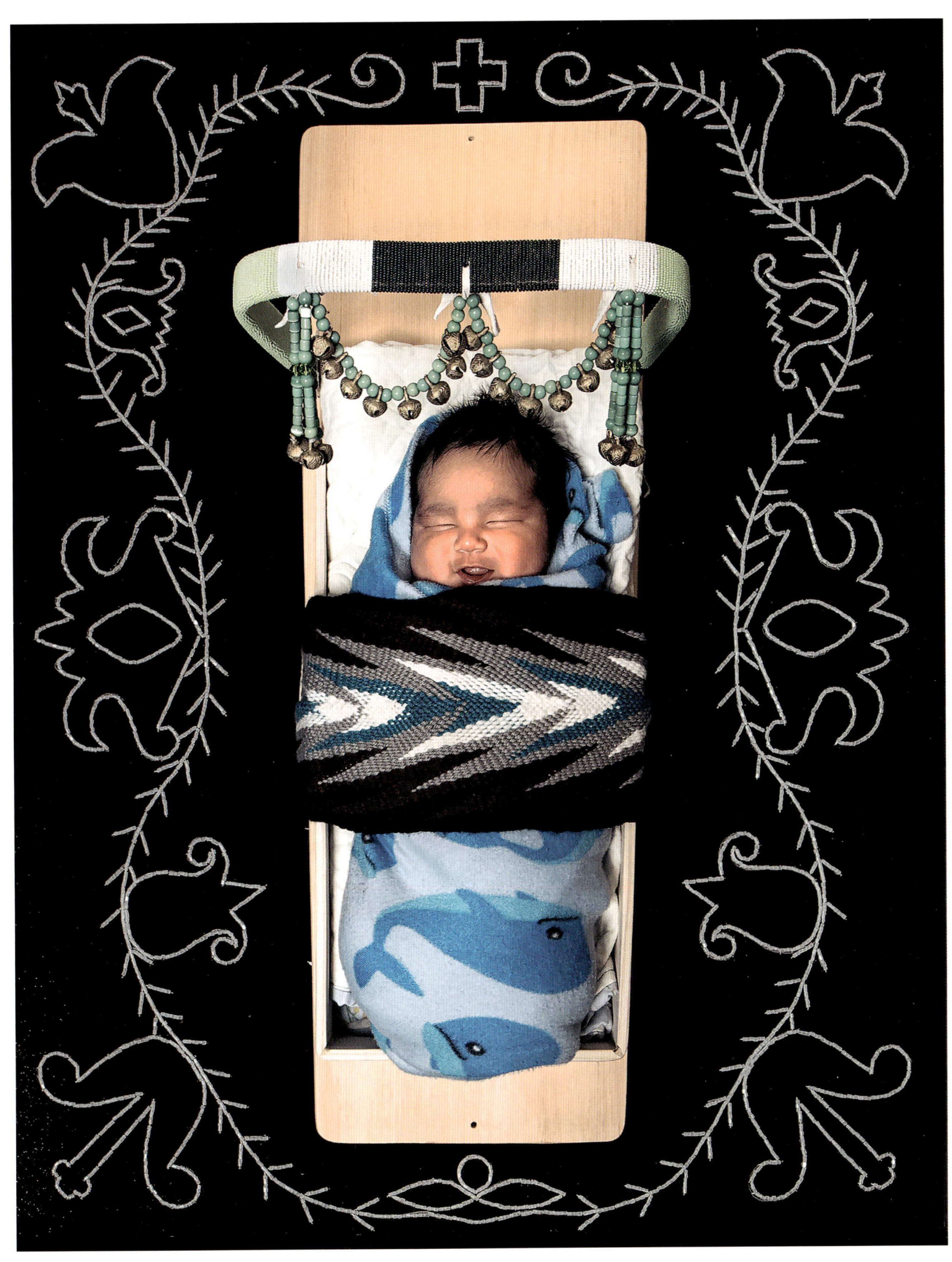

Brad Kahlhamer

Tribally ambiguous [b. 1956]

Next Level Figure 1, 2013
Acrylic on wood

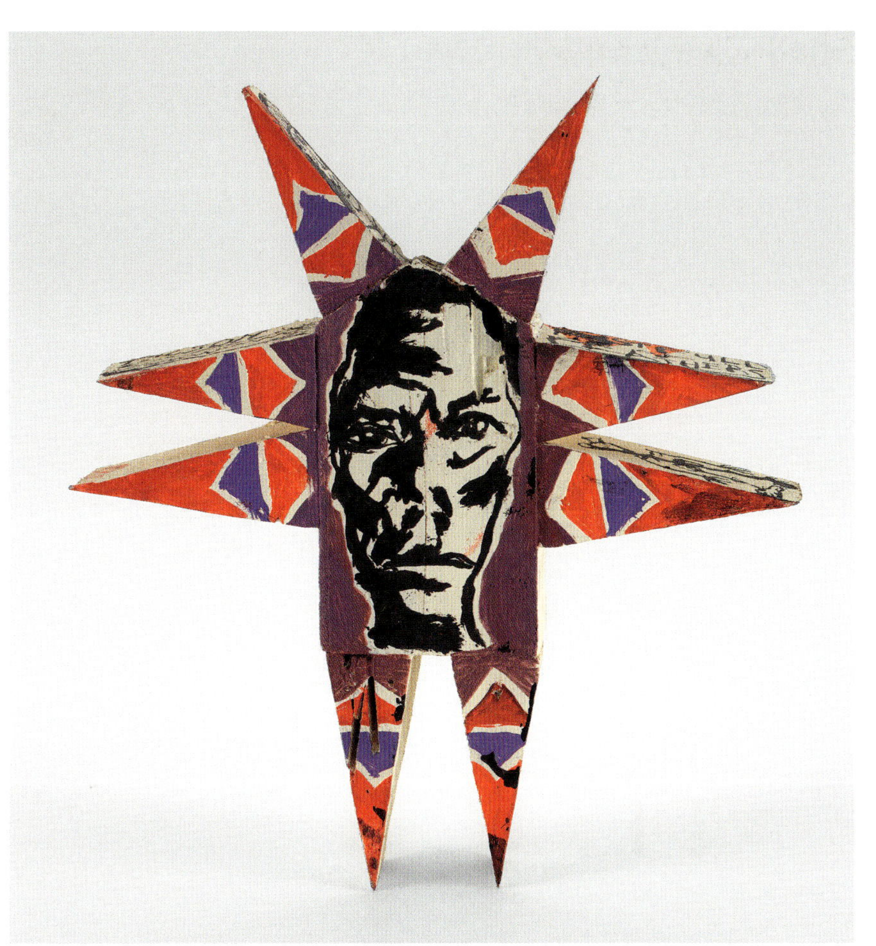

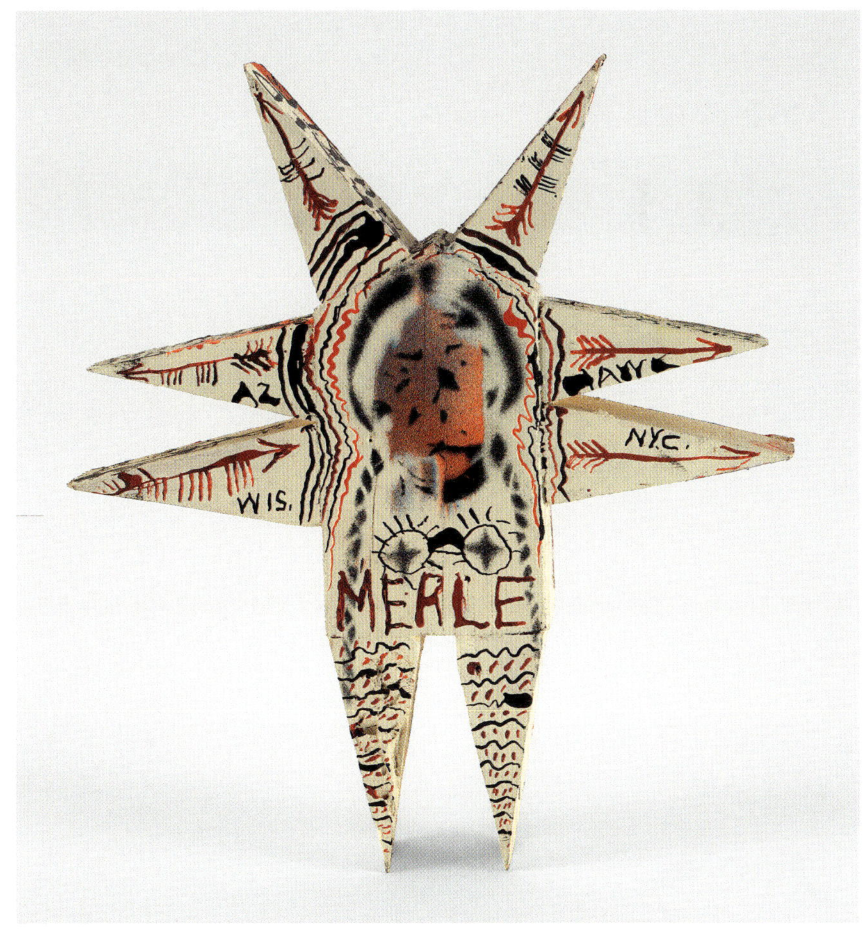
AZ
NYC.
WIS.
MERLE

Sonya Kelliher-Combs

Iñupiaq/Athabascan (b. 1969)

Remnant (Walrus Bone IV), 2019
Mixed media

Remnant

1) a: a usually small part, member, or trace remaining
   b: a small surviving group—often used in plural
2) an unsold or unused piece of goods
3) what is left of a community after it undergoes a catastrophe
   (a recurring theme throughout the Hebrew and Christian Bible.)

Remnant is a series commenting on the threatened state of the natural environment of Alaska, a location where the folly of our human-centric approach to industry is achingly clear. Within these works the viewer is surrounded by fragments and scraps of the world of the North—bits and pieces of animal hide, hair, clothing, and other detritus—submerged in synthetic media like so many specimens from a way of life that no longer exists. *Remnant* invites the viewer into a dialogue that exposes the tenuousness of our own existence. —S.K-C.

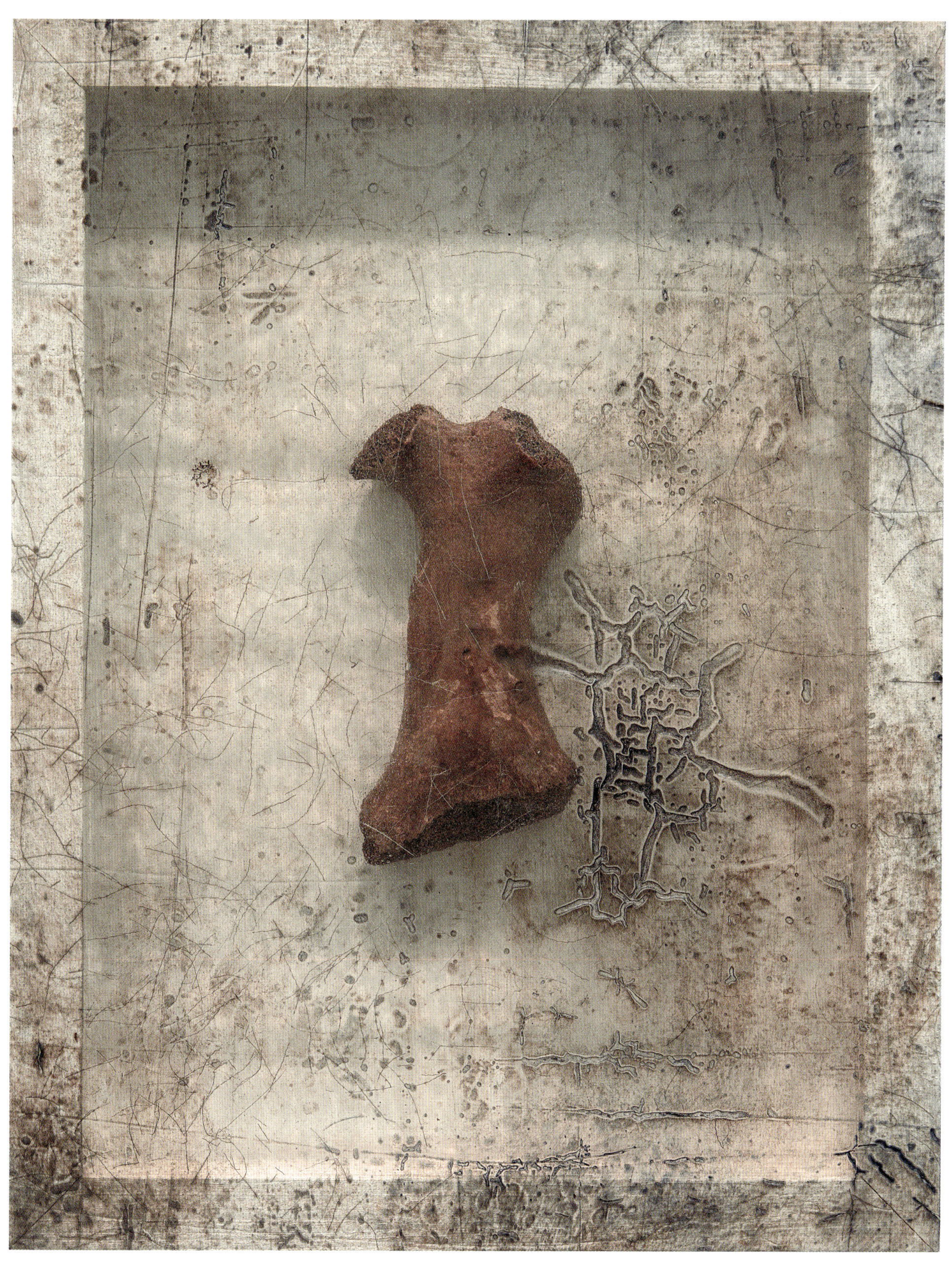

Linda King

Enrolled Member of the Confederated
Salish and Kootenai Nation (b. 1952)

Beauty Set, 2020
Beaded makeup brushes

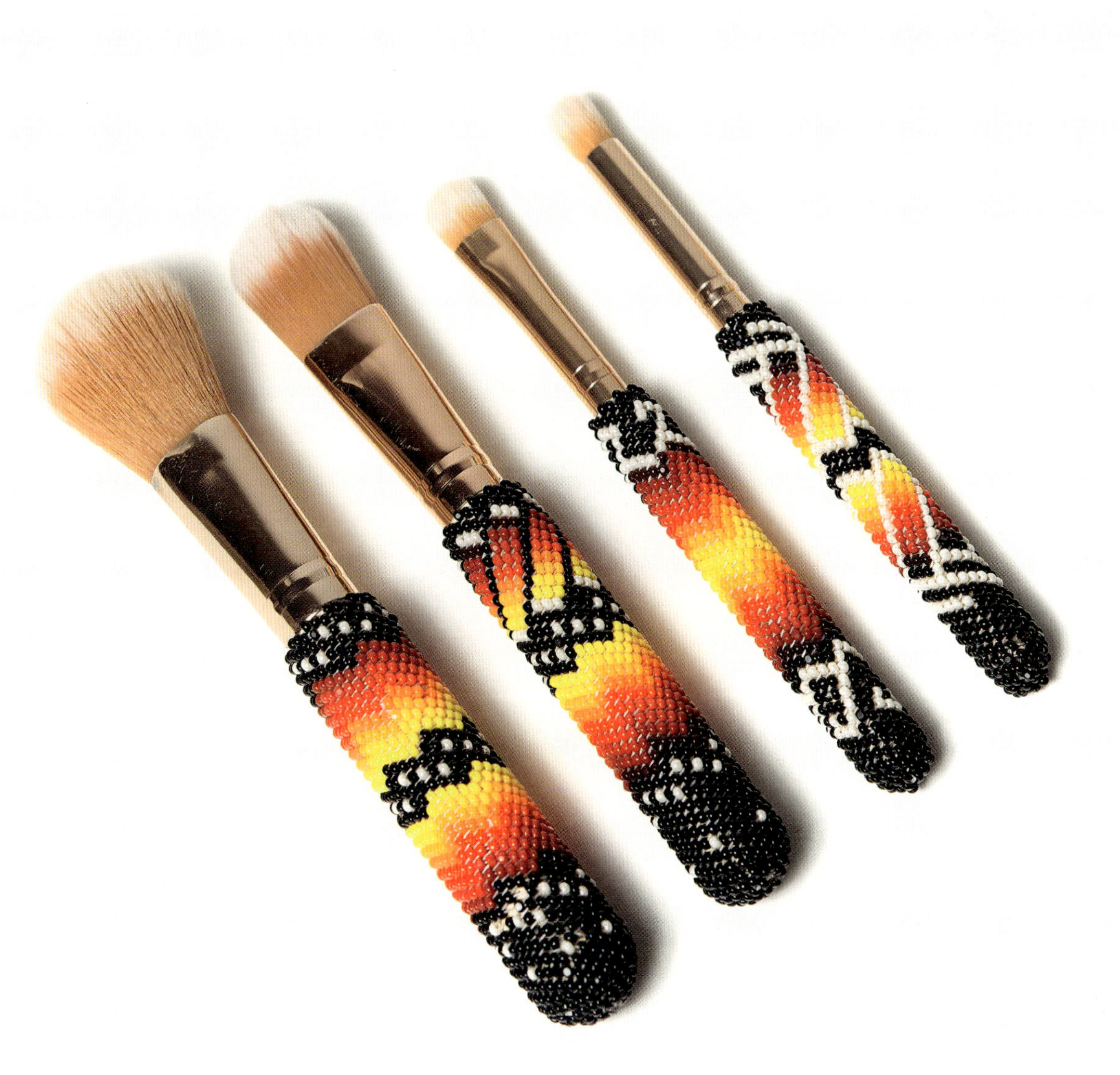

Terran Last Gun (Saakwaynaamah'kaa)

Piikani (Blackfeet) (b. 1989)

Nearing the Skybeings Lodge, 2021
Colored pencil on ledger book paper

Nearing the Sky Beings Lodge is a visual interpretation of what encountering the Sun and Moon's lodge or any other lodge in the cosmos could look like. Space maps of our solar system come to mind as well, and how we're all connected on a planetary level and moving in a circular motion around our star and creator, the Sun.
—T.L.G.

Form B 108
454

Distribution of County and Penalty Taxes

Collected *September* 19*26*

Delinquent Taxes 1924

COUNTY TAX

School District	Assessed Valuation	Page	Amount of Tax	Ledger Page	For County Purposes	Total Levy	Day's Collection	Amt. Per Mill
						22⅘	*50 85*	*2.2905*
1	*Prin 22 90 Int. 4 14*		*27 04*	*136*				
2								
3								
4								
5								
6								
7								
8								
9								
10								
11								

FUNDS		AMOUNT OF TAX
General Fund	*12⅘*	*27 95*
Poor Fund	*6*	*13 74*
Road Fund		
Sinking Fund	*4*	*9 16*
General School Fund		
Bridge Fund		
		50 85

PENALTY

Penalty Due General Fund

Interest
State 3 — 2.48
County 10 — 8.27
Gen. School 4 — 3.31
Sch. Dist. #1 5 — 4.14
22 — 18.20

RECAPITULATION

		Cash Book Page	
State Fund Tax	*Prin 801 Int. 248*	*5*	*10 49*
State War Defense Sinking			
Vets Welfare ½		*5*	*46*
Educational 7		*5*	*160*
Stock Inspector Tax			
State Sinking			
State I. A. and T. S. I. Bond			
Stock Indemnity Tax			
State Livestock Commission			
State Livestock Sanitary Board			
Stock Bounty Tax			
Fish and Game			
Warden Tax			
Sheep Inspector Tax			

		Cash Book Page	
General Fund Tax	*Prin 2795 Int. 827*		*36 22*
General Fund Penalty			*5 98*
General Fund Publication		*5*	*12 20*
Poor Fund Tax		*5*	*13 74*
Poor Fund Tax, Special			
Road Fund, Special			
Road Fund		*5*	*2 12*
Sinking Fund		*5*	*9 16*
General School Fund	*Prin 1374 Int. 331*	*5*	*17 05*
High School		*553*	*6 87*
District No. 1, Special		*515*	*4 58*
Text		*580*	*1 81*
Districts No. 1 to 11			*27 04*
Bridge Fund		*5*	*40 30*
City of Walkerville			
District No. 1, Special Improvement			

James Lavadour

Enrolled Member of the Confederated Tribes of the Umatilla Indian Reservation (b. 1951)

Stick House, 2006
Lithograph

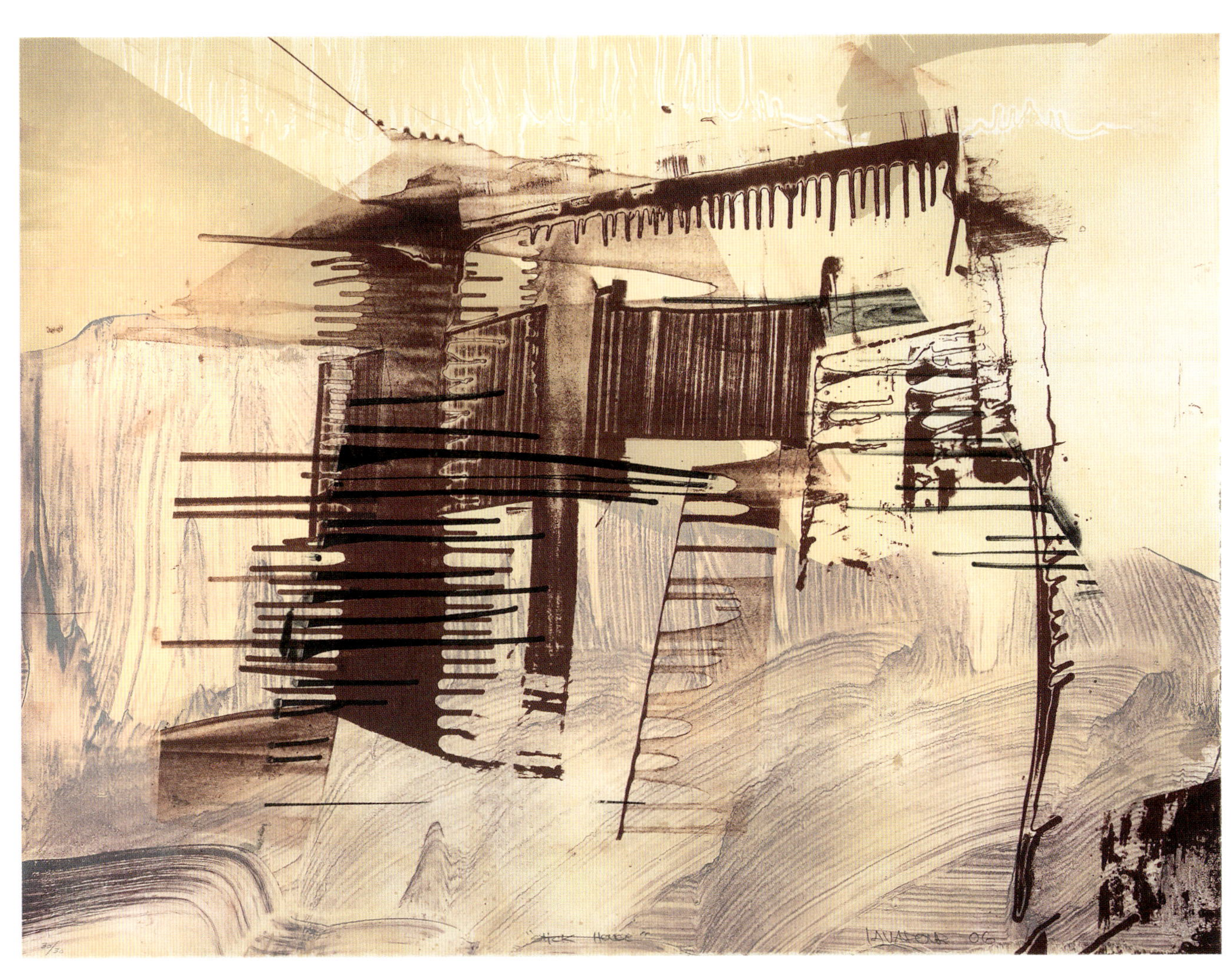

Linda Lomahaftewa

Hopi/Choctaw (b. 1947)

Ancestral Gulf Birds #3, 2010
Monotype

In the beginning, birds could speak. Everyone could understand each other—birds, humans, and animals—but over time we have lost the ability to communicate. The background of this print references the four rivers that the Hopi people had to cross before finding their homeland in north central Arizona and marks the passing of time. The red emblem comes from beadwork and is known as the Celestial Eye, which to me represents my connection to my Southeastern Woodland ancestors. Through our migrations and shifting relationships with our fellow creatures, Creator watches over us and is unchanging. —L.L.

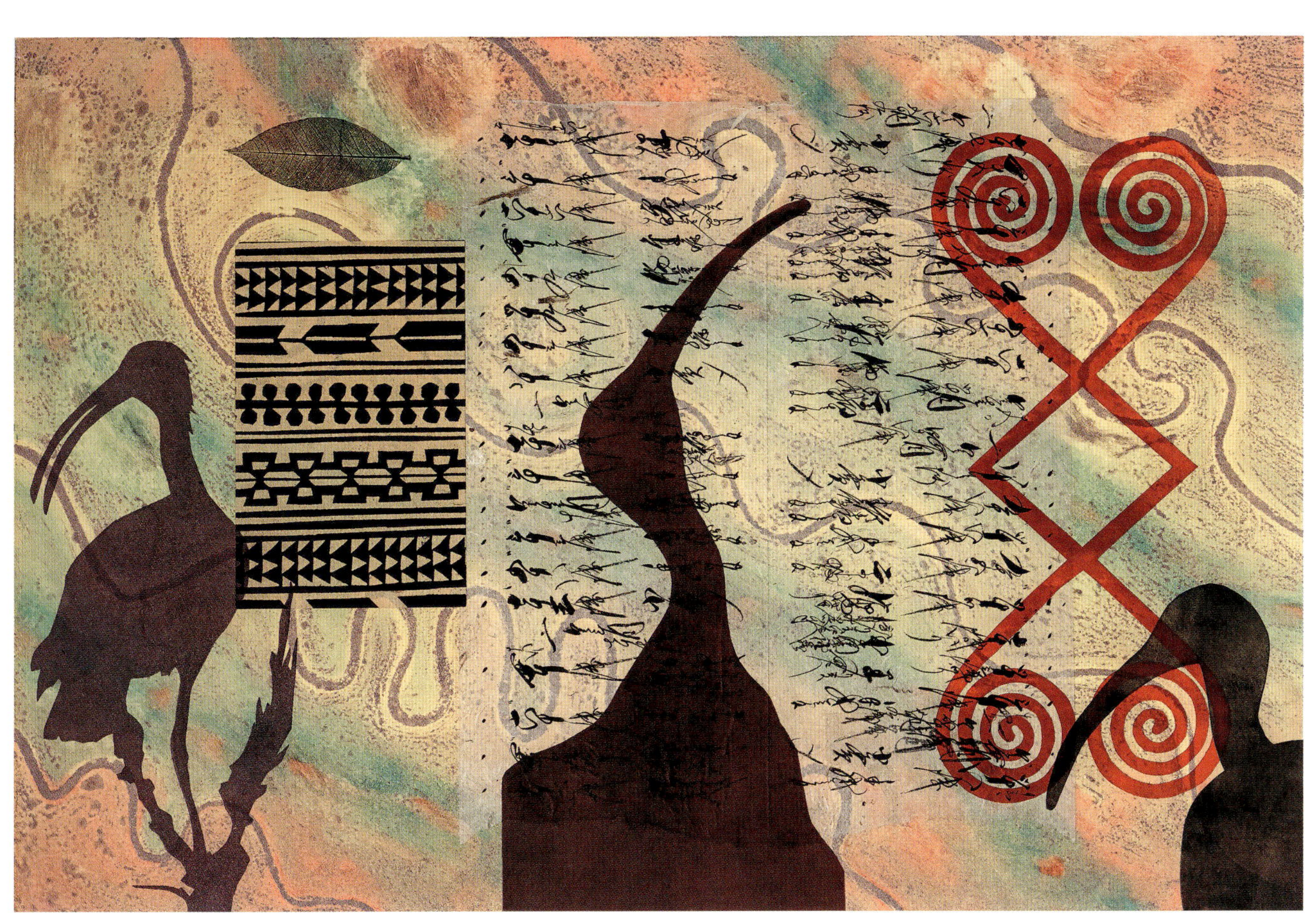

Michael McCabe

Diné (Navajo) (1961–2023)

Untitled, 2022
Monotypes

Michael McCabe made these prints in his studio, Fourth Dimension, in Santa Fe, New Mexico, which he ran for many years. He was a master printmaker who experimented often with different methods of printing, including collage and chine collé, and would often run the press making his own layered and colorful work in between clients. In the top image, Michael incorporated a family photo of Chishi Nez, who was born in Supai Canyon in 1837. The photo is from 1902 and became a frequent image that Michael printed with, often in series. Nez was Michael's great-grandfather.
—Grace Rosario Perkins

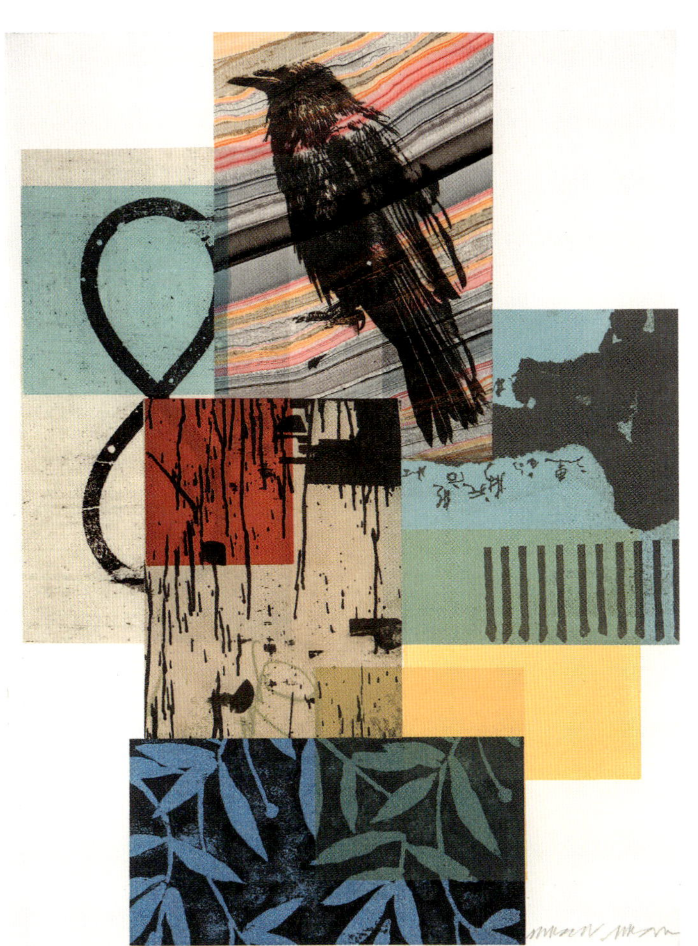

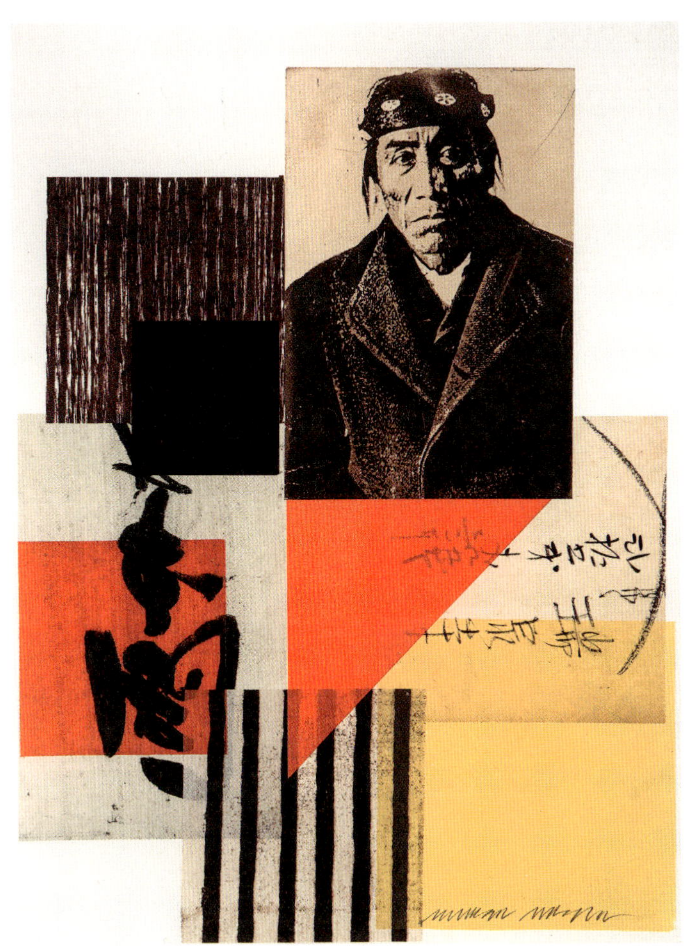

Bryson Goodrunner Meyers

Chippewa, Cree, Sicangu, Oglala, Hunkpapa, Dakota
(b. 1984)

Bandolier Bag of 1916, 2022
Mixed media

The textile designs and florals on this bandolier bag are symbols from the Northern tribes around the region where I grew up. Both are driven by history, stories, and traditional gatherings. We would tell stories with some of these designs. The designs come from Cree, Dakota, Lakota, and Ojibwe cultures—my choices of color and placement make them contemporary pieces. *Bandolier Bag of 1916* is an example of how the bags were designed during that time frame, and the utilization of the beads into the floral design is unique to the woodland region of the Chippewa. —B.G.M.

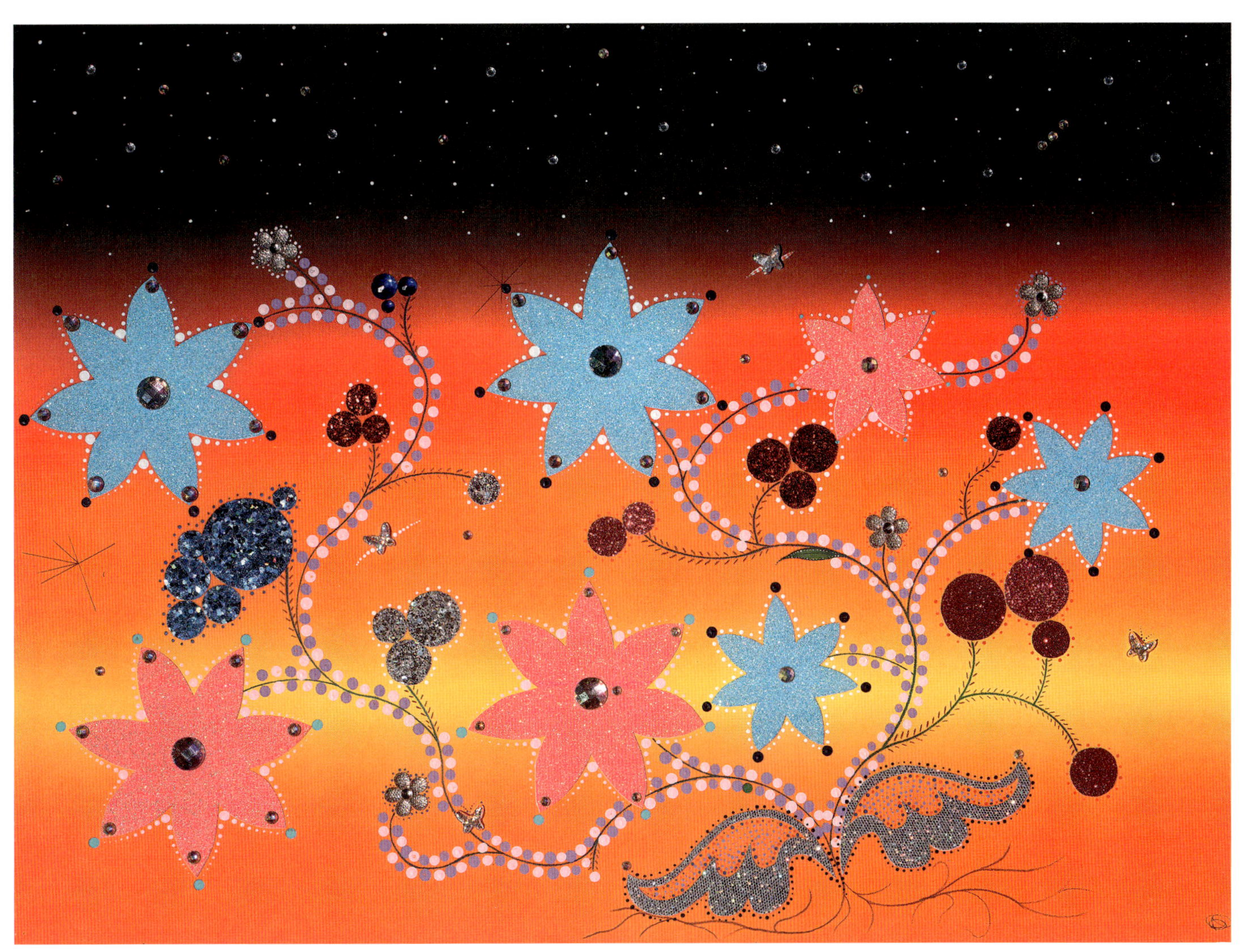

Nora Naranjo-Morse

Tewa, Santa Clara Pueblo (b. 1953)

What Was Taken and What We Sell, 2014
Video

The poverty rate for American Indians living on tribal lands is 29.4 percent compared with the national average of 15.3 percent. The early 1980s brought gaming casinos to tribal lands, promising unfathomable wealth for Indigenous people—since then, Native casinos have exceeded $30 billion in revenue. *What Was Taken and What We Sell* looks at the long-term effects of Native gaming to culture and land.

...I've been bingoed by my baby
no more aces up my sleeve
just one more lucky seven
so I can get off my knees.
Hay yah
Hay yah
Hay yah hey... —N.N-M.

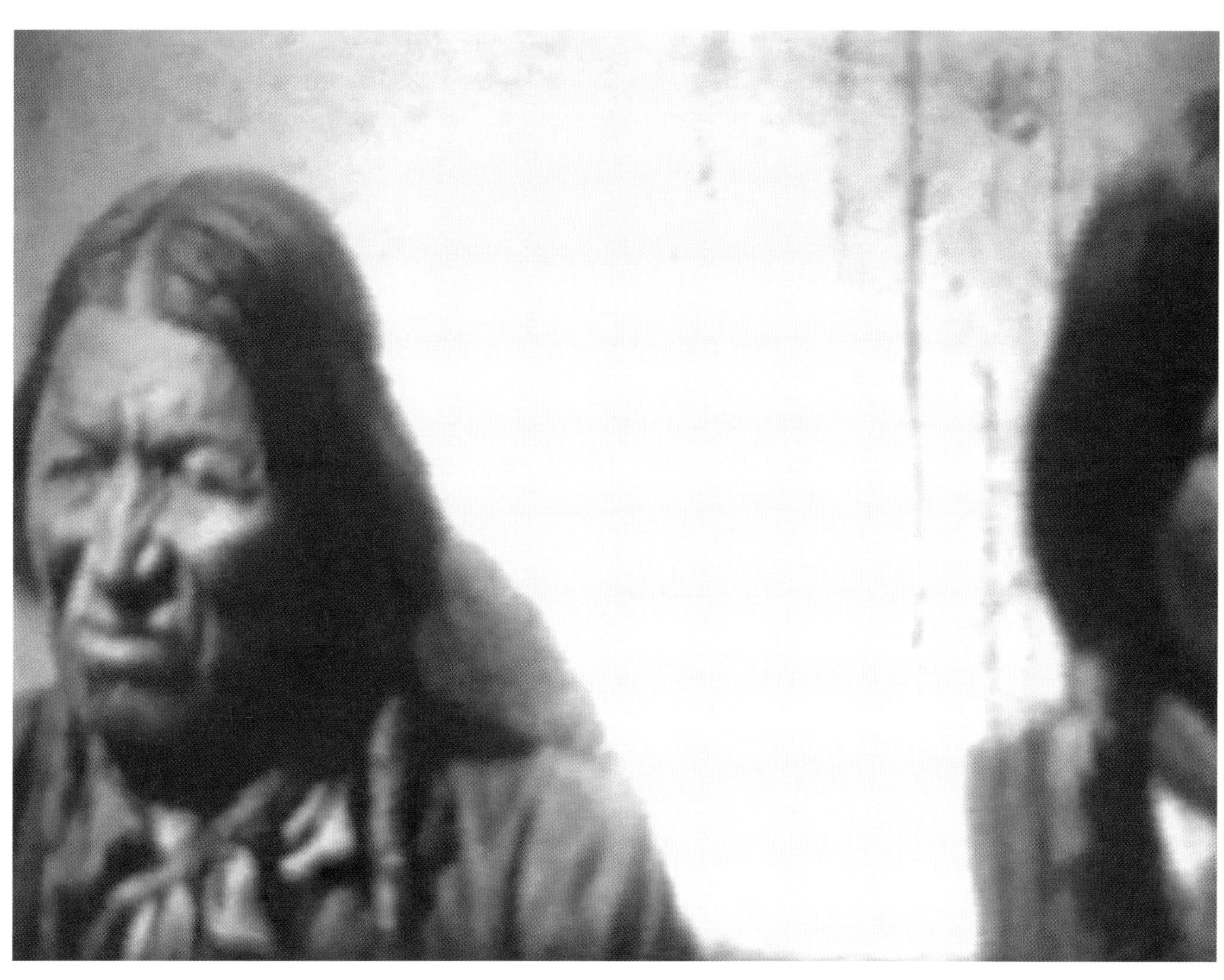

Chris Pappan

Kanza, Lakota (b. 1971)

Of White Bread and Miracles (Buffalo), 2020
Mixed media on embossed Evanston municipal ledger

This work is a response to the Boy Scout tradition of misappropriating Native American practices as "hobbies." The figures are from a manual titled *Here Is Your Hobby . . . Indian Dancing and Costumes* (Putnam, 1966). The book is an example of cognitive dissonance as it erases any vestiges of contemporary Native people and homogenizes all Native American cultures while making casual remarks such as "Get a local Indian to teach you singing and dancing." By appropriating the figures from the book and recontextualizing them, I am reclaiming the power of dance for our people; it is a sacred form of prayer and sacrifice that has deep roots and meaning for Native people everywhere. These works also deal with the idea of innocence (lost) and institutionalized racism. Interjecting the static poses (that are meant to teach movement) with elements of spirituality and authenticity, I am reclaiming that which has been erased. —C.P.

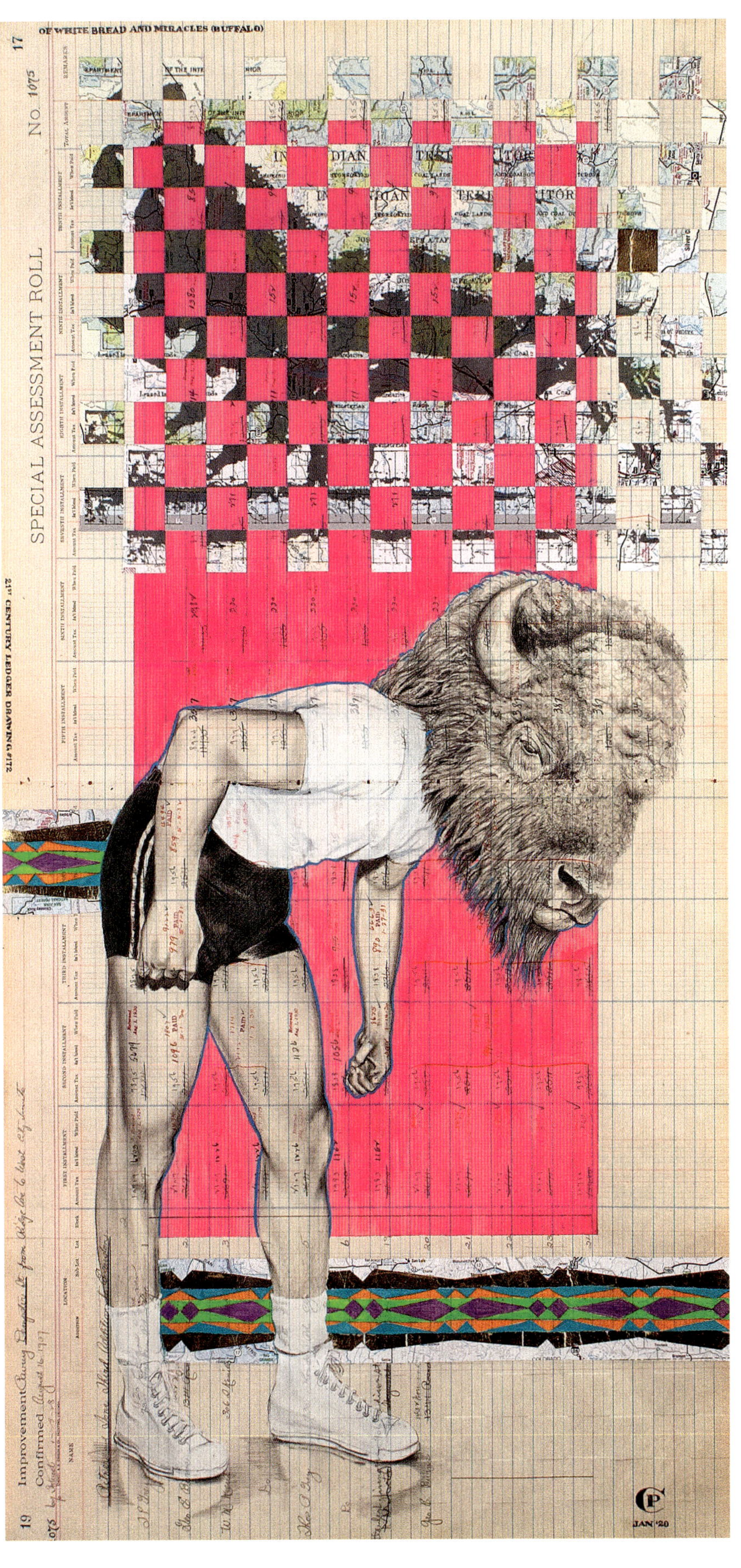
OF WHITE BREAD AND MIRACLES (BUFFALO)
SPECIAL ASSESSMENT ROLL
No. 1075
21ST CENTURY LEDGER DRAWING #172
JAN '20

Luanne Redeye

Seneca Nation of Indians/Hawk Clan (b. 1985)

I See You, 2018
Oil on panel

My works are visual narratives of the complexities of what it means to be Indigenous today. Primarily a figurative artist, I use paint and portraiture as a form of self-determination to claim portraiture for Indigenous identities. The paintings are from my gaze, sharing the stories of my family by weaving together personal narratives, home, identity, and culture. My work blends personal narrative with familial relationships, and because of its intimate nature, I carry memories, stories, and pictures of the people I depict. My practice involves working across the mediums of painting, print, bead-work, and textiles, drawing connections to land, place, and kinship and often intersecting autobiography and community. My work is always created through a Native lens, through which I share my experiences, knowledge, and perspective of navigating a modern world as a Native woman. —L.R.

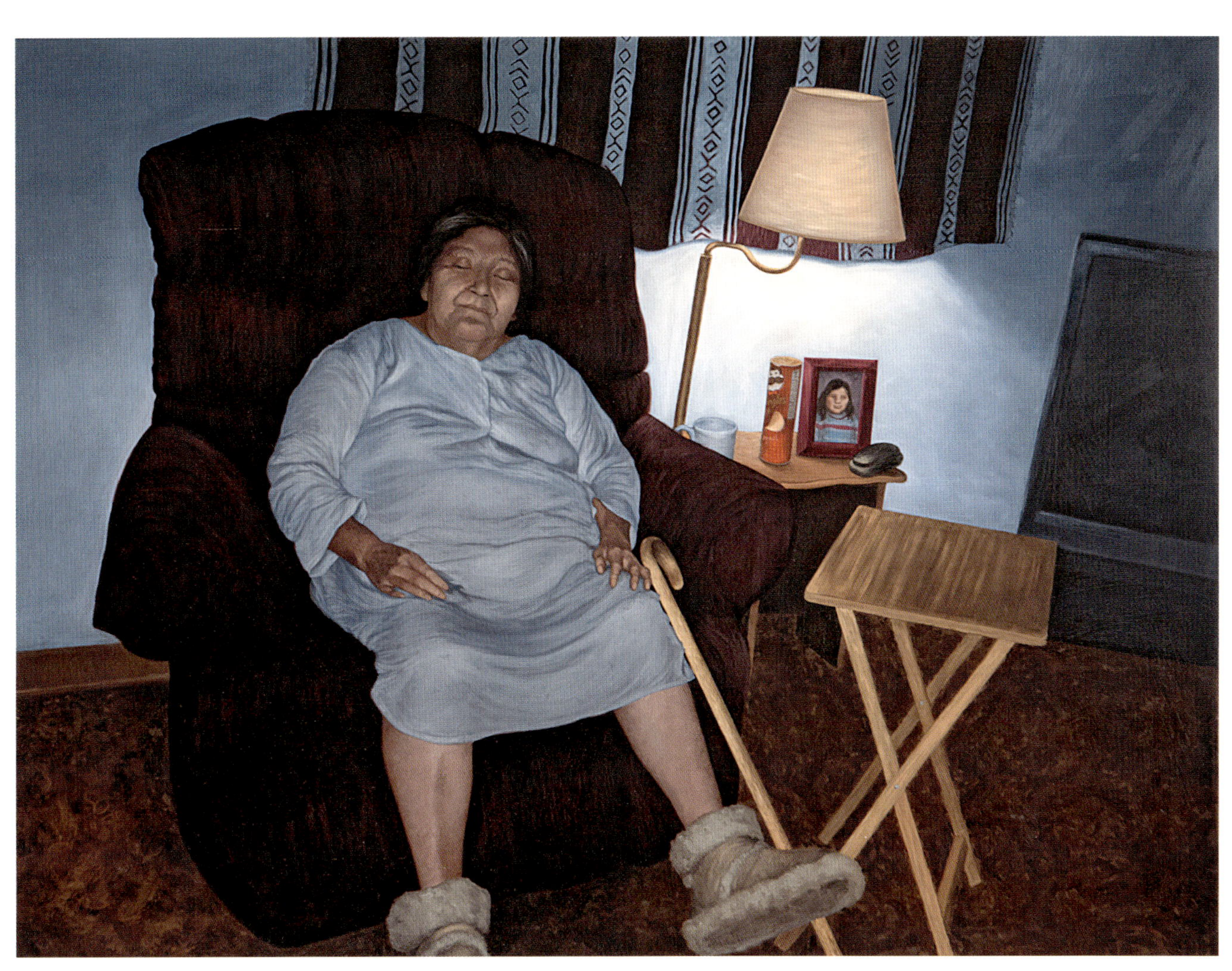

Wendy Red Star

Apsáalooke/Crow (b. 1981)

Dust, 2020
Lithograph

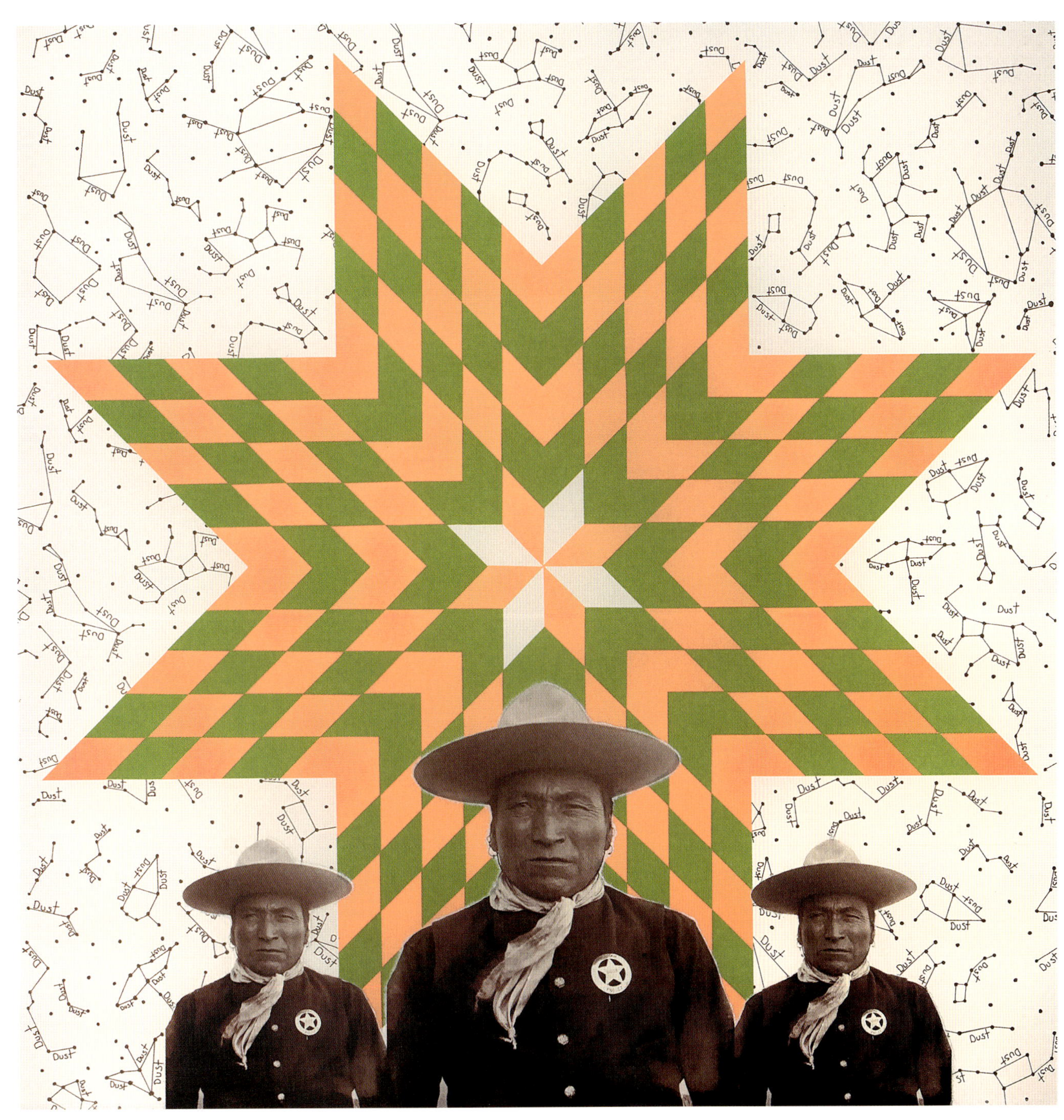

Sarah Sense

Chitimacha and Choctaw (b. 1980)

Dickens, 2022
Woven archival inkjet prints on
Hahnemuhle bamboo paper, tape

Dickens, part of the *Power Lines* series, draws inspiration from the British Library's collection of maps, rare books, and manuscripts. The series holds stories of British settler-colonialism in Native North America while reclaiming Indigenous place with landscape and space with traditional Chitimacha and Choctaw basket weaving. I am practicing familial patterning with photo-weaving of digitally reproduced images that retell settler-colonial stories. The use of maps along with settlers' letters to the British monarchy, layered over each other with photographs then interwoven with Chitimacha and Choctaw basket patterns re-Indigenizes the objects. Cutting the paper into strips and opening them, moving them apart to create space for differing interpretations, and reinserting Indigenous patterns is a process of decolonizing. —S.S.

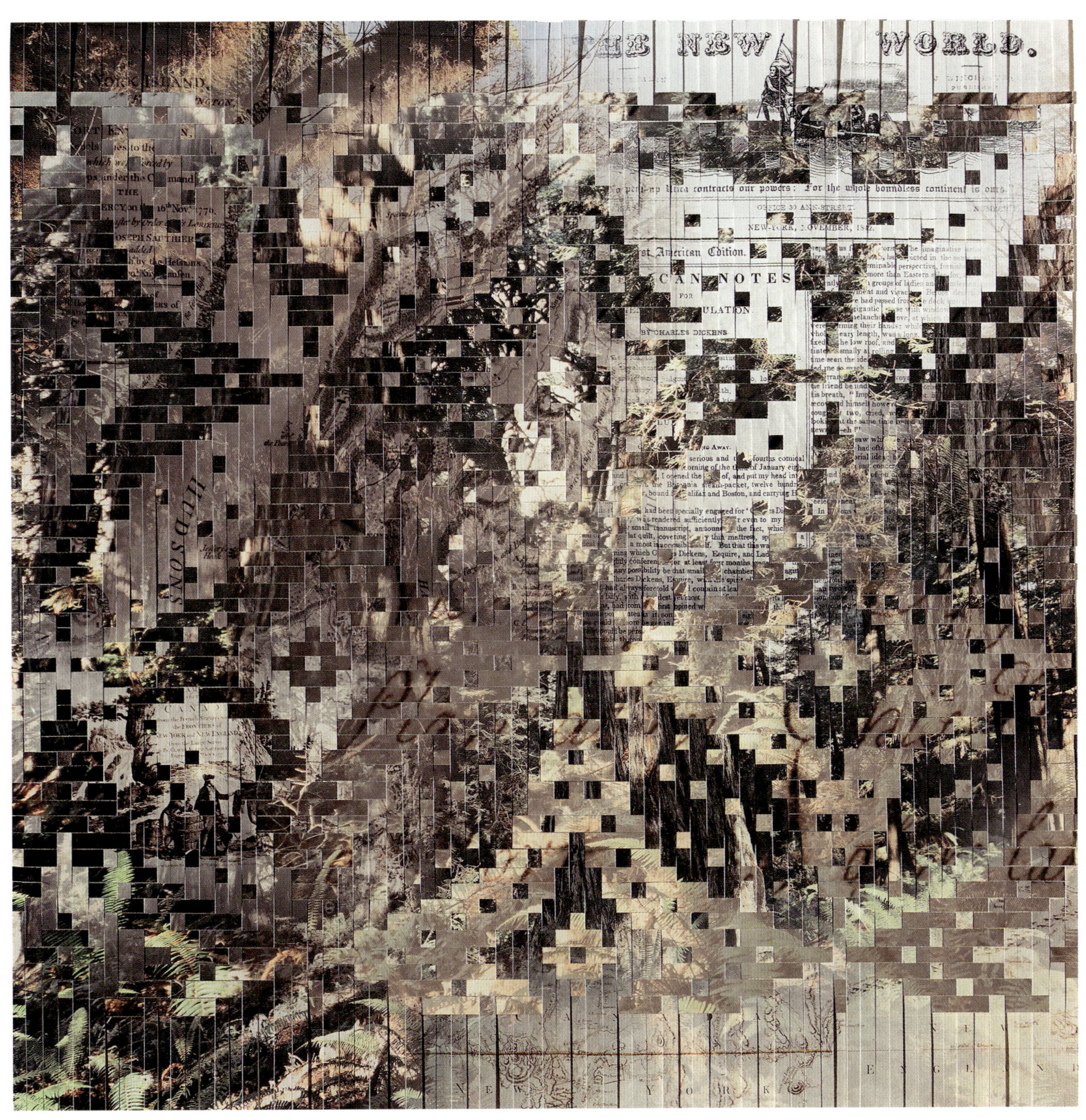
NEW WORLD.
contracts our powers: For the whole boundless continent is ours.
NEW-YORK, NOVEMBER, 1842.
American Edition.
CAN NOTES
BY CHARLES DICKENS
HUDSONS

Rose B. Simpson

Santa Clara Pueblo (b. 1983)

X-Ray, 2021
Ceramic and steel

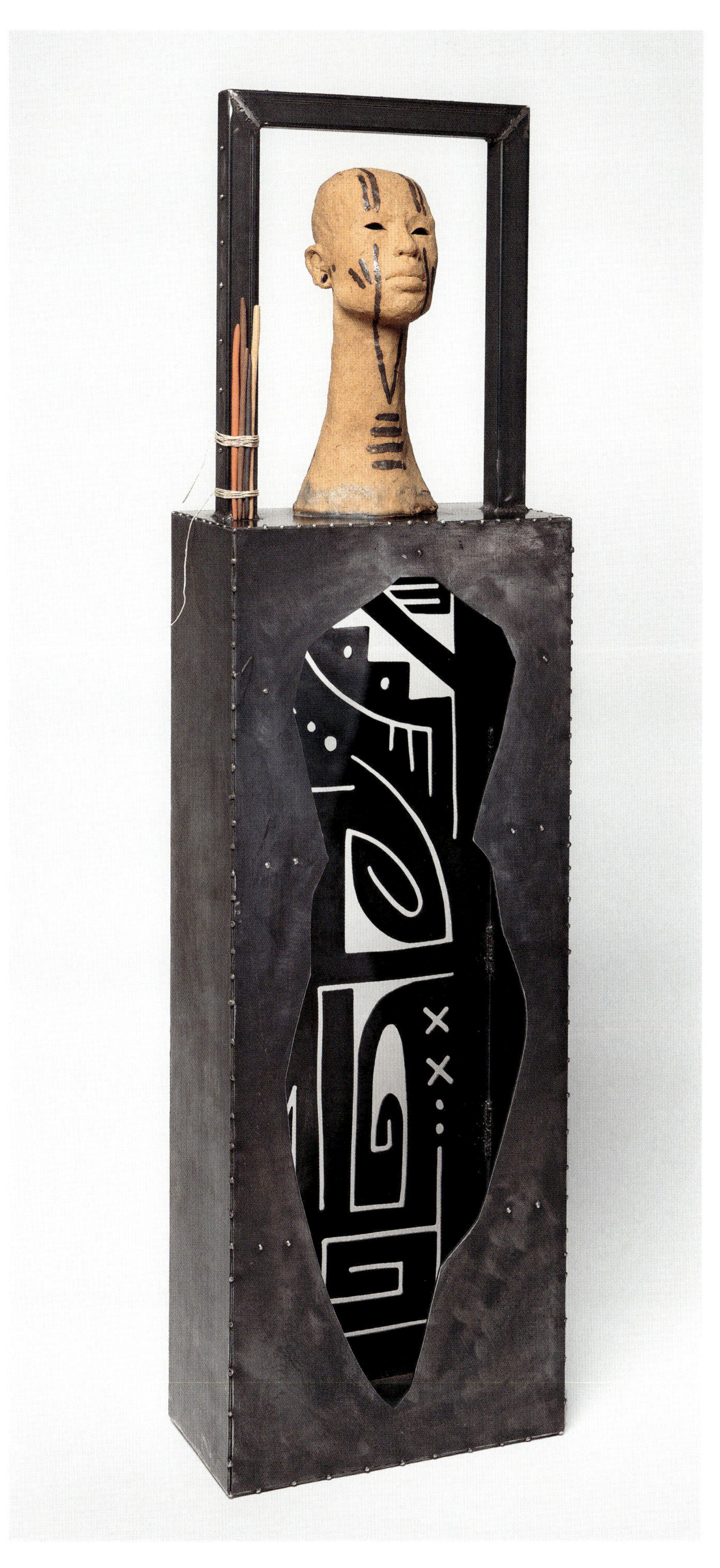

Duane Slick

Meskwaki/Ho-Chunk (b. 1961)

There Are No Endings, 2018
Acrylic on linen

There Are No Endings is part of a series of night paintings that began in 2018 and is ongoing today. They are interpretations, musings, and recollections of the experience of night on the Meskwaki and Ho-Chunk homelands in Iowa and Nebraska. The atmosphere of these spaces is active with textures, signaling noise and repetition to recall the sound of singing that carries through the darkness. The visual field of the painting is broken by the architecture of stripes that pick up rhythm as they move from top to bottom and left and right. Night becomes active in a way that negates the idea of nothingness, thus positing the notion that there are no endings. There never were. —D.S.

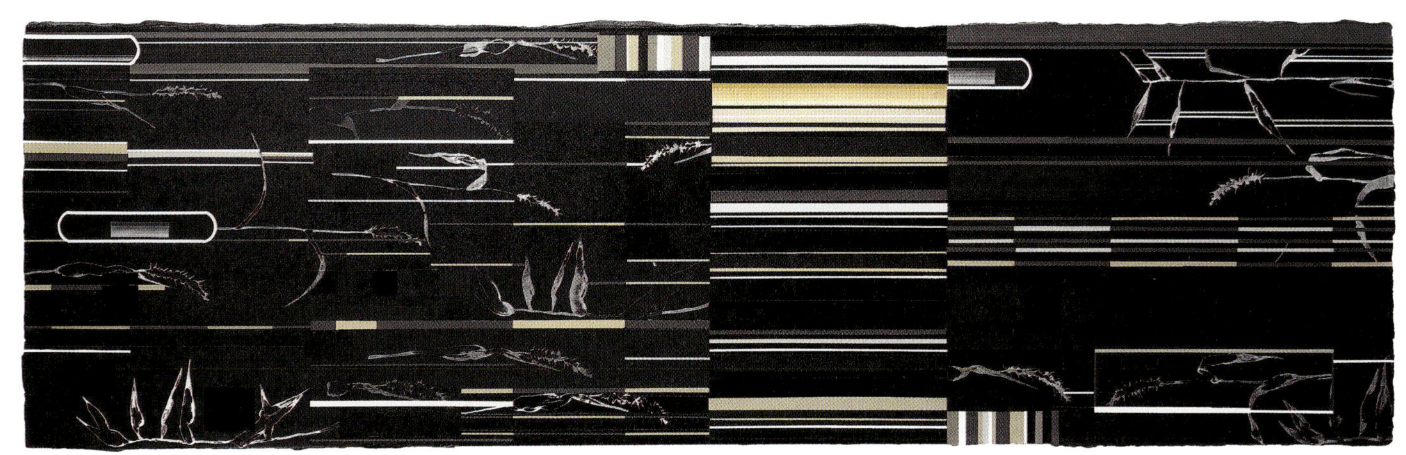

Roxanne Swentzell

Santa Clara Pueblo [b. 1962]

Touched, 2011
Original clay

This piece represents how the ways in which we interact with each other leave marks. It is a reminder to touch, speak, and treat each other with care and love so that our input makes the world better for us all. —R.S.

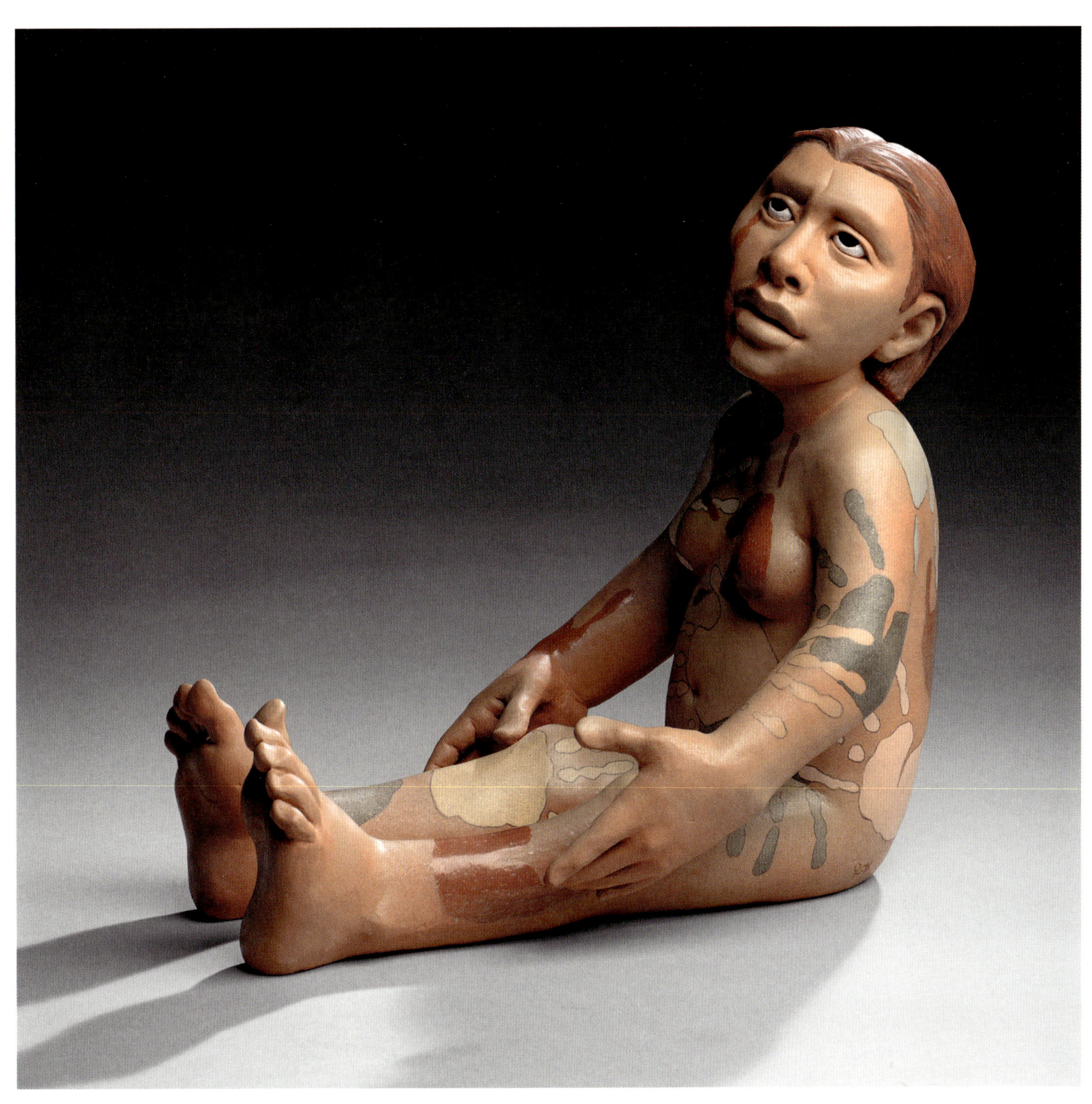

Zoë Urness

Tlingit (b. 1984)

Year of the Women, 2019
Analog capture-digital chromogenic output on Fuji crystal archive paper with UV over laminate mounted to Dibond aluminum substrate

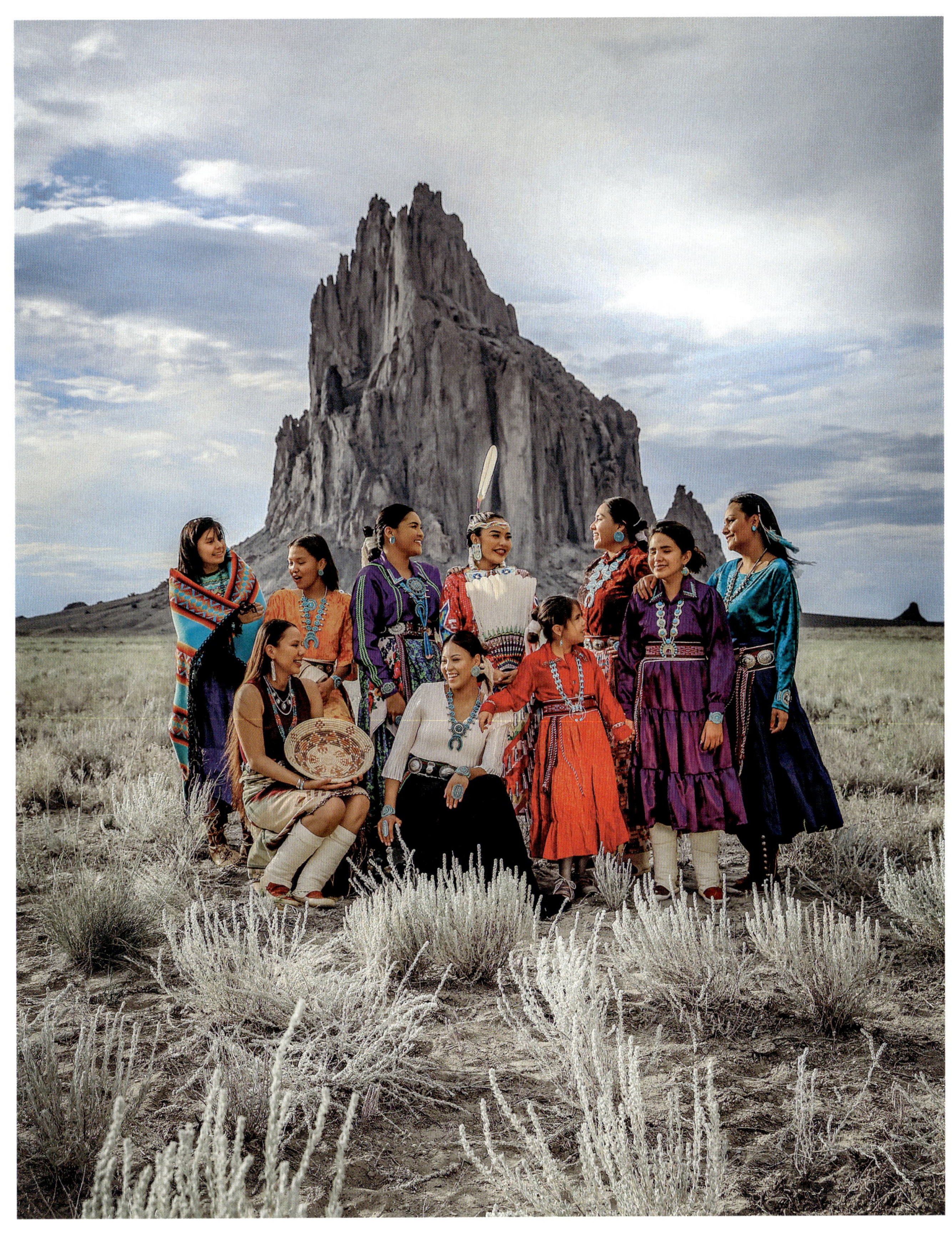

Melanie Yazzie

Diné (Navajo) (b. 1966)

Visions in Brittany, 2007
Print

I taught printmaking several summers at the Pont Aven School of Art in France between the years 1999 to 2003. One of the most beautiful places in the area is a place called Carnac. It is along the gulf of Morbihan on the south coast of Brittany and is known for the most extensive Neolithic menhir collections in the world. I come from the Southwest where we have ancient sites like Chaco Canyon, and I felt a connection to these stone menhirs. I often use the image of small animals as self-portraits in my work. In this print I am dreaming and being a part of the land with the formation of Carnac on my body. I also use the images of the profiles of the houses of the area in this work. These places I have been in Brittany, France, are always a part of me. —M.Y.

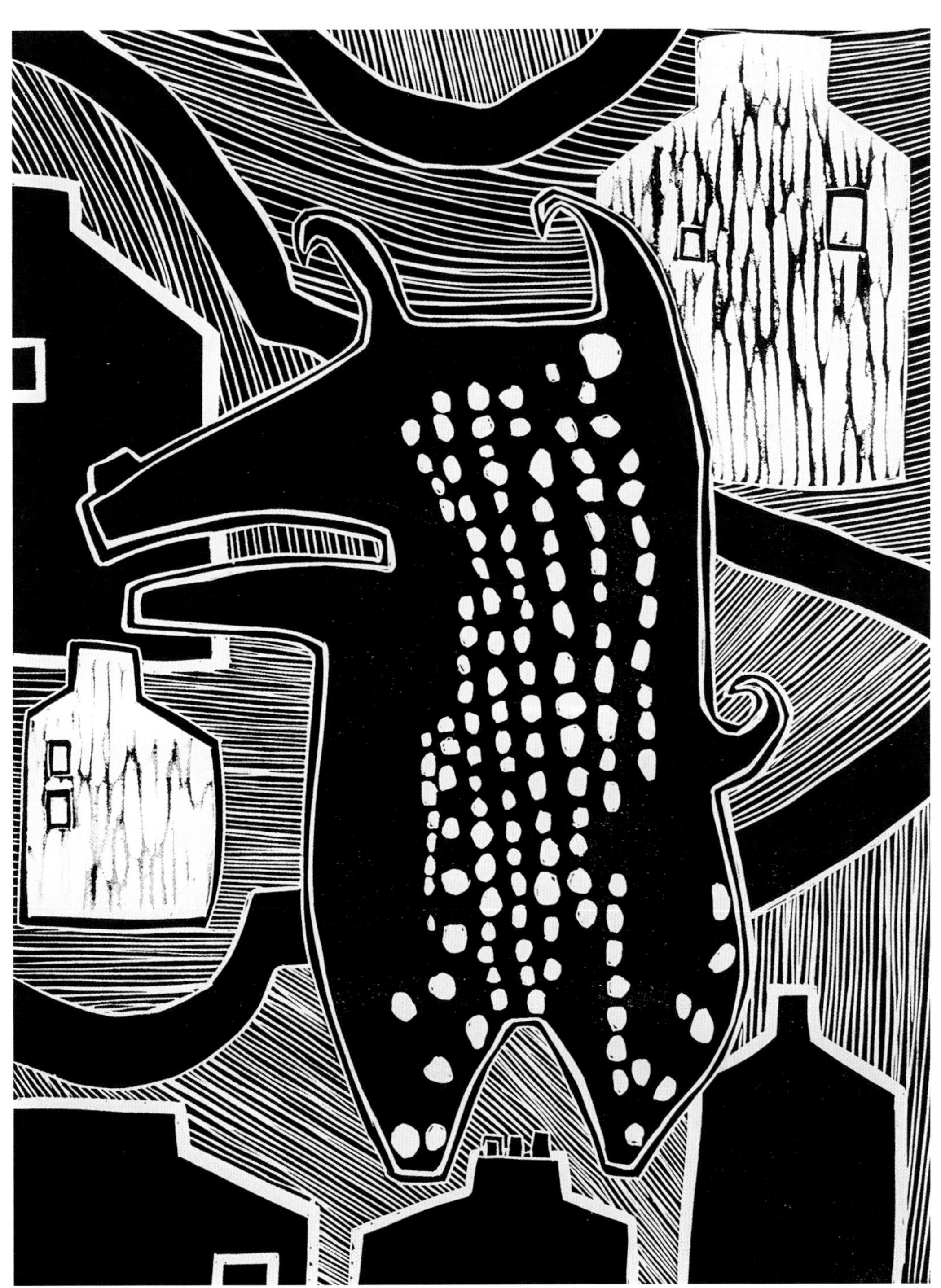

Native ideology insists that we are part of the sacred, from the solar dust on this planet as well as our bodies recycling with the ancestors and all other living things.
—Jaune Quick-to-See Smith

Native American artists often make artwork that documents daily happenings and regular activities such as powwows, making meals, and shopping at big-box stores. The frequent overlay of American popular culture adds to these narratives. Today, because of higher education and migration off reservations, American popular culture has greatly shaped the social aspects of Native American life. Native American artists frequently translate, internalize, and convert seemingly "all-American" narratives into newly adapted Native American stories.

SOCIAL

Frank Big Bear

Ojibwe (b. 1953)

Ghost Dance of the Great Mystery, 2022
Colored pencil on black illustration board

"In *Ghost Dance of the Great Mystery*, Frank Big Bear imagines the great interconnectivity of a prophecy. The Ghost Dance ceremony was initiated in the late 1800s by the Northern Paiute prophet Wovoka in response to and as a deterrent to prevent colonial incursions onto Native land and to revive traditional lifeways across Turtle Island for all Native people. While the US military violently retaliated in response to the Ghost Dance, most infamously at Wounded Knee, the movement and the prophecy ignited fierce and inextinguishable embers of hope across Turtle Island." —Erin Robideaux Gleeson

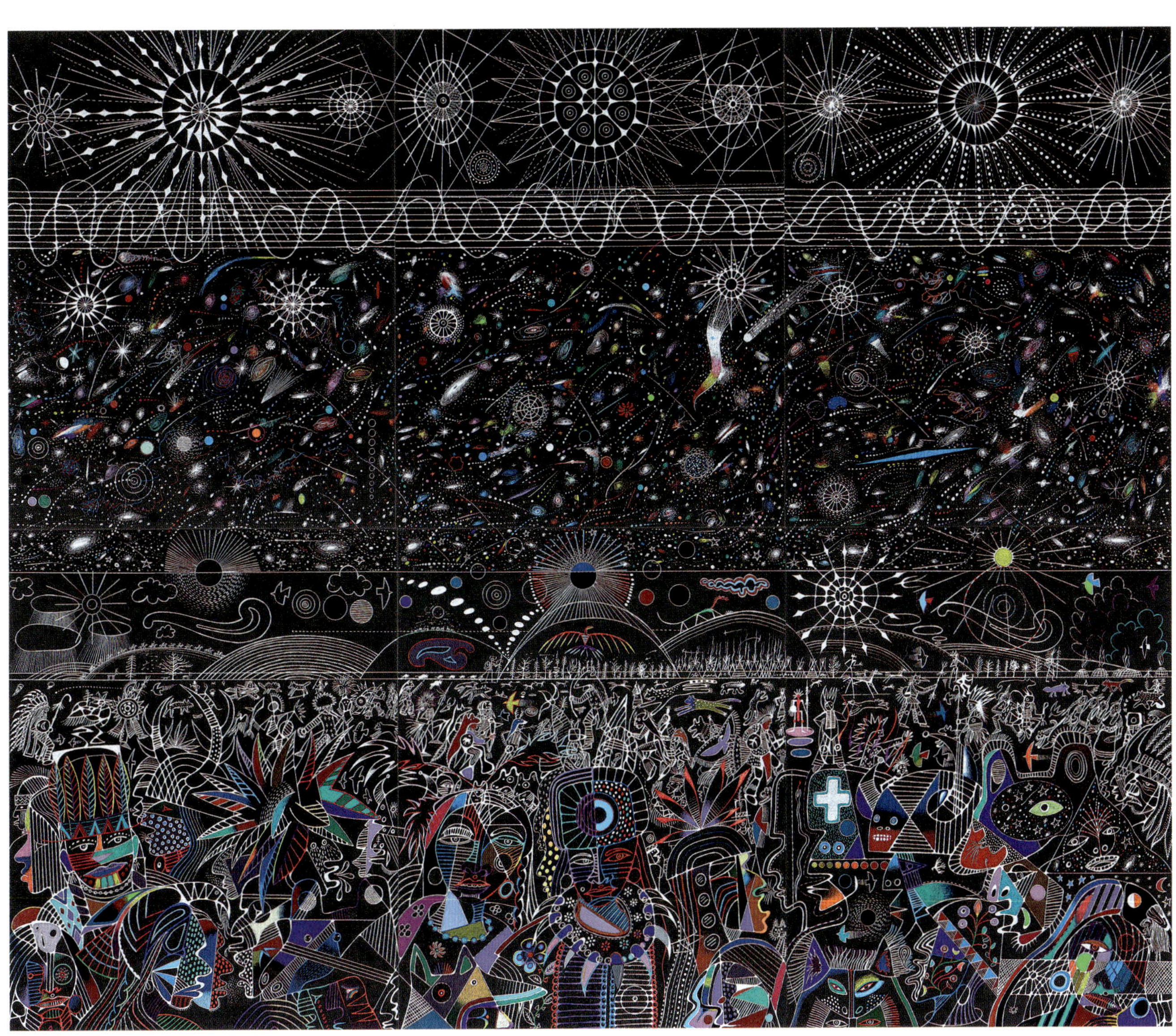

Julie Buffalohead

Enrolled Ponca Tribe of Oklahoma
[b. 1972]

The Great Divide, 2008
Acrylic, ink, and graphite on paper

This piece is part of a series of autobiographical works to encapsulate my emotions about motherhood and to deconstruct romanticized visions of childhood and growing up in the suburbs. These characters sometimes attack stereotypes about Native people, exposing their artificiality through children's games. The characters occupy a fictional territory that seems both out of place and time. They are not fairy tales, nor wholly products of fantasy, in the sense that they aren't simply just invented. In many ways, the characterizations are akin to staged facsimiles, presenting specific archetypes as a dramatist would. The narrative that emerges in this mythic space is mostly opaque. As a parallel to traditional knowledge, the animals come out of the woods to meet with humans. The cast of characters are drawn from Native stories about the rabbit and the coyote. There exists a rosy nostalgia in the work, but with a hard edge to it. —J.B.

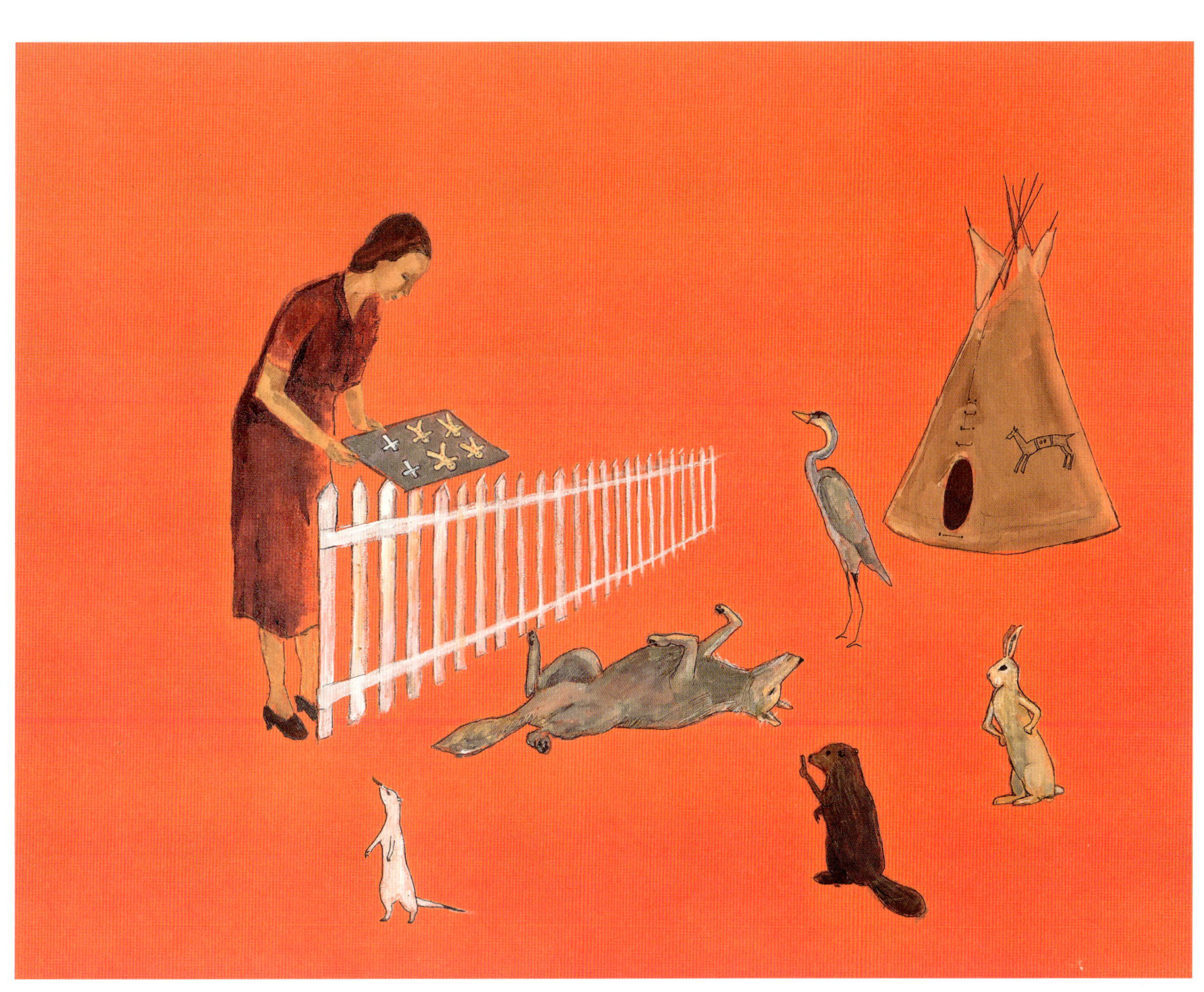

Nanibah "Nani" Chacon

Diné [Navajo] and Chicana [b. 1980]

Emersion into the Blue World, 2017
Acrylic on Polytab

In this work, Chacon references the Diné creation stories in which events take place across four worlds, with each world linked to a color. The Blue World talks about Sky People. This body of work is not a literal translation of the creation stories but instead an interaction of ideas presented in the stories. Chacon created this series to promote oral traditions. This work invites discussion, correction, questions, and relation to further promote the telling and retelling of traditional stories. —N.C.

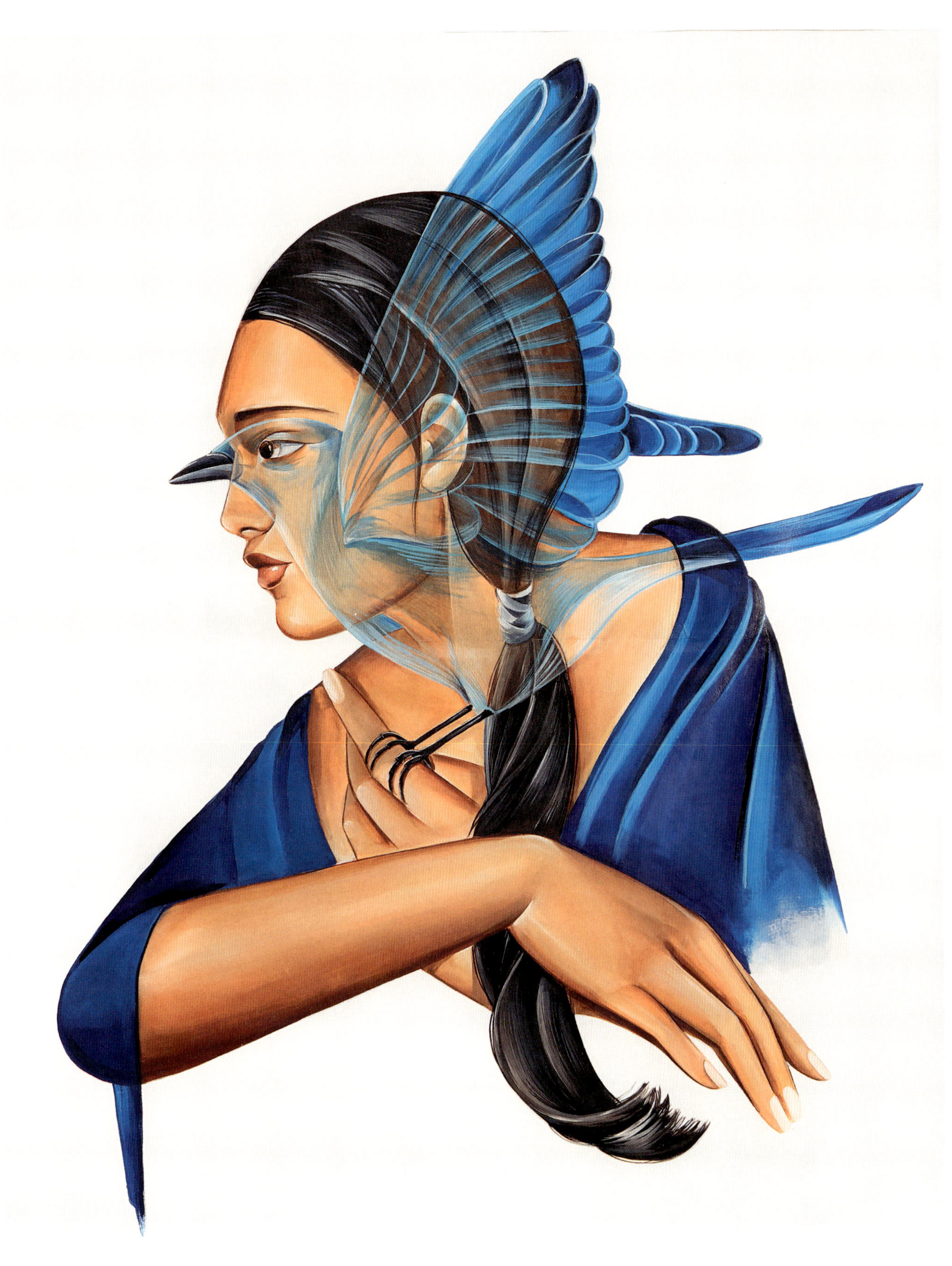

Lorenzo Clayton

Navajo (b. 1950)

Consciously Conscious Numbers, 2024
Mixed media

Consciously Conscious Numbers is a collaborative piece between George Sidebotham, an artist and professor of mechanical engineering at the Cooper Union's School of Engineering, Timothy Corbett, an artist and designer for manufacturing and production, and me. Central to the piece is the idea that at the very core of the base numbers 0–9 are individual, conscious entities—as fantastical as that may seem. Divine-like attributes are qualities I've always attributed to the field of mathematics, so thoughts of numbers possessing consciousness during a Gestalt-like experience I had some years ago seemed to make absolute, instinctive sense. I can say that what I experienced was culturally based, and that my Indigeneity was at the core of the experience. People like my ancestors have been acknowledging the consciousness of the natural world and that of the cosmos for millennia. —L.C.

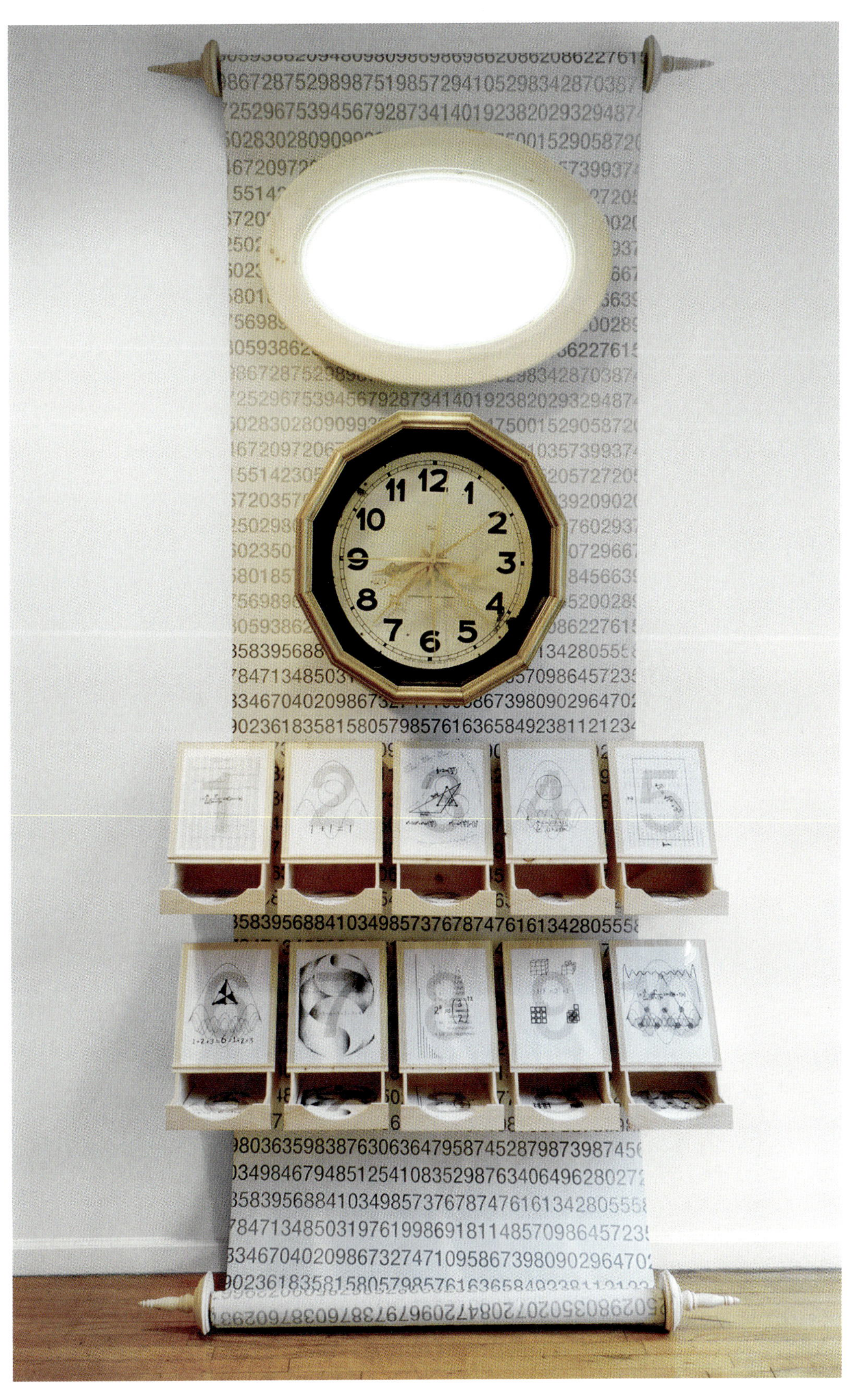

Jeremy Dennis

Shinnecock Indian Nation Tribal Member (b. 1990)

Ma's House: Reciprocity Project, 2022
Video

Making this film about Ma's House was a wonderful experience. After working to rehabilitate our family home over the past year, it was important to reflect on the progress and how far the house had come. The work was tiresome and financially draining, but it all came together thanks to the individual contributions of many friends and family members. When we began, there was so much love and passion behind the mission of turning the home into a future communal art space for artists of color on the Shinnecock Reservation. I hope the film conveys our gratitude toward those individuals, shows where the space is going, and provides a better image of what Ma's House is all about. —J.D.

MA’S HOUSE

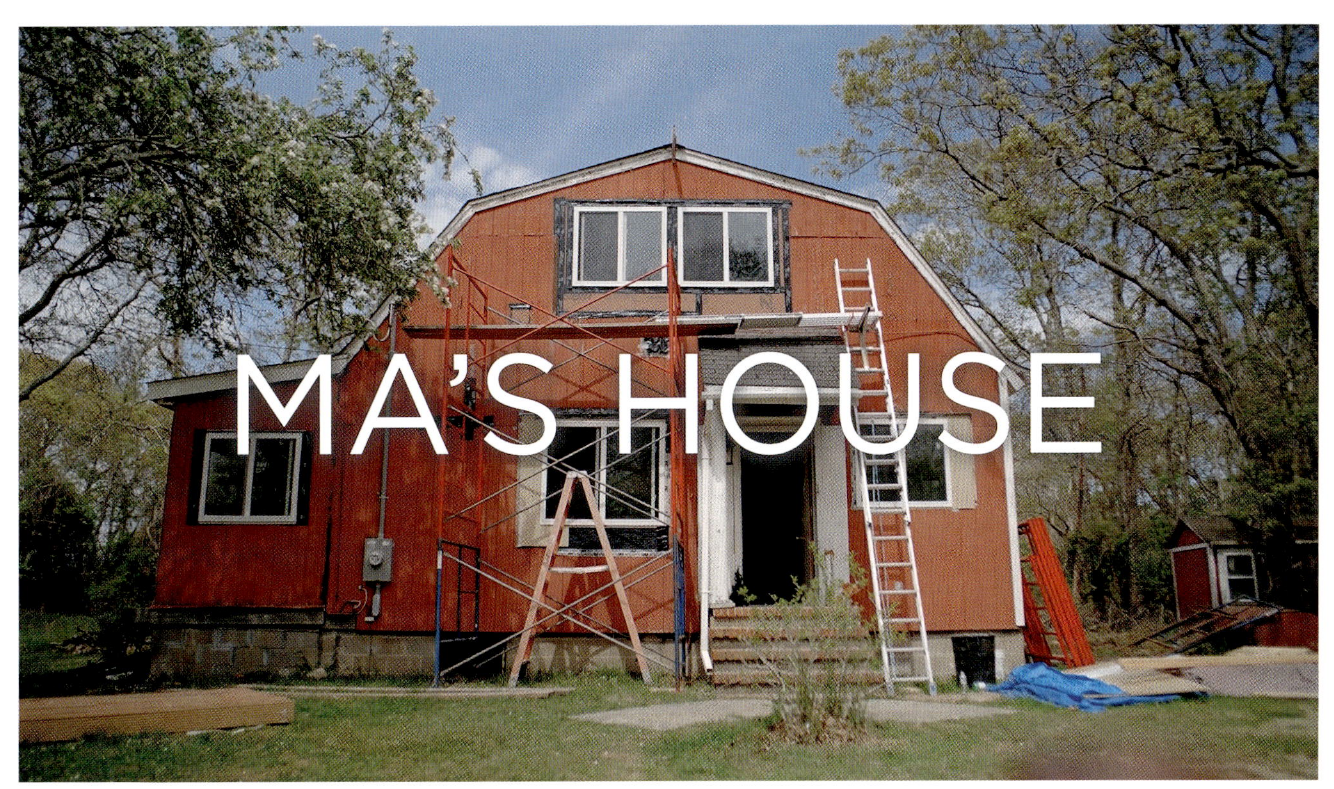

Raven Halfmoon

Caddo Nation (b. 1991)

E-a'-ti-ti, 2021
Stoneware, glaze

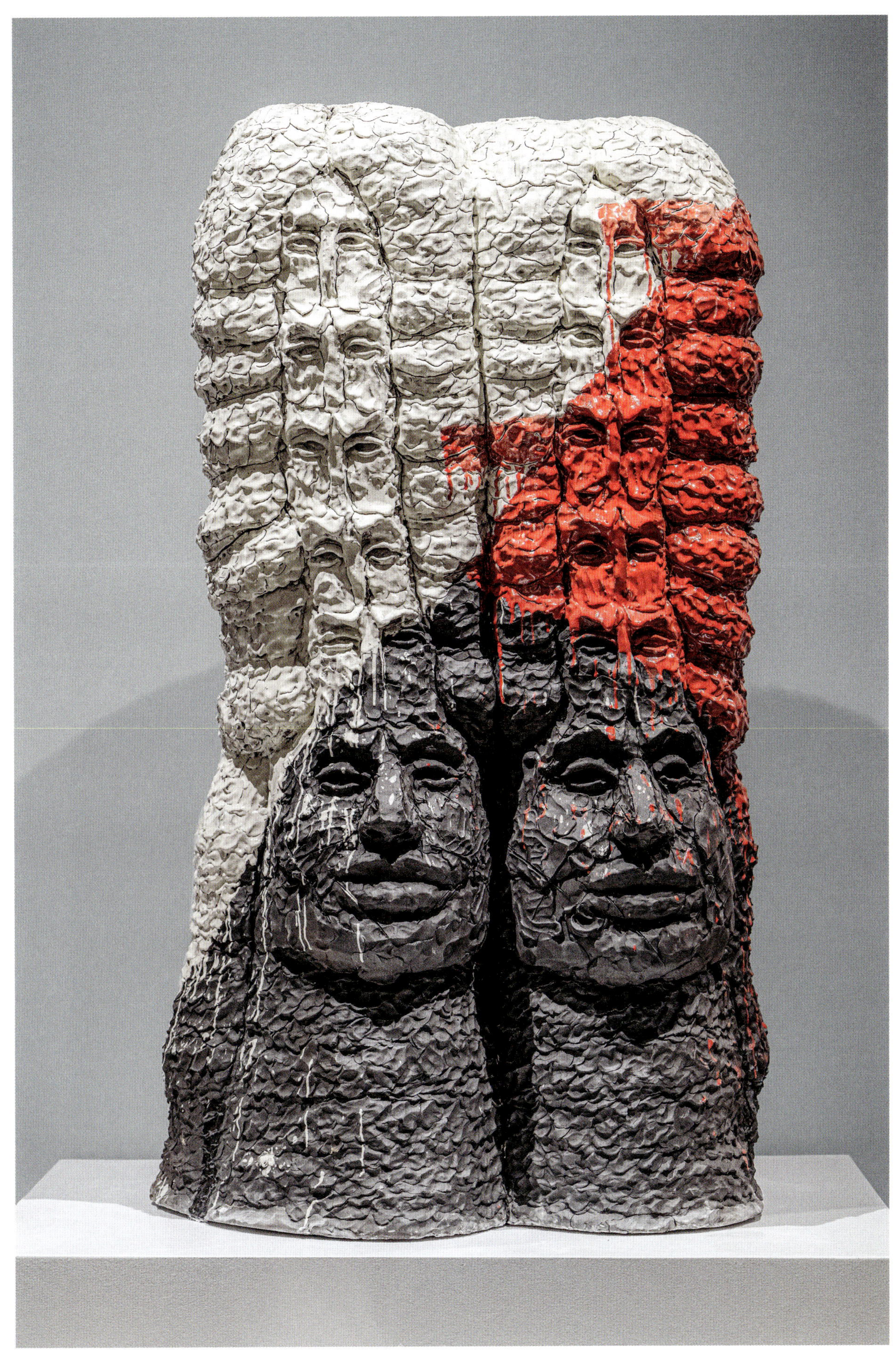

Bob Haozous

Chiricahua Apache Tribe of Oklahoma (b. 1943)

Sinful Dreams, 1993
Ink on paper

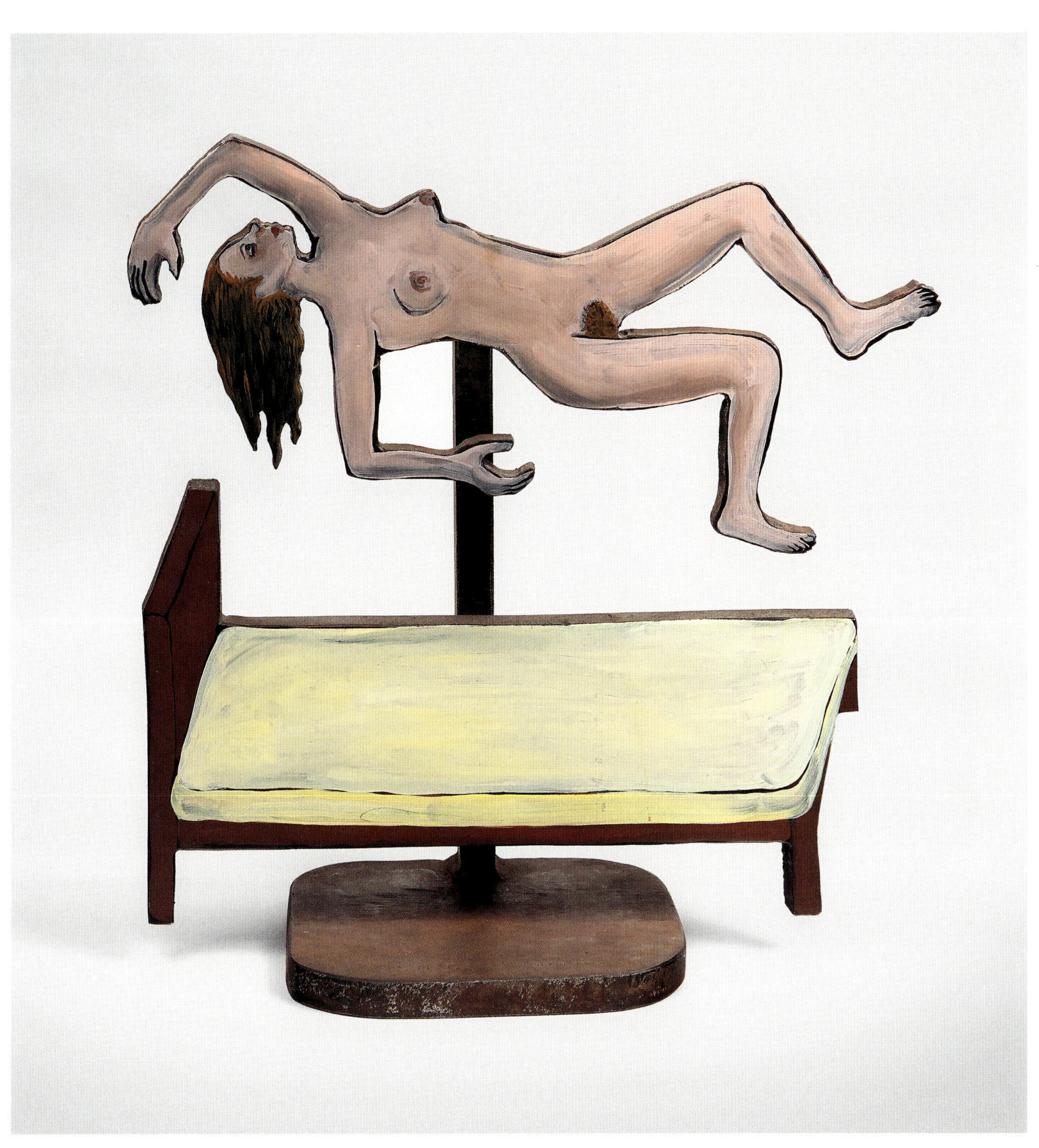

G. Peter Jemison

Seneca, Heron Clan (b. 1945)

Red Power, 1973
Acrylic on canvas

The year 1973 was for me a year of consciousness raising. Wounded Knee, South Dakota, was taken over by the American Indian Movement (AIM) and their supporters. Across the country we all faced questions about social justice, sovereignty, and Indigenous rights. The Ongweoweh, or "real human beings," come in many shades of brown, and the colors in the painting signify that. I equated the plant, the sand burr, with our issues with the federal government—painful to touch. It is a past the federal government doesn't want to talk about. And now states are trying to ban teaching a true history of America. The issues are thorny. —G.P.J.

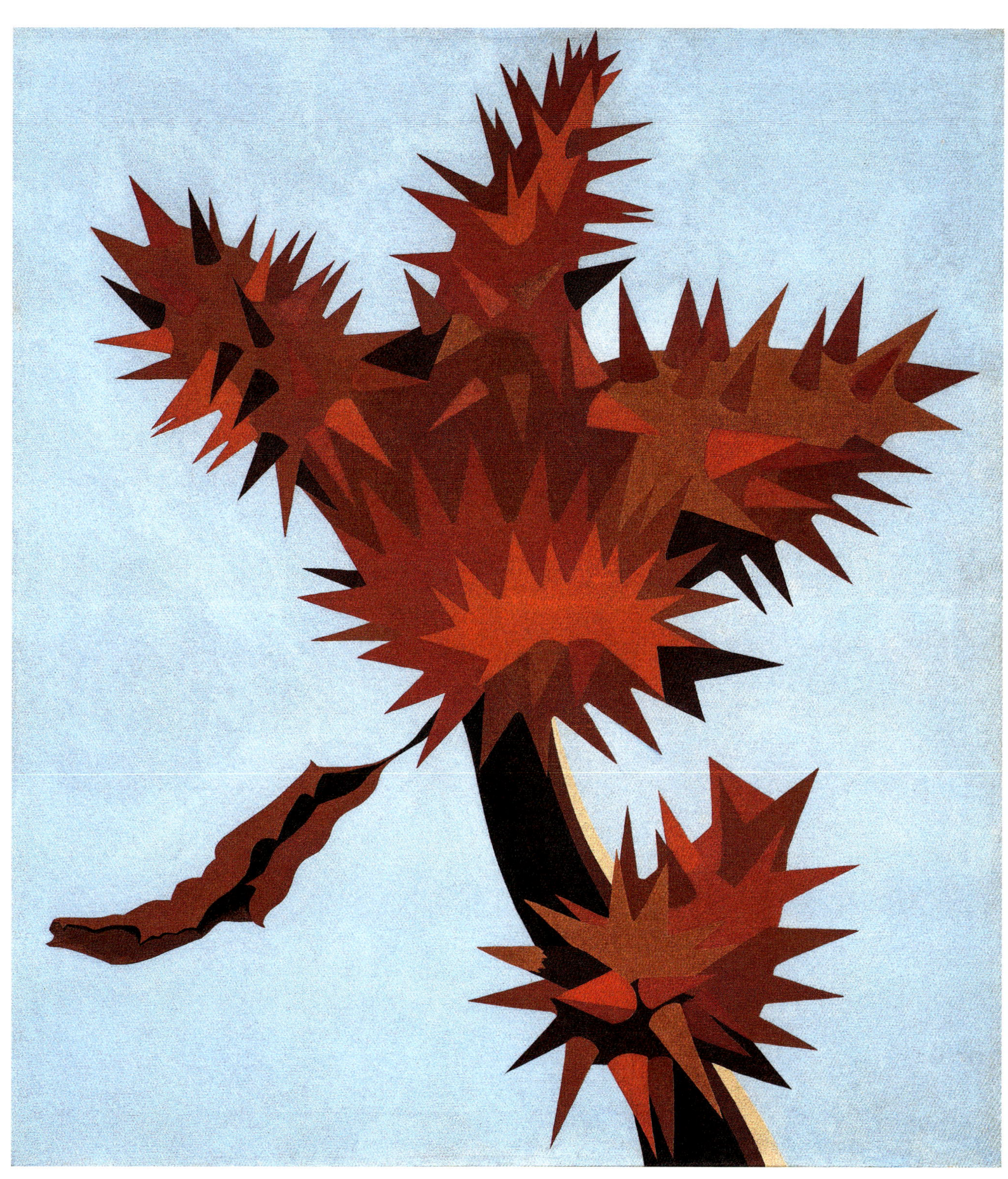

Emily Johnson

Yup'ik Nation (b. 1976)

inbetween Kwimiak, blue, 2020
Video

Intimacy became no longer about touch, but rather of separation, in-betweeness; they discovered the dark matter in between reaching out hands. And this in-between dark matter became the space that helped us find one another. —E.J. and Kai Recollet, 2020

This is a dance that is listened to and viewed through four images. They are slow, the images. But, then again, we are traversing more than a hundred years. I am often teleporting the past to the present in what I make. And we are very suddenly in an in-between. I welcome you to listen. To imagine with me a way to emerge and begin again and to view as you wish—with intense looking, or restful witnessing. —E.J.

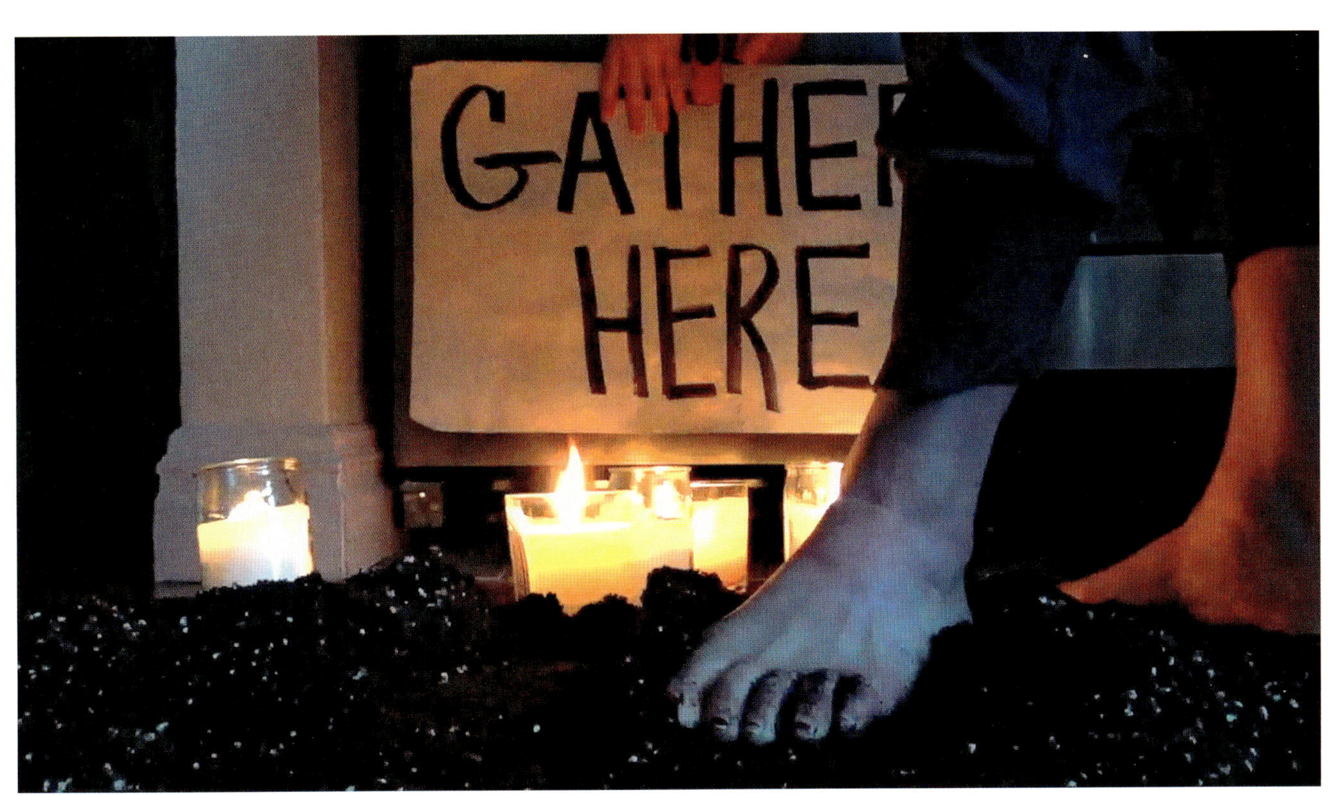
GATHER
HERE

George Longfish

Seneca and Tuscarora (b. 1942)

Long Fish, 1985
Acrylic

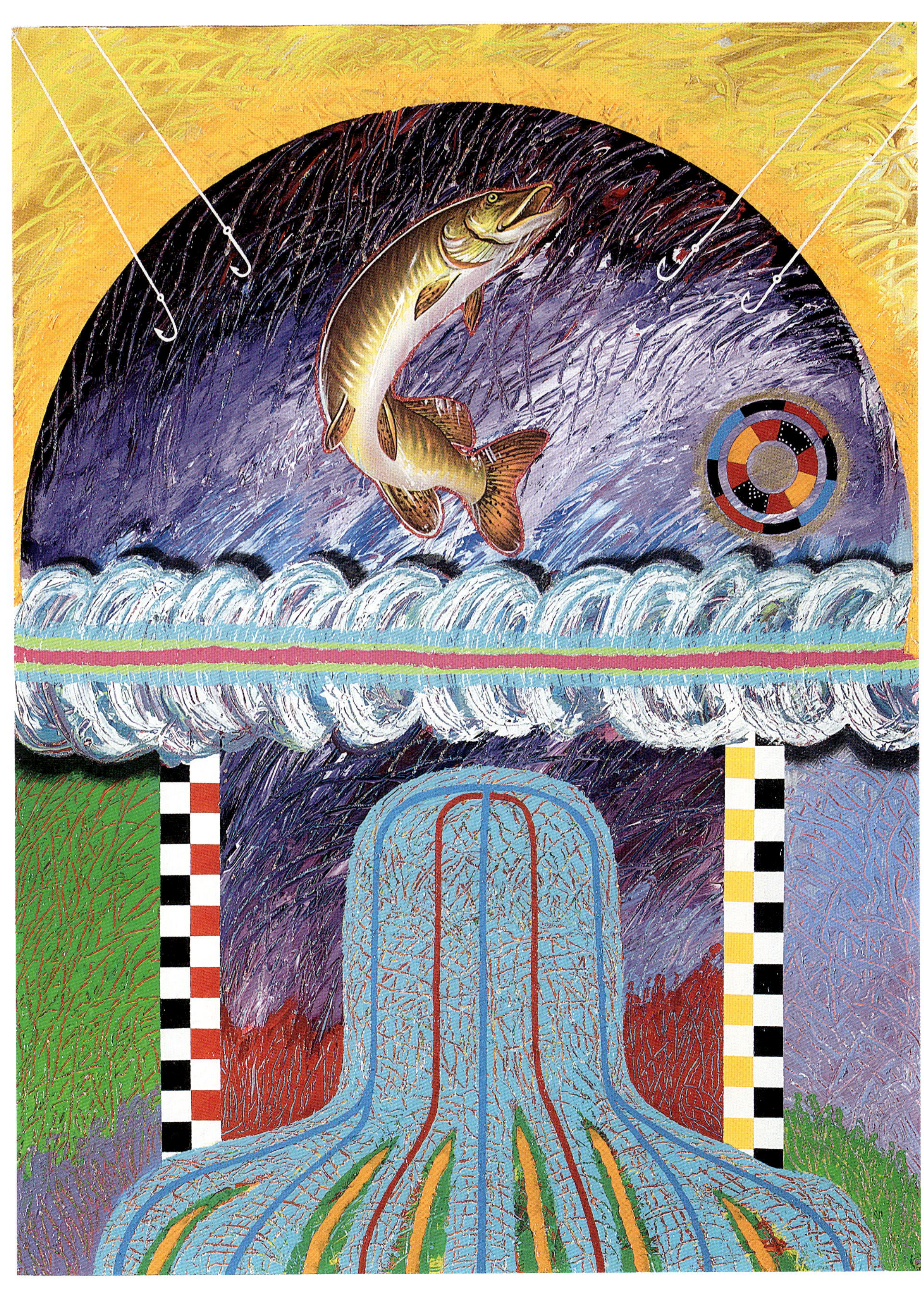

Judith Lowry

Hammawi Band Pit River/Mountain Maidu/Washo/
Scots-Irish Cultures (b. 1948)

Medicine Man, 1994
Acrylic on canvas

Judith Lowry prefers to "critique Native culture from within . . . because I believe it is good for the health of the culture." In *Medicine Man*, Lowry depicts a kind of reverse feminist painting about the sexual objectification of Indian men. It also confronts the internal issues of tribal censorship and self-censorship. Inspired by Jean Dominique Ingres's *Jupiter and Thetis* (1811), Lowry's version transforms Thetis into a White, blonde, New Ager, gazing up at a stereotyped Native American man. Lowry intended *Medicine Man* to "reveal aspects of illusion and hypocrisy that occur in both Native and non-Native societies. We as Native people need to resist the allure of false worship of our marketed image and critique ourselves honestly. . . . Otherwise, we may survive only as two-dimensional, cartoonlike parodies of our ancestors!" —Lucy R. Lippard

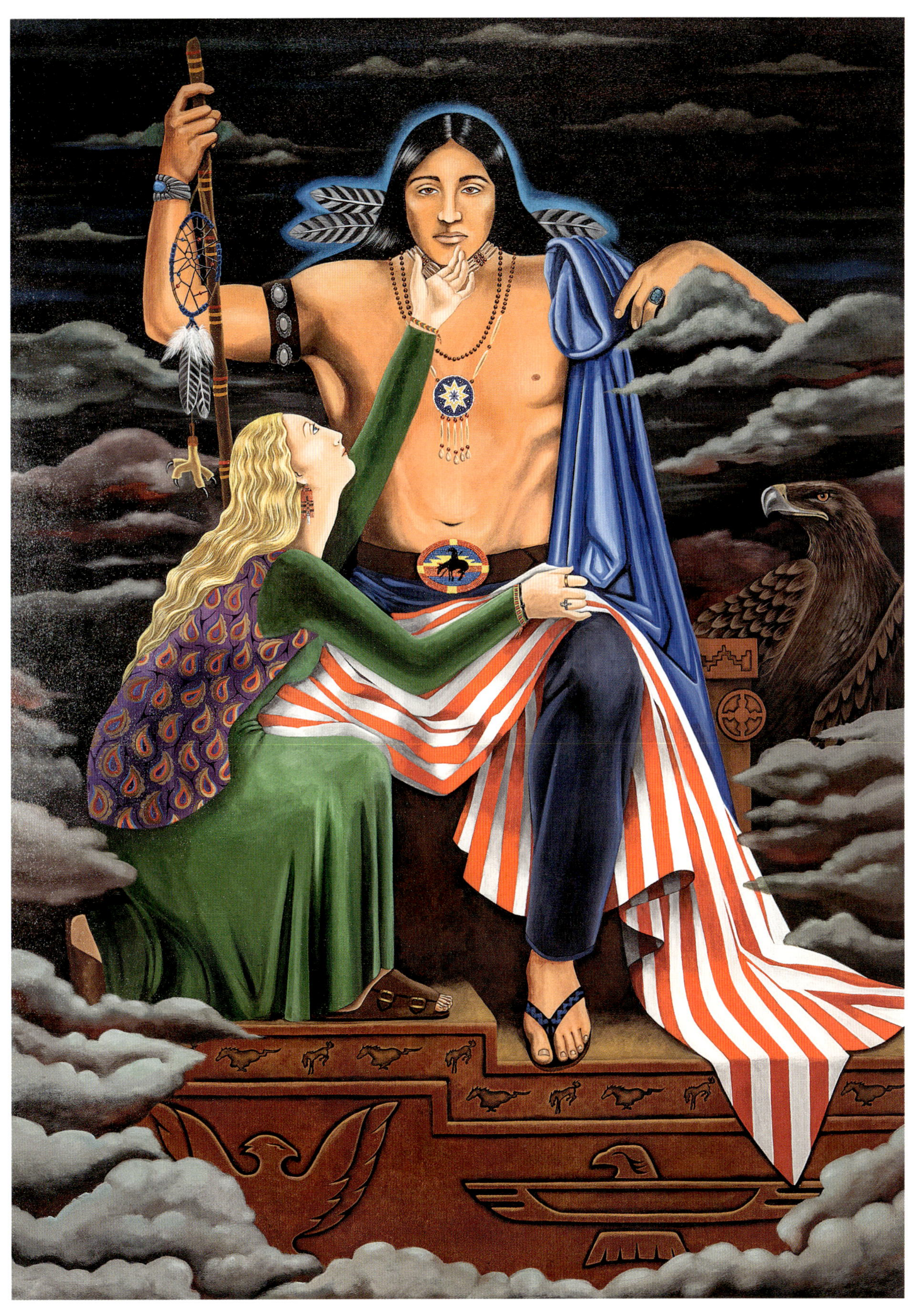

Mario Martinez

Enrolled Member of the Pascua Yaqui Tribe of Arizona
(b. 1953)

Native Modernist Reflection, 2021
Prismacolor and pastel on paper

I have always admired the New York School and abstract expressionists. In my practice, I try to channel the energy of works by Gorky and de Kooning. At the same time that I have these proximal influences, I see myself as part of a much older, more expansive tradition—one in which the Western painting tradition forms just a small part. While my works avoid overt Yaqui references, they do incorporate our traditions, concepts, and worldviews. Yaqui culture has a deep reverence for the natural world, and that reverence always finds its way into my work. Branching forms and cascading colors evoke natural elements like sunsets and water. Indigenous patterns and materials like lace and glitter make subtle references to Yaqui ceremonies. —M.M.

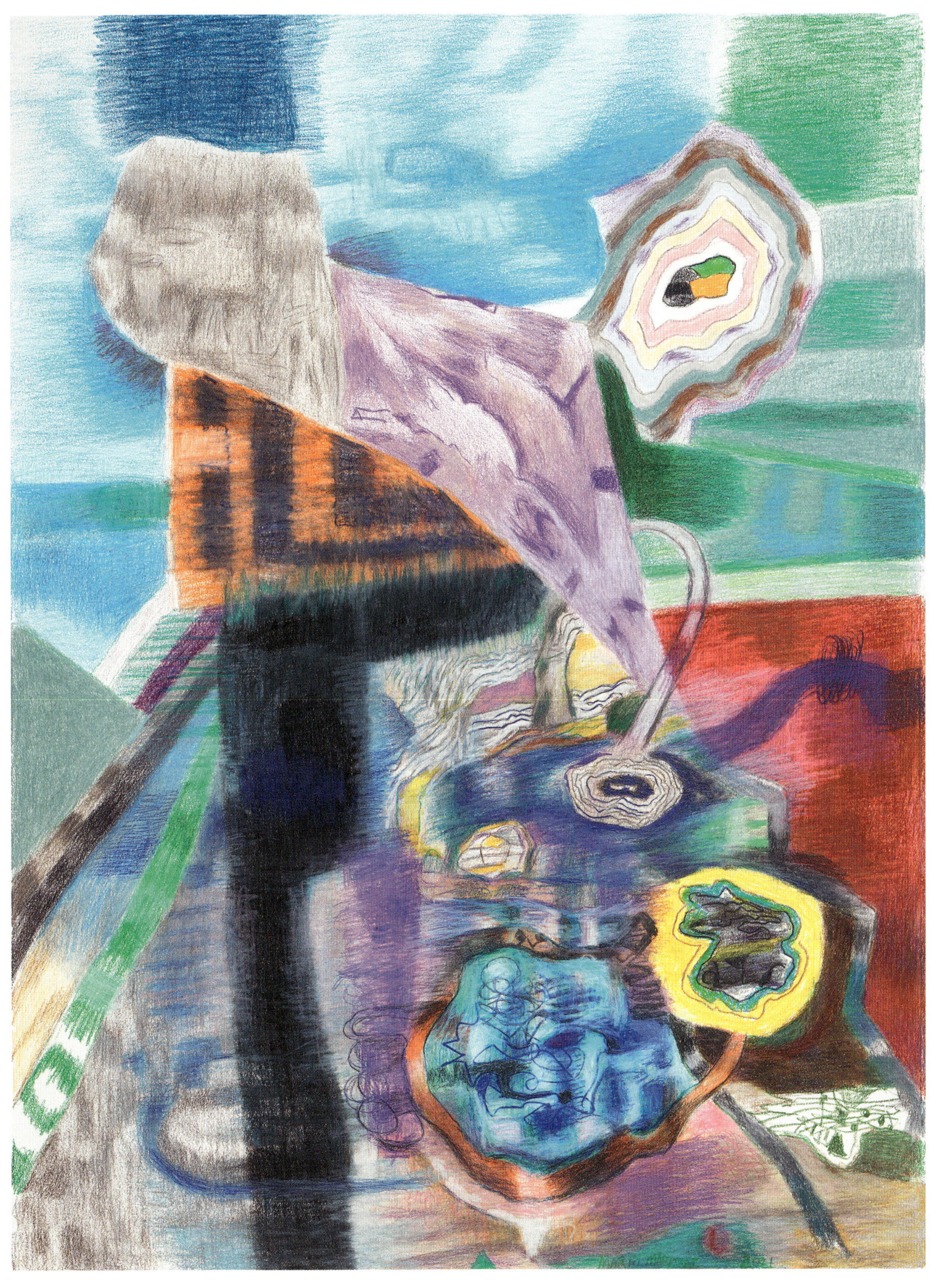

Da-ka-xeen Mehner

Tlingit, Nisga'a (b. 1970)

The Artist with His Thoughts, 2007
Digital photograph

Going through a museum's archive online, I stumbled across a description of an image of a Tlingit man named Da-yuk-hene, which is almost certainly a phonetic variation of my name, Da-ka-xeen. This image was taken by Case & Draper in Juneau, Alaska, in 1906 and is a perfect example of the constructed identity of Native-ness through the lens of the "other." I feel a need to deconstruct the images of the past. Reinterpreting the image, I reconstruct the pose but with the tools I use on a daily basis: the camera I received from my uncle, the adze I made for myself, and the jacket, a gift from my mother for my wedding day. I change the text to reflect my presence in the reinterpreted image. By mirroring this image, I attempt to reflect both the truth and fiction of this history. By reversing the archival image, I attempt to reverse the history constructed about Native peoples. —D.M.

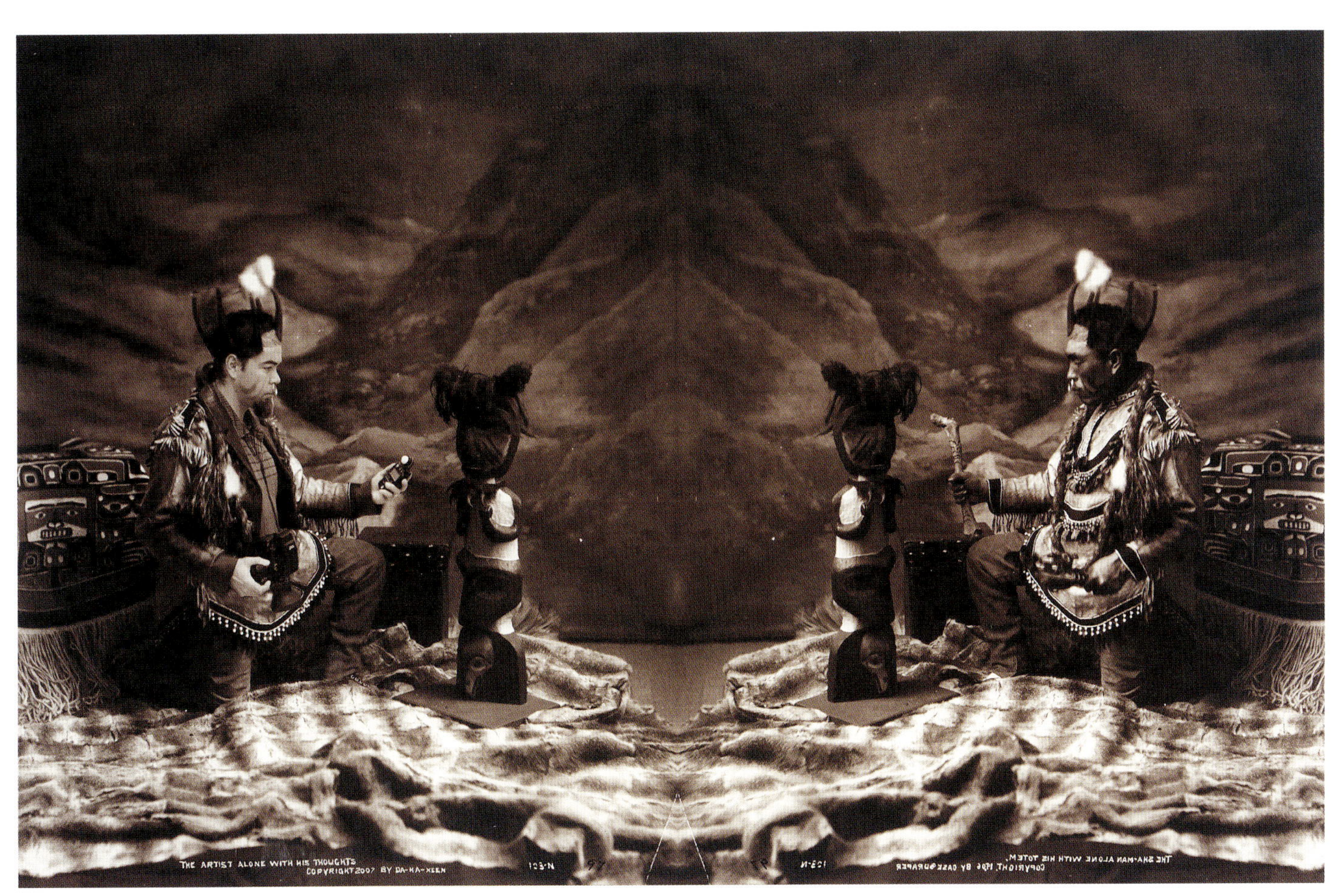
THE ARTIST ALONE WITH HIS THOUGHTS
COPYRIGHT 2007 BY DA-KA-XEEN
103-N

Alan Michelson

Mohawk Member of the Six Nations of the Grand River (b. 1953)

Pehin Hanska Ktpei (They Killed Longhair), 2021
Silent video and wool trade blanket

Pehin Hanska Ktpei (They Killed Longhair) is a silent, multimedia installation consisting of edited archival film projected onto a vintage wool trade blanket. The found footage depicts Indigenous veterans of the Battle of the Greasy Grass (1876), a.k.a. Custer's Last Stand, parading on horseback at a commemoration with the United States Army on the battle's fiftieth anniversary, in 1926. To honor them and their victorious resistance in defense of their people and land, I looped the remarkable footage into a continuously rotating procession of riding warriors that references the Winter Count, the pictographic calendar of the Plains nations often painted on buffalo hide or fabric. I titled the work after the Lakota entry for the 1876 Winter Count. —A.M.

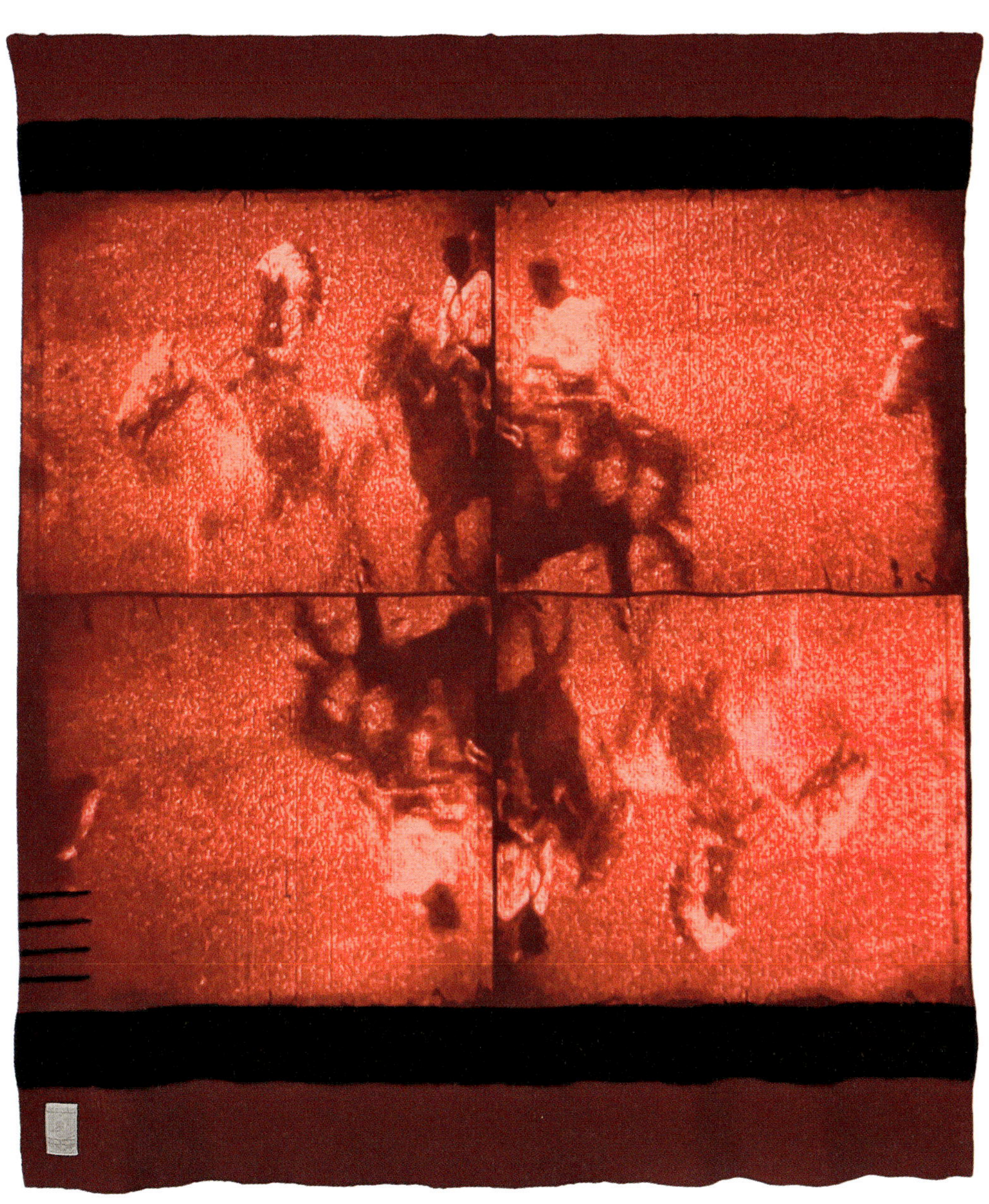

Native Art Department International (NADI)

Wasauksing First Nation and Chiricahua Apache Tribe/Mexican

Double Shift, 2018
Acrylic paint on custom canvas clothing

Maria Hupfield (Wasauksing First Nation) and Jason Lujan (Chiricahua Apache Tribe/Mexican), as Native Art Department International, created a reversible garment to perform in. It was sewn by Jason's mother, in Texas, at his request, and later one-side painted in Brooklyn, New York. The intention is to use the garment to highlight action and presence directed at creating manifestations of possibilities of cooperation in the context of Indigeneity. When not in use, its dormant state suggests art as a catalyst for reimagining our future and our (Native) communities. —NADI

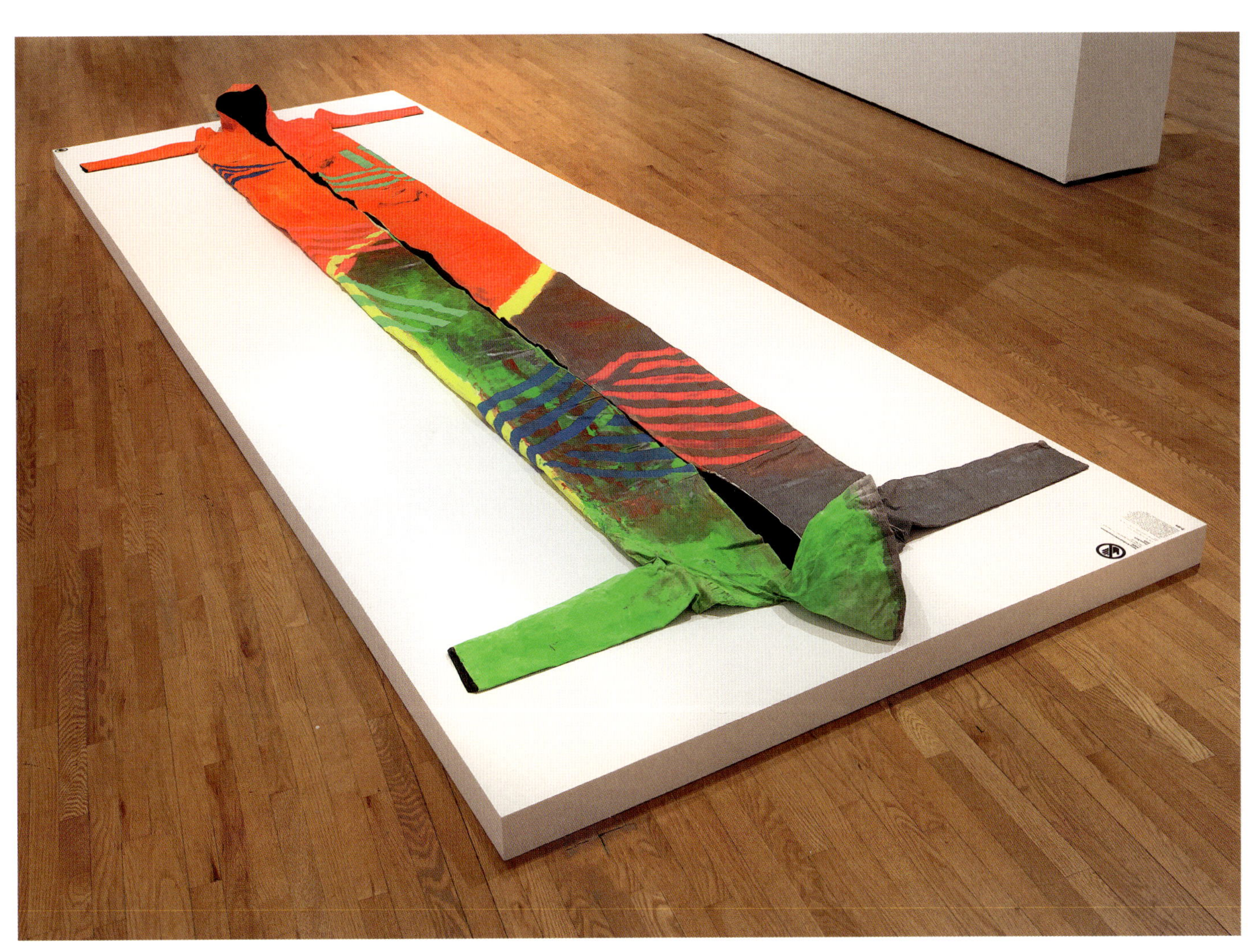

Grace Rosario Perkins

Diné/Akimel O'odham (b. 1986)

Mom Jokes to Make Her Hair Curly Like a Sheep, 2022
Acrylic, spray paint, rose petals, crushed mirror, and Xerox on canvas

This painting's title refers to a memory. It combines an enlarged family photograph of my mother in the front yard of our home, taken sometime in the 1970s, many years before I was born. She holds her cat in front of her face and the sense of anonymity that is created is what is appealing. While to anybody else she could be anyone and the photograph could be from anywhere, to me she is someone in a new place, a new home with a rosebush that still stands forty years later. Although the rosebush is much larger now, the yard is different, run-down, overgrown, or developed, and everyone has left the house. Roses are heart medicine, mirrors are protective, and webs are homes, and these symbols are rotated like letters in an alphabet. Beside these I let my young mother peek out and hold space. —G.R.P.

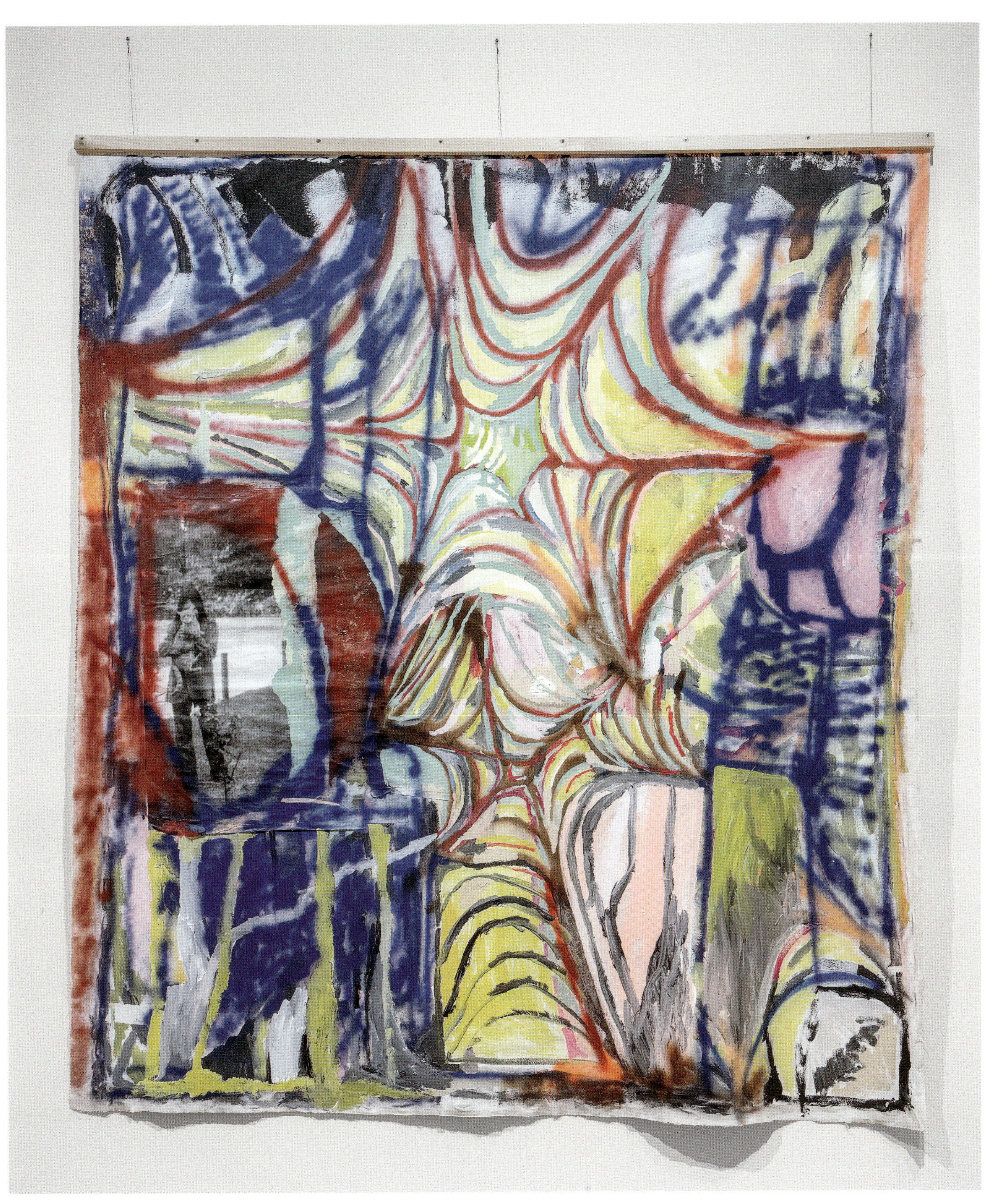

Cara Romero

Chemehuevi (b. 1977)

Arla Lucia, 2019
Photograph

The figure of a Native American woman as a superhero, modeled after Wonder Woman, stands boldly and proudly in this image. She wears the recognizable shorts, corset, and lasso of the comic character, but also moccasins, a beaded panel and earrings, braids, and a feather.

The title refers to her character or image as a beacon; it is a blend of the model's name, Arla Marquez (Seneca-Cayuga/Shoshone-Bannock/Blackfoot), and the name Lucia, which means light. —C.R.

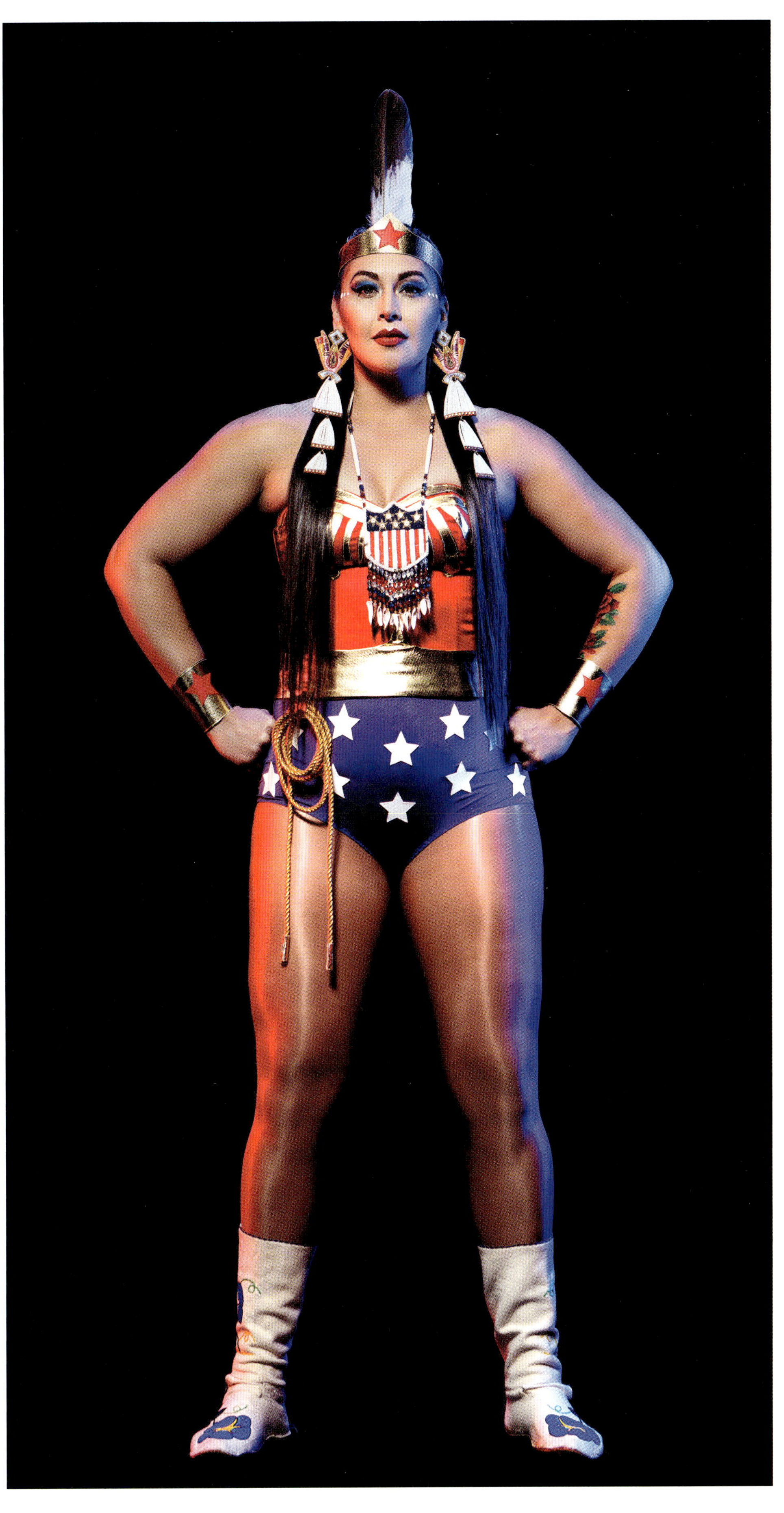

Cara Romero

Chemehuevi [b. 1977]

Starlight, Starbright, 2023
Archival pigment photograph

As a kid, roller-skating was a significant part of my life and I practiced competitively in freestyle and dance. I'm always deeply interested in challenging preconceived notions about who we are and how we are defined as Native people and artists. The truth is, we have a thousand stories about our experiences, our interests, our humor. We love hip-hop, metal, skateboarding, and sports, yet we are often cast into what I call "The One-Story Narrative" as a monolithic culture, stoic and mystic. While many of us are practicing spiritual peoples and purveyors of culture and lifeways, we are also multidimensional human beings. In a whimsical, playful bringing together of women, we styled ourselves to Indigenize the roller derby look, and I wanted there to be a Renaissance style of "conversazione silenzio" in the mayhem [a nod to Kent Monkman]. —C.R.

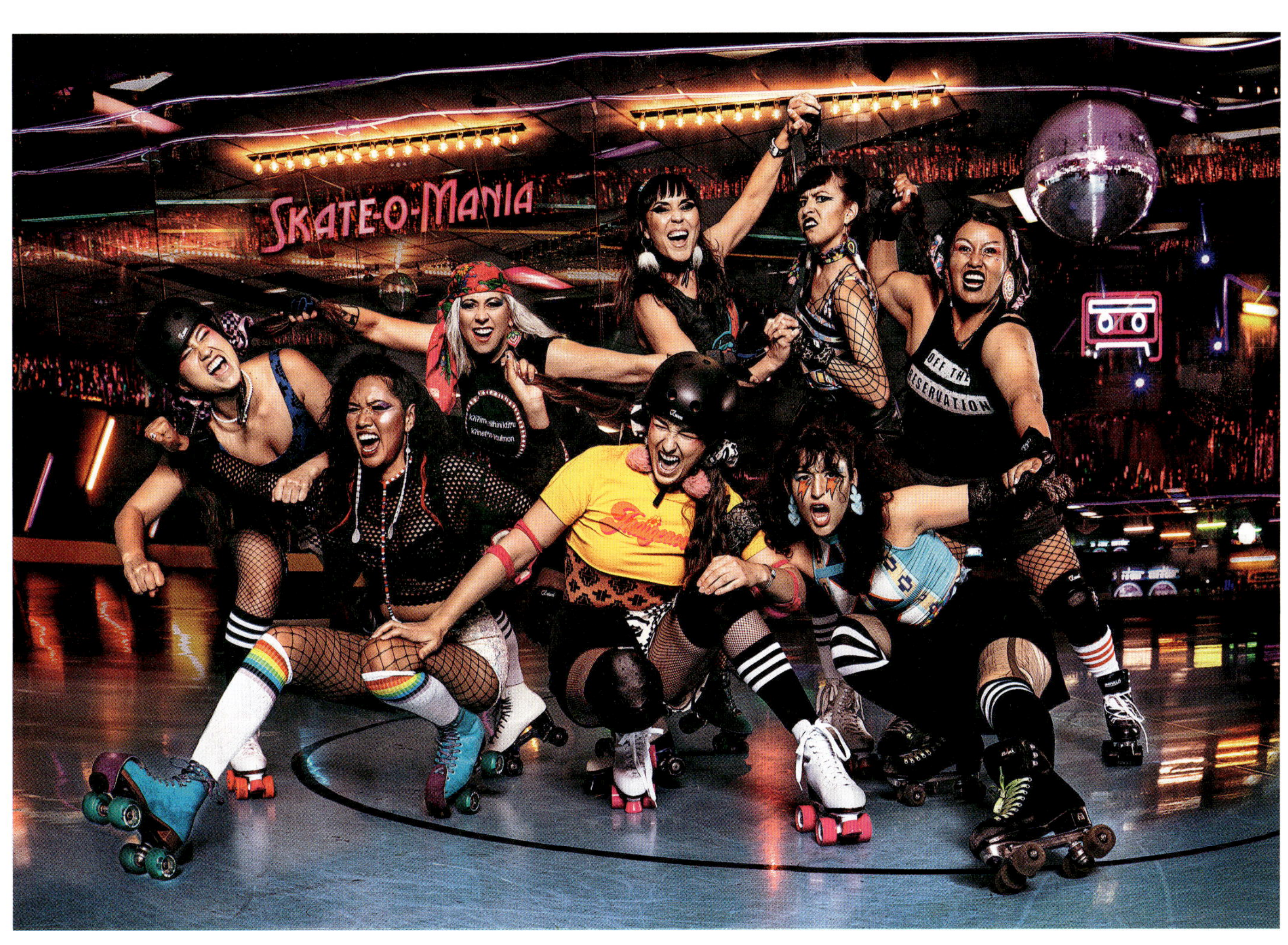
SKATE-O-MANIA
OFF THE
RESERVATION

Ryan Singer

Diné [Navajo] (b. 1973)

The Vendor, 2014
Acrylic on canvas

The main subject in this painting is the elderly Diné [Navajo] woman vendor walking with a cooler and carrying her purse. I used a black-and-white photo by my friend Albert Sloan as a reference for this piece. I wanted to show a bit of tension between the vivid colors versus the idea of an elderly woman working to support herself and her family. The concept of food is significant in Diné culture. Being a Diné person, I can tell those burritos she's selling are delicious. While there is a socioeconomic commentary underlying the piece, there is also an elegant resilience displayed by the woman as she works while the people in the background enjoy the parade. —R.S.

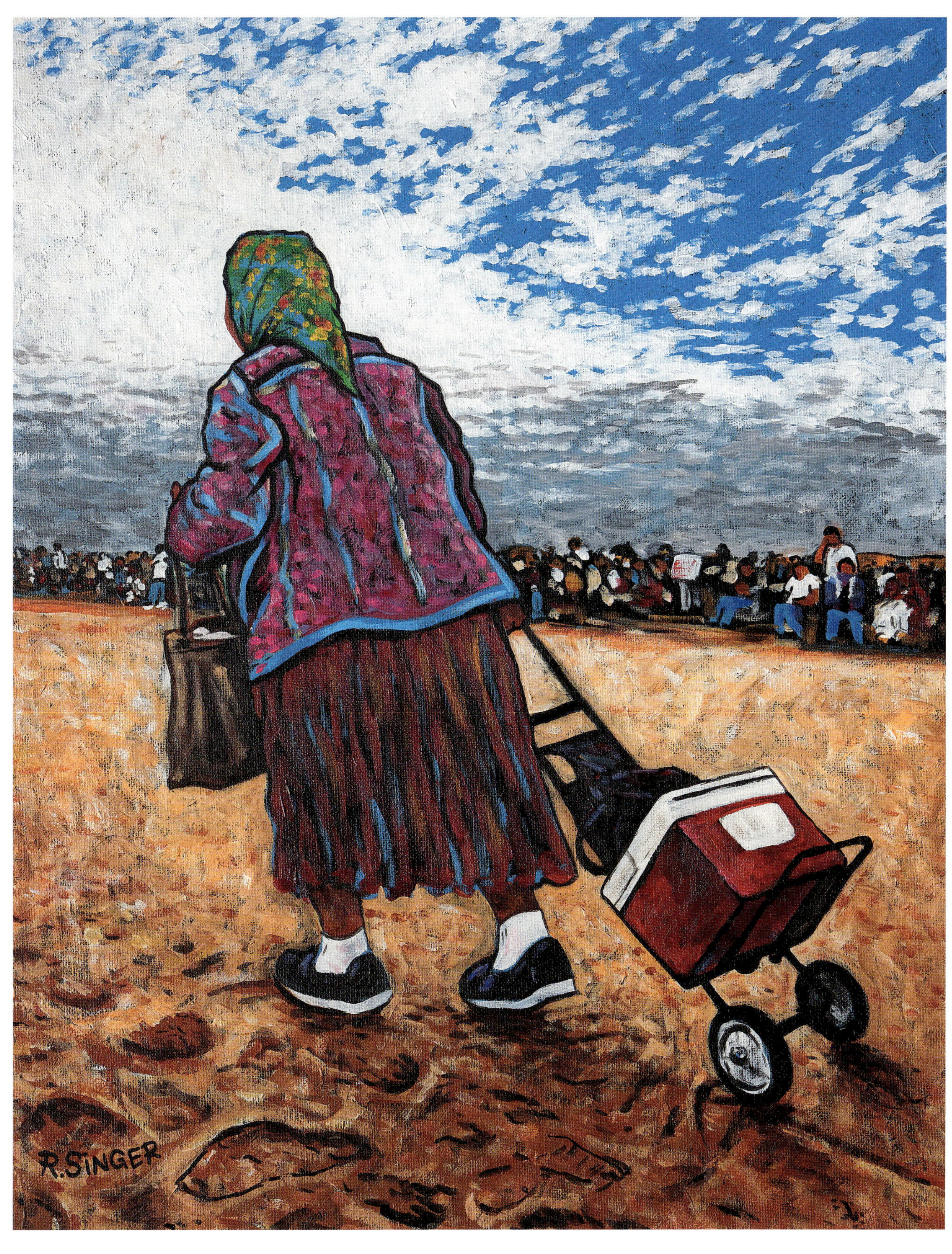
R. SINGER

Tyrrell Tapaha

Diné [b. 1999]

Adá Nítsíjíkees: Think for Yourself, 2022
Hand and commercial vegetal-dyed
Navajo Churro alpaca

Diné textiles have always been used for documentation. In this piece, the chaos in the lower portion is like the "TV-static" that comes with the overstimulation of our time. I incorporated the female and male lightning designs to pay homage to my community and my family. The middle portion is a glimpse of the roots in my life. To the left is my great-grandmother Mary Kady Clah, the third generation that allowed me to learn from our family's practice. To the right is my other great-grandmother, Fannie Yazziee, a renowned weaver and livestock holder. The weaving also expresses the vulnerability that I don't often give myself time to assess—it lived and breathed through every moment of what I was navigating. I wrapped all of this up with the Diné philosophy of "Ádá Nítsíjíkees," which is a deeper way of saying, "Think for yourself." —T.T.

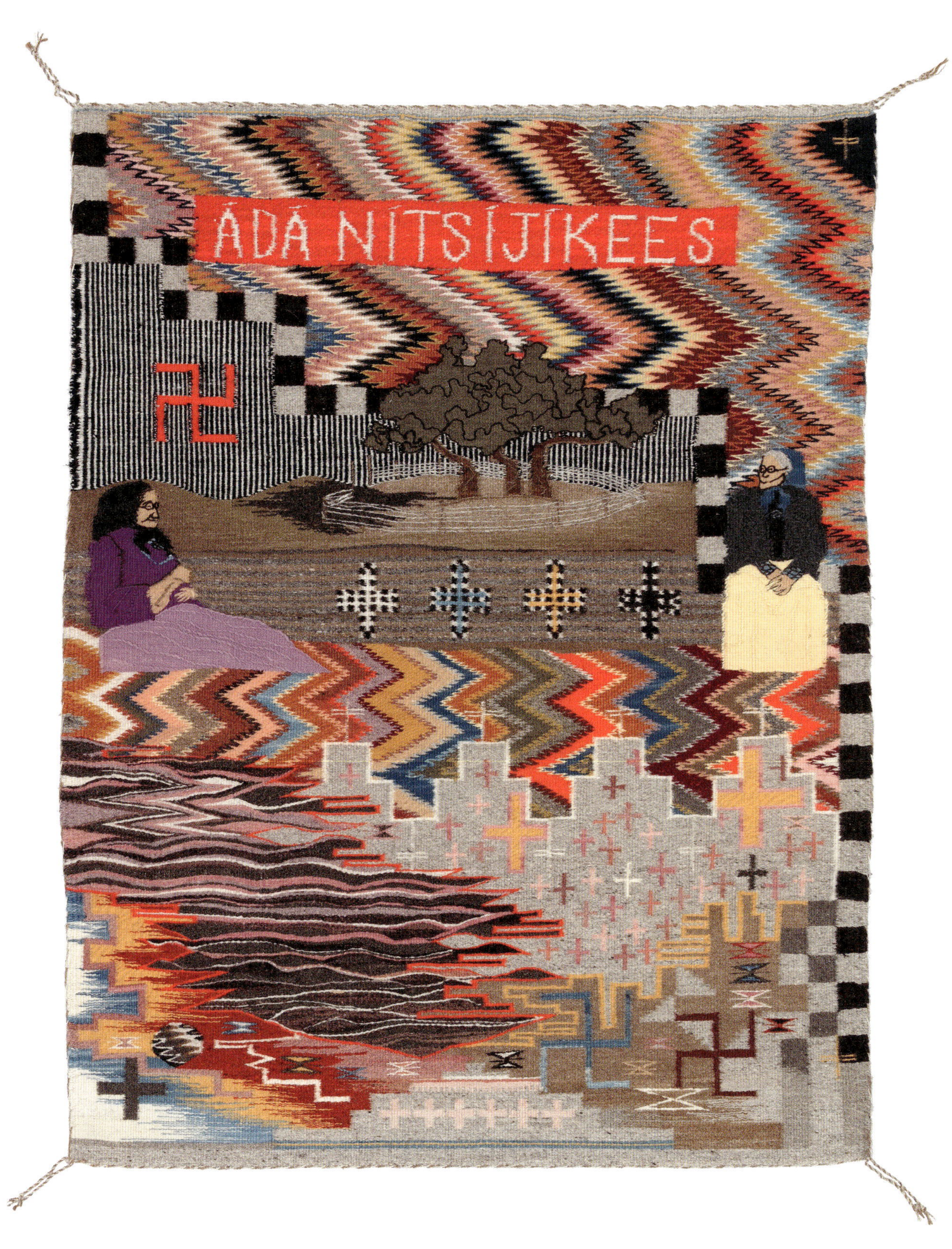
ÁDÁ NÍTSÍJÍKEES

Hulleah J. Tsinhnahjinnie

Taskigi/Diné (b. 1954)

Anticipation, 2006
Hand-pieced photo collage on paper

Anticipation

The spectrum of Anticipation.
Before physical, visual, colonial contact, change was anticipated.
The reverberation of genocidal intent proceeded the chaos of greed.

Anticipation of the most terrible of times.

Not drowned in the despair was the
Anticipated return of Love, Land, Language, and Beauty. —H.J.T.

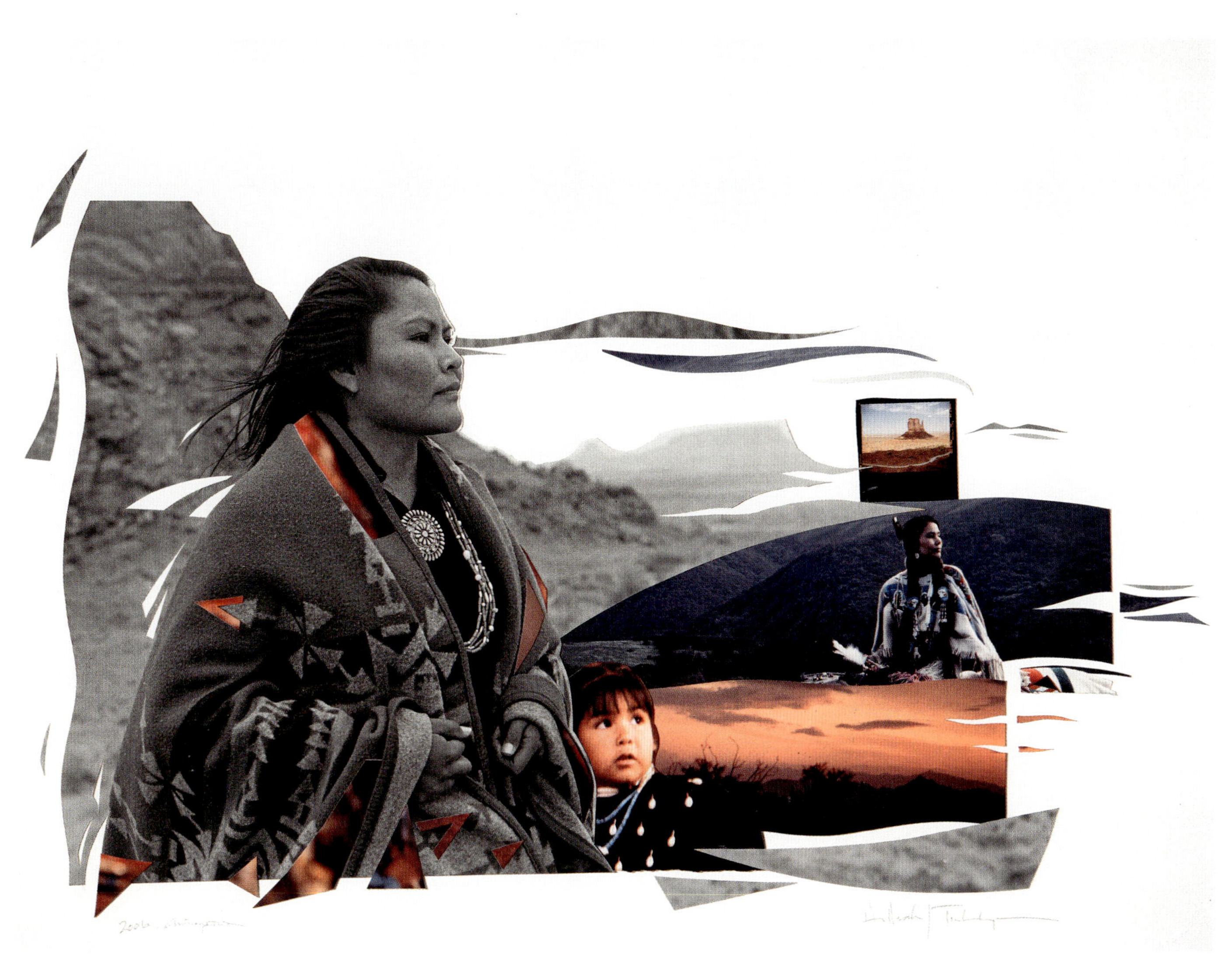

Jeffrey Veregge

Port Gamble Band of S'Klallam Tribe
(1974–2024)

Last Son, 2019
Digital print

My work is a reflection of a lifetime love affair with comic books, toys, TV, and film. I take my passions and blend them with my Native perspective, artistic background, and the desire to simply be me. Basically, I am just trying to have fun and get back to that kid that went to art school to begin with, wanting to create artwork that I wanted to see and make just for the hell of it. —J.V.

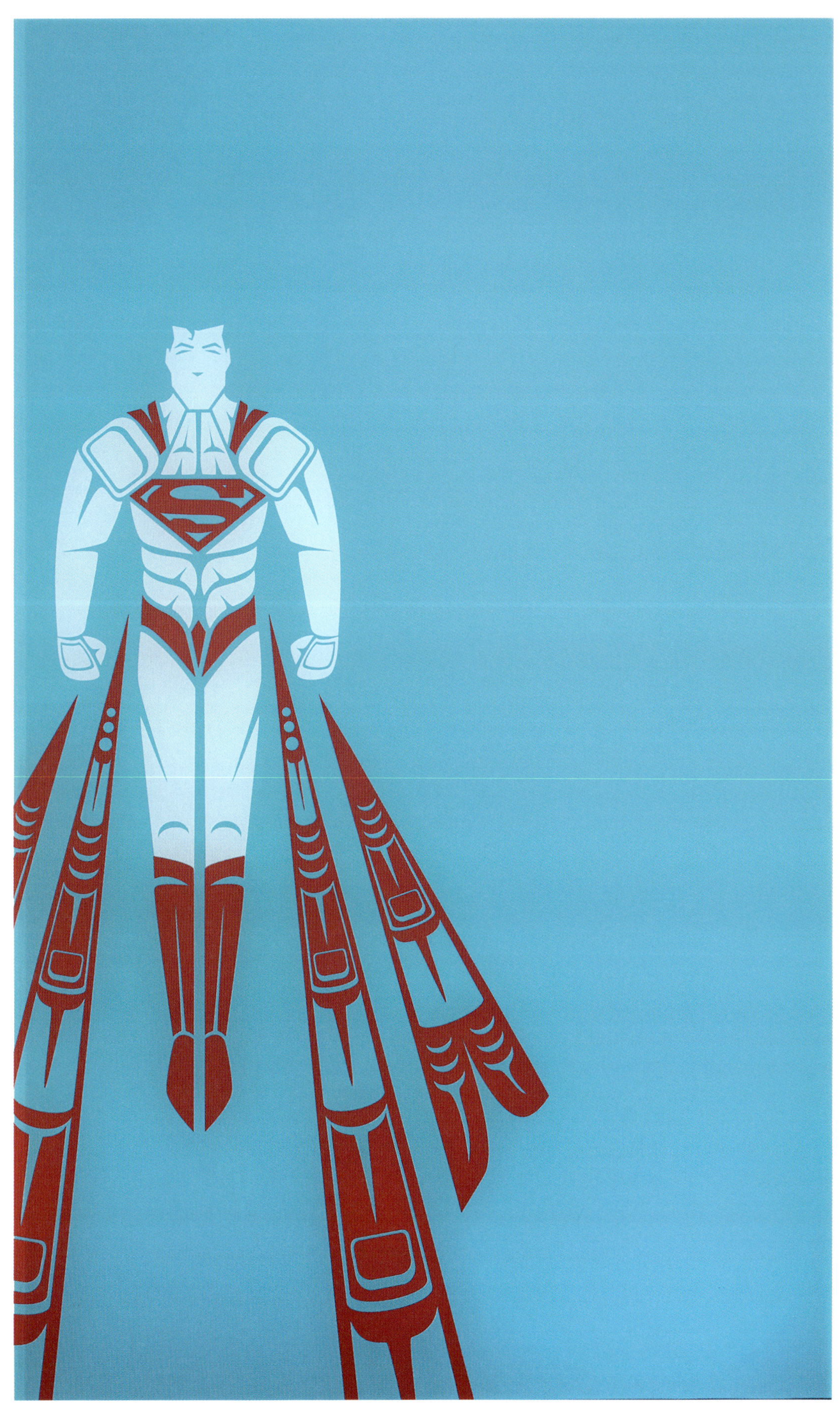

Star WallowingBull

Ojibwe/Arapaho (b. 1973)

Arapaho Man with Traditional Design, 2004
Colored pencil on paper

This drawing is an earlier work, from when I was starting out my art career. It refers to my identity as an Ojibwe and Arapaho person. The figure you see in this drawing is an Arapaho man from Wyoming, in the Wind River area, where my mother lived. I put an Ojibwe border around the figure, bringing in my mother's and my father's cultural identities to represent my own identity. At the time I made this work I was exploring different Native American groups and tribes. I would take portraits of Natives from history and redraw them—just exploring my own identity through my work. Nowadays, my work has changed: When I look at Native Americans in history books, I can see making them into robots now. It feels like I made a shift from making traditional work to making futuristic traditional work. —S.W.

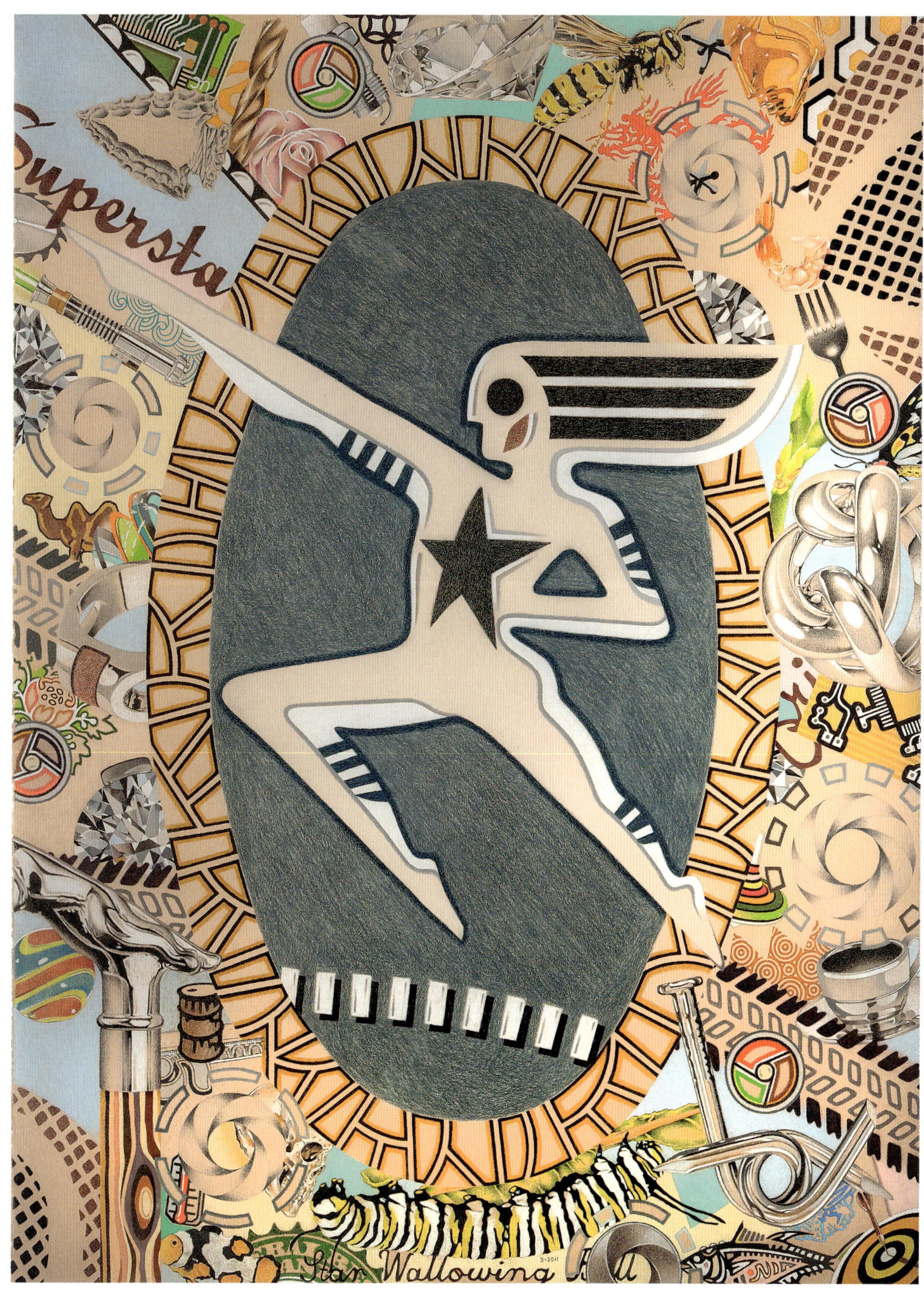

Holly Wilson

Enrolled Member of the Delaware Nation, Lenape and Descendant of the Delaware Tribe of Indians (b. 1968)

Red, 2015
Photograph

Red is my daughter; she wanted to be Deadpool, a fast-talking superhero, though at the time she was not much of a talker. In that moment I wondered how she will be seen or heard as she grows in our current world. What mask will she have to wear to be considered equal? As children, we make and wear masks to become anything we want or need to be. We can do anything in them, from being a superhero to a bird in flight. As adults, the layers and meaning of masks deepen and grow. They are a way to represent the different personas that we need or desire to be in life. Masks are an identity that one can live through or hide behind. —H.W.

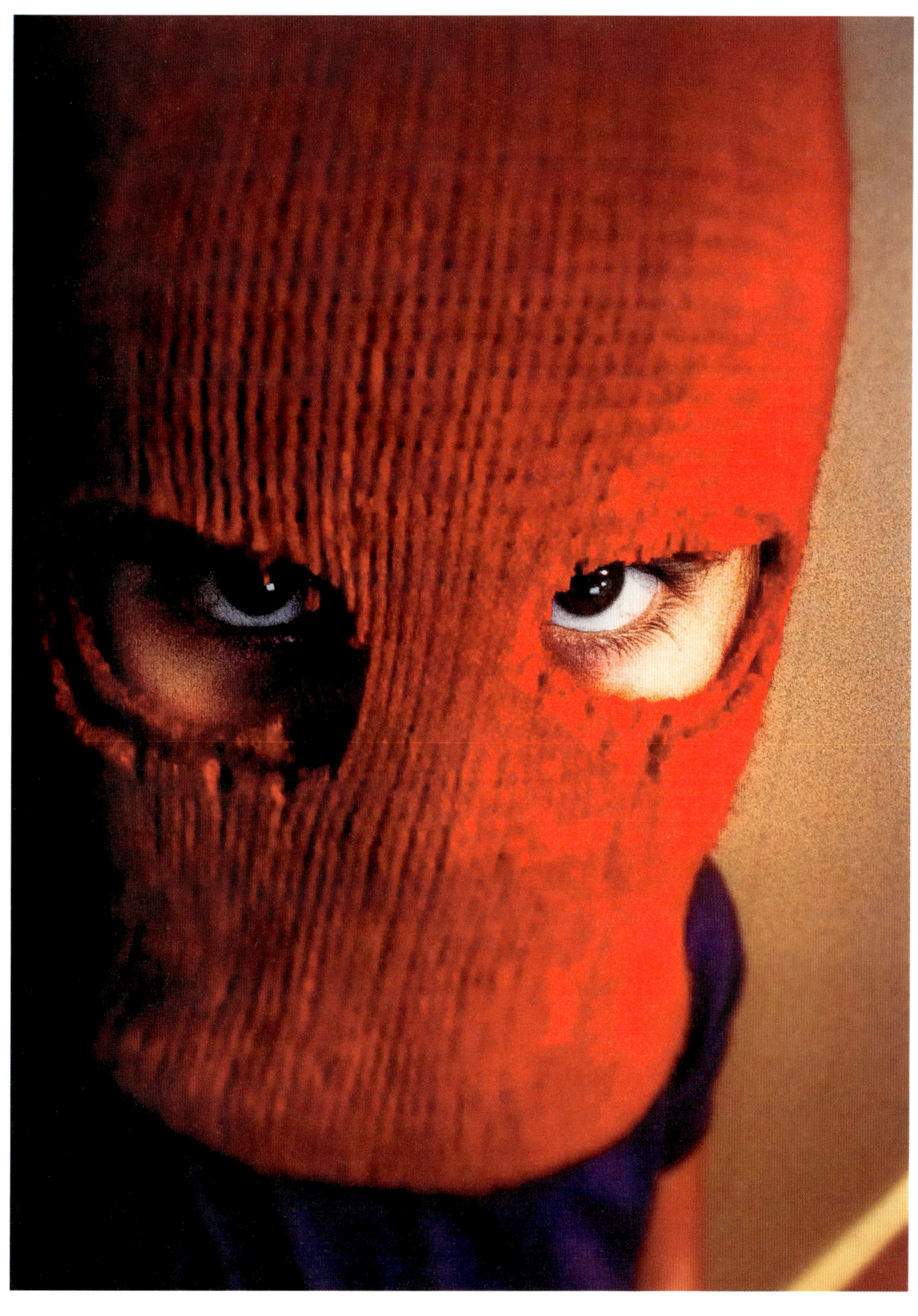

Will Wilson

Diné (b. 1969)

Self-Portrait—DAM, 2013
Tintype

Self-Portrait—DAM was created during an artist residency at the Denver Art Museum (DAM) in 2013. It is part of the Critical Photographic Exchange (CIPX) project, a challenge to Edward S. Curtis's oeuvre, which proposes "to create a body of photographic inquiry that will stimulate a critical dialogue and reflection around the historic and contemporary 'photographic exchange' as it pertains to Native Americans." My aim is to convene Indigenous artists, art professionals, and government leaders, as well as the general public, to engage in the performative ritual that is the studio portrait. This experience will be intensified and refined by the use of large format (8 × 10 inch) wet plate collodion studio photography. This beautifully alchemic photographic process dramatically contributed to our collective understanding of Native American people and, in so doing, our American identity. —W.W.

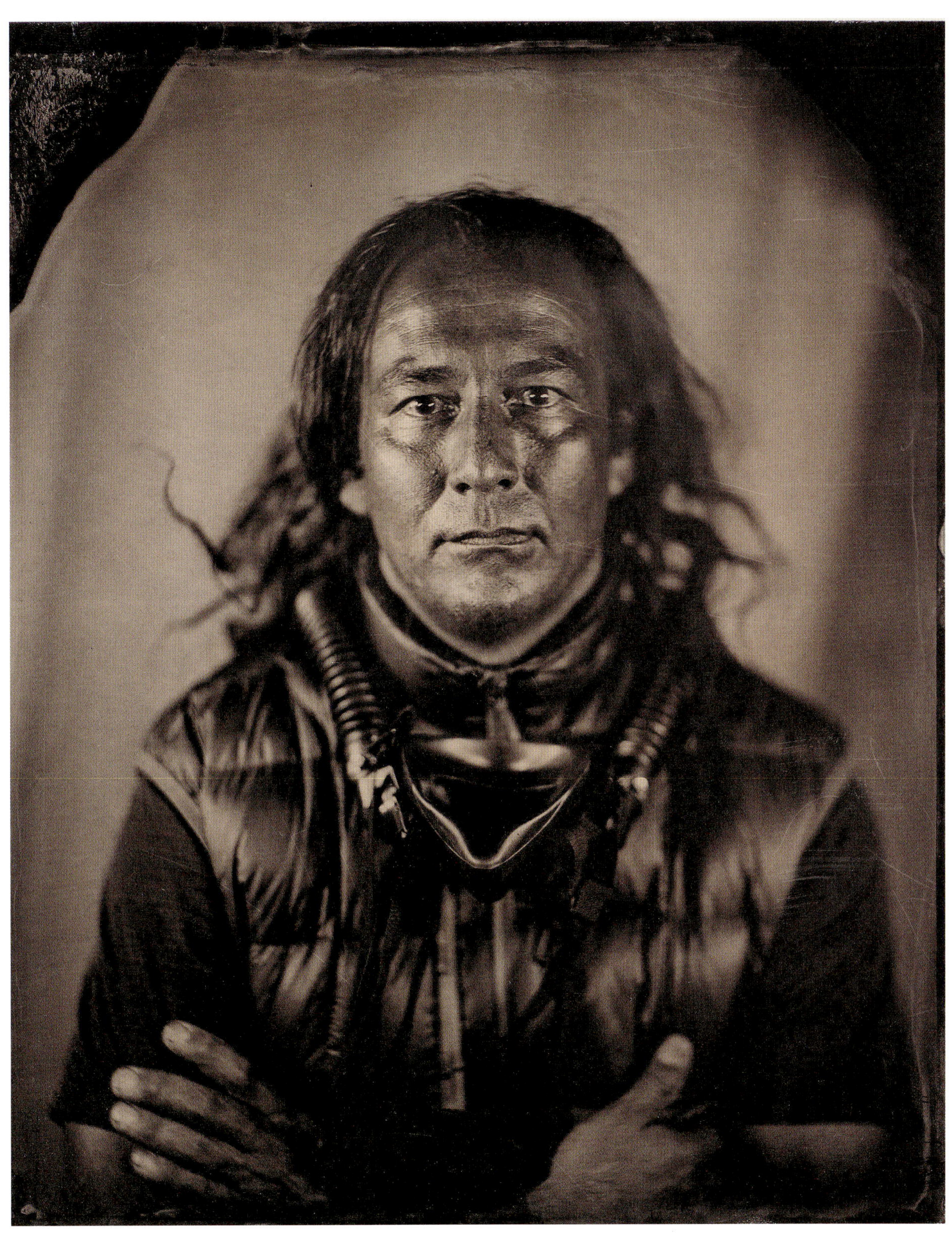

Will Wilson

Diné [b. 1969]

How the West Is One, 2012
Pigment print diptych

How the West Is One, part of the Critical Photographic Exchange [CIPX] project, was created for a show at SITE SANTA FE, in Santa Fe, New Mexico, and was part of their SITE LAB 4 initiative, where I worked with students from the New Mexico School for the Arts to develop different personae that interrogated the "Myth of the West." These "photographic personae" critically engage with New Mexican myths and stereotypes and reflect on the students' own self-representations as contemporary young New Mexicans with complex relationships to the region's history, geography, and culture. —W.W.

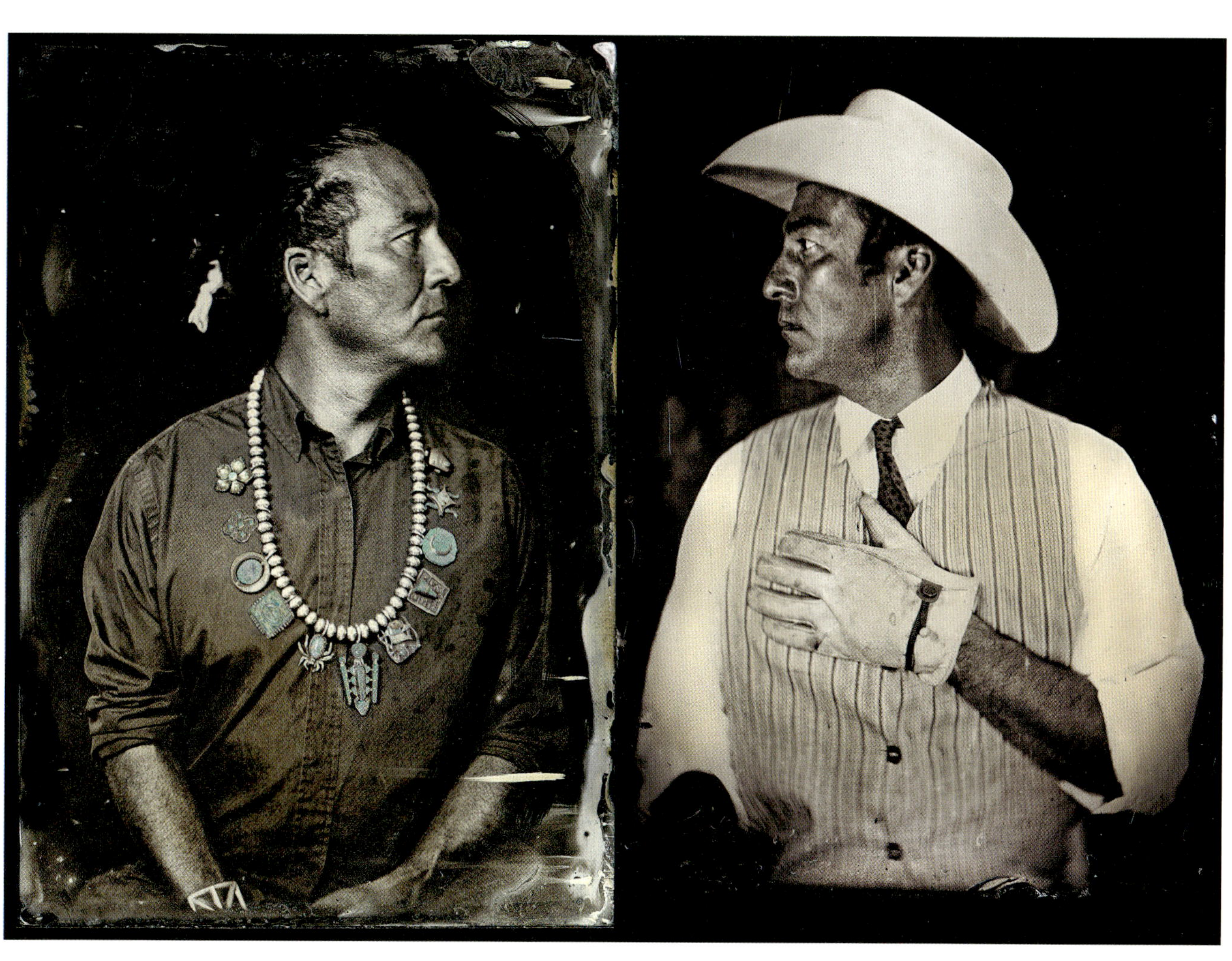

Natives of the Americas live in a holistic world without a horizon line. We are partners with the natural world; it is our kin.
—Jaune Quick-to-See Smith

Native American artists' work is often grounded in their relationship to their homelands and regularly explores themes of land, land rights, and treaties with the federal government. For Indigenous peoples, the natural and spiritual worlds are combined. People indigenous to the land are part of the sacred, from the cosmic dust that sustains the earth to their bodies blending with the ancestors and all forms of life. Artworks related to land pay homage to Mother Earth and distinct tribal cosmologies and remind viewers that we all are on Native land.

LAND

George Alexander

Muscogee (Creek) (b. 1990)

Urban #2, 2021
Acrylic on canvas

In *Urban #2*, a bison stands at a crossroads flanked by telephone poles and trees, symbolizing the complex interplay between tradition and modernity, rural and urban landscapes, and the evolving nature of cultural identity. This visual metaphor invites viewers to reflect on how we, like this bison, stand at the intersection of multiple worlds—honoring our past while embracing the present and future. It acknowledges that whether one grows up immersed in traditional culture or in an urban setting, their experience is equally valid and important to the ongoing story of Native American identity. —G.A.

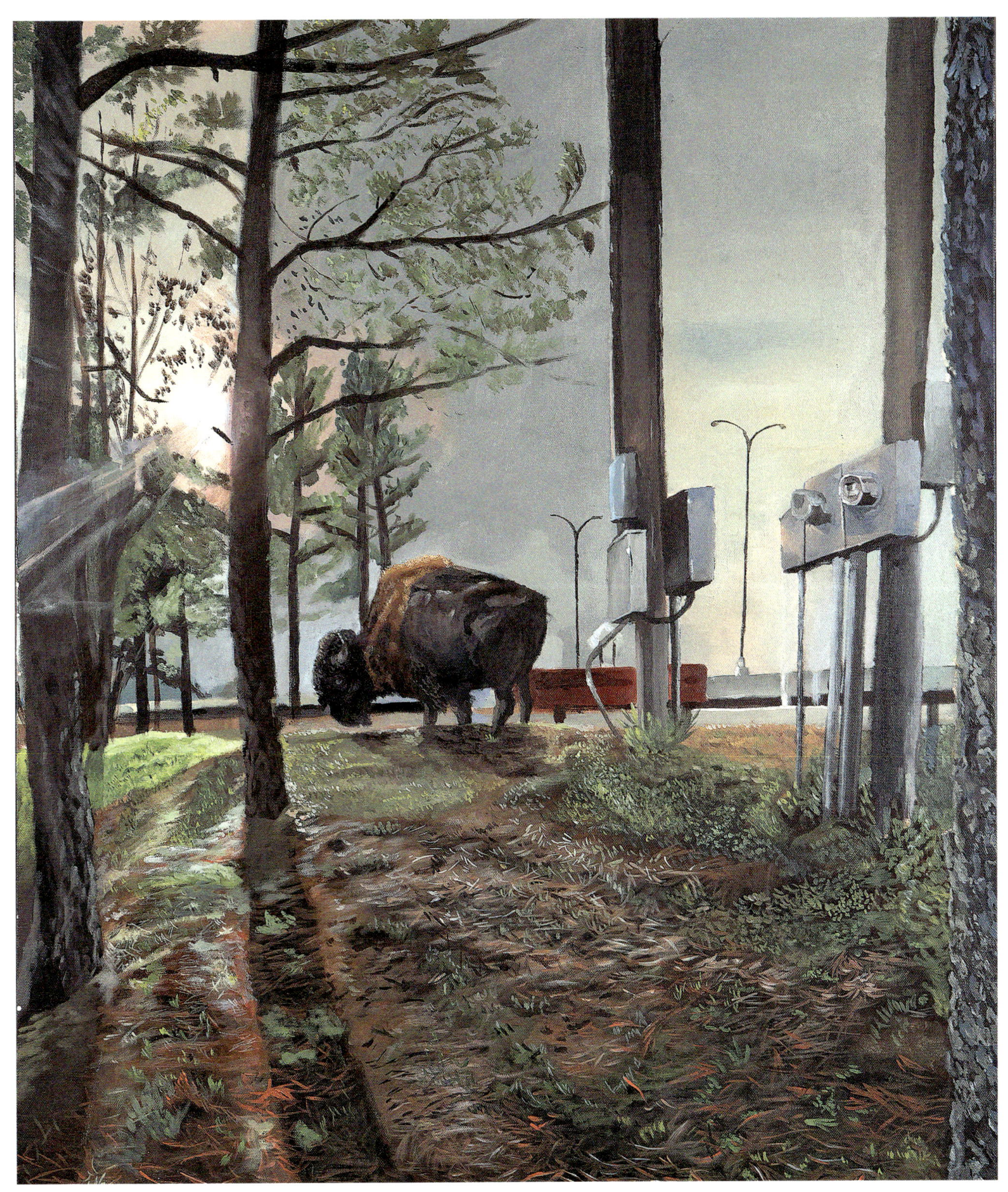

Esteban Cabeza de Baca

Indigenous Chicano (b. 1985)

Cieneguilla Caves, 2019
Acrylic on canvas

As a Chicano artist with mixed heritage and diasporic roots from Mexico and New Mexico, my work connects stories severed by neocolonial borders. I grew up between Tijuana, Mexico, and California, and often visited my paternal family in northern New Mexico. This painting explores the ideas of emergence from the earth as an origin story but also a viewpoint of how to live equitably. I made this painting in northern New Mexico as a way to connect to knowledge embedded in the land—knowledge that colonization couldn't destroy—and land art that predates modernism. I hope my work gets audiences to feel through color and space and reflect about potential futures and revisions toward critical race art history. —E.CdeB.

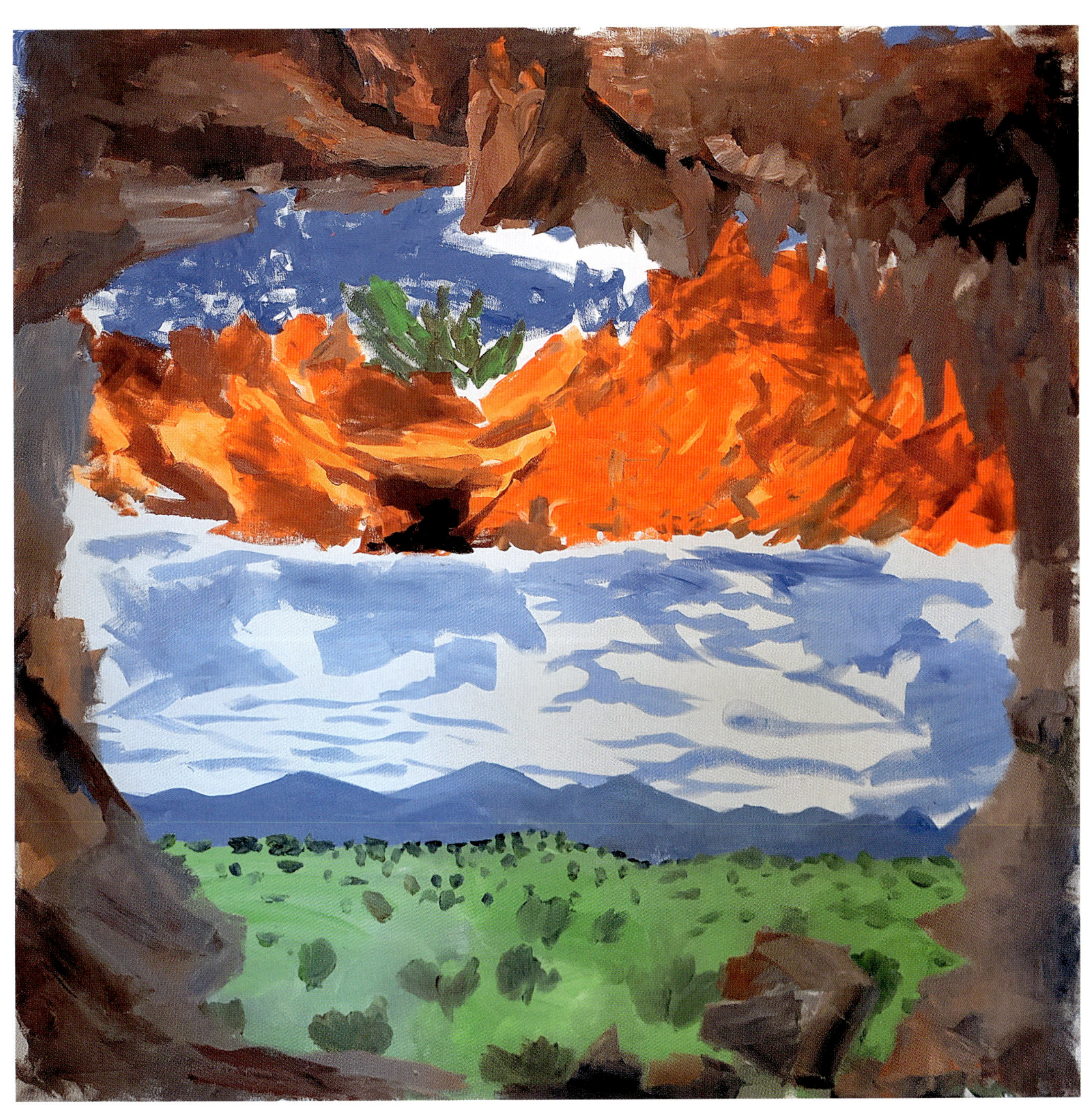

Andrea Carlson

Grand Portage Ojibwe Descent (b. 1979)

First Generation, 2016
Oil, acrylic, ink, colored pencil, graphite on paper

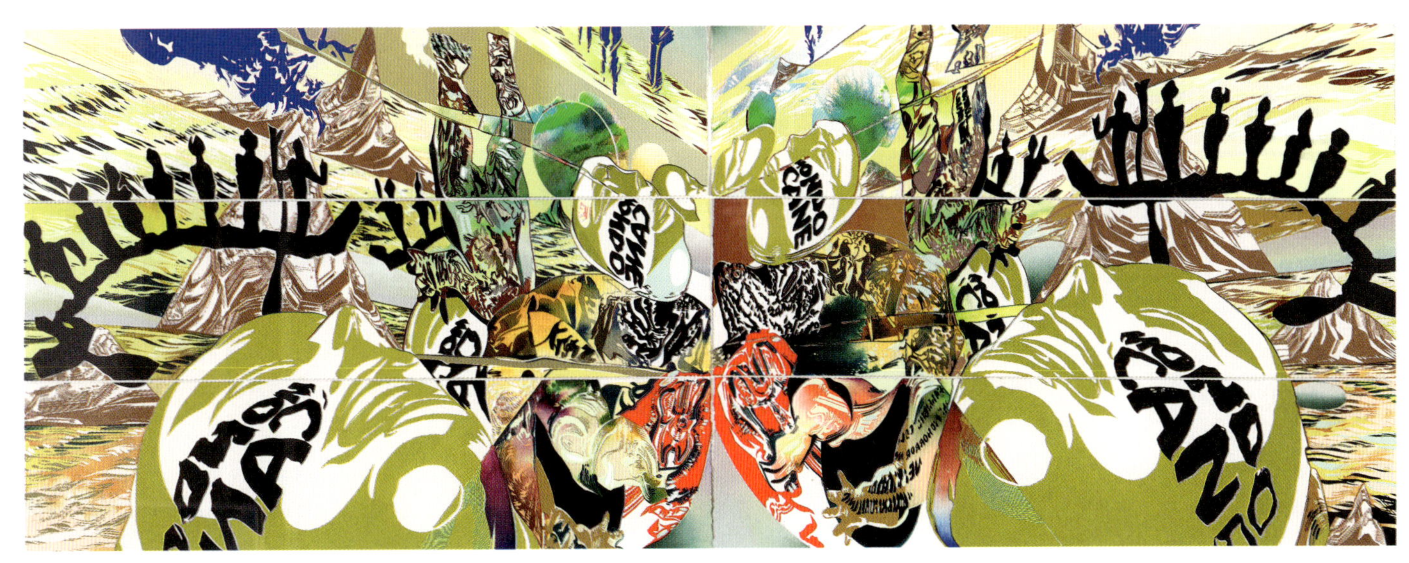

Kelly Caroline Frye

Tesuque Pueblo and Mescalero Apache Descent
(b. 1979)

Malevich Pueblo-Style #4, 2023
Watercolor on paper

The *Malevich Pueblo-Style* series was inspired by the avant-garde artist Kazimir Malevich and my fascination with the architecture and design of the ancient Pueblo world. My palette represents the colors of the Southwest desert landscape, yellow being the most visible from a distance, while both yellow and orange share meanings of worth and optimism. Red is the color of passion, brown the color of resilience. Turquoise shadow outlines the windows and doors, signifying protection, trust, and calmness. The Pueblo pottery designs tell their own stories, although I chose these designs for their universal use among all Pueblo cultures. —K.F.

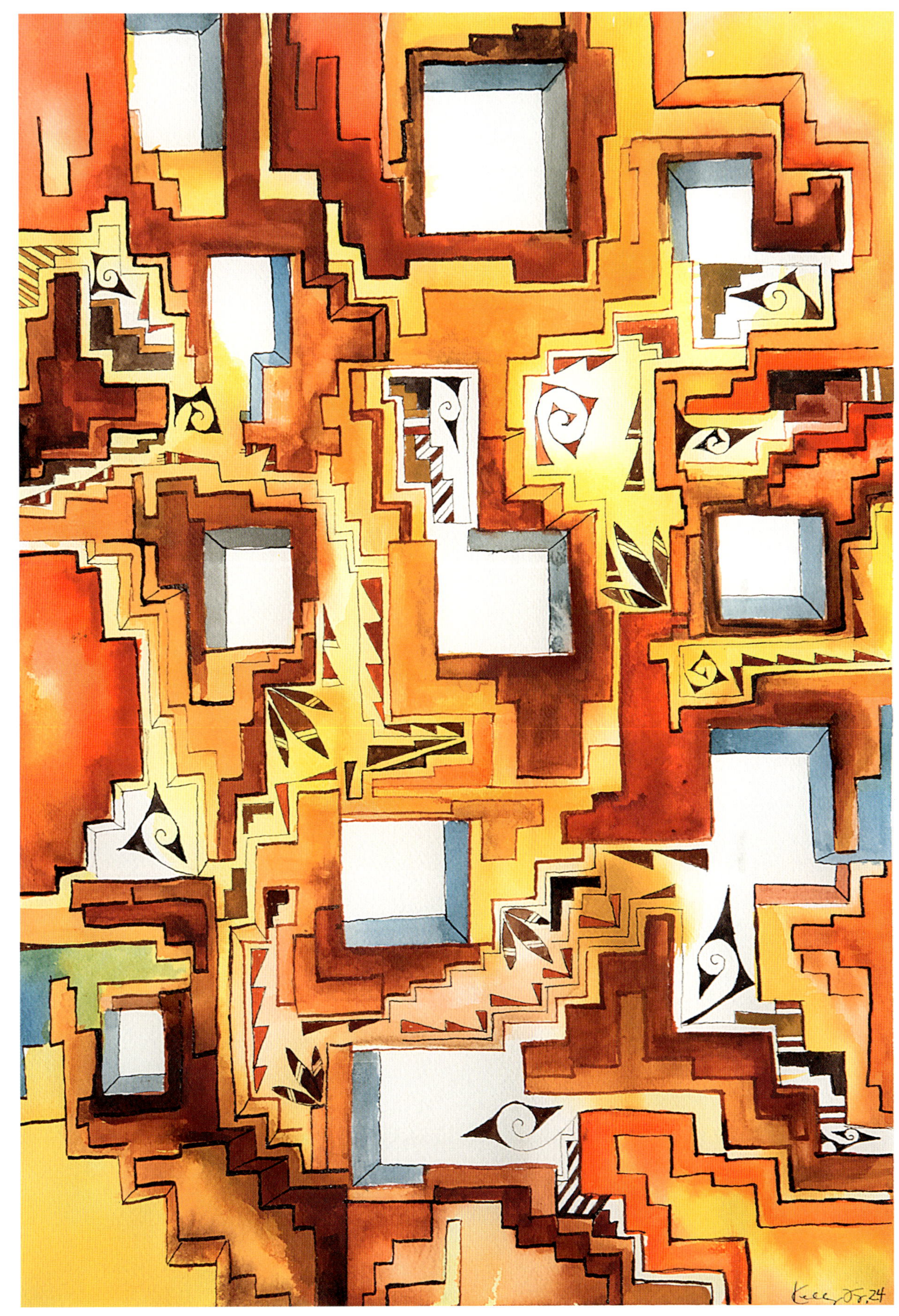

Darren Vigil Gray

Jicarilla Apache [b. 1959]

Motherland of the Basketmakers, 2000
Oil on canvas

Nature is my greatest influence. I see so much and feel so much with the land. What I see, what I've experienced there, that it is probably limitless. I only paint the landscape in and around Abiquiu, New Mexico, which is important to note as this is our native homeland, and the title of this painting refers to our true Indigenous art form of basket weaving. Concentrating on this one locale allows me to mold and shape it innumerable times, until I have come away with an idea of what is there. Georgia O'Keeffe, who so loved the Pedernal mesa [Peshlakai, White Mountain] that appears frequently in her paintings, said that God had promised she could have it if she painted it enough. But the fact remains that it belonged to the Jicarilla Apache long before that, and I am a natural heir. —D.V.G.

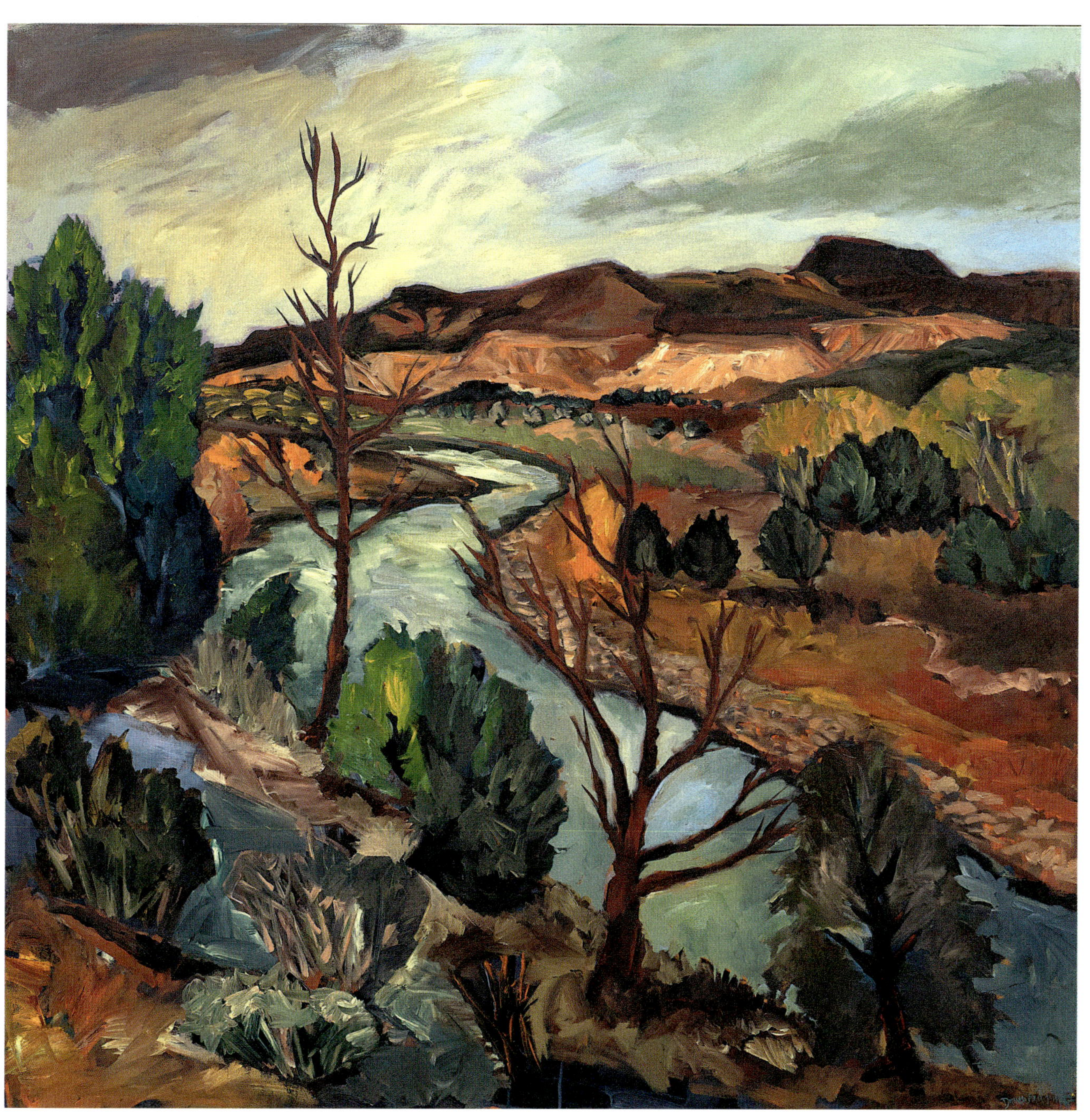

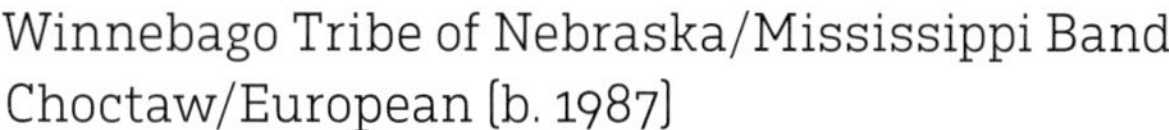

Chaz John

Winnebago Tribe of Nebraska/Mississippi Band Choctaw/European (b. 1987)

Tattooed Mississippian Effigy Head with Magnolias, 2022
Colored pencil

Effigy head pots may have been created as portraits of deceased relatives or representations of any enemy's severed head. For warriors, facial tattoos were used as snares for capturing the soul of someone they killed in battle. This head symbolizes the killing of a warrior's body, while the butterfly is the escape of his soul, avoiding the fate of assimilation by supernatural capture. —C.J.

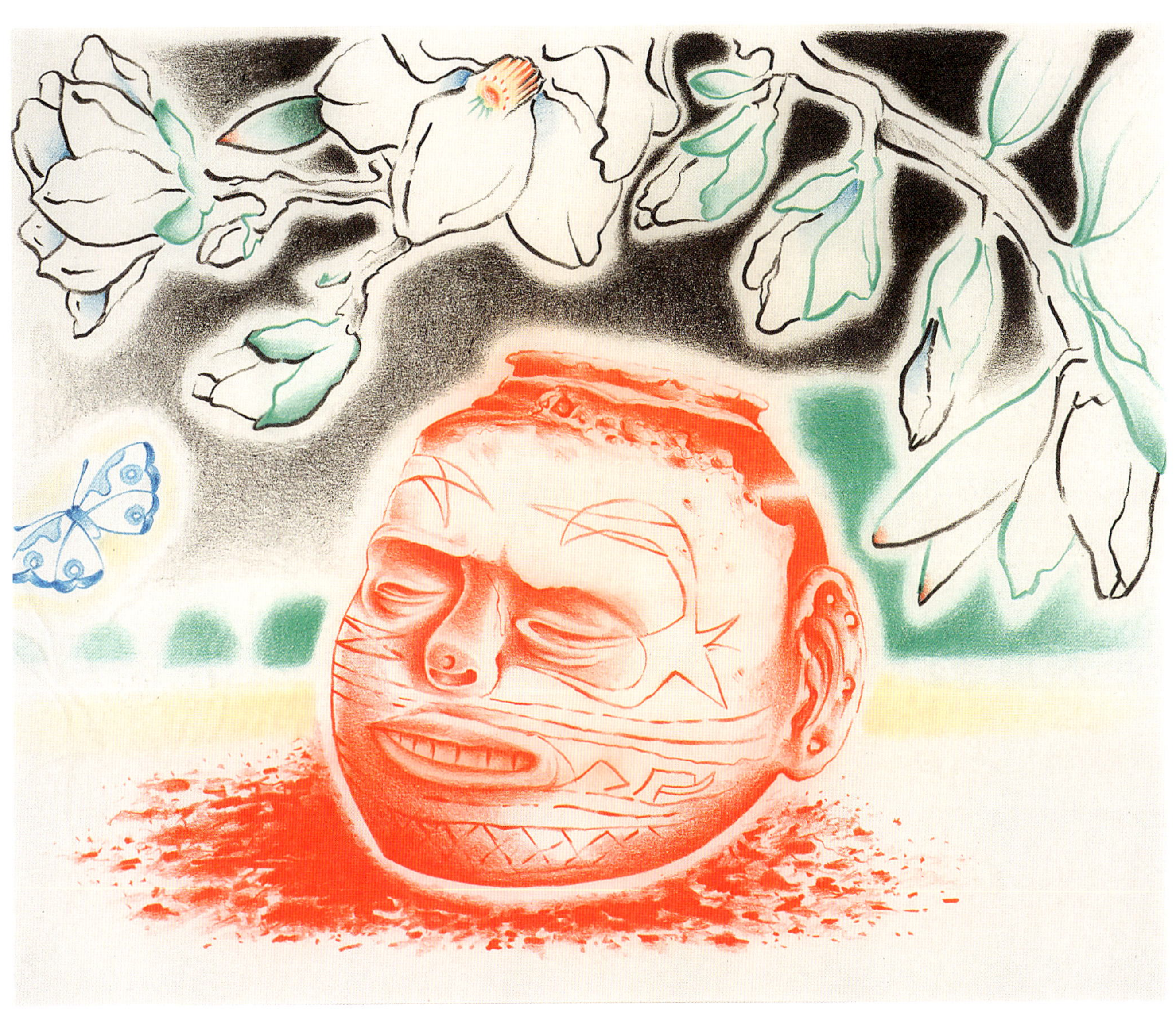

Athena LaTocha

Hunkpapa Lakota/Ojibway (b. 1969)

Murderers Creek, 2018–19
Ink and earth on paper, steel, lead, wood

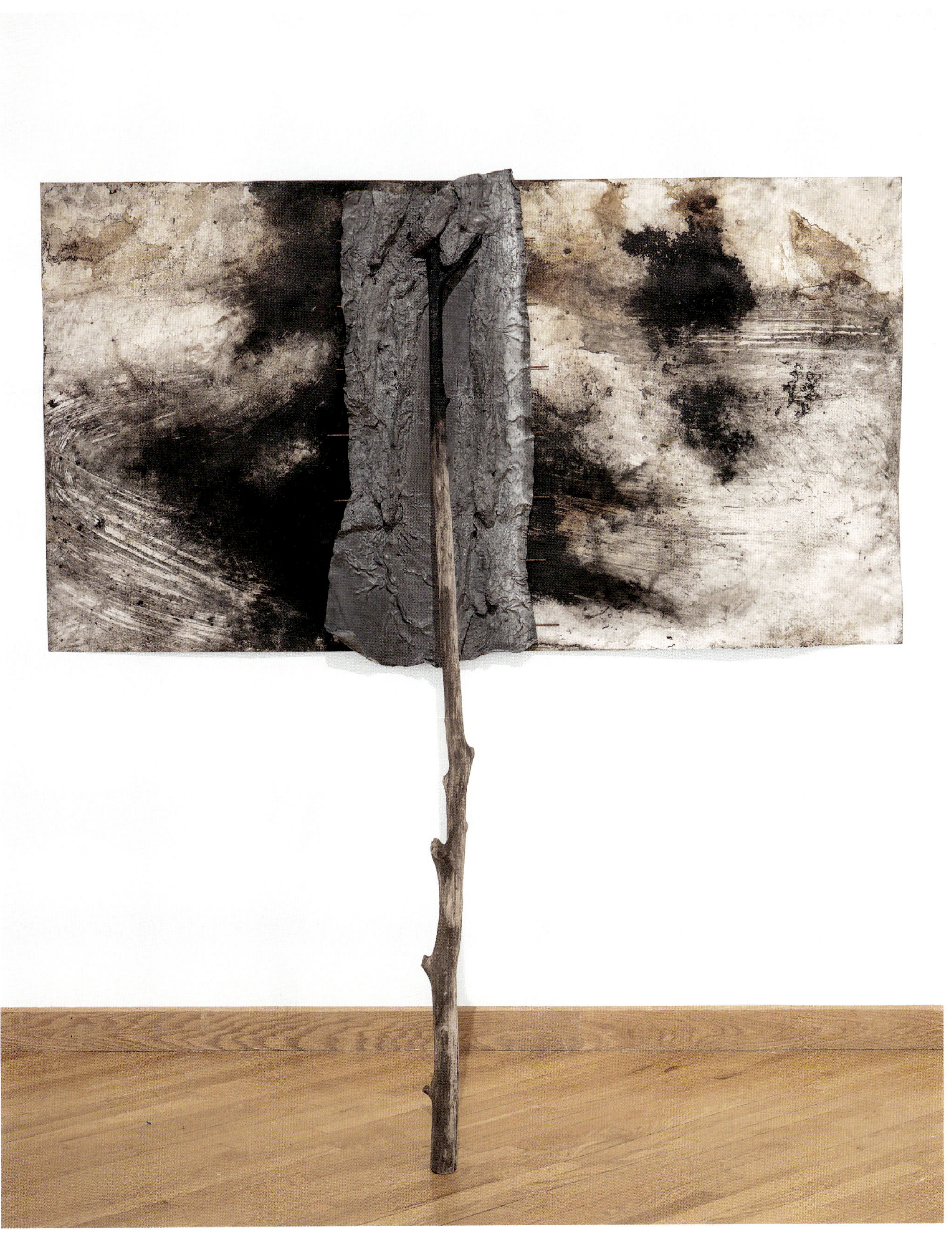

Dan Namingha

Hopi-Tewa (b. 1950)

Reservation Dusk, 2008
Acrylic on canvas

This painting is my impression of an evening in solitude as the sun sets quietly behind the Hopi mesa. —D.N.

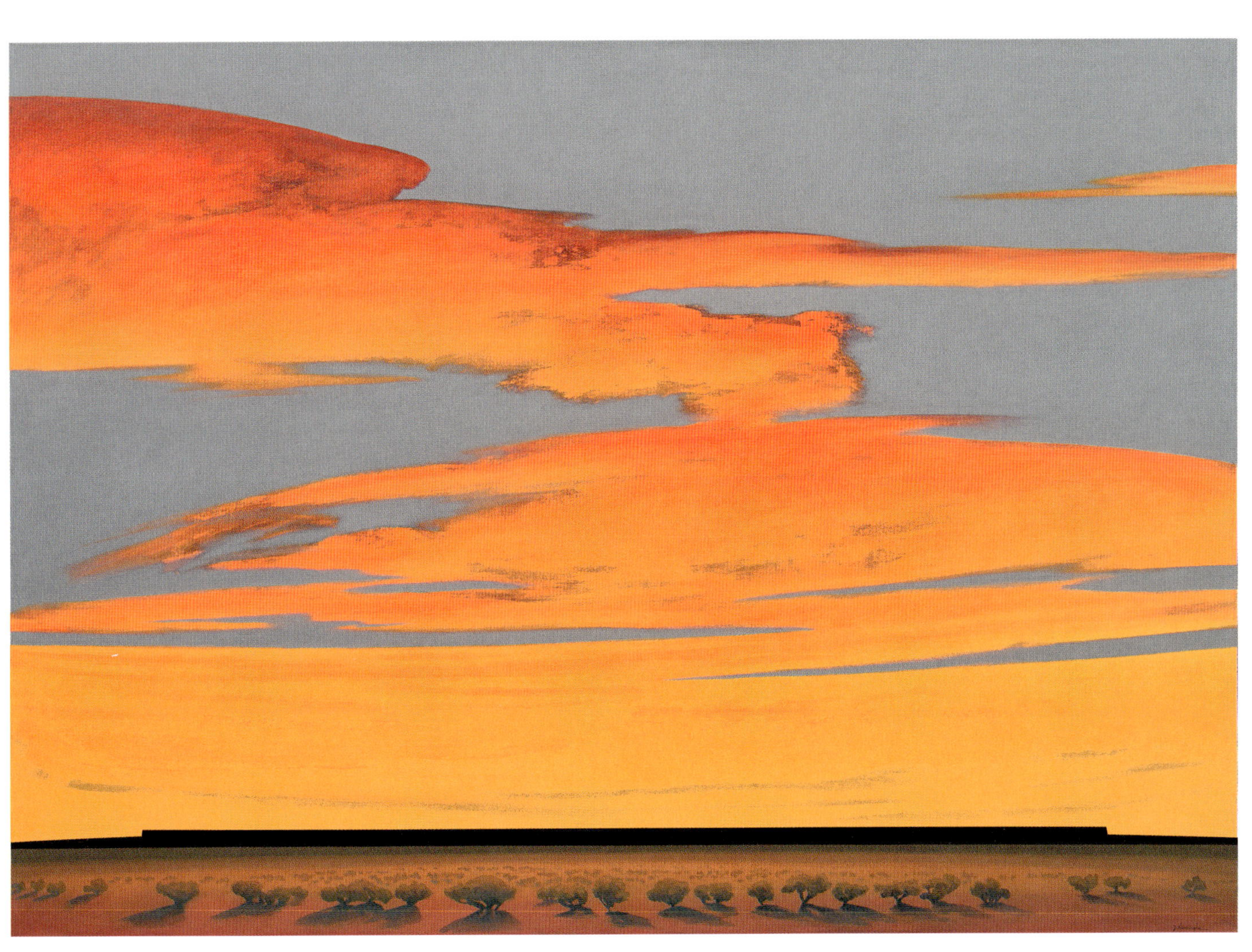

Michael Namingha

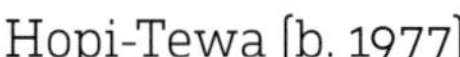

Hopi-Tewa (b. 1977)

Altered Landscape 14, 2022
C-print face mounted to shaped acrylic

Altered Landscape 14 is a photograph I took in May of 2022 in Santa Fe, New Mexico, when the state experienced its largest forest fire on record. The Calf Canyon/Hermits Peak Fire was the result of a prescribed burn; it burned 341,000 acres from April 6, 2022, to August 22, 2022. Much of the American West has experienced unprecedented fire seasons as a result of climate change. —M.N.

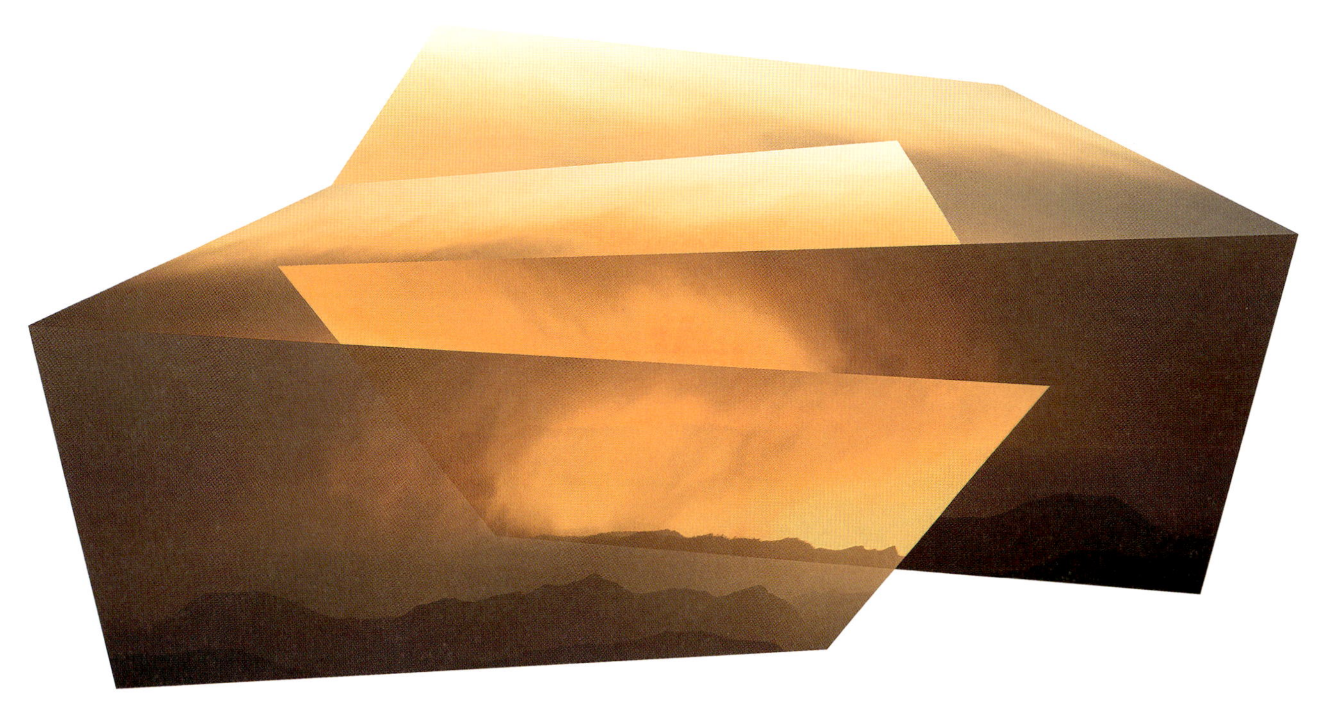

Laura Ortman (and Nanobah Becker)

White Mountain Apache (b. 1973); (Diné, b. 1970)

My Soul Remainer, 2017
Video

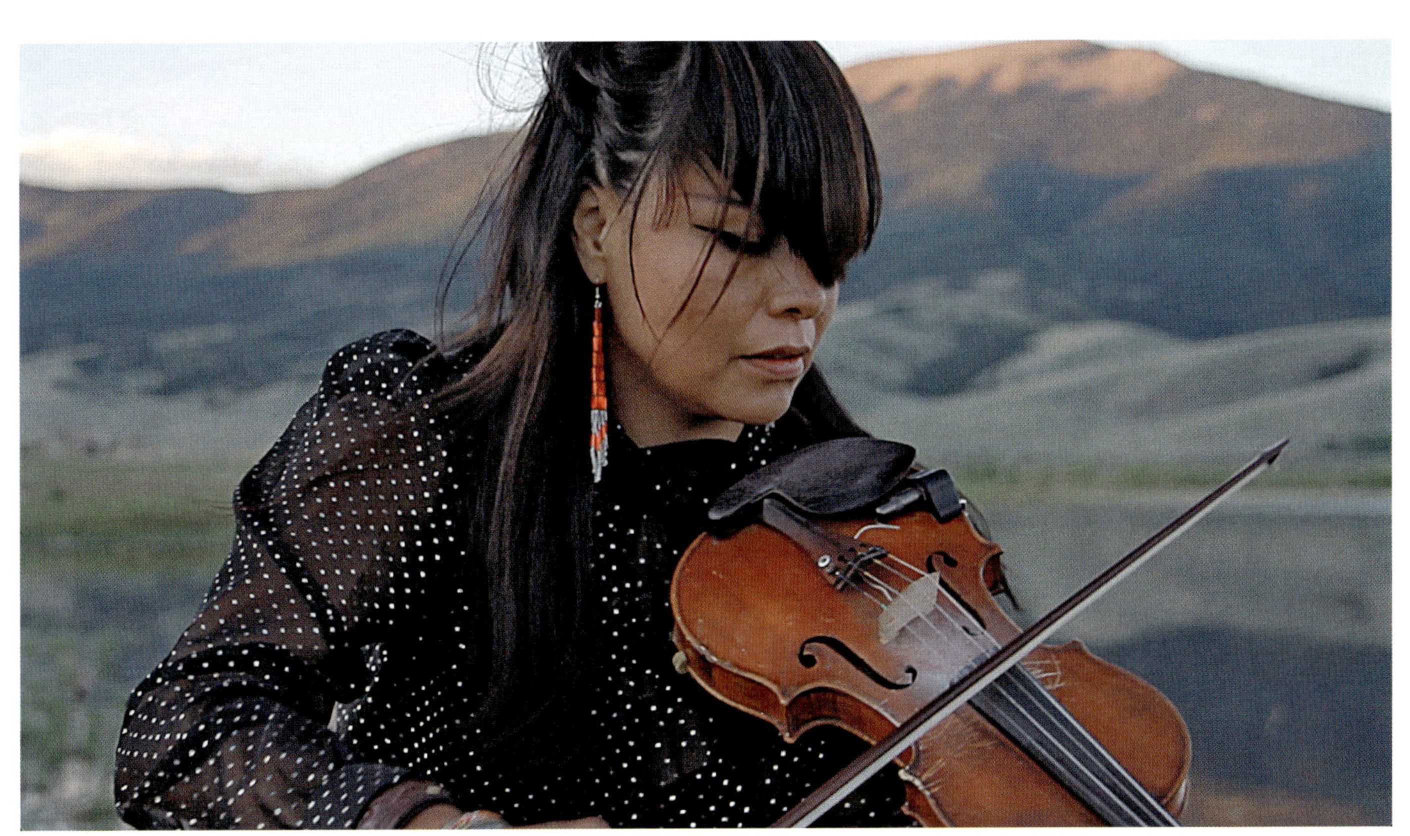

Wade Patton

Enrolled Member of the Oglala Lakota Tribe (b. 1966)

Lone, 2018
Mixed media

With the elegant line and an almost hypnotic use of pattern, I draw the viewer into my interpretation of the natural elements and seasonal changes of the land. The mastery of the triangle and circle work evokes the subtlest of phenomenon, and my spare use of color in the beadwork resonates with the lone power of the buffalo. —W.P.

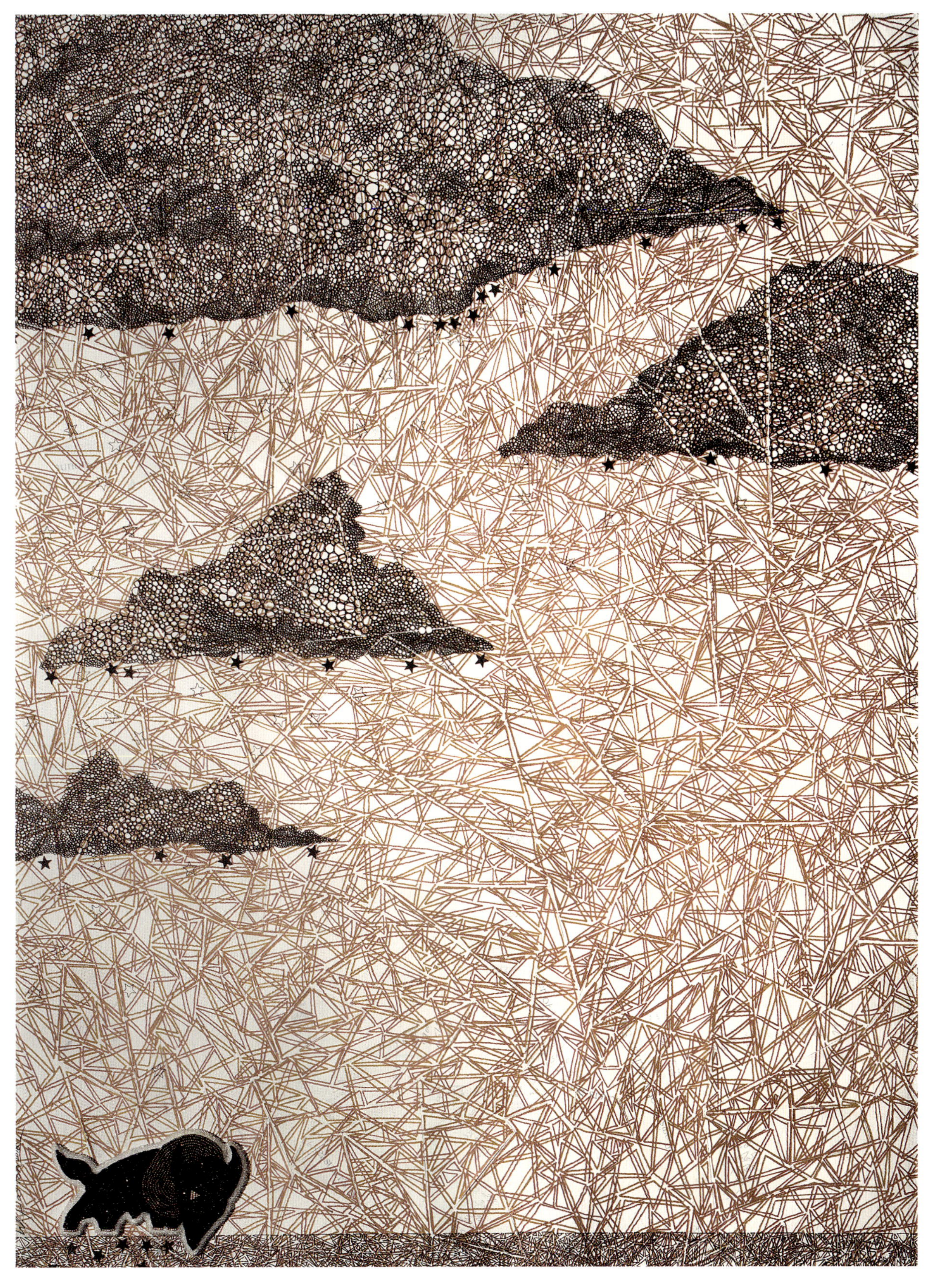

Kay WalkingStick

Member of the Cherokee Nation of Oklahoma and Anglo (b. 1935)

Buffalo Country (Diptych), 2018
Oil on panel

I have a deep and abiding respect for our beautiful indigenous bison. This painting is a tribute to them. In this oil painting, the foothills roll in the distance and the Rockies tower in the background. These particular buffalo I saw in Yellowstone, but there are many other buffalo living outside of national lands since the herds are regrowing after their near decimation in the nineteenth century. If you are very lucky, one day you will see a herd at one of the many wild locations throughout the northwestern part of the United States and Canada where they live. When you do, it will feel like a magical vision. A gift from the gods. I have added a pattern based on a Lakota parfleche bag to the painting because this is one of the tribes whose land was taken to form Yellowstone National Park. We are all living in Indian Territory. —K.W.

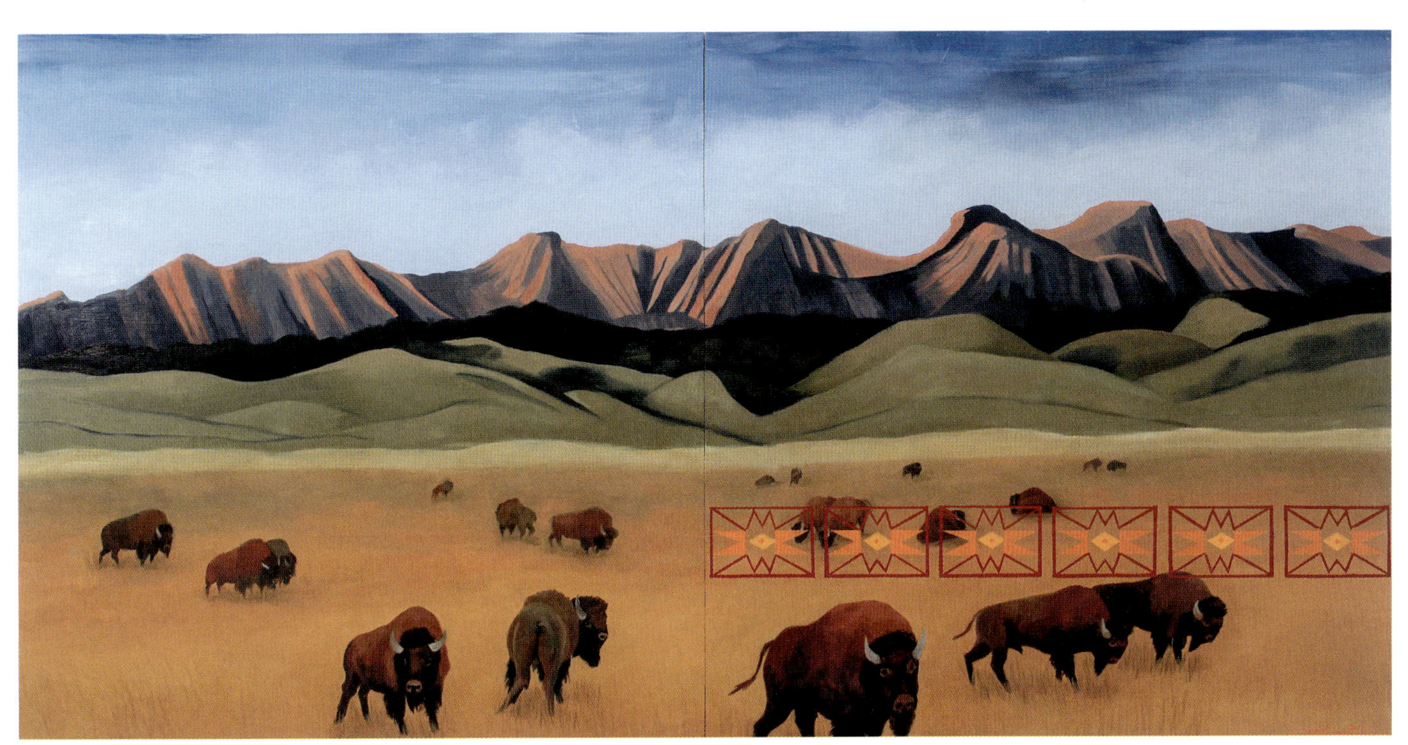

Emmi Whitehorse

Diné [b. 1957]

Rushing Water, 2000
Oil pastel on paper on canvas

The red painting *Rushing Water* was one in a series of works related to water. In my home area in the Navajo Nation, there was always a need for water. Water was scarce. Many other Native communities around us petitioned the Gods for water. We prayed for water, made songs for water, and dreamed rain would come. When it finally did come, it would turn red as the water rushed over the red sands. —E.W.

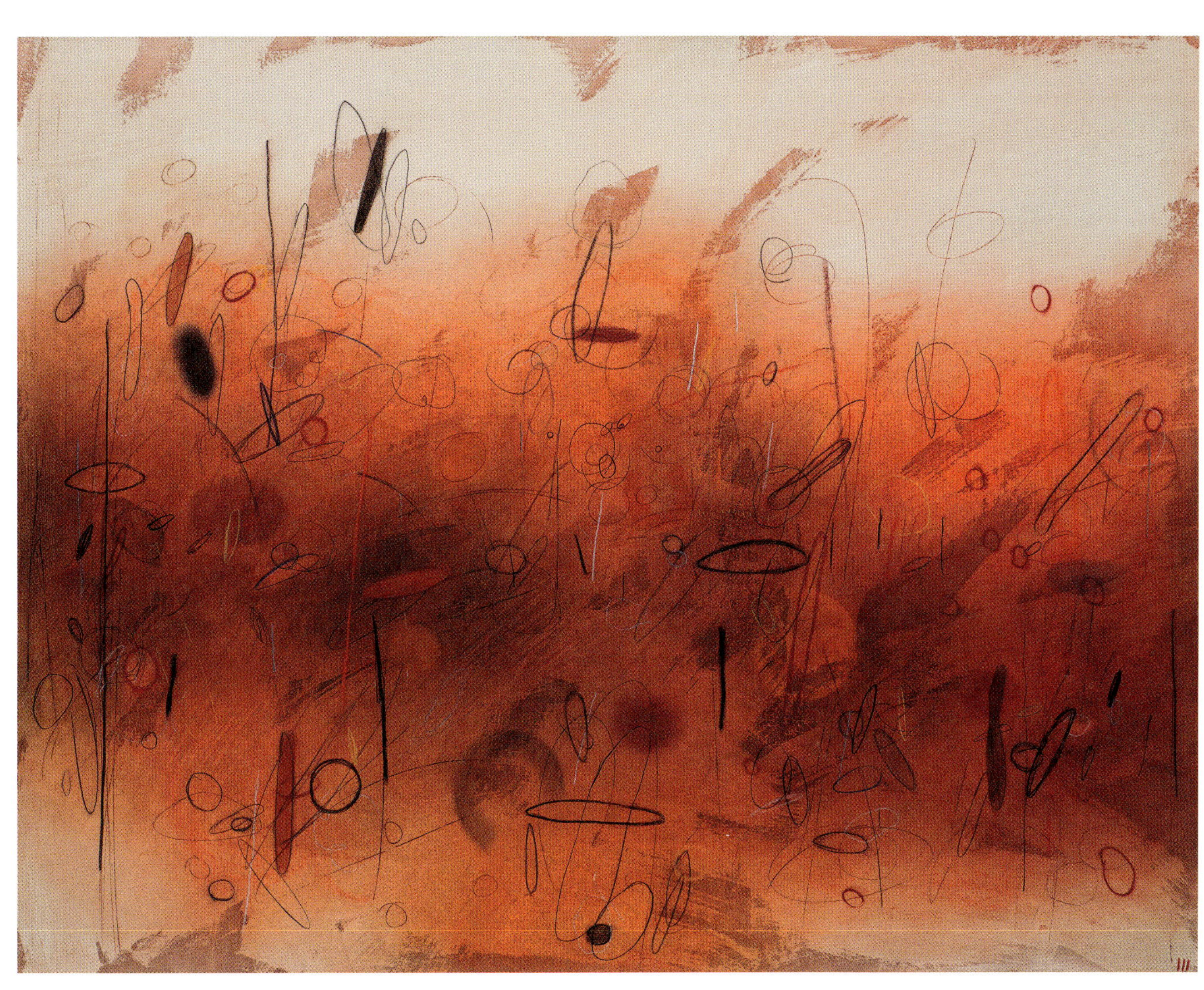

Catalogue of the Exhibition

Artwork images are Photo Peter Jacobs, unless otherwise noted.

Tony Abeyta
Diné (Navajo), (b. 1965)
Dispersion, 2018
Micaceous clay and acrylic medium, historical Native beads, encaustic wax on archival wood panels
24 × 71½ inches
Tia Collection
James Hart Photography
pp. 100–101.

Norman Akers
Citizen of the Osage Nation (b. 1958)
Drowning Elk, 2020
Oil on canvas
78 × 68 inches
Gochman Family Collection
Photo Aaron Paden
pp. 52–53

George Alexander
Muscogee (Creek), (b. 1990)
Urban #2, 2021
Acrylic on canvas
40 × 36 inches
Private Collection
© George Alexander/Artist
pp. 230–31

Neal Ambrose-Smith
Descendant of the Confederated Salish and Kootenai Nation of Montana (b. 1966)
Abstract in Your Home, 2009
Neon, mixed media
92 × 71 × 4 inches
Tia Collection
Chiaroscuro Contemporary Art, Santa Fe, NM
pp. 54–55

Keri Ataumbi
Kiowa (b. 1971)
Antler Earrings, 2022
Silver, gold, and diamonds
2 × ¾ × ½ inches (each)
Artist's collection, Underexposed Studios/Santa Fe, NM
pp. 102–3

Joe Baker
Enrolled Member of the Delaware Tribe of Indians of Oklahoma (b. 1946)
Bandolier Bag, 2014
Fabric, wool, and glass beads
34½ × 21 × ¾ inches
Collection of the artist
pp. 104–5

Natalie Ball
Klamath/Modoc (b. 1980)
Sheriff's Star, 2022
Neon glass, textiles, Billy Jack hats, ribbon, paint, deer hide
93½ × 68½ × 8 inches
Gochman Family Collection
pp. 56–57

Jamison Chās Banks
Enrolled Member of the Seneca-Cayuga Nation of Oklahoma (b. 1978)
Untitled, 2015
23-layer serigraph on cedar
3⅞ × 1½ × 7½ inches
Artwork on loan from the artist
pp. 106–7

Marwin Begaye
Navajo (b. 1970)
Columbia River Custodian, 2018
Lithograph
28¼ × 22¼ inches
Private Collection
© Marwin Begaye
pp. 108–9

Frank Big Bear
Ojibwe (b. 1953)
Ghost Dance of the Great Mystery, 2022
Colored pencil on black illustration board
80 × 96 inches
Tia Collection
© Frank Big Bear. Courtesy of the artist and Bockley Gallery
pp. 176–77

Roy Bigcrane (and Thompson Smith)
Séliš, Member of the Confederated Salish and Kootenai Tribes
(b. 1955)
The Place of the Falling Waters, 1990
Video
Part I—28:55, Part II—28:16, Part III—27:03
© Salish Kootenai College
pp. 110–11

Jackie Larson Bread
Amsakapi Pikunni/Blackfeet
(b. 1960)
Triangular Beaded Trinket Box, Chief Joseph, 2007
Beaded satin-lined box
6½ × 5½ inches
Tia Collection
James Hart Photography
pp. 112–13

Julie Buffalohead
Enrolled Ponca Tribe of Oklahoma
(b. 1972)
The Great Divide, 2008
Acrylic, ink, and graphite on paper
22 × 30 inches, framed: 26⅜ × 34½ inches
Private Collection
pp. 178–79

Esteban Cabeza de Baca
Indigenous Chicano (b. 1985)
Cieneguilla Caves, 2019
Acrylic on canvas
60 × 60 × 1 inches
Tia Collection
Photography courtesy of the artist and Garth Greenan Gallery, NY
pp. 232–33

Andrea Carlson
Grand Portage Ojibwe Descent
(b. 1979)
First Generation, 2016
Oil, acrylic, ink, colored pencil, graphite on paper
22 × 66 inches
JoAnn Gonzales Hickey Collection
© Andreas Carlson. Courtesy of the Artist and Bockley Gallery
pp. 234–35

Nanibah "Nani" Chacon
Diné (Navajo) and Chicana
(b. 1980)
Emersion into the Blue World, 2017
Acrylic on Polytab
117 × 95 inches
Tia Collection
pp. 180–81

Raven Chacon
For Zitkála-Šá (For Carmina Escobar), 2019
Lithograph
11 × 8½ inches
Private Collection
Courtesy of the Artist
pp. 58–59

For Zitkála-Šá [For Suzanne Kite], 2019
Lithograph
11 × 8½ inches
Private Collection
Courtesy of the Artist
pp. 60–61

Corwin Clairmont
Member of the Confederated Salish and Kootenai Tribes of the Flathead Nation (b. 1946)
Raven Speaks to His Friends, 2020
Serigraph
30 × 22 inches
Private Collection
pp. 62–63

Jason Clark
Non-enrolled Algonquin, Creek, Swiss, and Scottish
(b. 1967)
Winona and the Big Oil "Windigo," 2014
Woodcut
26 × 35 inches
Private Collection
pp. 114–15

Gerald Clarke Jr.
Cahuilla (b. 1967)
Native Land, 2019
Burnt paper
19¼ × 13¾ inches
Private Collection
© Collection of the artist
pp. 64–65

Lorenzo Clayton
Navajo (b. 1950)
Consciously Conscious Numbers, 2024
Mixed media
121 × 60 × 12 inches
James Hart Photography
Consciously Conscious Numbers: A collaboration between Lorenzo Clayton, George Sidebotham, and Timothy Corbett
pp. 182–83

Jordan Ann Craig
Northern Cheyenne (b. 1992)
Colliding Clouds, 2020
Acrylic on canvas
70 × 65 inches
Tia Collection
James Hart Photography
pp. 116–17

Jeremy Dennis
Shinnecock Indian Nation Tribal Member (b. 1990)
Ma's House: Reciprocity Project, 2022
Video, variable duration: 8 minutes
Ma's House | Jeremy Dennis
pp. 184–85

Demian DinéYazhi'
Diné (b. 1983)
my ancestors will not let me forget this, 2020
Letterpress print
18 × 24 inches
Gochman Family Collection
© Demian DinéYazhi'
Photo Max Yawney
pp. 66–67

Carly Feddersen
Enrolled Member of the Colville Reservation and of Mixed European Heritage (b. 1982)
[Dis] Embodied: Fingers Necklace II, 2023
Mixed media
18 × 16 × 2 inches
On loan courtesy of the artist
pp. 118–19

Joe Feddersen
Okanagan and Arrow Lakes (b. 1953)
Country Road, 2024
Sally bag
8½ × 5½ inches
Courtesy of the Artist and Studio @ Seattle, WA
pp. 120–21

RYAN! Feddersen
Confederated Tribes of the Colville Reservation and of Mixed European Descent (b. 1984)
Bison Stock Crane, 2018
Archival pigment print
34 × 44 inches
Private Collection
© RYAN! Feddersen
pp. 68–69

Kelly Caroline Frye
Tesuque Pueblo and Mescalero Apache Descent (b. 1979)
Malevich Pueblo-Style #4, 2023
Watercolor on paper
25 × 19 inches
Private Collection
© Chelsea Benally for Gallery Hózhó
pp. 236–37

Nicholas Galanin
Tlingit/Unangax̂ (b. 1979)
Never Forget, 2021
C-print
51¾ × 78¾ × 2¼ inches
Forge Project Collection, traditional lands of the Moh-He-Con-Nuk
Courtesy the artist and Peter Blum Gallery, New York
pp. 70–71

Jeffrey Gibson
Member of the Mississippi Band of Choctaw Indians and of Cherokee Descent (b. 1972)
SHE NEVER DANCES ALONE, 2021
Acrylic on canvas, archival pigment on cotton, archival pigment on rice paper, inset in custom wood frame, glass beads, artificial sinew
87⅞ × 79⁵⁄₁₆ × 2⁹⁄₁₆ inches
Gochman Family Collection
Photo Max Yawney
© Jeffrey Gibson
pp. 72–73

Richard Glazer-Danay
Caughnawaga Mohawk and Jewish Descent (b. 1942)
Divided We Stand, 2020
Ink on paper
22½ × 30 inches
Tia Collection
Photo Trotta-Bono Contemporary, Los Angeles, CA
pp. 74–75

Darren Vigil Gray
Jicarilla Apache (b. 1959)
Motherland of the Basketmakers, 2000
Oil on canvas
72 × 72 inches
Tia Collection
James Hart Photography
@darrenvgray
pp. 238–39

Tomahawk GreyEyes
Navajo (b. 1989)
Eyes Like Arrows, 2013
Digital media
14 × 11 inches
Gorman Museum of Native American Art Collection
pp. 122–23

Raven Halfmoon
Caddo Nation (b. 1991)
E-a'-ti-ti, 2021
Stoneware, glaze
63 × 38 × 25 inches
Forge Project Collection, traditional lands of the Moh-He-Con-Nuk
Photo by Trayson Connor
© Raven Halfmoon
pp. 186–87

Bob Haozous
Chiricahua Apache Tribe of Oklahoma (b. 1943)
Sinful Dreams, 1993
Ink on paper
16 × 15¾ × 8 inches
Tia Collection
© Bob Haozous
pp. 188–89

Edgar Heap of Birds
Cheyenne and Arapaho Nations (b. 1954)
Indian Never Safe, 2006–12
Monotype
67½ × 60 inches
Tia Collection
pp. 76–77

Luzene Hill
Enrolled Member of the Eastern Band of Cherokee Indians (b. 1946)
Enate, 2017
Video, duration: 5:46 minutes
Courtesy of the artist and Portland Art Museum
pp. 78–79

John Hitchcock
Comanche, Kiowa and Northern European Ancestry (b. 1967)
Shouting Lightning from Their Eyes (Winter Birds), 2021
Lithograph
34 × 25 inches
Private Collection
pp. 124–25

Anna Hoover
Norwegian/Unangax̂ (b. 1985)
Salmon Reflection, 2021
Video, duration: 4 minutes
On loan courtesy of the artist
pp. 126–27

Sky Hopinka
Ho-Chunk Nation/Pechanga Band of Luiseño Indians (b. 1984)
Here You Are Before the Trees, 2020
HD video, stereo, color, 3-channel synchronous loop; duration: 13 minutes
Forge Project Collection, traditional lands of the Moh-He-Con-Nuk
pp. 128–29

Norma Howard
Choctaw and Chickasaw (1958–2024)
Miniature Storefront, 2019
Watercolor on paper
9 × 11 inches
Private Collection
© Estate of Norma Howard
pp. 130–31

Patrick Dean Hubbell
Diné (b. 1986)
You Protect Us Day and Night, 2020
Oil, acrylic, spray, and natural earth pigment on canvas
63½ × 40¼ × 1 inches
Tia Collection
James Hart Photography
© Patrick Dean Hubbell
pp. 132–33

Erin Ggaadimits Ivalu Gingrich
Nome Eskimo Community, culturally affiliated Koyukon Denaa & Iñupiaq (b. 1990)
Spawning Iqalukpik Double from Tustumena Lake, 2022
Basswood, acrylic, glass beads, and salmon vertebrae
50 × 20 × 2 inches
Gochman Family Collection
pp. 134–35

G. Peter Jemison
Seneca, Heron Clan (b. 1945)
Red Power, 1973
Acrylic on canvas
40 × 38 inches
Tia Collection
James Hart Photography
pp. 190–91

Chaz John
Winnebago Tribe of Nebraska/ Mississippi Band Choctaw/ European (b. 1987)
Tattooed Mississippian Effigy Head with Magnolias, 2022
Colored pencil
14 × 17 inches
Private Collection
pp. 240–41

Emily Johnson
Yup'ik Nation (b. 1976)
inbetween Kwimiak, blue, 2020
Video, duration: 23 minutes
Commissioned by ENTER project, an initiative of Onassis Foundation, courtesy of the artist
pp. 192–93

Tom Jones
Ho-Chunk Nation of Wisconsin (b. 1964)
Forster Nash from the *Strong Unrelenting Spirits* series, 2015
Digital photograph with beadwork
25 × 20 inches
Private Collection
© Tom Jones
pp. 136–37

Brad Kalhamer
Tribally ambiguous (b. 1956)
Next Level Figure 1, 2013
Acrylic on wood
10¼ × 9⅞ × 1⅝ inches
Forge Project Collection, traditional lands of the Moh-He-Con-Nuk
pp. 138–39

Sonya Kelliher-Combs
Iñupiaq/Athabascan (b. 1969)
Remnant (Walrus Bone IV), 2019
Mixed media
18 × 12 × 1¾ inches
Gochman Family Collection
Photo Yao Zu Lu
© Sonya Kelliher-Combs
pp. 140–41

Linda King
Enrolled member of the Confederated Salish and Kootenai Nation (b. 1952)
Beauty Set, 2020
Beaded makeup brushes
10 × 10 × 2 inches
Private Collection
pp. 142–43

Terran Last Gun (Saakwaynaamah'kaa)
Piikani (Blackfeet) (b. 1989)
Nearing the Skybeings Lodge, 2021
Colored pencil on ledger book paper
Private Collection
© Terran Last Gun
pp. 144–45

Athena LaTocha
Hunkpapa Lakota/Ojibway (b. 1969)
Murderers Creek, 2018–19
Ink and earth on paper, steel, lead, wood
84 × 84 × 39 inches
JoAnn Gonzales Hickey Collection
© Athena LaTocha
pp. 242–43

James Lavadour
Enrolled member of the Confederated Tribes of the Umatilla Indian Reservation (b. 1951)
Stick House, 2006
Lithograph
26⅜ × 34½ inches
Private Collection
© James L. Lavadour
pp. 146–47

Linda Lomahaftewa
Hopi/Choctaw (b. 1947)
Ancestral Gulf Birds #3, 2010
Monotype
22 × 30 inches
Private Collection
© Linda Lomahaftewa
pp. 148–49

George Longfish
Seneca and Tuscarora (b. 1942)
Long Fish, 1985
Acrylic
45½ × 35½ × 2 inches
Gorman Museum of Native American Art Collection
© George Longfish
pp. 194–95

Judith Lowry
Hammawi Band Pit River/ Mountain Maidu/Washo Tribe/ Scots-Irish Cultures (b. 1948)
Medicine Man, 1994
Acrylic on canvas
94 × 69 × 2 inches
On loan from private collection
© Judith Lowry
pp. 196–97

Cannupa Hanska Luger
Enrolled Member of the Three Affiliated Tribes of Fort Berthold and is Mandan, Hidatsa, Arikara, and Lakota (b. 1979)
Mirror Shield Project–River (The Water Serpent), 2016
Single channel video
The video depicts a site-specific performance of Luger's *Mirror Shield Project*, which was organized by Luger in collaboration with Rory Wakemup. It took place on November 18, 2016, at Oceti Sakowin Camp, Standing Rock Indian Reservation, North Dakota; audio features a morning prayer sung by the Oceti Sakowin main camp announcer. Video courtesy the artist and Garth Greenan Gallery, New York City
pp. 80–81

Mario Martinez
Enrolled Member of the Pascua Yaqui Tribe of Arizona (b. 1953)
Native Modernist Reflection, 2021
Prismacolor and pastel on paper
30 × 22½ inches
Courtesy of the artist and Garth Greenan Gallery, New York
pp. 198–99

Michael McCabe
Diné (Navajo) (1961–2023)
Untitled, 2022
Monotypes
18⅞ × 15⅛ inches each
Private Collection
© Estate Michael McCabe
pp. 150–51

Da-ka-xeen Mehner
Tlingit, Nisga'a (b. 1970)
The Artist with His Thoughts, 2007
Digital photograph
15 × 24 inches
Gorman Museum of Native American Art Collection
pp. 200–201

Bryson Goodrunner Meyers
Chippewa, Cree, Sicangu, Oglala, Hunkpapa, Dakota (b. 1984)
Bandolier Bag of 1916, 2022
Mixed media
20 × 22 inches
Private Collection
pp. 152–53

Alan Michelson
Mohawk Member of the Six Nations of the Grand River (b. 1953)
Pehin Hanska Ktpei (They Killed Longhair), 2021
Silent video and wool trade blanket
90 × 72 inches, duration: 1:05 minutes
Courtesy of the artist
pp. 202–3

Douglas Miles
White Mountain Apache/San Carlos Apache/Akimel O'odham (b. 1963)
Forced Removal Series: Victoria in Blue and Gold, 2023
Vintage suitcase, spray paint, and appliqué
26 × 18 × 9 inches
Private Collection
© Douglas Miles
pp. 82–83

Dan Namingha
Hopi/Tewa (b. 1950)
Reservation Dusk, 2008
Acrylic on canvas
60 × 84 × 1½ inches
Tia Collection
James Hart Photography
pp. 244–45

Michael Namingha
Hopi/Tewa (b. 1977)
Altered Landscape 14, 2022
C-print face mounted to shaped acrylic
25 × 50 × 1 inches
On loan courtesy of the artist
© Michael Namingha
pp. 246–47

Nora Naranjo-Morse
Tewa, Santa Clara Pueblo (b. 1953)
What Was Taken and What We Sell, 2014
Video, duration: 10:26 minutes
On loan courtesy of the artist
© Nora Naranjo Morse
pp. 154–55

Native Art Department International (NADI)
Wasauksing First Nation and Chiricahua Apache Tribe/Mexican
Double Shift, 2018
Acrylic paint on custom canvas clothing
219 × 68½ inches
Forge Project Collection, traditional lands of the Moh-He-Con-Nuck
pp. 204–5

New Red Order (NRO)
Ojibway, Tlingit
Culture Capture: Crimes Against Reality, 2020
Video, duration: 7 minutes
Forge Project Collection, traditional land of the Moh-He-Con-Nuk
Photo by Filip Wolak Photography
pp. 84–85

Laura Ortman (and Nanobah Becker)
White Mountain Apache (b. 1973), (Nanobah Becker, Diné, b. 1970)
My Soul Remainer, 2017
Video, duration: 5:44 minutes
On loan courtesy of the artists
pp. 248–49

Chris Pappan
Kanza, Lakota (b. 1971)
Of White Bread and Miracles (Buffalo), 2020
Mixed media on embossed Evanston municipal ledger
36 × 18 inches
Tia Collection
pp. 156–57

Mikayla Patton
Enrolled Member of the Oglala Lakota Nation (b. 1991)
Enduring, 2023
Paper, deer lace, porcupine quills, medicine ash
Each 18 × 22 × 15½ inches with 10 feet hanging deer lace
70 × 156 × 156 inches overall
Tia Collection
Addison Doty, courtesy Chiaroscuro Contemporary Art
pp. 86–87

Wade Patton
Enrolled Member of the Oglala Lakota Tribe (b. 1966)
Lone, 2018
Mixed media
41 × 33 × 2 inches
Gorman Museum of Native American Art Collection
pp. 250–51

Grace Rosario Perkins
Diné/Akimel O'odham (b. 1986)
Mom Jokes to Make Her Hair Curly Like a Sheep, 2022
Acrylic, spray paint, rose petals, crushed mirror, and Xerox on canvas
97 × 88 inches
© Grace Rosario Perkins, Courtesy of the artist and Bockley Gallery
Photo McKay Imaging Photography
pp. 206–7

Luanne Redeye
Seneca Nation of Indians/Hawk Clan (b. 1985)
I See You, 2018
Oil on panel
30 × 40 inches
Courtesy of Ganondagan State Historic Site & The Friends of Ganondagan Inc.
© Luanne Redeye
pp. 158–59

Wendy Red Star
Apsáalooke/Crow (b. 1981)
Dust, 2020
Lithograph
24⅛ × 23⅞ inches
Private Collection
© Wendy Red Star
pp. 160–61

Cara Romero
Chemehuevi (b. 1977)
Arla Lucia, 2019
Photograph
30 × 23¾ × 1¼ inches
Gorman Museum of Native American Art Collection
© Cara Romero. Courtesy of the artist. All rights reserved.
pp. 208–9

Starlight, Starbright, 2023
Archival pigment photograph
16 × 23 inches
Private Collection
© Cara Romero. Courtesy of the artist. All rights reserved.
pp. 210–11

Diego Romero
Cochiti Pueblo (b. 1964)
Girl in the Anthropocene, 2017
Lithograph
19 × 24 inches
Private Collection
© Diego Romero
pp. 88–89

Sarah Sense
Chitimacha and Choctaw (b. 1980)
Dickens, 2022
Woven archival inkjet prints on Hahnemuhle bamboo paper, tape
24 × 24 inches
Courtesy of the artist and Bruce Silverstein Gallery, New York
© Sarah Sense
pp. 162–63

Rose B. Simpson
Santa Clara Pueblo (b. 1983)
X-Ray, 2021
Ceramic and steel
58 × 16 × 8 inches
Tia Collection
Photography courtesy of Chiaroscuro Contemporary Art.
Photo by Addison Doty.
Courtesy of the artist
pp. 164–65

Philip Singer
Diné (Navajo) (b. 1963)
Pink Triangle, 2019
Wool
Framed: 32 × 20 × 2½ inches
Forge Project Collection, traditional land of the Moh-He-Con-Nuk
pp. 90–91

Ryan Singer
Diné (Navajo) (b. 1973)
The Vendor, 2014
Acrylic on canvas
24 × 20 × 1 inches
Gorman Museum of Native American Art Collection
pp. 212–13

Duane Slick
Meskwaki/Ho-Chunk (b. 1961)
There Are No Endings, 2018
Acrylic on linen
18 × 60 inches
Tia Collection
© Duane Slick
pp. 166–67

Bently Spang
Enrolled Member of the Tsitsistas/Suhtai Nation (b. 1960)
Modern Warrior Series: War Shirt #3—The Great Divide, 2006
Mixed media
45½ × 55 inches
Montclair Art Museum; Museum purchase; Gifts made in honor of Elaine and Hal Sterling, and Acquisition Fund, 2006.9
© Bently Spang
pp. 92–93

Roxanne Swentzell
Santa Clara Pueblo (b. 1962)
Touched, 2011
Original clay
16 × 16 × 11 inches
Tia Collection
James Hart Photography
pp. 168–69

Tyrrell Tapaha
Diné (b. 1999)
Adá Nítsíjíkees: Think for Yourself, 2022
Hand and commercial vegetal-dyed Navajo Churro alpaca
54 × 42½ inches
Tia Collection
James Hart Photography
pp. 214–15

Charlene Teters
Spokane (b. 1952)
Way of Sorrows, 2020
Video
Duration: 3 minutes
Video documentation of a Charlene Teters installation *Way of Sorrows* by Frost Flower
© Charlene Teters
pp. 94–95

Hulleah J. Tsinhnahjinnie
Taskigi/Diné (b. 1954)
Anticipation, 2006
Hand-pieced photo collage on paper
33¼ × 33½ × 1½ inches
On loan from private collection
© Hulleah J. Tsinhnahjinnie
pp. 216–17

Zoë Urness
Tlingit (b. 1984)
Year of the Women, 2019
Analog capture-digital chromogenic output on Fuji crystal archive paper with UV over laminate mounted to Dibond aluminum substrate
40 × 30 inches
Tia Collection
Image courtesy of the artist
© Zoë Urness
pp. 170–71

Jeffrey Veregge
Port Gamble Band of S'Klallam Tribe (1974–2024)
Last Son, 2019
Digital print
24 × 15 × 1 inches
Gorman Museum of Native American Art Collection
© Estate of Jeffrey Veregge
pp. 218–19

Kay WalkingStick
Member of the Cherokee Nation of Oklahoma and Anglo (b. 1935)
Buffalo Country (Diptych), 2018
Oil on panel
30 × 60 inches
Tia Collection
Photo courtesy of Frolick Gallery, Portland, OR
© Kay WalkingStick 2018
pp. 252–53

Star WallowingBull
Ojibwe/Arapaho (b. 1973)
Arapaho Man with Traditional Design, 2004
Colored pencil on paper
21⅛ × 18 inches
Private Collection
© Star WallowingBull. Courtesy of the artist and Bockley Gallery
pp. 220–21

Marie Watt
Enrolled Member of the Seneca Nation of Indians/European Descent (b. 1967)
Skywalker/Skyscraper (Twins), 2020
Reclaimed wool blankets, steel I-beams, two textile towers
120 × 40 × 24 inches
Tia Collection
James Hart Photography
© Marie Watt, Courtesy of MARK STRAUSS, New York, Courtesy of Marie Watt Studio
pp. 96–97

Emmi Whitehorse
Diné (b. 1957)
Rushing Water, 2000
Oil pastel on paper on canvas
39½ × 51 inches
Tia Collection
James Hart Photography
© Emmi Whitehorse
pp. 254–55

Holly Wilson
Enrolled member of the Delaware Nation, Lenape and Descendant of the Delaware Tribe of Indians (b. 1968)
Red, 2015
Photograph
36 × 24 × 4½ inches
Gorman Museum of Native American Art Collection
© Holly Wilson
pp. 222–23

Will Wilson
Diné (b. 1969)
How the West Is One, 2012
Pigment print diptych
6¾ × 4¾ inches
Tia Collection
James Hart Photography
Courtesy of the artist: Will Wilson
pp. 226–27

Self-Portrait—DAM, 2013
Tintype
9⅜ × 7⅜ inches
Tia Collection
James Hart Photography
Courtesy of the artist: Will Wilson
pp. 224–25

Melanie Yazzie
Diné (Navajo) (b. 1966)
Visions in Brittany, 2007
Print
20 × 15 inches
Gorman Museum of Native American Art Collection
Permission given by Melanie Yazzie & Clark Barker
pp, 172–73

Artist Biographies
Raven Manygoats (Diné)

Tony Abeyta (b. 1965)
Diné (Navajo)
Tony Abeyta is a contemporary artist working in mixed-media paintings, large-scale drawings, and sculpture. His works are nature-based explorations tied to his Indigenous roots as a Diné artist. Abeyta holds an honorary doctorate degree from the Institute of American Indian Arts in Santa Fe and is a graduate of New York University. In 2012, he was a recipient of the New Mexico Governor's Award for Excellence in the Arts and recognized as a Native Treasure by the Museum of Indian Arts and Culture (MIAC) in Santa Fe. Abeyta was also awarded the prestigious US Department of State Medal of Arts in 2023.
→ *tonyabeyta.com*

Norman Akers (b. 1958)
Citizen of the Osage Nation
Norman Akers was born in Fairfax, Oklahoma. He is a citizen of the Osage Nation, Grayhorse district. He creates artworks that act like maps of culture, memory, and place, and through color, line, and visual form expresses deeply felt concerns regarding removal, disturbance, and the struggle to reclaim cultural context. Akers's paintings are held in numerous collections, including those of the Forge Project in Taghkanic, New York; the Gilcrease Museum in Tulsa; the Minneapolis Institute of Art; the Nerman Museum of Contemporary Art in Overland Park, Kansas; and the Heard Museum in Phoenix.
→ *normanakers.com*

George Alexander (b. 1990)
Muscogee (Creek)
George Alexander (a.k.a. Ofuskie) is a Muscogee (Creek) artist living in Santa Fe. He received an MFA from Studio Arts College International in Florence, Italy, in 2019 and a BFA from the Institute of American Indian Arts in Santa Fe in 2015. His artwork explores themes of global identity and cultural evolution. Through metaphor and surrealist figures, Alexander creates a vision for humanity that is not constricted by social complexes.
→ *ofuskie.com*

Neal Ambrose-Smith (b. 1966)
Descendant of the Confederated Salish and Kootenai Nation of Montana
Neal Ambrose-Smith is a contemporary Native American painter, sculptor, printmaker, and former professor at the Institute of American Indian Arts in Santa Fe. He has also developed an app, *Artist Ideas*, which offers one hundred ideas for making art, available for Android and Apple. His work is included in the collections of many national and international museums and institutions, including the New York Public Library in New York City; the Smithsonian National Museum of the American Indian in Washington, DC; the Galerie Municipale d'Art Contemporain in Chamalières, France; and Hongik University in Seoul. Ambrose-Smith holds an MFA from the University of New Mexico and a BA from the University of Northern Colorado.
→ *indianspacepainters*

Keri Ataumbi (b. 1971)

Kiowa

Raised on the Wind River Reservation in Wyoming, Ataumbi was exposed to both traditional Native American aesthetics and contemporary art theory and practice from an early age. Her Kiowa mother operated a trading post and her Italian American father is famous for his bronze sculptures. Ataumbi and her sister, artist Terri Greeves, were encouraged to pursue their individual interests in art. Ataumbi worked as a landscape designer while attending the Institute of American Indian Arts in Santa Fe and earned a BFA in painting with a minor in art history from the College of Santa Fe. She currently lives and works in Cerrillos Hills, just outside Santa Fe.

→ *ataumbi.com*

Joe Baker (b. 1946)

Enrolled Member of Delaware Tribe of Indians of Oklahoma

Joe Baker is an artist, educator, curator, and culture bearer who has been working in the field of Native Arts for the past thirty years. Baker is the cofounder and executive director of the Lenape Center in Manhattan and an adjunct professor at Columbia University's School of Social Work in New York. Baker earned an MFA from Harvard University and a BFA from the University of Tulsa. He also completed postgraduate study in the Management Development Program at Harvard University's Graduate School of Education. Baker's work is part of the permanent collection of the Metropolitan Museum of Art, among many others in the United States and Canada.

→ *thelenapecenter.com*

Natalie Ball (b. 1980)

Klamath/Modoc

Natalie Ball was born and raised in Portland, Oregon. She holds an MFA from Massey University in Aotearoa, New Zealand, an MFA in painting and printmaking from the Yale School of Art, and a BA from the University of Oregon. Her work has been shown nationally and internationally. In 2021, Ball was the recipient of the Native Arts and Cultures Foundation's Oregon Native Arts Fellowship and in 2020 was named a Ford Family Foundation's Hallie Ford Foundation Fellow. That same year she received the Joan Mitchell Painters & Sculptors Grant. She is now an elected official serving on the Klamath Tribal Council.

→ *natalieball.com*

Jamison Chās Banks (b. 1978)

Enrolled Member of the Seneca-Cayuga Nation of Oklahoma

Jamison Chās Banks is a multidisciplinary artist who creates films, paintings, performances, and installations. His work often explores the history of war and territorial expansion, both literal and psychological, and appropriates and alters symbols employed in propaganda and popular culture and redeploys them in contexts that subvert their original meanings. Banks is currently a visiting professor in the Studio Arts Department at the Institute of American Indian Arts in Santa Fe, where he has taught since earning a BFA from the school in 2012.

→ *chasbanks.blogspot.com*

Marwin Begaye (b. 1970)

Navajo

Marwin Begaye is an internationally exhibited printmaker and painter. As an associate professor of painting and printmaking at the University of Oklahoma's School of Visual Arts, his research has been concentrated on issues of cultural identity, especially those that lie at the intersection of traditional American Indian culture and pop culture. He has received numerous awards as an artist in residence and in juried exhibitions, and his work has been featured in many notable publications. Begaye's graphics have been shown in exhibitions in Argentina, England, Estonia, Italy, New Zealand, Paraguay, and Siberia and are held in private collections, museum collections, and the United States Library of Congress, Prints & Photographs Division.

→ *marwinbegaye.com*

Frank Big Bear (b. 1953)

Ojibwe

Drawing on a broad constellation of inspirations—family, popular culture, dreams, urban and rural landscapes, politics, and spirit worlds—Frank Big Bear's bright, allover compositions fuse Western modernism with Ojibwe and broader Native aesthetic and conceptual traditions. His recent exhibitions include *The Land Carries Our Ancestors: Contemporary Art by Native Americans*, a group exhibition at the National Gallery of Art in Washington, DC, in 2024, and *Ghost Dance of the Great Mystery* at Bockley Gallery in Minneapolis in 2023. In 2015, he received both the USA Knight Fellowship and the National Artist Fellowship. Big Bear's work has been collected by the British Museum in London, the Walker Art Center in Minneapolis, the Denver Art Museum, the Minneapolis Institute of Art, and the Des Moines Art Center, among others.

Roy Bigcrane (b. 1955)

Séliš, Member of the Confederated Salish & Kootenai Tribes

Roy Bigcrane is a documentary filmmaker and media specialist at Salish Kootenai College (SKC) in Pablo, Montana. Throughout his career, he has worked to preserve Indigenous cultures, histories, and languages. At SKC, Bigcrane has played a central role in the SKC Media Center, formerly KSKC-TV, a public television channel on the Flathead Indian Reservation.

Jackie Larson Bread (b. 1960)

Amsakapi Pikunni/Blackfeet

Jackie Larson Bread was born and raised on the Blackfeet Nation in Browning, Montana. Her grandmother taught her the art form of beadwork. Bread attended the Institute of American Indian Arts in the late 1970s, where she first studied painting before focusing solely on beadwork. She describes her artistic practice as "a bead worker who paints in beads." Over the course of her forty-year career, Bread has become known for her photorealistic style of beadwork. Her beaded images are rooted in the history and culture of her Blackfeet community. She often beads on utilitarian objects, such as bags and boxes, to emphasize the importance of art in daily life.

Julie Buffalohead (b. 1972)

Enrolled Ponca Tribe of Oklahoma

Julie Buffalohead is a visual artist living and working in St. Paul. She received an MFA from Cornell University in 2001 and a BFA from the Minneapolis College of Art and Design in 1995. Her many accolades include a Pollock-Krasner Foundation grant, a John Simon Guggenheim Fellowship, and a Joan Mitchell Foundation Painters & Sculptors Grant. Buffalohead has held notable public solo exhibitions at the Minneapolis Institute of Art, the Denver Art Museum, the Museum of Contemporary Native Arts in Santa Fe, and the Smithsonian National Museum of the American Indian in Washington, DC.

→ *juliebuffalohead.com*

Esteban Cabeza de Baca (b. 1985)

Indigenous Chicano

Esteban Cabeza de Baca employs a broad range of painterly techniques, entwining layers of graffiti, landscape, and pre-Columbian pictographs in ways that confound Cartesian single-point perspective. His recent solo exhibitions include *Let Earth Breathe* at Crystal Bridges Museum in Bentonville, Arkansas; *Nepantla* at Garth Greenan Gallery in New York City; and *Life is one Drop in Limitless Oceans* . . . at Kunstfort, Vijfhuizen in the Netherlands. Cabeza de Baca received an MFA from Columbia University in 2014 and a BFA from the Cooper Union in 2010. He currently lives and works in Queens, New York, and is represented by Garth Greenan Gallery in New York City.

→ *estebancabezadebaca.com*

Andrea Carlson (b. 1979)

Grand Portage Ojibwe Descent

Andrea Carlson is a visual artist who maintains a studio practice in Grand Marais, Minnesota. She works primarily on paper in drawing and painting. Institutional critiques, land-based narratives, and assimilation metaphors in film are major themes addressed in her work, which has been acquired for the permanent collections of the Whitney Museum of American Art in New York, the Walker Art Center in Minneapolis, the Museum of Contemporary Art Chicago, and the National Gallery of Canada. She is a recipient of a Joan Mitchell Foundation Painters & Sculptors Grant, a Chicago Artadia Award, and a United States Artists Fellowship. Carlson is a cofounder of the Center for Native Futures in Chicago.

→ *mikinaak.com*

Nanibah "Nani" Chacon (b. 1980)

Diné (Navajo) and Chicana

Nani Chacon is most recognized as a painter and muralist but expands across disciplines to include illustration and installation. Her most notable works have been in the public arts sector, in which she has a cumulative experience of more than twenty years. The focus of Chacon's work includes the integration of sociopolitical issues affecting women and Indigenous peoples. Creating murals and large-scale public works facilitates her work's content and personal philosophy that art should be an accessible and meaningful catalyst for social change.

→ *nanibahchacon.com*

Raven Chacon (b. 1977)

Diné/Chicano

Raven Chacon is a composer, performer, and installation artist born in Fort Defiance, Arizona, on the Navajo Nation. A recording artist for over twenty-two years, he has appeared on more than eighty releases on various national and international labels. In 2022, Chacon was awarded the Pulitzer Prize in Music for his composition *Voiceless Mass*. He is based in Albuquerque and the Hudson Valley, New York.

→ *Spiderwebsinthesky.com*

Corwin "Corky" Clairmont (b. 1946)

Member of the Confederated Salish and Kootenai Tribes of the Flathead Nation

Corwin Clairmont is a college professor, administrator, and professional artist. He received his MA from California State University, Los Angeles in 1971 and BA from Montana State University in 1970. He served as head of printmaking at the Otis/Parsons Art Institute and helped develop the Fine Arts department and degree program at Salish Kootenai College. Corwin's artwork has been exhibited both nationally and internationally. Awards include the Ford Foundation; National Endowment for the Arts; Eiteljorg Fellowship Award; Individual Artist Award, Arts Missoula, Montana; and the State of Montana 2008 Governors Award for Visual Arts. He currently serves on the State Board of the Montana Arts Council.

Jason Clark (b. 1967)

Non-enrolled Algonquin, Creek, Swiss, and Scottish

Jason Clark resides in Missoula, Montana. He is a printmaker, an adjunct professor, and the two- and three-dimensional technician at the School of Art at the University of Montana. His prints have been exhibited nationally and internationally, including at the Missoula Art Museum; the Turner Center for the Arts in Valdosta, Georgia; AppleStick Contemporary Art in Victoria, Australia; the Art at Wharepuke gallery in Kerikeri, Bay of Islands, New Zealand; and the 15th International Print Biennial Varna in Bulgaria. Clark's work has been collected by Artist Printmaker/Photographer Research Collection at the Museum of Texas Tech University, Lubbock; the Boise Art Museum; and Salish Kootenai College in Pablo, Montana.

Gerald Clarke Jr. (b. 1967)

Cahuilla

Gerald Clarke Jr. is a visual artist, educator, tribal leader, and cultural practitioner whose family has lived in the Anza Valley, in southwestern Riverside County, California, from time immemorial. He lives on the Cahuilla Indian Reservation in the home his grandfather built (c. 1940) and currently oversees the Clarke family cattle ranch. He is a professor of ethnic studies at the University of California, Riverside, where he teaches classes in Native American art, history, and culture. Clarke served on the Cahuilla Tribal Council from 2004 to 2008 and again from 2018 to 2021, where he advised on matters of cultural preservation, the Native American Graves Protection and Repatriation Act, and Indian Child Welfare Act cases.

→ *geraldclarke.net*

Lorenzo Clayton (b. 1950)

Navajo

Lorenzo Clayton received a BFA from the Cooper Union in New York City in 1976. He taught lithography there and at Parsons School of Design/The New School, also in New York. His studio practice evolved from abstract expressionist painting and assemblage to collaborative installations. As he is half Navajo, his Indigeneity has become the platform from which he perceives and engages in his work. Be it philosophical, scientific, religious, or otherwise, his Indigeneity helps him to be open to the possibilities of being. Clayton is a recipient of an Eiteljorg Contemporary Art Fellowship, a Pollock-Krasner grant, and a New Jersey State Council on the Arts grant. Clayton's work has been exhibited nationally and internationally.

Jordan Ann Craig (b. 1992)

Northern Cheyenne

Jordan Ann Craig is a Northern Cheyenne artist living and working in Pojoaque Valley, New Mexico. Craig grew up in the San Francisco Bay Area and received a BA from Dartmouth College. In 2017, Jordan was awarded the H. Allen Brooks Traveling Fellowship and that same year also received the Eric and Barbara Dobkin Fellowship at the School for Advanced Research in Santa Fe. In 2019, she was awarded artist residencies from the Institute of American Indian Arts and the Roswell Artist-in-Residence Program. Craig's work is shown nationally and internationally; currently, she is painting in Northern New Mexico.

→ *jordanannncraig.com*

Jeremy Dennis (b. 1990)

Shinnecock Indian Nation Tribal Member

Jeremy Dennis is a contemporary fine art photographer and founder of Ma's House & BIPOC Art Studio, Inc., in Southampton, New York. He explores Indigenous identity and culture in his work, as in his notable project *On This Site*, which documents Native American sites on Long Island. In 2016, Dennis received the Dreamstarter Academy Grant and in 2020 was awarded the Dreamstarter GOLD grant. His *Rise* and *Nothing Happened Here* series address decolonization and invisibility. He holds an MFA from Pennsylvania State University and has completed prestigious residencies. Dennis serves on several advisory boards and resides on the Shinnecock Indian Nations Reservation in Southampton, New York.

→ *jeremynative.com*

Demian DinéYazhi' (b. 1983)

Diné

Demian DinéYazhi' was born for the clans Naasht'ézhí Tábąąhá (Zuni Clan Water's Edge) and Tódích'íí'nii (Bitter Water). Their practice is a regurgitation of purported Decolonial praxes informed by the over-accumulative and exploitative supremacist nature of hetero cisgender communities. They are a survivor of attempted european genocide, forced assimilation, manipulation, sexual and gender-based violence, capitalistic sabotage, and hyper marginalization in a colonized country that refuses to center its politics and philosophies around the Indigenous peoples whose land it occupies and refuses to give back.

→ *@heterogeneoushomosexual*

Carly Feddersen (b. 1982)

Enrolled Member of the Confederated Tribes of the Colville Reservation and of mixed European heritage

Carly Feddersen was born and raised in Wenatchee, Washington, and comes from a long line of creative people. She is an enrolled member of the Confederated Tribes of the Colville Reservation and of mixed European descent. Much of her work emphasizes storytelling and making connections between her Plateau heritage and contemporary culture. Feddersen holds a BFA with a concentration in jewelry from the Institute of American Indian Arts in Santa Fe. Following a long tradition of stone carving, she uses stones collected from rivers near her home in the Columbia Basin as a focal point in her jewelry.

→ *@carlyfeddersen*

Joe Feddersen (b. 1953)

Okanagan and Arrow Lakes

Joe Feddersen trained at Wenatchee Valley College, the University of Washington, and the University of Wisconsin, Madison. He has been an active participant in the contemporary Native fine arts movement, exhibiting internationally and domestically since the early 1980s. Feddersen's work has been included in pivotal shows such as *Continuum: 12 Artists* at the Smithsonian's National Museum of the American Indian in New York. He was an art faculty member at the Evergreen State College in Olympia, Washington, from 1989 until his retirement in 2009. He works in an array of media, including painting, printmaking, photography, collage, and glass. Feddersen lives in his hometown of Omak, Washington, on the Colville Reservation.

Ryan! Feddersen (b. 1984)

Confederated Tribes of the Colville Reservation and of Mixed European Descent

Ryan! Elizabeth Feddersen specializes in creating compelling site-specific installations and public artworks that invite people to consider their relationships to the environment, technology, society, and culture. She earned a BFA from Cornish College of the Arts in Seattle in 2009. Feddersen recently completed several public artworks projects, including *Inhabitance* for the Portland International Airport, *Schema* for citizenM Seattle Pioneer Square Hotel, and *Antecedents* for the University of Washington, Seattle. She has created large-scale site-specific pieces and interactive installations throughout North America, working with the Seattle Office of Arts and Culture; the Seattle Art Museum; the University of Washington; the Wellin Museum of Art in Clinton, New York; the College of New Jersey; and Northeastern University in Boston, Massachusetts, among others.

→ *ryanfeddersen.com*

Kelly Caroline Frye (b. 1979)

Tesuque Pueblo and Mescalero Apache Descent

Kelly Caroline Frye is a contemporary visual artist who works in metal casting, painting, and ceramics. She graduated from the Institute of American Indian Arts in Santa Fe with a BFA in studio arts and is currently pursuing her MFA. Her paintings and sculptures explore themes of healing from trauma. As the artist writes, "The soul and spirit of my work springs from my curious nature, which has led me to many adventures. Self-discovery through the arts allows me to express a contemporary voice of my Indigenous world. I find limitless possibilities of expression in a combination of historical and personal narratives."

Nicholas Galanin (b. 1979)

Tlingit/Unangax̂

Nicholas Galanin engages past, present, and future to expose intentionally obscured collective memory and barriers to the acquisition of knowledge. His work critiques commodification of culture, while contributing to the continuum of Tlingit art. Galanin employs materials and processes that expand dialogue on Indigenous artistic production and how culture can be carried. His work is in numerous public and private collections and has been exhibited worldwide. Galanin apprenticed with master carvers and earned an MFA from Massey University and a BFA from London Guildhall University in New Zealand. He lives and works with his family in Sitka, Alaska.

→ *@nicholasgalanin*

Jeffrey Gibson (b. 1972)

Member of the Mississippi Band of Choctaw Indians and of Cherokee Descent

Jeffrey Gibson is an interdisciplinary artist based in Hudson Valley, New York. He grew up in major urban centers in the United States, Germany, and Korea. He received an MA in painting from the School of the Royal College of Art in London in 1998 and a BFA in painting from the School of the Art Institute of Chicago in 1995. Gibson has received numerous awards, notably a Joan Mitchell Foundation Painters & Sculptors Grant in 2012 and a John D. and Catherine T. MacArthur Foundation Fellowship Award in 2019. He also conceived and coedited the landmark volume *An Indigenous Present* (DelMonico Books, 2023), which showcases diverse approaches to Indigenous concepts, forms, and media.

→ *jeffreygibson.net*

Richard Glazer-Danay (b. 1942)

Caughnawaga Mohawk and Jewish Descent

Richard Glazer-Danay grew up in Coney Island, New York, and Hollywood, California. He earned an MFA from California State University, Chico; an MFA from California State University, Davis; and a BFA from California State University, Northridge. Having grown up around Mohawk ironworkers, Glazer-Danay often references them as inspiration for his work. Glazer-Danay's art is in the permanent collections of the British Museum in London; the Heard Museum in Phoenix; the Peabody Essex Museum in Salem, Massachusetts; the San Diego Museum of Art; the Seneca Iroquois National Museum; and the Smithsonian National Museum of the American Indian in Washington, DC, among others.

Darren Vigil Gray (b. 1959)

Jicarilla Apache

Darren Vigil Gray is a painter and musician who grew up on the Jicarilla Apache Reservation in Dulce, New Mexico. He began studying art at the Institute of American Indian Arts in Santa Fe at the age of fifteen and graduated from the school in 1977. Additionally, he studied art at the College of Santa Fe and the University of New Mexico. Vigil Gray works primarily with acrylic on canvas to craft abstract expressionist landscapes and dreamscapes. His work is part of the permanent collections of the Denver Art Museum, the Smithsonian American Art Museum (formerly the National Museum of American Art), the Heard Museum in Phoenix, and others around the globe.

Tomahawk GreyEyes (b. 1989)

Navajo

Tomahawk GreyEyes is an interdisciplinary artist from the Navajo Nation who was raised throughout the state of Arizona. In 2016, he graduated from California College of the Arts in San Francisco with an MFA in social practice, and he holds an undergraduate degree in intermedia from Arizona State University. GreyEyes uses site-specific installations, print, and video to convey intertribal autonomist messages to the dominant society. His work challenges Western ideas of what it means to be a human being and confronts stereotypical ideas about Native peoples in America.

→ *tomahawkgreyeyes.com*

Raven Halfmoon (b. 1991)

Caddo Nation

Raven Halfmoon is from Norman, Oklahoma. She attended the University of Arkansas, where she earned a double bachelor's degree in ceramics/painting and cultural anthropology. Her work has been featured in multiple exhibitions throughout the United States as well as internationally. Halfmoon most recently finished a long-term residency at the Archie Bray Foundation in Helena, Montana. She lives and works in Norman and is represented by Kouri + Corrao Gallery in Santa Fe, and Ross + Kramer Gallery in New York City.

→ *ravenhalfmoon.com*

Bob Haozous (b. 1943)

Chiricahua Apache Tribe of Oklahoma

Bob Haozous is an internationally recognized artist who works in a range of media, from drawing, painting, and printmaking to jewelry, but his primary focus is on sculpture, especially monumental public works. In 1971, he received a BFA in sculpture from California College of Arts and Crafts in Oakland. Haozous's art often focuses on his Apache heritage, climate change, and racism. In 1999 and 2001, he participated in the Venice Biennale. His works are included in institutions such as the National Museum of the American Indian in Washington, DC; the British Museum in London; and the Heard Museum in Phoenix, among others.

→ *bobhaozous.com*

Edgar Heap of Birds (Hock E Aye Vi) (b. 1954)

Cheyenne and Arapaho Nations

Edgar Heap of Birds is an artist and an advocate for Indigenous communities worldwide. His work includes multidisciplinary forms of public art messages, large-scale drawings, the Neuf series of acrylic paintings, prints, works in glass, and monumental porcelain enamel on steel outdoor sculpture. As a tribal elder, Heap of Birds serves as an instructor in the traditional Cheyenne Earth Renewal Ceremony at Concho, Oklahoma, and is one of the leaders of the Elk Scraper Warrior Society. His works have been acquired for the collections of some of the most prominent museums, both nationally and internationally. After thirty years of teaching at the University of Oklahoma, Heap of Birds now serves as a professor emeritus.

→ *eheapofbirds.com*

Luzene Hill (b. 1946)

Enrolled Member of the Eastern Band of Cherokee Indians

Through work informed by precontact culture of the Americas, Luzene Hill advocates for Indigenous sovereignty—linguistic, cultural, and individual. Employing early autochthonous motifs, she asserts female power and sexuality to challenge colonial patriarchy. Hill has exhibited throughout the United States, as well as in Canada, Russia, Japan, and the United Kingdom. Awards include a Ucross Fellowship, a Native Arts and Cultures Foundation Fellowship, an Eiteljorg Contemporary Art Fellowship, and a First Peoples Fund Fellowship. Her work is featured in two recently published books, *An Indigenous Present* (BIG NDN PRESS, 2023) and *Art, Activism, and Sexual Violence* (University of Washington Press, 2024).

→ *luzenehill.com*

John Hitchcock (b. 1967)

Comanche, Kiowa, and Northern European Ancestry

John Hitchcock earned an MFA in printmaking and photography from Texas Tech University, Lubbock, and a BFA from Cameron University in Lawton, Oklahoma. He is a recipient of the Robert Rauschenberg Foundation Artistic Innovation and Collaboration grant and a Jerome Foundation Grant, as well as a Creative Arts Award and an Emily Mead Baldwin Award in the Creative Arts from the University of Wisconsin–Madison. Hitchcock is currently an artist and a Vilas Distinguished Achievement Professor at UW–Madison, where he teaches screen printing, relief cut, and installation art.

→ *hybridpress.net*

Anna Hoover (b. 1985)

Norwegian/Unangax̂

Anna Hoover produces documentary, fiction, and art films via her home state of Alaska. She is on the faculty of the MFA program in studio arts at the Institute of American Indian Arts in Santa Fe and is a recipient of the Native Arts and Cultures SHIFT Grant. Hoover has also received support from the Alaska Humanities Forum, the Anchorage Museum, the International Sami Film Institute in Buletjavri, Norway, and the Rasmuson Foundation in Anchorage, and her work has been screened at the imagineNATIVE Film and Media Arts Festival in Toronto, the Berlinale International Film Festival/Berlinale: NATIVE in Berlin, the Northwest Filmmakers' Festival, the Museum of Contemporary Native Arts in Santa Fe, and the Maoriland Film Festival in Otaki, New Zealand. Additionally, Hoover has written four episodes of the PBS television show *Molly of Denali*, an Emmy-nominated animated children's show set in Alaska.

→ *annahoover.net*

Sky Hopinka (b. 1984)

Ho-Chunk Nation/Pechanga Band of Luiseño Indians

Sky Hopinka was born and raised in Ferndale, Washington, and spent a number of years in Palm Springs and Riverside, California; Portland, Oregon; and Milwaukee, Wisconsin. In Portland, he studied and taught Chinuk Wawa, a language Indigenous to the Lower Columbia River Basin. Hopinka's video, photo, and text work centers around personal positions on Indigenous homeland and landscape and focuses on designs of language as containers of culture expressed through nonfictional forms of media.

→ *skyhopinka.com*

Norma Howard (1958–2024)

Choctaw and Chickasaw

Norma Howard was a self-taught watercolorist who crafted scenes inspired by Choctaw and Chickasaw history in Oklahoma. Her style of layered brushwork produced works of vibrancy and depth that are rarely seen in watercolors. Throughout her career, she won numerous awards at the Red Earth Native Culture Festival and at Santa Fe Indian Market. Howard's work has been acquired by numerous institutions including the Gilcrease Museum in Tulsa.

Patrick Dean Hubbell (b. 1986)

Diné

Patrick Dean Hubbell is from Navajo, New Mexico, located on the Navajo Nation. He earned an MFA from the School of the Art Institute of Chicago. His work is inspired by cultural methodologies, references to traditional Indigenous art and philosophy, and the abstractness of language, nature, time, and place. Hubbell draws on a variety of media, including natural earth pigments collected from his Diné homelands and two-dimensional painting and drawing media. His work aims to challenge the imposition of categorizations and amplify aspects of Indigenous identity within the Western ideologies of contemporary art. He currently lives and works on the Navajo Nation.

→ *patrickdeanhubbell.com*

Erin Ggaadimits Ivalu Gingrich (b. 1990)

Nome Eskimo Community, culturally affiliated Koyukon Denaa & Iñupiaq

Erin Ggaadimits Ivalu Gingrich is a Koyukon Denaa and Iñupiaq carver and interdisciplinary artist working and subsisting on the Dena'ina homelands in Southcentral Alaska. Honoring her arctic and subarctic ancestral homelands, Ivalu's work represents what has tied her and her ancestors to the North. Through carved, painted, and beaded sculpture and mask- and lens-based forms, Ivalu creates representations of the revered wild relatives that have provided for her, her family, and her ancestors since time immemorial. Connection to the realities of subsistence lifeways and arctic survival is vital to Ivalu's work, which mirrors what keeps us fed and present in the North.

→ *ggaadimitsivalu.com*

G. Peter Jemison (b. 1945)

Seneca, Heron Clan

G. Peter Jemison's works navigate political and environmental themes. In 2022, he gained acclaim at MoMA PS1's Greater New York exhibition and was recognized by *ARTnews* and the *New York Times* for his paper-based art referencing the Treaty of Canadaigua, signed in 1794. In 2023, Jemison received the Johnson Fellowship and showcased a solo booth at the Armory Show and was featured in *Art in America*'s 2023 Fall icon edition. His art is held in prestigious collections including the Museum of Modern Art in New York, the Whitney Museum of American Art in New York, the Heard Museum in Phoenix, and the Buffalo AKG Art Museum (formerly known as the Albright-Knox Art

Gallery]. Jemison's academic journey includes studies at the University of Siena in Tuscany, Italy, and honorary doctorates from Buffalo State College; Hobart and William Smith Colleges in Geneva, New York; and Rochester Institute of Technology.

→ *gpeterjemison.com*

Chaz John [b. 1987]

Winnebago Tribe of Nebraska/
Mississippi Band Choctaw/European

Chaz John was born in Topeka, Kansas, and currently lives in Santa Fe. His multidisciplinary work presents a vibrant collection of images composed of cultural iconography, raw dreams, and a personal quilt of archetypal patterns that make up the collective American psyche.

→ *chazjohnart.com*

Emily Johnson [b. 1976]

Yup'ik Nation

Emily Johnson is an artist who makes body-based work. She is a land and water protector and an organizer for justice, sovereignty, and well-being. A Bessie Award–winning choreographer, Guggenheim Fellow, and recipient of the Doris Duke Artist Award, Johnson is based in Lenapehoking/New York City and on Haudenosaunee lands. Her large-scale performance gatherings insist on thrivance, radical reworlding, and just futures. Johnson is trying to make a world where performance is a part of life, instilling an integral connection to each other, our environment, our stories, our past, our present, and our future.

→ *catalystdance.com*

Tom Jones [b. 1964]

Ho-Chunk Nation of Wisconsin

Tom Jones is a professor of photography at the University of Wisconsin–Madison and an artist, curator, writer, and educator. He graduated with an MFA in photography and an MA in museum studies from Columbia College in Chicago and holds a BFA in painting from UW–Madison. Jones's artwork examines how American Indian culture is represented through popular culture and raises questions about these depictions of identity by non-Natives and Natives alike. His artwork is included in numerous private and public collections, most notably in those of the Smithsonian National Museum of the American Indian in Washington, DC; the Nerman Museum of Contemporary Art in Overland Park, Kansas; the Minneapolis Institute of Art; and the Museum of Contemporary Native Arts in Santa Fe.

→ *tomjonesho-chunk.com*

Brad Kahlhamer [b. 1956]

Tribally ambiguous

Brad Kahlhamer is an artist working in a range of media including sculpture, drawing, painting, performance, and music to explore what he refers to as the "third place"—a meeting point of opposing personal histories. Kahlhamer's work draws on his tripartite identity, navigating his Native American heritage, the influence of his adoptive German American family, and his adult life in New York City. His work explores his own displaced identity and straddles notions of authenticity and representation within the discourse of Native American art. Kahlhamer's work features in numerous public collections, including those of the San Francisco Museum of Modern Art, the Whitney Museum of American Art, and the Museum of Modern Art, New York.

→ *bradkahlhamer.net*

Sonya Kelliher-Combs [b. 1969]

Iñupiaq/Athabascan

Sonya Kelliher-Combs is a mixed-media visual artist from Alaska. Her work focuses on the changing North and our relationship to nature and each other. Customary women's work taught her to appreciate the intimacy of intergenerational knowledge and material histories; these experiences and skills allow her to examine connections between Western and Indigenous cultures. Recent exhibitions include *Arctic/Amazon* at Powerplant Gallery in Toronto, *Agency, Feminist Art and Power* at the Museum of Sonoma County, and *Hearts of Our People: Native Women Artists* at the Minneapolis Institute of Art. Kelliher-Combs is a United States Artist Fellow, a Native Arts and Cultures Fellow, an Eiteljorg Fellow, a Joan Mitchell Foundation Fellow, and a Rasmuson Foundation Fellow.

→ *sonyakellihercombs.com*

Linda King [b. 1952]

Enrolled Member of the Confederated Salish
and Kootenai Nation

Linda King has served as a cultural arts instructor at Salish Kootenai College for twenty years. In 1992, she was selected by the state of Montana as a highlighted artist who gave lectures and demonstrations with the traveling exhibition *Bridles Bits and Beads*. In 2017, King was invited to participate in *Tears of Duk'Wibahl*, an international gathering of Pacific Rim Indigenous visual artists and to *Teaching of the Tree People*, held at the Evergreen State College Long House in Olympia, Washington, in 2018. Additionally, she was featured in *The Land Carries Our Ancestors* at the National Gallery of Art, Washington, DC, in 2023–24.

Terran Last Gun / Saakwaynaamah'kaa (b. 1989)
Piikani (Blackfeet)
Terran Last Gun's work centers around the process of color exploration and visual documentation of nature, the cosmos, cultural narratives, and recollections of home. Often employing geometric aesthetics, he is contributing to an ancient Indigenous North American narrative through various media that include ledger drawing, printmaking, painting, and photography. In 2016, Last Gun received a BFA in museum studies and an AFA in studio arts from the Institute of American Indian Arts in Santa Fe. Most recently, he was named one of twelve 2022 New Mexico Artists to Know Now by *Southwest Contemporary* (formerly *THE Magazine*). Last Gun currently lives and works in Santa Fe.
→ *terranlastgun.com*

Athena LaTocha (b. 1969)
Hunkpapa Lakota/Ojibway
Athena LaTocha is an artist whose massive works on paper explore the relationship between human-made and natural worlds. In the wake of Earthworks artists from the 1960s and 1970s, her works are inspired by her upbringing in the wilderness of Alaska. LaTocha's process is about being immersed in these environments while responding to the storied and at times traumatic cultural histories that are rooted in place. LaTocha's work has been shown across the country, including at the Museum of Contemporary Native Arts in Santa Fe, the International Gallery of Contemporary Art in Anchorage, and the Visual Arts Center of New Jersey in Summit.
→ *athenalatocha.com*

James Lavadour (b. 1951)
Enrolled Member of the Confederated Tribes of the Umatilla Indian Reservation
James Lavadour, a descendant of the Walla Walla, lives and works on the Umatilla Reservation, near Pendleton, Oregon. He starts each day in his studio, rising before the sun to begin painting. Just when the sun begins to rise, he leaves his studio to go for a walk or a drive to witness the land waking up. Although Lavadour's paintings are not based on direct observation, the time spent looking, hearing, and feeling the natural world that surrounds him—his Native homeland—deeply informs his work.
→ *pdxcontemporaryart.com/james-lavadour*

Linda Lomahaftewa (b. 1947)
Hopi/Choctaw
Linda Lomahaftewa is a painter, printmaker, and mixed-media artist residing in Santa Fe. Her work is strongly influenced by the Southwest desert and high plateau landscapes and her decades-long research of her matrilineal Choctaw ancestors, the ancient mound builders of Oklahoma. For her contributions in the arts and academia, Lomahaftewa was awarded an honorary doctorate of fine arts from the San Francisco Art Institute in 2022 and an honorary doctorate of humanities from the Institute of American Indian Arts in Santa Fe in 2017. She holds both an MFA and a BFA in painting from SFAI, and her work has been exhibited in solo and group exhibitions since the 1960s.
→ *lomahaftewa.weebly.com*

George Longfish (b. 1942)
Seneca and Tuscarora
George Longfish is professor emeritus of Native American studies at the University of California, Davis (UCD), where he taught for thirty years. He was also the director of the Gorman Museum of Native American Art at UCD from 1973 to 2003. Longfish earned an MFA and a BA from the School of the Art Institute of Chicago. As an artist, he is best known for his vivid, mixed-media paintings that explore Native American identities, cultures, and politics. He has exhibited his work internationally and held solo exhibitions, including *George Longfish: A Retrospective* at the Montana Museum of Art and Culture and *CONTINUUM: George Longfish* at the Smithsonian National Museum of the American Indian in New York.

Judith Lowry (b. 1948)
Hammawi Band Pit River Tribe/Mountain Maidu/Washo Tribe/Scots-Irish Cultures
Judith Lowry earned an MFA in painting and drawing from California State University, Chico (CSUC), and a BFA from Humboldt State University (Cal Poly Humboldt). Primarily painted in oils and acrylics, her works often reference themes of consumerism, relationships, and representations of Native Americans in contemporary

culture. Lowry's paintings have been featured in exhibitions across the country and are part of the permanent collections of the Smithsonian's National Museum of the American Indian in New York; the Peabody Essex Museum in Salem, Massachusetts; and the Nevada Museum of Art, among others. She is based in Nevada City, Nevada, and Susanville, California.

Cannupa Hanska Luger (b. 1979)
Enrolled Member of the Three Affiliated Tribes of Fort Berthold and is Mandan, Hidatsa, Arikara and Lakota
Cannupa Hanska Luger is a New Mexico–based multidisciplinary artist creating monumental installations, sculpture, and performance to communicate urgent stories of twenty-first-century Indigeneity. His bold visual storytelling presents new ways of seeing our collective humanity while foregrounding an Indigenous worldview. His work has been exhibited at the National Gallery of Art in Washington, DC; the Metropolitan Museum of Art in New York; the Whitney Museum of American Art in New York; the Gardiner Museum in Toronto; and the National Center for Civil and Human Rights in Atlanta. Luger has been awarded fellowships from the Guggenheim Museum in New York, United States Artists, Creative Capital, the Smithsonian Institute, and the Joan Mitchell Foundation.
→ *cannupahanska.com*

Mario Martinez (b. 1953)
Enrolled Member of the Pascua Yaqui Tribe of Arizona
Mario Martinez received an MFA from the San Francisco Art Institute in 1985 and a BFA from the School of Art at Arizona State University in 1979. A great admirer of the New York School and abstract expressionism, Martinez creates expansive canvases with writhing forms that often echo the turbulent surfaces of Arshile Gorky or Willem de Kooning. Though he often avoids direct references to Yaqui traditions, cultural allusions and visual references permeate his work. Since 1991, Martinez's work has appeared in more than fifty solo and group exhibitions at prestigious venues, and he has received numerous grants, fellowships, and awards.

Michael McCabe (1961–2023)
Diné (Navajo)
Michael McCabe was a monotype artist, master printmaker, and educator. He was born in Fort Defiance, Arizona, on the Navajo Nation, of the Táchii'nii clan (Red Running into the Water) and for the Hashk'aa Hadzohi clan (Yucca Fruit Strung Out in a Line). He studied printmaking, ceramic arts, and creative writing at the Institute of American Indian Arts in Santa Fe and went on to study poetics and spiritual practices at the Naropa Institute in Boulder, Colorado. McCabe taught at Santa Fe Community College, the Institute of American Indian Arts, the California Correctional Center in Susanville, and for several private studios. His works are included in the permanent collections of the Museum of Contemporary Native Arts in Santa Fe and the Portland Art Museum in Oregon, among others.

Da-ka-xeen Mehner (b. 1970)
Tlingit/Nisga'a
Da-ka-xeen Mehner is a transdisciplinary artist whose work explores Indigenous identity and equity and examines power structures through a lens of personal narrative. Mehner received an MFA in Native arts from the University of Alaska Fairbanks (UAF), a BFA from the University of New Mexico, and an AA from the Institute of American Indian Arts in Santa Fe. He has been recognized for his work through several fellowships, including the Rasmuson Foundation Fellowship, the Native Arts and Cultures Fellowship, the Eiteljorg Contemporary Art Fellowship, and the United States Artists Fellowship. He is the director of the Native Art Center and chair of the art department at UAF.
→ *da-ka-xeen.com*

Bryson Goodrunner Meyers (b. 1984)
Chippewa, Cree, Sicangu, Oglala, Hunkpapa, Dakota
Bryson Goodrunner Meyers is an award-winning graphic designer and textile artist and a two-time Native American Music Award nominee. A flutist from the Rocky Boy Reservation in Montana, Meyers is also a Northern-style hand-drum singer, drum maker, and printmaker. In his art, Meyers incorporates Cree, Dakota, Lakota, and Ojibwe designs. These works are driven by history, stories, and traditional gatherings; Meyers's choices of color and placement make them contemporary pieces.

Alan Michelson (b. 1953)
Mohawk Member of the Six Nations of the Grand River
Alan Michelson is a New York–based multimedia artist, curator, writer, and lecturer. For more than twenty-five years, he has been a leading practitioner of socially engaged, site-specific art grounded in local context and informed by the retrieval of repressed histories.

His work is included in the permanent collections of the Whitney Museum of American Art in New York, the National Gallery of Canada in Ottawa, and the Smithsonian National Museum of the American Indian in Washington, DC, among others. Michelson was cofounder and cocurator of the groundbreaking series *Indigenous New York* at the Vera List Center, which raised the visibility of contemporary Indigenous art in New York and beyond.

→ *alanmichelson.com*

Douglas Miles (b. 1963)

White Mountain Apache-San Carlos Apache-Akimel O'odham

Douglas Miles is a painter, printmaker, photographer, curator, and founder of Apache Skateboards and Apache Skate Team. Miles draws corollaries between skateboarding and the Apache warrior tradition, as both involve increased concentration, stamina, and the ability to withstand pain. Founded in 2002, Apache Skateboards is one of the earlier Native American–owned skateboard companies. Apache Skate Team gives skating demonstrations, organizes skateboard contests and concerts, and curates art shows around the country, especially on Indian reservations in the American Southwest. Miles's works are included in the collections of the Smithsonian National Museum of the American Indian in Washington, DC; the Eiteljorg Museum of American Indians and Western Art in Indianapolis; and the Museum of Contemporary Native Arts in Santa Fe, among others.

→ *douglasmiles.co*

Dan Namingha (b. 1950)

Hopi-Tewa

Dan Namingha is an internationally known contemporary painter, sculptor, printmaker, and instructor. His work is included in several major national and international museums and embassies throughout the world. In 1989 his work was aired on CBS *Sunday Morning*, and two PBS documentaries were aired on his work, one of which won a local Emmy. He's held exhibitions at the Fogg Art Museum in Cambridge, Massachusetts, Carnegie Mellon University in Pittsburg; the Palm Springs Art Museum, among many others. He attended the Institute of American Indian Arts, Santa Fe; University of Kansas, Lawrence; and the American Academy of Art, Chicago.

→ *namingha.com*

Michael Namingha (b. 1977)

Hopi/Tewa

Michael Namingha was raised in and currently lives and works in New Mexico. He graduated from Parsons School of Design in New York. Through his photography, Namingha merges realism and abstraction. His two-part *Altered Landscapes* series documents the fire seasons of 2020 and 2022 in New Mexico. In 2020, the American West experienced one of the worst fire seasons on record with a total of eight million acres burned and 13,000 buildings destroyed at a cost of $2.7 billion. Our changing climate is leading to the severity of these wildfires, and we, the human race, are contributing to the altering of our landscapes.

→ *michaelnamingha.com*

Nora Naranjo-Morse (b. 1953)

Tewa, Santa Clara Pueblo

Nora Naranjo Morse is an artist best known for her work with clay. She makes pottery and figurines as well as installation exhibits and large-scale public art. Beyond Santa Fe, her work can be seen at the Heard Museum in Phoenix, the Minneapolis Institute of Art, and the Smithsonian National Museum of the American Indian in Washington, DC. Naranjo-Morse is the recipient of an honorary doctorate from Skidmore College in Sarasota Springs, New York, and a Native Arts and Cultures Foundation Artist Fellowship. She is the author of the poetry collection *Mud Woman: Poems from the Clay*, which combines poems with photographs of her clay figures.

→ *noranaranjomorse.squarespace.com*

Native Art Department International (NADI)

NADI is a collaborative long-term project created and administered by Maria Hupfield (Anishinaabe Nation) and Jason Lujan (Chiricahua Apache/Mexican) that began in Brooklyn in 2016 and is now based in Toronto. Hupfield is Canadian and belongs to Wasauksing First Nation; Lujan is American, originally from Marfa, Texas. NADI seeks to circumvent easy categorization through a diverse range of undertakings such as unannounced actions, curatorial projects, video screenings, paintings, collective art making, and mixed-use installations. NADI has been featured in exhibitions at the Varley Art Museum in Markham, Ontario, and the Museum of Contemporary Art and Mercer Union, both in Toronto. Their works are present in private and museum collections including Markham Public Art and the Art Gallery of Guelph, as well as several corporate collections.

→ *nativeartdepartment.org*

New Red Order (NRO)
New Red Order is a public secret society facilitated by core contributors Adam Khalil (Ojibway), Zack Khalil (Ojibway), and Jackson Polys (Tlingit). Working with an interdisciplinary network of informants, NRO coproduces video, performance, and installation works that confront settler colonial tendencies and obstacles to Indigenous growth. They have presented their work at the Art Sonje Center in Seoul, Artists Space (The Artist Studio) in Albuquerque, Counterpublic in St. Louis, Creative Time in New York City, the Haus der Kulturen der Welt Berlin, the Kunsthal Charlottenborg in Copenhagen, the Kunstverein in Hamburg, the MOMENTA Biennale de l'image festival in Montreal, the Museum of Modern Art (MoMA), the Museum of Contemporary Art Detroit, the Sundance Film Festival, the Toronto Biennial 2019, Walker Art Center in Minneapolis, and the Whitney Biennial 2019 in New York, among others, expanding the public secret society network across numerous institutional platforms.
→ *newredorder.org*

Laura Ortman (b. 1973)
White Mountain Apache
A soloist musician, composer, and collaborator, Laura Ortman creates across multiple platforms, including recorded albums, live performances, and filmic and artistic soundtracks. She has collaborated with artists such as Raven Chacon, Nanobah Becker, Jeffrey Gibson, and Demian DinéYazhi', and is a member of In Defense of Memory (IDOM). An inquisitive and exquisite violinist, Ortman is versed in Apache violin, piano, electric guitar, keyboards, and amplified violin, often sings through a megaphone, and is a producer of countless field recordings. She has performed at the Whitney Museum of American Art in New York, the Guggenheim in New York, the Museum of Modern Art in New York, the Musée d'Art Contemporain de Montréal, and many other renowned institutions.
→ *thedustdiveflash.bandcamp.com*

Chris Pappan (b. 1971)
Kanza, Lakota
Chris Pappan's work taps into the American cultural roots of 1970s underground comics, punk, and hot rod cultures. His art reflects the dominant culture's distorted perceptions of Native peoples and is based on the Plains Native art tradition known as ledger art. He is a graduate of the Institute of American Indian Arts in Santa Fe and a nationally recognized painter and ledger artist. Pappan's work is held in numerous prestigious collections such as the Smithsonian National Museum of the American Indian in Washington, DC; and the Tia Collection in Santa Fe, and others. He is represented by Blue Rain Gallery in Santa Fe.
→ *chrispappan.com*

Mikayla Patton (b. 1991)
Enrolled member of the Oglala Lakota Nation
Through the interplay of recycled papermaking and earth elements, Mikayla Patton creates sculptural objects that explore Indigenous intimacies, personal narratives, and the transformative power of repurposing materials. While utilizing her Lakota knowledge of creative methodologies and adornment, she aims to address shared themes of healing, growth, and renewal. In 2019, Patton obtained a BFA with a focus in printmaking from the Institute of American Indian Arts in Santa Fe. Patton's work has been exhibited at the Texas Tech School of Art in Lubbock, All My Relations Gallery in Minneapolis, and the Contemporary Arts Center in New Orleans. Additionally, she has won numerous fellowships, awards, and residencies.
→ *mikaylapatton.com*

Wade Patton (b. 1966)
Enrolled member of the Oglala Lakota Tribe
Wade Patton grew up on the Pine Ridge Reservation, surrounded by a rich culture of music and art. After obtaining a BA in art from Black Hills State University in Spearfish, South Dakota, and having his first solo exhibition at the Sioux Indian Museum in Rapid City, South Dakota, he moved away to explore other artistic endeavors. It took leaving South Dakota for Patton to find a voice in his recent body of work. Living on the East Coast, he began expressing what he missed—the beautiful splendor of the Black Hills, the landscape and skies of South Dakota—and started to draw the landscapes and clouds as a reminder of home.
→ *wadepatton.com*

Grace Rosario Perkins (b. 1986)
Diné/Akimel O'odham
Based in Albuquerque, Grace Rosario Perkins has spent most of her life moving between city centers, the Navajo Nation, and the Gila River Indian Community, near Phoenix. She is interested in using maximal painting to create works that are imbued with cultural and autobiographical metaphor. Though a self-taught painter, Perkins considers her time as an educator her

"art school," having worked alongside youth, adults with disabilities, and elders in hospice and teaching painting and drawing courses at the university level for more than a decade.

→ *gracerosarioperkins.com*

Luanne Redeye (b. 1985)

Seneca Nation of Indians, Hawk Clan

Luanne Redeye grew up on the Allegany Indian Reservation in western New York. It is from here that she draws inspiration. Redeye received an MFA from the University of New Mexico and has exhibited in museums and galleries throughout the United States and abroad, including Kent State University in Ohio; the Rainmaker Gallery in Bristol, United Kingdom; and the European Museum of Modern Art in Barcelona. She has been featured in *First American Art Magazine* and has been a participant in various residencies including the Truth and Reconciliation Residency at the Santa Fe Art Institute. Redeye currently lives and works in Binghamton, New York.

→ *luanneredeye.com*

Wendy Red Star (b. 1981)

Apsáalooke/Crow

Raised on the Apsáalooke (Crow) Reservation in Montana, Wendy Red Star's work is informed by both her cultural heritage and her engagement with many forms of creative expression, including photography, sculpture, video, fiber arts, and performance. An avid researcher of archives and historical narratives, Red Star seeks to incorporate and recast her research, offering new and unexpected perspectives in work that is at once inquisitive, witty, and unsettling. Red Star holds an MFA in sculpture from the University of California, Los Angeles, and a BFA from Montana State University in Bozeman. She lives and works in Portland, Oregon.

→ *wendyredstar.com*

Cara Romero (b. 1977)

Chemehuevi

Growing up in contrasting settings of rural reservation and urban sprawl, Cara Romero now possesses a bicultural Indigenous identity. She pursued an undergraduate degree in cultural anthropology at the University of Houston but became disillusioned by the way Native Americans are portrayed in academia and media. Realizing that photography could do more in images than anthropology did in words, she trained in photojournalism, editorial portraiture and film, and digital, commercial, and fine art photography. Romero travels between Santa Fe and the Chemehuevi Indian Reservation in Chemehuevi Valley, California, where she maintains close ties to her tribal community and ancestral homelands.

→ *cararomerophotography.com*

Diego Romero (b. 1964)

Cochiti Pueblo

Diego Romero has built a career constructing ceramic vessels that elevate Pueblo life to Olympian stature. A third-generation professional artist, Romero was born to a Cochiti father and a non-Native mother. He attended the Institute of American Indian Arts in Santa Fe before attaining a BFA from Otis College of Art and Design in Los Angeles and an MFA from the University of California, Los Angeles. Since earning a master's degree in 1993, Romero has developed an extensive exhibition record with works housed in significant public collections including the Metropolitan Museum of Art in New York; the Cartier Foundation for Contemporary Art in Paris; the Peabody Essex Museum in Salem, Massachusetts; the Denver Art Museum; the Heard Museum in Phoenix; and the British Museum in London.

Sarah Sense (b. 1980)

Chitimacha and Choctaw

Sarah Sense lives and works in California. She has traveled extensively through the Americas, Europe, and Southeast Asia; her landscape photography is an essential part of her travel and visual art practice. Sense's weaving practice began in New York while she was a master's student at Parsons School of Design–The New School from 2003 to 2005. As the director and curator of the American Indian Community House Gallery in New York, she catalogued the gallery's thirty-year history, inspiring her search for Indigenous art internationally. Her world travels were charged with archive research, a photo-weaving project that expanded to community programming, international Indigenous artist interviews, and her first book, *Weaving the Americas: A Search for Native Art in the Western Hemisphere* (Pascoe, 2012).

→ *sarahsense.com*

Rose B. Simpson (b. 1983)

Santa Clara Pueblo

Rose B. Simpson earned an MFA from Rhode Island School of Design and an MA in creative writing from the Institute of American Indian Arts in Santa Fe. Her works are held in numerous museum collections, including the Metropolitan Museum of Art, the Guggenheim, and the Los Angeles Museum of Modern Art. Along with numerous group exhibitions, Simpson has enjoyed solo shows at ICA Boston, the Nevada Art Museum, and the SCAD Museum of Art, among others, and her art was featured in the 2024 Whitney Biennial. Simpson is represented by Jessica Silverman in San Francisco and Jack Shainman Gallery in New York.

→ *rosebsimpson.com*

Philip Singer (b. 1963)

Diné (Navajo)

Philip Singer attended Arizona State University School of Art, where he studied printmaking and various other art forms before making a transition into weaving. He moved home to be a caretaker only to find that he had a teacher—his mother—and an abundant source of wool to make his art. Like his mother, Singer considers himself a self-taught weaver/tapestry maker. Having studied fine arts, he has relied on his training in the use of color, proportion, and balance. Singer weaves to create simple, nontraditional designs and to be innovative. His weaving is about exploration and how to use traditional tools and construction methods to achieve a visual masterpiece.

→ *@singer_philip*

Ryan Singer (b. 1973)

Diné (Navajo)

Ryan Singer is an artist-painter based in Albuquerque. He weaves stories of his childhood memories with nostalgic iconography. He has been included in the Indigenous Futurism movement but has been drawing *Star Wars* characters since 1977. He also enjoys creating portrait realism of Native subjects with a contemporary appeal. Singer's artwork is held in private and museum collections worldwide, and he has been the recipient of several awards from some of the nation's leading art institutions, including the renowned Southwestern Association for Indian Arts' Santa Fe Indian Market. He is currently attending the University of New Mexico to acquire a BFA in art studio and plans on working toward an MFA.

→ *facebook.com/RSingerArt*

Duane Slick (b. 1961)

Meskwaki/Ho-Chunk

Duane Slick is an artist of Native American descent from the Meskwaki Nation of Iowa and the Ho-Chunk Nation of Nebraska. His paintings blend the subjects of oral and visual Native American traditions with a focus on trickster strategies and modernist/post-modernist painting histories. Born in Waterloo, Iowa, Slick earned an MFA from the University of California, Davis, and a BFA from the University of Northern Iowa. His recent exhibition venues include the Aldrich Museum of Contemporary Art in Connecticut, the Eiteljorg Museum of American Indians and Western Art in Indianapolis, and the National Museum of the American Indian in New York. Slick lives and works in Providence, Rhode Island.

→ *duaneslickstudios.com*

Bently Spang (b. 1960)

Enrolled Member of the Tsitsistas/Suhtai Nation

Bently Spang is a multidisciplinary artist, writer, curator, and educator who works in a variety of media including video, mixed-media sculpture, performance, photography, and installation. His work confronts and confounds the persistent, romantic, and inaccurate role crafted for Native peoples in the false narrative of "The West." Spang uses the historical art-making methodologies, and sometimes reimagined art forms of his people, to explore issues of cultural continuity and to debunk the "mythology of the vanished" created for his and many other Native communities. His work has been exhibited and collected widely in North America, South America, and Europe.

→ *bentlyspang.com*

Roxanne Swentzell (b. 1962)

Santa Clara Pueblo

Swentzell holds an honorary doctorate of fine arts from the Institute of American Indian Arts in Santa Fe. She exhibits her work at the Tower Gallery in Pojoaque, New Mexico. Her work has been acquired for the permanent collections of the British Museum in London; the Auckland Museum in New Zealand; the National Museum of the American Indian in Washington, DC; and the Denver Art Museum, among others. Swentzell has received numerous awards, including first place in sculpture at the Southwestern Association for Indian Arts' Santa Fe Indian Market and the New Mexico Governor's Award for Excellence in the Arts. She has been recognized as a Native Treasure by the Museum of Indian Arts and Culture in Santa Fe. She is known for her figurative sculptures that capture human emotions in playful, and sometimes eerie, lifelike gestures that speak of the human condition.

→ *roxanneswentzell.net*

Tyrrell Tapaha (b. 1999)

Diné

Tyrrell Tapaha is a Diné weaver and fiber artist whose work encompasses the intergenerational pastoral living handed down to him through his grandfather, great-grandmother, and other relatives willing to teach. Tapaha's work acts as a tangible bank of feelings, memories, and experiences, a practice that not only sustains his life force but is the powerhouse to many lifeways of his people. Culture isn't stagnant, it's living and breathing, and every generation within the Tapaha family has had its own experience with what this media means to them. "We give ourselves to our weaving, and it gives itself to us."

→ *@tyrrelltapaha*

Charlene Teters (b. 1952)

Spokane

Charlene Teters is a mother, a grandmother, a wife, a college graduate, a professor, an academic dean, a speaker, an artist, and an activist for Native rights. She holds an honorary doctorate in fine art from Mitchell College in New London, Connecticut; an MFA from the University of Illinois Urbana-Champaign; a BFA from the College of Santa Fe; and an associate's degree from the Institute of American Indian Arts in Santa Fe. Teters's art, lecturing, and teaching have centered around achieving a national shift in the perception of Native people.

→ *charleneteters.com*

Hulleah Tsinhnahjinnie (b. 1954)

Taskigi/Diné

Hulleah Tsinhnahjinnie was born into the Bear Clan of the Taskigi Nation and born for the Tsinajinnie (Blackstreak) clan of the Diné (Navajo Nation). Exhibited nationally and internationally, Tsinhnahjinnie claims photography and video as her primary languages. Creating fluent images of Native thought, her emphasis is art for Indigenous peoples. She is the recipient of an Eiteljorg Fellowship for Native American Fine Art, a First Peoples Community Artist Award, and a Rockefeller Foundation artist in residence. She is currently the director of the Gorman Museum of Native American Art at the University of California, Davis (UCD), and a professor in the Native American Studies Department at UCD.

→ *hulleah.com*

Zoë Urness (b. 1984)

Tlingit

Zoë Marieh Urness is an award-winning Alaskan Tlingit photographer whose work focuses on Indigenous communities living and thriving through their traditions and in relationship with their lands. She is well known for *No Spiritual Surrender*, her 2016 photograph taken during the pipeline protests at Standing Rock Indian Reservation in North Dakota, which was nominated for a Pulitzer Prize in Feature Photography. Urness attended the Brooks Institute of Photography in Santa Barbara, California, and has presented work at Art Basel Miami Beach, the Heard Museum Guild Indian Fair & Market, and the Southwestern Association for Indian Arts' Santa Fe Indian Market, and she was the recipient of the 2022 Sony Alpha Female+ Grant in support of her project *Indigenous Motherhood*.

→ *zoeurnessphoto.com*

Jeffrey Veregge (1974–2024)

Port Gamble Band of S'Klallam Indians

Jeffrey Veregge was an award-winning Native American artist and writer known for his "Salish Geek" style, which used form-line design to blend traditional Coast Salish aesthetics and references to popular culture. He designed over a hundred comic book covers for Marvel Comics, IDW Publishing, Valiant Comics, Dynamite Entertainment, Boom! Studios, and Dark Horse Comics. Additionally, his work has been exhibited throughout the United States in institutions such as the Museum of Contemporary Native Art and the Center on Contemporary Art in Seattle. Solo exhibitions include *Of Gods and Heroes* at the Smithsonian National Museum of the American Indian in New York.

→ *jeffreyveregge.com*

Kay WalkingStick (b. 1935)

Member of the Cherokee Nation of Oklahoma and Anglo

Kay WalkingStick has held over thirty solo shows in the United States and Europe. Her work is in the permanent collections of the Metropolitan Museum of Art in New York, the National Museum of Canada in Ottowa, the Whitney Museum of American Art in New York, and many others both nationally and internationally. Now a professor emerita, WalkingStick held full professorship at Cornell University for seventeen years. In 2015, her retrospective of seventy-five paintings and drawings spanning the years from 1970 to 2015 opened at the Smithsonian National Museum of the American Indian in Washington, DC. The exhibition traveled to much acclaim to five additional venues across the country. WalkingStick is represented by Hales Gallery in New York City and London.

→ *kaywalkingstick.com*

Star WallowingBull [b. 1973]

Ojibwe/Arapaho

The vividly intricate colored-pencil drawings and acrylic paintings of Star WallowingBull explore intersections of Indigeneity and United States pop culture to expose fundamental mechanisms of control. WallowingBull's solo exhibitions include *Mapping and [Meta]Morphing* at Bockley Gallery in Minneapolis; *Transformer* at the Plains Art Museum in Fargo, North Dakota; and *Mechanistic Renderings* at the Museum of Contemporary Native Arts in Santa Fe. He has been included in group exhibitions at the Smithsonian National Museum of the American Indian in New York, Art Gallery of Ontario in Toronto, and October Gallery in London, among others. WallowingBull's work is included in numerous permanent collections, including those of the British Museum in London; the Plains Art Museum; the Tweed Museum of Art in Duluth, Minnesota; and the Walker Art Center in Minneapolis. In 2024, he was the recipient of the third annual Jim Denomie Memorial Scholarship.

Marie Watt [b. 1967]

Enrolled Member of the Seneca Nation of Indians/European Descent

Marie Watt was born in Seattle. She currently lives and works in Portland, Oregon. Watt's interdisciplinary work draws from biography, conversations across cultures and generations, Hodinöhsö:ni' protofeminism, and Indigenous teachings. In it, she explores the intersection of history, community, and storytelling. Watt holds an MFA in painting and printmaking from Yale University as well as degrees from the Institute of American Indian Arts in Santa Fe and Willamette University in Salem, Oregon. In 2016, she received an honorary doctorate from Willamette University. Watt serves on the board for VoCA [Voices in Contemporary Art] and joined the board of trustees of the Portland Art Museum in 2020.

→ *mariewattstudio.com*

Emmi Whitehorse [b. 1957]

Diné

Emmi Whitehorse grew up in Whitehorse Lake, New Mexico. She attended the University of New Mexico in Albuquerque and graduated in 1982 with an MA in art and printmaking. For over forty years, Whitehorse has captured abstract and meditative works inspired by the landscapes of the Southwest. Her work is held in the permanent collections of the Brooklyn Museum of Art, the Whitney Museum of American Art in New York, and the New Mexico Museum of Art in Santa Fe, among many others.

Holly Wilson [b. 1968]

Enrolled Member of the Delaware Nation, Lenape and Descendant of the Delaware Tribe of Indians

Multimedia artist Holly Wilson creates figures as her storytellers, conveying stories of the sacred and the precious, capturing moments of the day, our vulnerabilities, and our strengths. She holds an MFA in sculpture and an MA in ceramics from Stephen F. Austin State University in Nacogdoches, Texas, and a BFA in ceramics from the Kansas City Art Institute. Wilson's works are part of the collections of the Virginia Museum of Fine Arts in Richmond; the Gorman Museum of Native American Art at the University of California, Davis; the Eiteljorg Museum of American Indians and Western Art in Indianapolis; and the Nerman Museum of Contemporary Art in Overland Park, Kansas.

→ *hollywilson.com*

Will Wilson [b. 1969]

Diné

Will Wilson's projects foster the continuation and transformation of customary Indigenous cultural practice. He holds an MFA in photography from the University of New Mexico and studied photography, sculpture, and art history at Oberlin College. He is the recipient of the Joan Mitchell Foundation Award for Sculpture, the Pollock-Krasner Foundation Grant for Photography, and the Native Arts and Cultures Foundation SHIFT grant. Wilson has taught at the Institute of American Indian Arts, Oberlin College, University of Arizona, and Santa Fe Community College. In 2020, he was Doran Artist in Residence at Yale University Art Gallery, and recently cocurated *Speaking with Light: Contemporary Indigenous Photography*, at the Amon Carter Museum of American Art. Wilson is associate professor of photography at the University of Texas, Austin.

→ *willwilson.photoshelter.com*

Melanie Yazzie [b. 1966]

Diné [Navajo]

Melanie Yazzie is professor of art practices and head of printmaking at the University of Colorado in Boulder. Her works belong to many collections including those of the Denver Art Museum; the Art Museum of Missoula, Montana; the Museum of Contemporary Native Arts in Santa Fe; and the Kennedy Museum of Art in Athens, Ohio. She has exhibited nationally and internationally in countries such as New Zealand, France, Russia, the United Kingdom, and Australia. Yazzie is known for organizing print exchange projects that connect communities across the world. She makes prints, sculptures, paintings, surface, and jewelry design. She is represented by Glenn Green Galleries in Tesuque–Santa Fe.

→ *glenngreengalleries.com/melanie-yazzie*

Contributors

Mario A. Caro is the founding director of the MFA in Studio Arts program at the Institute of American Indian Arts. He is a researcher, curator, and critic of contemporary art and has published widely on the history, theory, and criticism of contemporary Indigenous arts. Previously, Dr. Caro taught in the Art, Culture, and Technology graduate program at the Massachusetts Institute of Technology. He also taught at New York University's John W. Draper Interdisciplinary Program in Humanities and Social Thought and at Indiana University, where he held the post of Public Scholar for Civic Engagement. He earned his doctoral degree in cultural analysis from the University of Amsterdam. His work within the academy complements his endeavors within various Indigenous communities to promote global cultural exchanges.

Lou Cornum, born in Arizona in 1989, is a Navajo writer and assistant professor of Native American studies in the Department of Social and Cultural Analysis at New York University. They are a founding editorial member of *Pinko: A Magazine of Gay Communism*, and their writing can be found in *Art in America*, *Frieze*, the *New Inquiry*, and *Triple Canopy*.

Heid E. Erdrich authored seven poetry collections, including *Little Big Bully*, a National Poetry Series winner. Erdrich edited the *New Poets of Native Nations* anthology from Graywolf Press. Her honors include two Minnesota Book Awards, the Rebekah Johnson Bobbitt National Prize for Poetry from the Library of Congress, and a National Artists Fellowship from the Native Arts and Cultures Foundation. An interdisciplinary artist and curator, Heid serves on the board of Minneapolis-based Rosy Simas Danse as well as Indigenous Nations Poets (IN-NA-PO). Along with Minnesota poet laureate Gwen Nell Westerman, Heid is a scholar-editor for Minnesota Humanities Center. Heid is Ojibwe enrolled at Turtle Mountain.

Lara M. Evans is an art historian, curator, and enrolled citizen of Cherokee Nation. Dr. Evans is a board member of the College Art Association and the National Committee for the History of Art (US affiliate, Comité International d'Histoire de l'Art). In 2023, Dr. Evans joined First Peoples Fund as vice president of programs after eighteen years as an art history professor, most recently at the Institute of American Indian Art. Dr. Evans has developed arts infrastructure designed to serve Native American communities, including artist-in-residencies, internship/apprenticeship programs, and fellowships for artists/researchers. Dr. Evans's recent curatorial projects include Smithsonian American Art Museum's Renwick Invitational 2023 and cocuration of *Action/Abstraction Redefined*. Publications include "Indigeneity and the Posthumous Condition," coauthored with Mique'l Dangeli, in *Posthumous Art, Law and the Art Market: The Afterlife of Art* (2022). She was executive producer of the short documentary *Cara Romero: Following the Light* (2023), airing on PBS.

Chelsea M. Herr, a citizen of the Choctaw Nation of Oklahoma, is the inaugural Jack & Maxine Zarrow Curator for Indigenous Art and Culture at Gilcrease Museum in Tulsa, Oklahoma. Her work at Gilcrease is focused on advocacy, inclusion, and self-representation of Indigenous peoples and cultures in museum spaces. She holds a BA in art history from Seattle Pacific University and an MA in art history with an emphasis on Native studies from the University of California, Riverside. In 2020, Herr earned a doctorate in Native American art history from the University of Oklahoma, writing a dissertation on Indigenous Futurisms in the work of Native North American artists. With cocurator Janet Berlo, she recently guest curated *Past Forward: Indigenous Art from Gilcrease Museum*, which traveled the United States between 2024 and 2025.

Raven Manygoats is a Diné PhD candidate in history at Rutgers University, New Brunswick. Her research focuses on the role of women within the history of the Red Power movement. She is the curatorial assistant in art of the Americas at the Zimmerli Art Museum.

Anya Montiel is a curator at the Smithsonian's National Museum of the American Indian. Recently, she has curated the exhibition *Ancestors Know Who We Are* (2022) and cocurated *The Future of Clay* (2024), *Pulse: Weavings and Paintings by Marlowe Katoney* (2023), and *This Present Moment: Crafting a Better World* (2022). She received her PhD and MA in American studies from Yale University and a BA in Native American studies from the University of California, Davis. She has written for *American Indian* magazine, *Art in America*, *First American Art* magazine, *Journal of Modern Craft*, and the *Oxford Handbook of American Indian History* as well as essays for Crystal Bridges Museum of American Art, the Heard Museum, the Hood Museum of Art, and the Smithsonian American Art Museum. She is of Mexican and Tohono O'odham descent.

Stacy Pratt is an enrolled citizen of the Mvskoke (Creek) Nation. She is a poet, art writer, and book reviewer, specializing in Indigenous arts. She holds a BA in English from Northeastern State University (Tahlequah, Oklahoma), an MA in literature from the University of Arkansas, and a PhD in creative writing from the University of Southern Mississippi. She is a regular contributor to *First American Art Magazine* and has written interpretive texts and catalogue essays for numerous Indigenous art exhibitions. She received a 2022 Dorthea and Leo Rabkin Prize in Art Journalism and a 2023 Andy Warhol Art Writing Fellowship. Stacy is also the singer and lyricist of the Tulsa metal band Everything That Kills.

Kathleen Sleboda is a graphic designer, illustrator, and design educator whose work crosses disciplines and often weaves together the acts of making, curating, collaborating, and documenting. She cofounded Draw Down Books and Text Field Office with her partner, Christopher Sleboda. For the past fifteen years she has designed books and printed materials for cultural institutions while lecturing and writing about graphic design, independent publishing, Indigenous knowledge systems, and the preservation of cultural heritage. Sleboda is also a principal of Gluekit and has worked on illustrations for clients in publishing across a range of media. Originally from San Francisco, she graduated from Yale University and the University of British Columbia. She now splits her time between Boston and Connecticut, on the traditional homelands of the Quinnipiac, Pawtucket, and Massachusetts. She currently teaches graphic design at Boston University and the Rhode Island School of Design. She is Nlaka'pamux and an enrolled member of the Coldwater Indian Band of Merritt, British Columbia.

Jaune Quick-to-See Smith was a citizen of the Confederated Salish and Kootenai Nation. She called herself a cultural arts worker. Her artwork uses humor and satire to examine myths, stereotypes, and the paradox of American Indian life in contrast to the consumerism of American society, and it is philosophically centered on strong traditional beliefs and political activism. Smith is internationally known as an artist, curator, lecturer, printmaker, freelance professor, and mentor. In 2023, Smith was the first Native American to have a solo show, *Memory Map*, at the Whitney Museum of American Art; it is currently traveling across the United States. Additionally, over her career, Smith organized and curated over thirty Native exhibitions in forty-plus years. During her lifetime, she gave more than 200 lectures at museums and universities internationally and her work was shown in more than 125 solo and 650 group exhibitions. Her work is in collections worldwide, such as the Victoria and Albert Museum, London; the Brooklyn Museum; the Museum of Modern Art, Quito, Ecuador; and the Whitney Museum, New York, to name only a few. Smith earned an art education degree at Framingham State, Massachusetts (now University), and a master's degree in art at the University of New Mexico.

Jennifer Woodcock-Medicine Horse is the program director for *IndigenEyes: Contemporary Native American Art of the Rocky Mountains and Plains*. Her PhD dissertation in American studies/museum studies, *Green Museums Waking Up the World: Indigenous and Mainstream Approaches to Exploring Sustainability*, focused on climate change and traditional ecological knowledge. Her MA thesis in Native American studies from Montana State University Bozeman, *Lewis and Clark in the Cities and Suburbs*, documented the cultural landscape of the Lewis and Clark trail, deconstructing "exploring the wilderness." Her BA in anthropology with emphasis in art history from the University of California, Berkeley, launched a lifelong interest in contemporary Native art, Indigenous representation in museums, and strengthening tribal sovereignty in relationship to rematriating/repatriating nonconsensually held cultural materials in museum and university collections. She teaches graduate and undergraduate classes at Montana State University, curates contemporary Native art exhibitions and events, and writes quarterly articles for the Montana Arts Council journal, *State of the Arts*.

Index

Published on the occasion of the exhibition *Indigenous Identities: Here, Now & Always*, organized for the Zimmerli Art Museum at Rutgers, The State University of New Jersey, by guest curator Jaune Quick-to-See Smith (Confederated Salish and Kootenai Nation).

Zimmerli Art Museum
February 1 to December 21, 2025

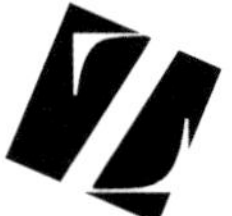

Zimmerli Art Museum
71 Hamilton Street
New Brunswick, NJ 08901
zimmerli.rutgers.edu

The exhibition, publication, and correlating public programs are supported by the National Endowment for the Arts, Nissan Foundation, the Middlesex County Board of County Commissioners through a grant award from the Middlesex County Cultural and Arts Trust Fund, and Rutgers University. Additional support is provided by donors to Zimmerli's Major Exhibitions Fund: Kathrin and James Bergin, Sundaa and Randy Jones, and Heena and Hemanshu Pandya.

The Zimmerli's operations, exhibitions, and programs are funded in part by Rutgers, The State University of New Jersey, and income from the Avenir Endowment Fund and the Andrew W. Mellon Endowment Fund, among others. Additional support comes from the New Jersey State Council on the Arts, Bloomberg Philanthropies, and the donors, members, and friends of the museum.

Published by
Hirmer Publishers
Bayerstrasse 57-59
80335 Munich
Germany
hirmerpublishers.com

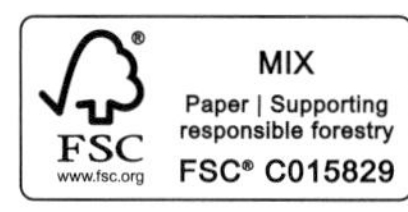

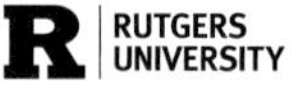

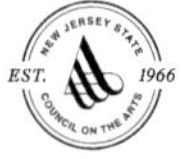

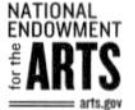

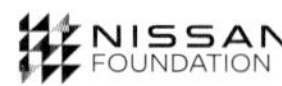

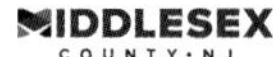

Library of Congress Control Number: 2025933294
ISBN: 978-3-7774-4536-6

General Editor: Jaune Quick-to-See Smith (Confederated Salish and Kootenai Nation)
Curatorial Assistant: Raven Manygoats (Diné)
Content Editor: RoseMary Diaz (Santa Clara Pueblo)
Design: Kathleen Sleboda (Nlaka'pamux) and Text Field Office

Set in November
Prepress: Reproline Mediateam, Munich
Printed and bound in Italy by Printer Trento s.r.l.
Printed on Gardamatt Ultra 150 g/m2 and
Wibalin Natural 120 g/m2

Hirmer Senior Editor: Elisabeth Rochau-Shalem
Hirmer Project Manager: Rainer Arnold
Zimmerli Project Manager: Stacy Smith
Zimmerli Rights and Reproductions: Kiki Michael
Copy Editor: Carolyn Vaughan
Proofreader: Carrie Wicks
Indexer: Emily Bowles

Front cover: G. Peter Jemison, *Red Power* (detail), 1973 (pp. 190–91)

Back cover: Zoë Urness, *Year of the Woman*, 2019 (pp. 170–71)

All photography of works in the exhibition is by Peter Jacobs, unless otherwise noted. Installation photography is by McKay Imaging Photography. Photograph of Jaune Quick-to-See Smith is by Grace Roselli.